# SOUTHERN NIGERIA
# IN TRANSITION
## 1885–1906

# SOUTHERN NIGERIA IN TRANSITION
## 1885-1906

*Theory and Practice in a Colonial Protectorate*

BY

## J. C. ANENE

*Professor of History in the*
*University of Ibadan*

CAMBRIDGE
AT THE UNIVERSITY PRESS
1966

PUBLISHED BY
THE SYNDICS OF THE CAMBRIDGE UNIVERSITY PRESS
Bentley House, 200 Euston Road, London, N.W. 1
American Branch: 32 East 57th Street, New York, N.Y. 10022
West African Office: P.M.B. 5181, Ibadan, Nigeria

©

CAMBRIDGE UNIVERSITY PRESS
1966

*Printed in Great Britain at the University Printing House, Cambridge*
*(Brooke Crutchley, University Printer)*

LIBRARY OF CONGRESS CATALOGUE
CARD NUMBER: 66-11280

*This book has grown out of my thesis for the Internal degree of Master of Arts in the University of London. It is dedicated to the Department of History, University of Ibadan.*

# CONTENTS

# LIST OF ILLUSTRATIONS

# PREFACE

The politico-territorial unit originally designated the Protectorate of Southern Nigeria was in time absorbed into what is known today as Nigeria. The emergence of Nigeria was due to two amalgamations which occurred in 1906 and 1914. A reversal of this process leaves Nigeria a country composed of semi-autonomous regions. The portion of Nigeria covered by this study—the territory which was historically Southern Nigeria—embraces the Mid-West State and Eastern Nigeria. Its outline was more or less clear when Britain in 1885 successfully secured international recognition of her 'freedom of action' on the Lower Niger and in the Oil Rivers.

Non-Nigerian writers are wont to refer to the inhabitants of the territory as 'a mere conglomeration of groups whose former associations with one another were, at best, artificial'. This view completely ignores the cultural and other unities which were quite pervasive. Contact with Europe was at first confined to the coast, and except for the ancient kingdom of Benin, the European agents who were destined to become rulers knew little or nothing about the Ibo and Ibibio who occupied the hinterland. They knew even less about the political institutions of these groups.

This study of Southern Nigeria in transition therefore begins by attempting to analyse the structure of an indigenous society, without becoming involved in the intricate problems of academic anthropology. The simple analysis helps to explain not only the ineptitude with which British agents applied the so-called policy of protection but also the disruption of indigenous institutions which inevitably resulted from British occupation and rule. The long period from 1849 to 1884 during which Britain imperceptibly entrenched herself in the politics of the coast forms a natural starting point of the modern history of Southern Nigeria. As a result of the Berlin West African Conference of 1884–5, the British position was internationally recognised.

The next phase of British policy has often been described as a 'paper protectorate'. Legally and morally, the internal sovereignty of the coast city-states was apparently safeguarded. It required the intelligence and tenacity of King Jaja to expose the hypocrisy which shrouded the theory of the colonial protectorate. The curtain was drawn and the policy of avowedly overthrowing indigenous independence was inaugurated.

It was easy enough for Britain to pave the way for occupying the Nigerian coast by treaties of protection with the merchant princes of the coast city-states. The hinterland was to be a different proposition. No blandishments could overcome the sturdy independence of the Binis, the Ibo and the Ibibio. British agents had therefore to adopt the paradoxical policy of extending British 'protection' by means of military expeditions. The process was indeed one of conquest and makes nonsense of the term 'protectorate'.

In one sense, however, the idea of protection persisted. The land and the forest resources of the territory were preserved to their owners, in spite of the importunities of alien speculators and concession-mongers. This policy may or may not have been the product of justice and fair-play on the part of the British rulers. The density of the population; the passionate attachment of the people to the land; the climate; and the expediency of avoiding provocative measures were all important factors. British rule unleashed forces which almost completely transformed the social and economic life of the peoples of Southern Nigeria. The resulting pattern of politics and economics is analysed up to 1906 when the territory was merged with Lagos and Yorubaland.

The material for this study comes principally from two sources, local and documentary. The documents are available at the Public Record Office, London, the British Foreign Office Research Library, and the British Museum. Exhaustive use has been made of the Intelligence Reports deposited in the National Archives, Ibadan. All the sources used are of course acknowledged in the appropriate places.

My thanks are due to the late Dr E. C. Martin of the University of London, who supervised the research out of which this book has emerged. Miss Marjorie Nicholson, formerly Secretary of the Fabian Colonial Bureau, helped enormously with suggestions during my research work. My gratitude is also due to the staff of all the research institutions where the invaluable documents are deposited. Lastly, I owe immense gratitude to Mr J. Ramsaran and Dr E. A. Ayandele who have, at great cost to their time, undertaken the final scrutiny of the typescript and made useful alterations.

J. C. A.

*Department of History*
*University of Ibadan*

# LIST OF ABBREVIATIONS

| | |
|---|---|
| A.D.C. | Assistant District Commissioner |
| Asst. | Assistant |
| Calprof | Calabar Province Archives |
| Capt. | Captain |
| C.-in-C. | Commander-in-Chief |
| C.O. | Colonial Office |
| Col. | Colonel |
| C.M.S. | Church Missionary Society |
| C.S.O. | Chief Secretary's Office (Nigeria) |
| D.C. | District Commissioner |
| F.O. | Foreign Office |
| F.O.C.P. | Foreign Office Confidential Prints |
| H.B.M. | His/Her Britannic Majesty |
| H.M. | His/Her Majesty |
| H.M.S. | His/Her Majesty's Ships |
| H.M.S.O. | His/Her Majesty's Stationery Office |
| *J.A.S.* | *Journal of the Royal Anthropological Society* |
| *J.H.S.N.* | *Journal of the Historical Society of Nigeria* |
| Lt. | Lieutenant |
| *Parl. Pap.* | *Parliamentary Papers* |
| *W.C.A.* | *West Coast of Africa.* |

# CHAPTER I

# THE TRADITIONAL STRUCTURE OF INDIGENOUS SOCIETY

It is not intended in this chapter to attempt a detailed anthropological history of the peoples who occupied the territory designated the Protectorate of Southern Nigeria. It is, however, necessary to describe briefly the basic features of the social and political institutions of the indigenous peoples involved in the process of establishing and consolidating British political domination. Only thus can the background be provided for appreciating the reactions of the peoples against the imposition of British sovereignty. The consequences of British rule cannot be assessed objectively without reference to the confrontation between the traditional indigenous institutions and the new. It is a generally accepted thesis that when 'backward' peoples were suddenly confronted by a powerful modern state and were not given time to adjust themselves to the new situation, the peoples invariably lost their stability and became disorganised. It is therefore important to single out and discuss the vital social and political institutions which the methods adopted in imposing British rule helped to undermine.

When the British Protectorate was established in 1885, it cannot be claimed that (leaving aside the coast city-states) Britain and her agents knew much about the major linguistic groups which occupied the territory Britain undertook to 'protect'. As a matter of fact, no professional anthropologist was appointed until 1909. A few political officers, for instance Partridge and Leonard,[1] did undertake amateurish investigations into traditional institutions, but their work was neither thorough nor above the distortions of prejudice. Policies based on utter ignorance of indigenous institutions were bound to produce consequences which the intruders hardly anticipated. It is of interest that a committee of the

---

[1] Partridge, *Cross River Natives* (London, 1905); Leonard, *The Lower Niger and its Tribes* (London, 1906).

Royal Anthropological Institute, London, at a meeting in 1910, emphasised the importance of the pioneer work undertaken by the first professional anthropologist, N. Thomas, in Southern Nigeria. The committee's report claimed that 'in the interests of the efficient administration of these territories, it is most desirable that enquiries of the kind carried out by Mr Thomas should be undertaken on a larger scale and for a more extended period...if mistakes which may entail serious consequences are to be avoided'.[1] This warning came too late because by 1906 the process of consolidating British rule had been virtually completed.

The British agents who undertook the responsibility began and continued their task on the basis of preconceptions which were both prejudiced and ignorant. The absence of extensive political integration was construed as evidence of anarchy. Their basic task, as they saw it, was to establish order and stability where anarchy had hitherto prevailed. The complexity and subtlety which characterised the social and political institutions of the indigenous peoples were not appreciated. The desire for quick results led to punitive expeditions where the theory of 'protection' should have suggested a less dramatic policy which enlisted the co-operation of existing institutions in the self-appointed British task of promoting the welfare and progress of the 'protected' peoples. In consequence, British intervention inevitably unleashed disintegrating forces whose results are only now being recognised and rectified.

In the study of the pre-colonial indigenous scene and of the immediate consequences of British rule, it is misleading to generalise. The peoples involved were diverse and their social and political institutions were more or less the products of environmental and other circumstances which were peculiar to the various groups. This is not to deny that the groups and their institutions had in many respects striking similarities. The differences between the indigenous institutions on the coast, in the hinterland east of the Niger, and in Benin district fully demonstrated the futility of the absence of discrimination in applying to the whole Protectorate 'reforms' and administrative innovations which the situation prevailing on the coast appeared to justify.

The Protectorate of Southern Nigeria in 1906 was officially the

---

[1] C.O. 520/99, R.A.I. to C.O., 21 June 1910.

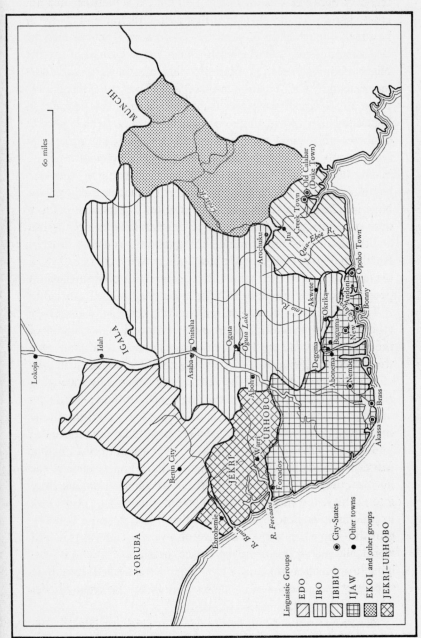

1. Sketch-map showing the coast city-states and the linguistic groups of Southern Nigeria, 1885–1906

territory between 5° and 9° east longitude and between the sea coast, known as the Bights of Benin and Biafra, and 7° north latitude. But up to 1900 the territory was arbitrarily partitioned for the benefit of two sets of British controlling agencies—the Royal Niger Company and the administration of the Oil Rivers Protectorate appointed by the Foreign Office. The result was that for about fifteen years the traditional commercial and ritual links which bound together widely scattered groups were sundered. The study of these groups and their antecedents should begin with some reference to their geographical environment. The claim that the history of a region is 'written clearly in its geographical features'[1] has not inconsiderable corroboration in the Protectorate of Southern Nigeria. The territory as originally constituted embraced three types of tropical vegetation—the mangrove swamps, the evergreen forest, and the deciduous forest thinning into grassland as one approaches Northern Nigeria. The geographical limit between the swamps and the firm land represented a significant demarcation between the coast peoples and the more coherent linguistic groups of the hinterland.[2]

The most striking feature of the Nigerian coast is the mangrove type of vegetation which is most fully developed at the mouths of the many rivers and creeks which form an almost continuous network from the Benin river to the Cross river. At about the middle of this stretch of coast lies the delta of the Niger. The waterways and channels which make up the Niger delta produce 'countless others, turning and twisting in fantastic contours until the whole country is honey-combed to such an extent as to become converted into an interminable series of islands'. One cannot resist quoting Morel's vivid description of the Niger delta: 'The vastness of the horizon, the mass of interlacing streams and creeks winding away into infinity, the sombre-coloured waters, the still more sombre impenetrable mangrove forests—here and there relieved by taller growth—impress one with a sense of awe.... It is the primeval world, and man seems to have no place therein.'[3] The land is low-lying, for the most part only a few feet above sea-level. The whole stretch of the coastal zone suggests a land built up from alluvial

[1] Hailey, *African Survey* (Oxford, 1938), p. 1.
[2] Unwin, *West African Forests and Forestry* (Unwin, 1920), pp. 151–2; Talbot, *Tribes of the Niger Delta* (London, 1932), p. 5 (Introduction).
[3] Morel, *Nigeria, Its Peoples and Problems* (London, 1911), p. 49.

4

deposits brought down by the rivers and held back by the mangroves. It has been estimated that the mangrove zone is in places up to ten miles in width. This environment of water and mangrove swamps was the home of the coast peoples of Southern Nigeria, who exploited this environment for the development of their remarkable commercial and political organisations.

One of the earliest, and perhaps the most diffusive, of the ethnic groups occupying the Nigerian coast are the Ijaw-speaking peoples. Talbot's derogatory reference to the Ijaw as 'a survival from the dim past, beyond the dawn of history'[1] may be dismissed as no more than a confession of ignorance. Talbot made no attempt to analyse the traditions of the people he designated the Ijaw nor did he seem to realise that the coast peoples to the east of the Niger delta as far the Ibibio coast contained a strong substratum of the Ijaw. The people who today are specifically called Ijaw are confined to the delta of the Niger, south of Abo. They are divided into clans whose traditions of origin vary. For instance, the Ijaw immediately south of Abo claim Patani as their original home; the Ijaw at Ase claim Onitsha. The largest of the Ijaw clans—and these are historically the most important—occupy the Brass–Nembe districts enclosed by the rivers Nun and Santa Barbara. Local histories of these groups contain traditions which are assumed to trace the origin and early migrations of the Ijaw.[2]

The traditions referred to above are clearly inconclusive evidence. They have many variations and all that can be done in the present state of research into the antecedents of these people is to summarise these traditions while leaving open the question as to which of the traditions of origin is most reliable. In due course the disciplines of comparative linguistics and archaeology may throw considerable light on what is now very obscure. The first and most popular tradition which the Ijaw often cling to claims that the Ijaw had a Benin origin. The king of the latter place allegedly sent out an army on an expedition in the direction of the Niger delta. Without his knowledge, the expedition was accompanied by his son. When this son of the Benin king was killed in battle, the members

---

[1] Talbot, *The Peoples of Southern Nigeria* (Oxford, 1926), I, 318.
[2] Tepowa, A., 'A Short History of Brass and its People', *J.A.S.* VII, 1907–8; Ockiya, Rev. D., *Nembe History* (in manuscript); see also Leonard, *The Lower Niger and its Tribes*.

of the expedition, quite understandably, decided not to return to Benin. The presence of the Benin war leaders in the delta is claimed to be the explanation for the foundation of the kingdoms which developed and flourished in the delta, of which the outstanding example was Nembe.

The second tradition points also to a Benin origin, but while the first took the form of military conquest, the second was a succession of peaceful emigrations from Benin by the aborigines of the area later consolidated by the incoming Edo-speaking aliens as Benin territory. The aborigines are claimed to have been responsible for giving the name Edo to the area they vacated. The Ijaw had the habit of using *Do* in their greetings and these greetings were interminable. The immigrants nicknamed the aborigines *Indo* and this word was later corrupted to *Edo*, which became the name of the area even after the Ijaw had been crowded out. The first exodus of the Ijaw from Benin was followed in due course by waves of fugitives from the tyranny of the new rulers of Benin.

The third tradition is interesting because it connects the Ijaw with the Yoruba. It is, however, not clear whether this connection is through Benin or independent of an assumed Benin connection with the Yoruba. It is not without some significance that Yoruba traditions include a claim that one of the Yoruba princes founded and consolidated a kingdom somewhere in the Niger delta. In any case, the Ijaw tradition being considered here quite clearly claims that after a short settlement at Ile-Ife, the celebrated place of origin of the Yoruba, the Ijaw moved into Itsekiri country and subsequently into the delta. The Itsekiri themselves also claim a Yoruba origin, and it is far from absurd to assume a common origin for the Yoruba, the Itsekiri and the Ijaw, with the differences of today explained by the inevitable disappearance of earlier affinities owing to the influence of new environmental and historical circumstances. With respect to all these traditions pointing to Benin or Yoruba origin, a note of warning is not out of place. The traditions may be in fact no more than an indication of the widespread influence and prestige of the empires built up by the Yoruba and Benin.[1]

[1] Even if it is assumed that the ruling families came from Benin or from the Yoruba, it would not necessarily prove that the people (the Ijaw) had the same origin. Onitsha on the Niger is another interesting case in this respect.

Local traditions are in agreement about the early foundations of settlements and petty kingdoms in the Niger delta. As regards these kingdoms, the names of the founders are remembered but whether these are mythical or real is a matter of conjecture. Two calamities led to the eastward dispersion of Ijaw groups. These groups encountered the Andoni who were already in occupation of the coast. Some were pushed back and some were absorbed by the Ijaw to form new groups known today as the Kalabari (around Degema) and the Ibeno (Bonny). Leonard is wrong in classifying the communities of Brass, New Calabar, Bonny and the 'Oru' as distinct tribes, but he was nearer the truth when he described their languages as 'dialects of the Ijo'. The traditions of origin preserved in Bonny and by the Kalabari clearly point to their close connections with the Ijaw. In the languages spoken by the Kalabari and the Ibeno there is a strong and unmistakable Ijaw substructure.

There was yet another movement of peoples which substantially affected the ethnic character of the communities of the Nigerian coast east of the Niger delta. The Ibo to the north must have been pressing southwards for centuries. It is probable that Ibo pressure had the result of confining the aborigines to the swamps of the coast. Then Ibo elements began to infiltrate into the already mingled Ijaw and Andoni communities of the coast. The Atlantic communities which ultimately emerged were therefore the result of the mingling of diverse elements—Ijaw, Andoni and Ibo. There is today the phenomenon of bilingual groups on the periphery of the Ijaw-dominated communities. Okrika is the outstanding example of a community where Ibo and Ijaw are regarded as native tongues.

East of the Ijaw-dominated portion of the coast is the stretch roughly bounded on the west by the Qua-Eboe river and on the east by the Cross river. The most important coast peoples here were the Efik who split from the Ibibio of the hinterland and moved to the estuary of the Cross river. The aboriginal inhabitants are represented by the Ibeno of the Qua-Eboe river and the Kwa of the Cross river, but they were completely overshadowed by their more dynamic neighbours, Opobo to the west and the Efik to the east. The similarities in language and culture between the Efik and the Ibibio are clearly indicated in studies undertaken on the groups concerned.[1]

[1] See Forde (ed.), *Ethnographic Survey*, part IX, pp. 9–20

Beyond the mangrove belt of the coast, the environment is dominated by the thick evergreen rain forest. Large evergreen trees are found in the districts between Warri and Benin City (west of the Niger), in the Owerri district and in the region north of Calabar as far as the Oban Hills. Beyond this, there is a transitional belt of deciduous vegetation which finally gives way to an open park-like environment at the north-eastern borders of Southern Nigeria. The greater part of this hinterland is composed of fertile palm land, whence spring a variety of timber trees and, as a result of industrious cultivation, an abundance of yams, cassava, and other food crops. The Lower Niger runs through this extensive hinterland. West of the Niger are the various sections of the Edo-speaking peoples and small groups of Ibo-speaking Ika. To the east of the Niger lies the territory of the predominant Ibo groups. East and south-east of the Ibo are the Ibibio; north and north-east, the Igarra and the Munchi.

The human groups which occupy the eastern border of Southern Nigeria, north of the Efik territory, defy classification. These groups are best described as human clusters. The Ekoi include the Akazu, Banyangi, Ezagham, Keaka, Manta, Nde, Nkumm and Obang. There are also non-Ekoi intrusive groups, like the Uwet, the Uyanga, the Akunakuna and the Ekuri. In the region north of the bend of the Cross river there are the Boki, the Nkim, the Iyache, the Iyala and the Yakoro. Most of these groups were probably fugitives from the Jukun conquerors of the Benue valley region to the north and so included diverse ethnic elements. The complexity of the linguistic pattern and the diversity of origin are perhaps without parallel in any African territory.[1] In this part of the Protectorate of Southern Nigeria, the linguistic hetereogeneity is so marked that neighbouring villages speak languages which are mutually un-intelligible. It is not without reason that the area has been described as a 'splinter zone'.

The distribution of the linguistic groups of Southern Nigeria having been briefly described, it is time to examine the mechanisms with which the peoples ordered their political and commercial life.

[1] Buchanan and Pugh, *Land and People in Nigeria* (London, 1955), see map 3; Jones, *Report on the Position, Status, and Influence of Chiefs, etc., in S. Nigeria* (1956); Forde (ed.), *Ethnographic Survey*, part X, pp. 91–2 and 128–30.

Once again a broad distinction can be made between the coast communities and the dwellers of the forest belt. The Itsekiri, the Ijaw, the Kalabari, the Ibeno and the Efik were destined by their environment to become first-class fishermen and traders. 'Whenever a few feet of solid land are found amid the mangrove swamps, fishing huts may be seen. After landing, the catch is at once smoked over bush fires, and the monopoly of dried fish, which is so greatly in demand in the interior, gives them a practical command of the inland marts.'[1]

Here indeed was the basis of the great city-states which flourished along the whole stretch of the coast of Southern Nigeria. The slave trade in due course provided a more lucrative source of wealth and the city-states attained remarkable political and social developments. West of the Niger delta, the Itsekiri settlements included Ebrohemie, Warri and Sapele. The Ijaws of the delta founded and developed their settlements in Brass, Twon, Akassa, Ogbolomabiri and Bassambiri. The Kalabari founded Buguma, Abonema and Bakana. Then there was Bonny, which became the most celebrated of the coast city-states. The Efiks evolved the 'republics' of Creek Town, Henshaw Town, Duke Town and Obutong.

Thus at every river mouth, at every centre of trade, a city-state developed with its own mechanism for self-rule, for the maintenance of law and order, and for energetic commercial activities.[2] The Ibeno of Bonny and the Efik afford the best illustrations of the types of political organisation which the native genius of the coastal communities evolved. In due course the stimulus of the slave trade and the impact of external trade with Europeans transformed the political evolution of these peoples.

No description of the political life of the coast is intelligible without an analysis of the social structure known as the 'House' system. A House was more or less a trading association of freemen and slaves under a head of House or chief, and each city-state comprised a number of Houses. There were therefore usually four social classes—the 'chief', the sub-chief, the freemen, and the slaves. The hierarchy was not a very rigid one. A dynamic and successful slave could rise to become a sub-chief or even head of a House.

[1] Talbot, *Southern Nigeria*, I, p. 317.
[2] Diké, *Trade and Politics in the Niger Delta* (Oxford, 1956); Jones, *The Trading States of the Oil Rivers* (Oxford, 1963).

Bonny provided many examples of slaves becoming chiefs and leading personalities in the political life of the city-state.[1]

Bonny became a kingdom probably as early as the fourteenth century. Thus over the chiefs who controlled Houses there was a king. The earliest of the Bonny kings of whom we have record was Perekule (a name corrupted to 'Pepple' by Barbot in the seventeenth century). Perekule acquired great power through the absorption into his House of men of energy and through his alliance with the powerful priestly class identified with the Bonny national cult, the Ikuba juju.[2] Another factor was the revenue obtained from the trade duty called 'comey'.

The Bonny king was traditionally the temporal and spiritual head of the state. Technically, the heads of Houses formed a sort of advisory council but the king held the balance between the Houses. On the whole, the king with the council of principal chiefs and the support of the priestly class was in charge of national affairs, responsible for wars and their conduct, and the founder and director of markets and trade. Inter-House rivalry was the perpetual menace to solidarity. Thus when there was a weak king, civil war invariably threatened. The nineteenth century clearly revealed this weakness.

The Efiks evolved 'republics', rather than kingdoms—the princes and dukes notwithstanding. The supreme authority was the Egbo[3] society, which was a sort of freemasonry. The society enforced peace and order, safeguarded the interests and privileges of the nobility, and kept the women, slaves and the masses of the population in subjection. For all practical purposes the Egbo order was the supreme political power among the Efiks, and exercised not only executive and legislative functions but was also the highest court of appeal in the land.[4] So pervasive was the influence of the Egbo society that the hinterland communities north of the Efik settlements bought from the Efiks the right to establish their own Egbo societies, often described as 'all-purposes clubs'.[5]

[1] Maduka, Oko Jumbo and Jaja, to name a few examples.

[2] Webber, *Intelligence Report on Bonny*, no. 27226.

[3] The term Egbo is in fact an Ibibio, rather than an Efik, designation. The Efik called their society the Ekpe, but the term that is in common use today is Egbo and, for this reason, it is retained in the text.

[4] Waddell, *Twenty-nine Years in the West Indies and Central Africa* (London, 1863), p. 314.

[5] Partridge, *op. cit.* pp. 35–7.

The early Europeans who arrived at the coast all left very depressing records of the Nigerian Coast settlements. For instance, Lander's Journal describes Brass as 'wretched, filthy and contemptible' and concludes that '...the mangrove itself can never be extirpated and the country will, it is likely enough, maintain its present appearance till the end of time'. De Cardi considered the Kalabari towns as 'being without exception the most squalid and dirty of any to be found in the Delta'. A Roman Catholic missionary who travelled through the delta in 1885 recorded that what left an indelible impression on his mind was 'evil smelling ooze and mud...'. At a much later date Talbot suggested that the environment of water and mangrove 'might seem a fitting symbol of all that is darkest and most terrible in West African beliefs,...[and] a fitting background for dark stories of lust and blood, while the very air seems heavy with the agony of victims'.[1] Squalid or not, the coast city-states developed to the full the opportunities which offered themselves for the commercial exploitation of the hinterland. The Itsekiri exploited the trade of the Urhobo country. The Ijaw organised trading expeditions on the Niger. The Kalabari tapped the resources of the Oguta lake basin. Bonny controlled the commerce of the region immediately to the north. The Efiks built up a vast commercial empire embracing the whole of the Cross river basin.

The political organisation of the coast communities was easily appreciated, though with considerable misgivings, by the aliens who intruded into coast affairs during the nineteenth century. On the other hand, the manner in which the large Ibo and Ibibio groups in the hinterland organised their political life was to baffle the British agents. In the end, it seemed more convenient to assume that anarchy prevailed or, at best, that the people were leaderless.[2] This facile assumption was destined to lead to tragic blunders and to the disorganisation of the traditional life of the Ibo and the Ibibio.

To avoid confusion, it is proposed to confine the present analysis of indigenous political structure to the Ibo east of the Niger. The

[1] Talbot, *Life in Southern Nigeria* (London, 1923), pp. 83–4; Lander, *Journal of an Expedition...*, II, 234; see also Tilby, *Britain in the Tropics*, footnote, p. 174; Jordan, *Bishop Shanahan of Southern Nigeria* (1949), p. 9.
[2] Ormsby-Gore, Cmd. 2744, *Report of a Visit to West Africa* (1926), p. 19.

Ibo along the Niger and to the west of it were absorbed into a different political system of which Benin was the centre. This system is discussed in due course.

For many centuries before the Europeans arrived, the Ibo had been settled in their present home. Nothing very definite is known about their earlier migrations. What is known is that when they moved in, the pressure of their numbers pushed the Ijaw and the Andoni to the less hospitable delta and coast swamps. The Ekoi and their neighbours were driven beyond the Cross river. As already explained, the physical environment is one dominated to a large extent by thick forest. On the one hand, the heavy vegetation was excellent defence against large-scale invasion from outside. On the other hand, its inaccessibility did not aid movement and easy intercourse among people who were primarily agriculturists.[1] The Ibo, therefore, never came under a single pyramidal system.

The Ibo lived in small village communities, often described as village 'democracies'. The political unit was the village-group consisting of lineage segments bound together by the belief in the common descent of all the segments from one ancestor. These localised lineage groups were structurally equal units. They had a corporate unity derived from a single lineage genealogy. The study of political authority among the Ibo is not concerned with formal institutions. There is no purely political or governmental organisation and there is no clearly delimited sphere of political affairs. But as Ottenberg argues in his study of the Afigbo Ibo, it is necessary to analyse how the Ibo communities did what they felt should be accomplished and how activities, not necessarily political, were organised and directed. The most crucial questions in all this are obviously the solidarity of the group as a political unit and the formulation of rules and standards of social behaviour.[2]

No study of the Ibo is intelligible without a clear appreciation of the pervasive reality of the supernatural world. Among the Ibo, religion, law, justice and politics were inextricably bound up. Law and custom were believed to have been handed down from the spirit world, from time immemorial, from ancestor to ancestor.

[1] Herbertson and Howarth, *The Oxford Survey of the British Empire, Africa*, p. 453.
[2] Meek, *Law and Authority in a Nigerian Tribe* (Oxford, 1937), p. 20; Evans-Pritchard, *African Political Systems* (Oxford, 1962), pp. 202–4.

The spirit world comprised a hierarchy of gods; the most important was perhaps the god of land—the unseen president of the small localised community. No community is complete without a shrine of the god of the land.

The nearest one gets to what may be regarded as an organ of government is the council of elders who were 'fathers' of component family segments. The elders were fundamentally the representatives and mouthpiece of the ancestors. Their sacred staff of office, called the *ofo*, symbolised the authority of the ancestors and was venerated as the embodiment of the supernatural world and all the spirits of the ancestors. Each elder possessed domestic authority because he was the intermediary between the family and the ancestors on whose good will the members of the kindred set great store.[1]

As regards the government of the lineage group, the centre of control lay in the council of elders. This council was not a legislative body in the orthodox sense of the word.

The meetings of the elders were neither formal nor frequent. The elders met when it was necessary to take a common action like sacrifice or war, or to settle an internal dispute which if allowed to continue would undermine the solidarity of the community. There was no law-making in the ordinary sense of the word. It was not necessary to prescribe formally any laws as deterrents against bad behaviour, because everyone accepted implicitly that any departure from the behaviour approved by the gods and the ancestors was likely to incur the displeasure and vengeance of the ancestors. When emergency 'laws' were promulgated by the elders, these laws were invariably given a divine sanction by a sacrifice to the god of the earth.[2]

In the same way, there was no institutionalised judiciary. Judicial proceedings were informal and were aimed at restoring solidarity. Within the family group, 'trial' was a matter of conciliation and a purification ceremony. In inter-lineage dispute, the elders met, but technically nobody was excluded from their assembly. Because a breach of the standard of behaviour would evoke the displeasure of the spirit world, the police and the secret service—services

---

[1] Meek, *op. cit.* p. 105.
[2] Basden, *Niger Ibos* (London, 1938), see ch. VII.

so characteristic of modern European society—formed no part of judicial control among the Ibo.[1]

Lastly, the institutions of age-groups were the nearest to formalised groups the Ibo ever found necessary for the services today performed by the executive organs of government. The senior grade, including members of titled societies, was usually concerned with the vital questions of war and peace. From among the members, there usually emerged the kind of personality to provide the leadership necessitated by the exigencies of external danger. The junior age-grade of young men was charged with social services which included sanitation and related services. There were lower age-grades for music, play and so on which were important agencies of socialisation.[2] An additional value of the age-group institution should be noted. Each group guarded its prestige very jealously and collectively ostracised a member who through continual misbehaviour brought his grade into disrepute. The institution thus played an important part in upholding standards of behaviour so vital to stability and peace in an Ibo community.

Generally speaking, the Ibo communities were democracies in the sense that the government of the communities was the concern of all. It can be seen then that the attempt by the British officials to select 'warrant' chiefs as the principal authorities among the Ibo was bound to produce an air of artificiality which contributed substantially to the disintegration of traditional Ibo society.

The subtlety, complexity and stability which characterised the manner in which the Ibo communities organised their political life may be said to apply to the Ibibio. Available evidence from Intelligence Reports shows that many Ibibio lineage groups also formed a large grouping best described as clan organisation. The term 'clan', like 'tribe', is difficult to define. Generally speaking, the Ibibio clan comprised lineage groups which recognised a remote and unascertainable common ancestor. The clan did not, however, represent a political structure nor did it constitute a central authority, involving the permanent or even occasional submission of the localised lineage groups. In conclusion, it can be said that among the Ibibio the ties of clanship hardly provided

[1] Green, *Ibo Village Affairs* (1947), p. 145; Meek, *op. cit.* pp. 88–115.
[2] *Ibid.* p. 200.

14

a framework of political significance.[1] Local traditions indicate, however, that clan consciousness considerably facilitated military, economic and ritual collaboration. Secret societies were an important institution in the life of Ibibio communities. The Idiong society enjoyed the executive powers and prestige which the Egbo society had among the Efik of the Calabar republics.

In emphasising the political fragmentation of the Ibo and the Ibibio peoples, it is easy to draw a misleading picture of isolation and a complete absence of integrative mechanisms. A definable political framework and subjection to one political authority are not necessarily the most effective criteria of group cohesiveness and unity. Among the Ibo, common interests in mythical values, common sacred places and so forth were more important unifying factors than the secular sanction of force—which is invariably the prerequisite of large-scale political consolidation. In addition, trade, migration patterns, marriage, and long-range contacts did bind the linguistic groups discussed above more closely than had until recently been acknowledged.[2]

The pervasive influence of religion among the Ibo, already emphasised, provided a basis for the important role of priests who mediated between god and man. Religion had another significance in the sphere of inter-group relations. In the first place, the ritual power formerly exercised by the king of Nri (in the Awka district) was an integrative force uniting, perhaps loosely, a large part of Iboland. The origin and precise nature of Nri kingship have not yet had the thorough study they deserve. In any case, the king enjoyed the special privilege of performing, personally or through his representative, sacrifices which were imperative in all cases of abomination perpetrated in an Ibo village. Nri influence was, however, not sustained by any formal social organisation and so it probably never provided a comprehensive relationship between independent Ibo political units.[3]

More important in this respect was the Aro Oracle—the Long Juju at Aro-Chukwu. The shrine was accepted by the Ibo and their

[1] See Evans-Pritchard, op. cit. pp. 20–3.
[2] Ottenberg, 'Ibo Oracles and Inter-group Relations', Southwestern Journal of Anthropology, XIV, 3 (1958), pp. 295 f.
[3] Thomas, An Anthropological Report on the Ibo-speaking Peoples of Nigeria, part I (London, 1913), p. 48; Jordan, op. cit. p. 37; Basden, op. cit. p. 115.

neighbours as the home of the supreme god and the Aro who owned it naturally occupied a very influential place among the communities from the Cross river westwards to the river Niger. The Long Juju shrine was the court of appeal to which serious internal and inter-group disputes were referred. There is a strong tradition[1] that before the final site was chosen for the foundation of Bonny on the coast, the migrating Ijaw group consulted the Long Juju and carried out the sacrifices prescribed by the juju. Up to 1925 the British administrators were firm in their belief in the local 'omnipotence'. They informed Ormsby-Gore that the British destruction of the Long Juju shrine had left the Ibo and the Ibibio leaderless.[2]

Who were the Aro and how did they exploit the Long Juju they possessed? What was the nature of the hegemony they enjoyed over a large section of Southern Nigeria?

The Aro territory and Aro-Chukwu are on the eastern periphery of the Ibo country. The Aro originally consisted of nineteen towns into which were incorporated Ibibio elements.[3] Other groups were closely associated with the Aro, for instance, the Adas and Abams who were useful as mercenaries effectively used by the Aro. The Aro were both juju agents and clever traders. In both capacities, they travelled and traded extensively in Ibo and Ibibio land. Various Aro settlements were established by means of which the Aro dominated the local market and specialised in the buying and selling of slaves and other commodities.

There were three types of Aro settlements outside the Aro home. There were settlements strategically established on important trade routes. Larger settlements were located in the neighbourhood of central markets. Lastly, there were settlements involving permanent occupation of land for farming and trading purposes. Aro settlements in various parts of Iboland include Bende, Ohaffia, Okigwi, Ajalli, Ndizuogu, Amaokwe, Achi, Ihiala and Umunoha.[4] Trade routes dominated by the Aro radiated in all directions, running northwards to the Ibo of the North and Ida, north-eastwards to Obubra, south-eastwards to Itu, southwards through

---

[1] See Fombo, *The History of Bonny* (in manuscript).

[2] Ormsby-Gore, *op. cit.* p. 19.

[3] *Intelligence Report on the Aro Clan.* See Resident's Covering Report, no. C.P. 502/10 (1933).

[4] Umo, *History of Aro Settlements* (Lagos, 1945).

Aba to the coast, and westwards through Awka to Onitsha and Oguta.

Aro influence did not in any way get near to being a political structure within the Ibo country. As oracle agents and as traders, the Aro wielded tremendous influence. They deployed mercenaries in inter-group wars to facilitate the availability of slaves for export. Local historians speak with considerable fear of the Abam 'wars', or more literally of the flight from the Abams. There is, however, no suggestion that the Aro controlled the affairs of independent Ibo village units.[1]

There were many sources for the supply of slaves to the Aro from among the Ibo and the Ibibio groups. There is no doubt that petty inter-village wars provided prisoners of war who were subsequently sold. There were two categories of domestic slaves who might also have provided commodities for Aro slave traffic. The first category consisted of slaves owned by a member of the community, but these could not have been many in a normal village. The second category —the Osu—belonged to the gods but it is extremely doubtful that any of them were ever sold. Another, major, source of the Aro slave supply was judicial litigation which took place in the sacred grove of Aro-Chukwu, where the guilty were seized and undoubtedly sold as slaves. Lastly, inveterate criminals in the Ibo villages were deliberately handed over to the Aro to safeguard peace and order.

Thus, although the influence of the Long Juju afforded protection to far-ranging Aro traders, oracle agents and settlements, there was no question of political domination of Ibo and Ibibio land by the Aro. The Aro did not even in their homeland evolve a centralised organisation with which to build an empire. Nor were the Aro primarily interested in political control. The Aro did not impose local rulers nor did they attempt to integrate village groups. There were also some sections of the territory east of the Niger that remained outside the ramifications of the Aro oracular and commercial activities, for instance, the Nigerian coast[2] and the Cross river. The Aro were primarily land traders.[3] The Niger trade was

[1] The points made here are based on extensive inquiries among Ibo groups most exposed to Abam raids in the Awka and Onitsha districts and among neighbours of existing Aro settlements.

[2] There is little evidence to show that Aro influence persisted there up to the nineteenth century.  [3] Ottenberg, *op. cit.* pp. 295 f.

dominated by Ibo groups, at Aboh, Ndoni, Osomari and Onitsha. The Cross river trade was in the hands of the Efik, the Umon and the Akunakuna. In spite of these limitations, the integrative influence of the Long Juju and the Aro was considerable.

Among the Ibo and the Ibibio, there was a complex network of integrative activities such as trade, ritual ties, marriage links, religious contacts, military alliances and craft distribution. Most important was the pervasive influence of the Aro Oracle. The political independence of the small units was not affected. Inter-group contacts in matters of trade and religion facilitated cultural diffusion and fostered fundamental unities among the peoples.

From the standpoint of British administrative intrusion, the role of the Aro in Ibo and Ibibio affairs was grossly exaggerated, and this ignorant assumption was partly responsible for the large-scale military expedition undertaken at the beginning of the century against the Aro and the Ibo and Ibibio peoples.[1] The result was to antagonise the groups concerned and to make more difficult the establishment of friendly relations between the intruder and the indigenous inhabitants.

To the east of the Ibo and the Ibibio, in the region of the Upper Cross river basin, the Ekoi and their neighbours formed a heterogeneous cluster of peoples. In their political life there was greater fragmentation than among the Ibo and the Ibibio. Talbot's reference to the Ekoi 'country' suggests that as one approaches it, one 'glides backward through the ages up the stream of time to the childhood of the world'. The Scottish missionaries spoke of the Ekoi communities as the 'fragments of an earlier world'.[2] What all these derogatory remarks amount to is simply that Ekoi communities were indeed small isolated communities. Small Ekoi groups seemed to be perpetually on the move through a heavily forested zone predominantly inhabited by monkeys. The small village of Atam provides an example of ritual rule and isolation. The 'chief' of Atam explained to an early British agent that:

[1] C.O. 520/8, Probyn to C.O. no. 200, 6 June 1901. See also Minutes by Butler.
[2] Talbot, 'The Land of the Ekoi', *The Journal of the Royal Geographical Society*, vol. XXXVI (December, 1910); Goldie, *Calabar and Its Mission* (Edinburgh, 1890), p. 282.

the whole town forced me to be head-chief. They hanged big juju (the buffalo's horns) round my neck....I have been shut up ten years, but being an old man, I don't miss my freedom, I am the oldest man of the town, and they keep me here to look after the jujus....By the observance and performance of these ceremonies, I bring game to the hunter, cause the yam crop to be good, bring fish to the fisherman, and make rain to fall....The other Atam towns do not acknowledge me—each has its own chief.[1]

Non-Ekoi groups, probably fugitives from elsewhere, moved into the Ekoi 'country' and the result was that the small communities were not only fragmented politically, but also lacked the linguistic and cultural affinities which gave a measure of homogeneity to the Ibo and Ibibio peoples.

To the north of the Cross river bend and along the Aweyong tributary of the river, splinter groups lived in small communities. The difficulty of classification apart, the groups recognised no inter-group association whatsoever. Each small community regarded itself as a separate and independent political unit. Those adventurous enough to occupy a river strip allowed no one else to pass through without paying tolls. This traditional practice was to earn the indigenous communities many punitive expeditions. To the British agents, the levying of tolls was no more than 'anarchic freedom'. Thus, after distributing flags and treaty forms among them, in spite of the doubts of the head of the African Section of the British Foreign Office as to whether 'these boisterous cannibals are...fit for British protection',[2] the British agents punished their trustees for not keeping the peace.

The portion of the Protectorate of Southern Nigeria west of the Niger was traditionally dominated by the kingdom of Benin. The Bini belong to the Edo linguistic group. Other Edo-speaking groups are the Kukuruku (north-east of the Bini), the Ishans (east) and the Urhobo and Itsekiri (south-east and south respectively). The Ibo along the Niger and west of it, dominated perhaps for centuries by Benin, trace their origin variously from Benin itself and from localities east of the Niger. For instance, Issele-Uku claims Benin ancestry. So do Onicha-Olona and Agbor. On the other hand, many clans in the Asaba district believe that their ancestors descended

---

[1] Partridge, *Cross River Natives*, pp. 200–2.
[2] F.O. 84/1881, see Minutes by Anderson on no. 6, 9 February 1888.

2-2

from an Ibo woman of Nteje across the Niger, although she also had Igala blood in her veins and finally married a Benin husband.[1]

The origin of the Benin kingdom is shrouded in myth, but the second kingdom, about which there exists abundant material in the form both of traditions and of documentary sources, began in the fourteenth century. The genealogy of Benin kings has been admirably traced by Egharevba, the Benin historian.[2] At the centre of the remarkable system evolved by the Bini was the Oba. In theory the Oba held absolute authority. In practice, the chiefs who formed a complicated hierarchy wielded more or less extensive influence according to the personality of the Oba. There were also juju priests who alone could perform the religious ceremonies essential to the Oba's welfare.

The Bini comprised two categories of people—the nobility and the common people. The nobility, from whom all the officers of state were drawn, were organised into three societies. The Iwebo society was charged with the Oba's regalia. The Iweguae society was in charge of the Oba's private appartments and provided the personal attendants of the king. The Ibiwe society supervised the harem. Outside of the palace societies, there were also title-holders who were important state functionaries, for instance, the Iyashere, the Ebohon, and the Ologboshere. The Uzamas, among whom was the Oba's eldest son, lived outside the walls of Benin in their own villages—'little Benins'.[3]

The title-holders and the leaders of the palace societies formed in practice, if not in theory, a council which the king consulted on major state questions. Every day the Oba held an open court in the palace, to which the title-holders had access and in which they could voice their opinions.

The extent of the empire built up by the Bini cannot be determined precisely, as Bradbury has pointed out.[4] To the north, the empire embraced the Kukuruku, and it is also claimed to have stretched north-eastwards to within forty miles of Lokoja. West-

---

[1] *Intelligence Report, Asaba Division* (1935). See Covering Report by H. F. M. White.

[2] Egharevgba, *A Short History of Benin*, 3rd ed. (Ibadan, 1960).

[3] *Intelligence Report on the Ancient Administrative System in Benin* (1939), by Marshall.

[4] *Ethnographic Survey*, no. XIII, pp. 14, 22.

wards, the empire in its heyday included Lagos, Badagri and the Ekiti and much of what is now Ondo division in Yorubaland. The Niger was the eastern boundary. Southwards, the Kwale-Ibo, the Isoko, the Urhobo and the Itsekiri were all subordinated to Benin rule and influence.

The origins of the extensive empire have been ascribed to many circumstances. The princes of the palace led expeditions to outlying places and settled there as local rulers. This explanation is inconclusively supported by the tradition among the Ishan and western Ibo ruling dynasties. Thus Idah, Ora, Uromi, Agbor, Issele-Uku, Warri and Aboh are believed to have been founded by Benin princes. Another explanation points to mass emigration from Benin during a period of oppression. Onitsha and many centres in the Kukuruku country have traditions which support the claim.

The important thing is that, at one time or another, Benin did effectively rule its empire and reproduce small replicas of its political system over a wide area. In the Ishan area the administrative unit was under the Enogie, whose title was conferred by the king of Benin. The Enogie was surrounded by a number of court or state officials whose offices, like that of the Enogie, became hereditary. The Enogie also had representatives in the outlying villages of the administrative unit. Usually each administrative unit had a protector in the person of a member of the Benin nobility. The Benin potentate who thus supervised the affairs of the unit acted as a link between the Oba and the Enogie. At the death of the Enogie, the eldest son and heir would send a message to the Oba to announce the death. The Oba would in return send a white cloth to·signify his assent to the burial. The heir of the late Enogie then sent a number of presents (usually slaves) to the Oba to beg for the *ada*—the staff of office which was the token of the Oba's recognition. The ceremony clearly illustrates the effective control which the Oba exercised.[1]

The subject districts paid annual tribute to the Oba of Benin. For instance, the Ora chief paid 10 goats, 10 fowls and the skin of all leopards killed. In addition, to kill a Benin man involved the payment of four male and five female slaves as compensation. There

[1] *Intelligence Report on the Irrua Peoples of Ishan Division* (1932). See the Resident's Covering Report.

were also regular presents of livestock and farm produce and slaves from local rulers who sought special favours from the Oba.[1]

The Ibo groups were ruled by an Obi. In Ogwashi-Uku, Ubulukwu, Issele-Uku, Agbor and Onicha-Olona, it is claimed that the title 'Obi' was originally obtained from the Oba of Benin. During the nineteenth century many of the outlying portions of the Benin empire became virtually independent. The centralising influence of Benin remained. Thus under the Obi there was a hierarchy of councillors who acted as administrative officers. Onitsha was an admirable example. But the records of the European explorers who visited Aboh, Onitsha and other towns along the Niger contain no suggestion that the local potentates still recognised the authority of Benin. The Itsekiri chiefs were also virtually independent of Benin. In the north of the empire, the latter half of the nineteenth century witnessed the incursions from Bida by Nupe agents. In many places, Nupe titles superseded those of Benin.[2]

The British agents who accompanied the expedition against Benin in 1897 have left on record the most appalling picture of the state of Benin. Bacon wrote: 'Truly has Benin been called the city of blood. Its history is one long record of savaging of the most debased kind.' Moor reported that 'on every path a freshly-sacrificed corpse was found lying....One large open space, 200 to 300 yards in length, was strewn with human bones and bodies in all stages of decomposition.'[3]

It is undoubtedly true that after many centuries of Benin rule, the central authority progressively deteriorated. Benin ceremonies involved human sacrifice, but it is possible the enormity was exaggerated by those who had to justify the Benin expedition. Before the slave trade inaugurated by the Europeans, we have a different picture of Benin. Then the Portuguese royal agent, Pires, had paid a glowing tribute to the peace and order which prevailed in Benin in the early decades of the sixteenth century. The later records left by Portuguese missionaries are not consistent and probably reflect their hopes and failures in the attempt to convert Benin to Christianity. The same thing may be said of the records of French mis-

[1] *Assessment Report, Benin Division* (1928), by H. N. Newns.
[2] *Ethnographic Survey*, no. XIII, pp. 101 f.
[3] Bacon, *The City of Blood* (London, 1897). F.O. 2/121, Moor to F.O. no. 17, 24 February 1897.

sionaries charged with missionary activities on the Guinea coast during the seventeenth and early eighteenth centuries.[1]

Human sacrifices there certainly were in Benin especially during the 'coral feast', and during the eighteenth and nineteenth centuries constant rebellions against Benin authority did occur. It is reasonable to assume that the Benin invaded by the British was no more than the shadow of the great Benin of old. To say this is not to suggest that nothing was left of the influence of Benin over extensive territories west of the Niger. As late as the twenties of this century, most Ishan youths were brought up in the belief that there were only two worlds—that owned by the white man, and that owned by the Oba of Benin. The significance of this was brought home to the British agents when the overthrow of the Oba of Benin was not followed by the enthusiastic submission which they had expected from the Enogies in the Ishan districts and the Obis among the Ika-Ibo. The difficulties encountered in the British attempt to organise native councils stemmed from the persistence of Benin influence which the British military victory over the Oba had undermined.[2]

The picture of the indigenous systems of government for the purposes of this study will be incomplete and probably misleading without some reference to the possible effects on the indigenous peoples of the long centuries of the slave trade across the Atlantic. On the coast, the slave trade and the wealth it brought to the coast middlemen contributed to the consolidation and prosperity of the coast kingdoms and republics. Barbot has left on record a typical commercial procedure in Bonny at the height of the slave traffic.

On the first of July, the King (Pepple) sent for us to come ashore, we staid there till four in the afternoon, and concluded the trade on the terms offered them the day before; the King promising to come the next day aboard to regulate it, and be paid his duties....Since our coming hither, none of the natives have dared to come aboard of us, or sell the least thing, till the King had adjusted trade with us.[3]

[1] For details, see Ryder, 'The Benin Missions', in *Journal of the Historical Society of Nigeria*, II, no. 2 (December 1961), 231–57; also Hodgkin, *Nigerian Perspectives* (London, 1960), pp. 122–30.

[2] See Watt, *Resident's Report in 1914* (B.P. 16/14 of 5 October 1924).

[3] Barbot, *An Abstract of a Voyage to New Calabar River or Rio Real in the year 1699*—quoted in Hodgkin, *op. cit.* p. 140.

On this occasion, the European merchants completed their transaction by purchasing five hundred slaves at two copper rings a head, and advancing the king and other principal men loans in the form of sundry goods, 'each in proportion to his quality and ability'.

The great wealth enjoyed by King Pepple of Bonny in the early decades of the nineteenth century is clearly revealed in the fantastic dowry paid to the king of Warri who offered Pepple a daughter in marriage. 'Gold and Silver Plates, costly Silks and fine Cloths' were mere presents to the king of Warri on his arrival at Bonny. 'My Queen Father stand for beach—his foot no touch ground—he stand on cloth—all way he walk, he walk for cloth.'[1] To a smaller extent the city-states of Brass, New Calabar and the republics of Calabar throve on the slave trade and on the trade in palm oil, palm wine and provisions in exchange for the fire-arms, gunpowder and beads which the hinterland peoples demanded. The pre-eminence, in European eyes, of the coast city-states and of the kingdoms along the Lower Niger produced the wrong impression that these city-states ruled Iboland and Ibibioland.[2]

The centuries-old contact which coastal society had with the European slavers and traders of all types left its mark. But one should not accept Johnston's prejudiced view that 'the degraded coast tribes...seem to have lost all their ancient culture, and have not yet become thoroughly imbued with European civilisation'.[3] The leaders of the city-states had certainly learnt a great deal about European liquor and other destructive concomitants of European civilisation. The chiefs had adopted ridiculous European names, such as Jewjew Tiger, John Africa, Indian Queen, Tom Tom, Jack Brown, Dublin Green, Strong Face, Fine Bone, Bony Face, My lord Willyby, Duke of Manmouth. The absurd way in which the local chiefs tried to ape the Europeans in dress was another example of the corroding effects of the contact with European ruffians.[4]

The condition of the people was one thing and good trade another.

[1] For the rest of the graphic description, see Jackson, *Journal of a Voyage to Bonny River on the Coast of West Africa*, quoted in Hodgkin, *op. cit.* p. 234.

[2] See Lander, *Journal*, vol. III, pp. 176–8; Dike, *Trade and Politics in the Niger Delta*, p. 26. For the Calabar area, see Anene, *The Boundaries of Nigeria* (unpublished Ph.D. thesis, London, 1960), pp. 93–7.

[3] Johnston, *Report on the Oil Rivers District*, W.C.A. (December 1888), p. 302.

[4] Baikie, *op. cit.* p. 326.

The coast communities did good business and remained great trading corporations of 'chiefs' and 'boys' for many centuries. When the slave trade was prohibited by Britain at the beginning of the nineteenth century, the coast communities had to find new commodities with which to sustain both the prosperity and the social and political structure of society. The presence of British agents on the coast in a new role, and one supported by gunboats, introduced a new situation: a situation which was destined to undermine the independent status of the indigenous communities.

Except along the Lower Niger, the new situation created on the coast had at first little or no serious impact on the hinterland. There was no doubt a great deal of incomprehension of the ways of the white man who had hitherto encouraged the capture of slaves and then quite suddenly decided that the transaction was iniquitous.

# CHAPTER II

# THE EMPIRE OF INFORMAL SWAY: BEFORE 1885

The abolition of the British slave trade on 1 January 1808 naturally transformed the character of British activities on the west coast of Africa. When Pitt the Younger asked, rather rhetorically, in the House of Commons how they could hesitate to abolish the commerce in human flesh which had so long disgraced their country, he was neatly summarising the history of more than three centuries of British connection with the west coast. The new task undertaken by Britain prescribed measures calculated to terminate the slave trade and encourage legitimate commerce. These objectives provided a basis for the juxtaposition of altruistic and materialistic motives which inspired Birtish policy towards West Africa during the first three-quarters of the nineteenth century.

A practical measure undertaken by the humanitarians during the years of the relentless struggle for the abolition of the slave trade was the settlement of emancipated slaves on a spot which became Freetown in 1787. A company was formed by the humanitarians to combine the control of the settlement with the enterprise of legitimate trade. On the Gold Coast, the European nations had built forts in the interest of the slave trade. In 1821 the British government took over, temporarily in the event, responsibility for the British forts from the 'Company of Merchants'. In this region, British policy of protecting the enervated Coast Fantis from the expansionist kingdom of Ashanti was destined to inaugurate a long period of intermittent warfare with the Ashanti rulers. On the Nigerian coast, Britain had no forts and none had been necessary because the city-states afforded both the trade and the protection the foreign merchants needed. But it was here that the role of the British preventive naval squadron was most direct in the struggle against the slave trade.[1]

[1] This subject is exhaustively discussed by W. L. Mathieson in *British*

During this period, the philanthropists and their friends propounded the theory that the best plan for striking at the root of the slave trade and its evils was to explore the hinterland, establish friendly relations with African chiefs and thus lay the foundations which would permit the infiltration of Christianity, social progress, and beneficent trade. The result was the financing of many expeditions to West Africa of which the central objective was the Niger. The most celebrated of the voyages of exploration were those of Mungo Park who attempted in 1795 and 1805 to trace the source, course and terminus of the mysterious Niger.[1] Final success, as far as the Niger was concerned, had to await the efforts of the Lander brothers who having reached Aboh were taken from there to the mouth of one of the distributaries of the Niger.

Of more immediate consequence to the Nigerian coast was the British acquisition from Spain in 1827 of the right to use Fernando Po as a naval base. It was from here that British naval commanders operated in their dealings with the chiefs of the Nigerian coast. Colonel Edward Nicolls was the first British 'governor' of Fernando Po. Nicolls conceived his duties to embrace more than the apparently negative task of intercepting slavers. He therefore inaugurated the policy of negotiating treaties with the potentates of the Bights of Benin and Biafra as the best means of exterminating the slave trade. The chiefs were, according to these treaties, to undertake to throw the weight of their authority on the side of Britain against the slavers. Nicolls was determined to make the area under his surveillance 'a glory and advantage both to British commerce and the cause of Humanity'.[2]

Nicolls's successor, Captain W. Owen, was in full agreement with the policy of treaty making. His advocacy issued in action. In 1839 the first 'slave trade' treaty between Britain and Bonny was signed. The local potentates of Calabar presented no difficulty. After all, one of them was described as 'a man of great knowledge and humanity'. But it was not to be expected that the new trade, with the inducement of an uncertain subsidy from Britain, could constitute, in the eyes of the coast chiefs, adequate compensation for the

*Slavery and its Abolition 1823–1838* (London, 1926); *Great Britain and the Slave Trade, 1832–1865* (London, 1929).

[1] See Mungo Park, *Travels in the Interior Districts of Africa*, 1797.
[2] Diké, *Trade and Politics in the Niger Delta*, quoted p. 66.

fabulous wealth which had hitherto accrued from the slave trade. Nor did non-British slave-dealers immediately react favourably to the belated admonitions of the British humanitarians on the iniquity of the slave trade. The slave-dealers resorted to all kinds of devices to elude capture and consummate their nefarious transactions. The local chiefs were not all unwilling partners in these transactions. For instance, when the British preventive squadron effectively controlled the slave trade through Bonny, Brass and New Calabar, which were less accessible to the Navy, became flourishing centres for the slave trade.[1] In due course, the treaty system was successfully extended to these places.

It is easy enough to argue demonstrably that during the first half of the nineteenth century the role of the British government in the affairs of the Nigerian coast was that of an impartial guardian solely interested in exterminating the foul trade in slaves and in encouraging legitimate trade. The navy was the sole instrument in implementing this policy and it proved an effective argument against local chiefs who might not have wished to sign the slave treaties. The only element of complication was the natural belief on the part of the British merchants attempting to develop the new trade that, with the British navy behind them, they could defy the authority of the local potentates and indulge in all kinds of commercial machinations which brought enormous profit. The naval commanders recognised the character of the merchants engaged in the coast trade and refused to do their bidding.[2]

The British Commodore in charge of the African station did in fact refuse to come to the assistance of the British merchants in Bonny. He pointed out that while he was prepared to protect their lives and property, he was not going to be a party to their trade malpractices. The complaints of the British merchants flooded the Foreign Office—and these complaints usually emphasised the wickedness and the slaving propensities of the local rulers. Palmerston, who now presided over the British Foreign Office, had no doubt in his mind that 'the best mode of preserving wealth is power...to enforce the *pax Britannica*'.[3] Britain was therefore

[1] Diké, *op. cit.* p. 87.
[2] See Hotham's dispatch to the Admiralty in F.O. 2/3, no. 125, Ward to Addington, 5 July 1847.
[3] Webster, *The Foreign Policy of Lord Palmerston*, (London, 1951) II, 751.

shortly to inaugurate a new policy in her relations with the potentates of the Nigerian coast, the policy of 'informal sway'.

As regards the river Niger, in the first half of the nineteenth century, limited attempts were made to penetrate the Nigerian hinterland. After the Landers' spectacular success in 1830, Macgregor Laird founded the African Steamship Company to exploit the commercial potentialities of the Niger basin. Laird's commercial ambitions were supported by the humanitarians. The next step, although Laird opposed it, was the much publicised enterprise, jointly sponsored by the British government and the philanthropists in 1841, to establish a mission station and a model farm at Lokoja and also to stimulate the export of Manchester goods in exchange for local produce.[1] The enterprise ended calamitously, yet the Niger as a field of immense economic possibilities was never lost sight of by the British government. Thus the Niger and the coast were destined to be the bases from which Britain attempted to consolidate her commercial interests in the second half of the nineteenth century.

But to go back to the coast. The pleadings of the British merchants for protection against 'mushroom kings' were not to be lost on Palmerston who had stated unequivocally that 'it is the business of Government to open and secure the roads for the merchant'. The formal appointment of John Beecroft in June 1849 as the British Consul for the Bights of Benin and Biafra hardly came as a surprise.[2] Beecroft was already very familiar with the affairs of the coast where he had himself traded and explored for nearly two decades. In fact, he had been much praised by the naval commanders, and was himself not above asserting that he specially understood the character of the Africans.

As was to be expected during a period when British governments disavowed territorial ambitions, the Foreign Office did not acknowledge that the appointment of Beecroft signified a change of policy towards the Nigerian coast. Nevertheless, Beecroft was enjoined to travel from one river mouth to another in men-of-war. Although the letter of appointment which reached him spoke innocently of 'the influence which you appear to have acquired over the native

[1] See Buxton, *The African Slave Trade and its Remedy* (London, 1840).
[2] For details see *Parl. Papers*, 1852, vol. LXXXIV.

29

chiefs of the places to which your jurisdiction will extend',[1] it was not without significance that Palmerston himself had rescinded from the draft letter of appointment any reference to Britain's unwillingness to make territorial acquisitions in the region which the Consul was expected to supervise.

With the possible exception of one or two, the local potentates who knew Beecroft well entertained no immediate misgivings about the appointment of a British Consul. Maybe as merchants they welcomed the presence of a man they believed they trusted in their often riotous dealings with the supercargoes. In any case, Beecroft began his new assignment in a manner which appealed to the pecuniary interests of the local rulers. He persuaded the British government to pay the subsidies which had formed an important stipulation in the slave treaties.

The complacent acceptance of Beecroft as Consul by the coast rulers—some even called him governor—provided an excellent opportunity for the Consul to lay the foundations of British authority on the Nigerian coast. There were of course many other circumstances which assisted the transformation of the role of the Consul. In the process, cajolery, bombardment and even deportation became the essential elements in the policy of informal empire building.[2] Neither Beecroft nor his immediate successors received formal instructions from Palmerston to make territorial additions to the British empire. There is no evidence that Beecroft and others entertained any imperialist dreams. Nevertheless, the Consuls progressively dominated the politics of the Nigerian city-states. It has to be admitted that the local politics indeed exhibited weaknesses which in no small measure contributed to the enhancement of consular authority.

Beecroft's first assignment in Dahomey proved abundantly that, in the absence of any willingness on the part of the British government to embark on what Lord Salisbury at a later date described as expensive West African expeditions, the mere appointment of a Consul was not necessarily inconsistent with the independence of the indigenous Nigerian states. In May 1850 Beecroft, accompanied by Commander Forbes, went on an official mission to Gezo, the

---

[1] F.O. 84/775, Palmerston to Beecroft, draft no. 1, 30 June 1849.
[2] Diké, *op. cit.* See ch. VII for details.

king of Dahomey. Beecroft promised Gezo a subsidy of £3000 for three years and solicited a treaty of good behaviour on the part of the king. The mission failed and Gezo quite complacently informed Beecroft that Dahomey had already planned its raids for the following year. All Britain subsequently did was to blockade Whydah, a Dahomian port.[1] The Dahomian king and state remained intact.

The next Dahomian king refused to accept a British agent at any of his ports. The mission undertaken by Burton, a British Consul, was treated discourteously. To Burton, the Dahomians were a 'flatulent, self-conceited herd of barbarians...vermin with a soul apiece'.[2] In spite of the circumstances indicated above, Britain, through the Consul, did not establish an empire of informal sway over Dahomey. On the other hand Beecroft's dealings with Lagos and the city-states to the east were on an entirely different basis and produced far-reaching consequences. The comparative smallness in size and the greater accessibility of these states to the British navy do not afford adequate explanation for the predominance of consular authority.

Beecroft's action in Lagos should have served as a warning to the rulers of the Nigerian coast states. But the point really is that, whether or not the significance of Beecroft's intervention in the affairs of Lagos was appreciated, the realities of coast politics would still have served the Consul's purposes. In the case of Lagos, it was easy enough for the Consul to find a rival to the throne. Kosoko, an ally of Dahomey, had probably continued to indulge in the slave trade. He, however, was not prepared to accept British influence. In the meantime, Akitoye, the rival, pleaded: 'I rejoice very much to see the day which has brought you, the Representative of England, to this town.... Indeed, I very much need your protection, as my life is every moment at stake.'[3]

After the bombardment of Lagos and the flight of Kosoko, Beecroft began his career as king-maker, and on 1 January 1852 obtained a treaty from the king he installed in Lagos. The treaty provided for the abolition of the slave trade and human sacrifices, the promotion of peaceful trade, the protection of British subjects

[1] F.O. 84/816, Palmerston to Beecroft, 12 February; Beecroft to Palmerston, 4 May and 22 July 1850.
[2] Burton, *A Mission to Gelele, King of Dahomey* (London, 1864), p. 250.
[3] Akitoye's letter to Beecroft, quoted in Burns, *op. cit.* p. 111.

and missionaries. Beecroft's policy was, from the British point of view, eminently successful. There is hardly any wonder that the policy of interference with local politics was extended to the city-states of the Niger delta and eastwards.

To understand what happened here under Beecroft and his successors it is necessary to discuss the political weaknesses outlined earlier. The first weakness was involved in the 'House' system. As explained earlier, the House was composed of chiefs, freemen and slaves bound together under a head for purposes of local government, mutual welfare and, most important, highly competitive trade. The strength and influence of a House depended on the wealth derived from trade. It thus happened that the king who owned his own House had to compete in trade with subjects who also owned their own Houses. Bonny in the fifties clearly demonstrated the pernicious effects of the system outlined above. A poor king could not hope to command respect in a society preoccupied with trade.[1]

During the reign of William Dappa Pepple (Pepple V), who became king in 1837, the Houses of Manilla Pepple and Annie Pepple progressively outstripped the royal House in wealth. The two powerful, because wealthy, Houses were under slaves who had risen to be heads of Houses. The opposition which the powerful chiefs led against the king stemmed directly from the manœuvres of the king to revive the fortunes of his House through manipulating the trade of the inland markets. In the meantime the growing weakness of the central authority in Bonny persuaded the white merchants to form what came to be called 'Courts of Equity'. Baikie described a Court as 'a commercial or mercantile association...the members being the chief white and black traders in the place, and the chair is occupied by the white supercargoes in monthly rotation'.[2]

In 1854 Beecroft deported the king of Bonny. He, however, reported to the British government that the king had himself asked to be rescued from the danger to his life threatened by the powerful chiefs of his kingdom. Beecroft once again exercised his new authority by selecting a puppet successor on whom he

---

[1] Diké, *op. cit.* p. 164.
[2] Baikie, *op. cit.* p. 356.

imposed the supremacy of the 'Court of Equity'. The European traders, and indeed the principal local chiefs, had naturally no respect for the puppet ruler.[1]

The puppet successor of Pepple V died in 1855 and for a time Bonny was left without an indigenous ruler. Then the Consul and the white traders agreed on the four leading native chiefs who should form a regency. It was not to be expected that four rival trading chiefs could agree among themselves or give Bonny political stability. Once again the Consul had to intervene to elect one of the chiefs, Manilla Pepple, as head regent. The reports of the British agents on the spot do not always give a satisfactory picture of the extent to which consular authority had superseded indigenous rule. For instance, in the midst of the political confusion consequent on the deposition of Pepple, the Acting Consul, Lynslager, still pretended to believe that 'no white man had any right to interfere in any of their country affairs'.[2]

The Consul who succeeded Beecroft was Hutchinson. In his dispatch to the Foreign Office, he reported the political vacuum which existed in Bonny. He enclosed a letter from the head regent of Bonny. It is necessary to quote part of this letter because it revealed the effective position occupied by the British Consul. '...I come for man-of-war to ask you for give me book to make me free, and then no man can call me slave, for Queen of England make me free.'[3] The return of Pepple V did not restore the former stability or independence of Bonny. In fact, after the death of Pepple in 1866, the posture of affairs in Bonny progressively deteriorated. The next king, George Pepple, who reigned between 1866 and 1888, hardly exercised any influence over his far too powerful chiefs, who in due course embarked on a civil war. Throughout the period, successive Consuls, Burton, Charles Livingstone and Hopkins, were virtual governors. No Foreign Office dispatch took cognisance of this status. Nevertheless, what the Consuls were able to do without even the threat of naval bombardment bears out the contention that the House system

---

[1] Kingsley, *West African Studies* (London, 1899), see appendix 1, p. 524, written by de Cardi, a trader in the Niger delta for about thirty years.

[2] F.O. 84/975, Lynslager to Clarendon, 5 October 1855.

[3] F.O. 84/1061, see Enclosure in no. 9, Manilla Pepple to Hutchinson, 4 January 1858.

and its preoccupation with trade played into the hands of the British agents.

In Calabar, much earlier than in Bonny, Beecroft had intervened in the vital matter of selecting and confirming a successor to the throne. Waddell noted that the rulers of the Calabar dukedoms from Ephraim to Eyamba, Eyo Honesty and Archibong were personal friends of the Consul.[1] That might be so. The significant thing was that an alien should in 1852 preside over the election of the successor of King Archibong. There were, however, more serious weaknesses in the local situation in Calabar which did much to strengthen the grip of the supercargoes and the Consul on the local rulers.

The Calabar rulers had, in addition to the slave members of the trading corporations or Houses, plantations in the neighbourhood which were occupied and cultivated by Calabar-owned slaves. In the fifties, the plantation slaves organised themselves under their own leaders to protect their members against the arbitrary exactions of their masters in the Calabar 'republics'. It has been explained earlier that, although the Calabar states had dukes and princes, the effective executive and legislative body was the Egbo society. It was largely through the instrumentality of the secret society that the slave population had hitherto been held in complete subjection. The slave population in the plantations now organised their own society known as 'the order of blood'. The slave society not only defied Egbo authority, but threatened to invade Duke Town.[2]

The prospect of civil war in the Calabar states was one hardly compatible with the security of British merchants and property. As in Bonny, the weaknesses in the social structure of Calabar created a political vacuum which the British merchants and Consul had perforce to fill. Thus, naturally, the supercargoes summoned Beecroft and the warships to Calabar to deal with 'certain alarming symptoms of revolt among the slaves'. Beecroft had no doubt about his ability and authority to restore stability to the government of Duke Town. He claimed that he alone could 'allay the storm'.[3]

At the 'peace' conference to which Beecroft invited the leaders

---

[1] Waddell, *op. cit.* pp. 378–9, 476 f.
[2] F.O. 84/858, no. 70, Beecroft to Palmerston, 27 October 1851.  [3] *Ibid.*

of the factions, he threw the weight of his authority on the side of the chiefs and the Egbo society. His so-called peace treaty stipulated that the slaves should not form associations without the approval of their masters, and should respect the Egbo society. The only provision which theoretically favoured the slaves was the clause which abolished human sacrifices. The effectiveness of, and the justification for, consular intervention in the politics of Calabar were, according to Beecroft, amply vindicated. 'I took advantage to do away with a law that had been a disgrace to a partially civilized place....It saved the loss of an immense sum (£200,000) to English merchants....'[1]

Beecroft's 'treaty' could not stop the movement for emancipation on the part of the slave population of the Calabar republics. The subsequent political history of Calabar saw the progressively successful vindication of the political rights of the slave-born communities.[2]

The situations in Lagos, Bonny and Calabar which helped to transform a British Consul into a king-maker had elements of similarity and dissimilarity. The three states exhibited dynastic and political weaknesses, although the manifestations of these weaknesses varied. In Lagos, Beecroft had found a rival and pliable claimant to the throne. In Bonny, powerful heads of Houses had nullified the authority of the king, who had no means of resisting deportation. In Calabar, the slave population had threatened to reduce political and commercial life to paralysis. In all the states, the interests of English trade were jeopardised. The merchants, the Consul and the British Foreign Office knew what the Consul was expected to do in the circumstances. Except in Lagos and belatedly in Bonny, the action of the Consul was not questioned by the indigenous rulers involved.

In the conditions prevailing along the Nigerian coast in the nineteenth century, trade and politics were hardly separable in the affairs of the city-states. In the circumstances, trade practices such as 'comey' and the trust system had considerable bearing on the political fortunes of the city-states. Before the middle of the

[1] *Ibid.*
[2] Jones, 'The Political Organisation of Old Calabar', in Forde, *Efik Traders of Old Calabar* (London, 1956), pp. 148–50.

3-2

nineteenth century, the local potentates levied on the white traders a duty called 'comey', for permission to trade in their territories and with their subjects. 'Comey' amounted to about 2s. 6d. per ton of the palm oil exported.[1] The payment of 'comey' to the king implicitly meant the recognition of the sovereignty of the city-state. But under consular jurisdiction, it came to be accepted that the kings or dukes were paid 'comey' because they were responsible to the Consul for the security of the lives and property of white merchants, and for the promotion of trade in the hinterland. The local chiefs did not stop to make fine distinctions and so they accepted the new basis without any misgivings.

The chiefs and the supercargoes were responsible for two dangerous developments in respect of the 'comey' system. The chiefs, probably more as traders than as rulers, introduced other exactions from the supercargoes. De Cardi has enumerated five such duties or taxes—Ex-Bar, Custom Bar, Work Bar, Gentlemen's Dash and Boys' Dash. In the first place, the proceedings involved in these payments enormously derogated from the status of local rulers. The kings were involved in situations where they virtually begged for presents, misnamed duties. The categories of duties which the supercargoes had to pay became inextricably mixed up with the fluid social structure of the city-states. In time, kings, heads of Houses and petty traders all claimed one kind of duty or another. In the face of this sort of confusion over the payment of irregular duties, the supercargoes began to manipulate even the original and well established 'comey' payment to uphold the political standing of Houses which did good business with them against the interests of the rulers.[2]

More pernicious in its effects than the distortion of the 'comey' was the 'trust' system. The system was probably a very old one because there is a record of it in Bosman's *New and Accurate Description of the Coast of Guinea*, published in 1705. The evils of the system became apparent in the nineteenth century. The practice of 'chopping oil' introduced lawlessness in the affairs of the city-states. In practice, the white merchants who had given out credits and did not receive in time the goods for which credits

---

[1] Kingsley, *op. cit.* p. 523.
[2] *Ibid.* pp. 524, 531.

were given took the law into their own hands. 'Thereupon that agent...armed his Krooboys and lay in wait beside a frequented creek; when a sufficiently rich canoe-train came down he laid violent hands upon it, and informed the owner that so-and-so owed him a certain quantity of oil, and he could collect the debt with interest from the defaulter.'[1]

Even the merchants recognised the iniquitous consequences of the 'trust' system. The rivalry between the Houses was accentuated and the supercargoes exploited this rivalry. The supercargoes themselves also suffered from the malpractices of indigenous traders who accepted 'double trusts'. It was partly to allay the evils of the 'trust' system that the unofficial 'Courts of Equity' had come into existence to usurp the authority of the local potentates. When Eyo Honesty of Calabar attempted to break the system, the British Consul intervened on the grounds that Eyo had not paid his debts incurred under the 'trust' system. Eyo was not allowed by the Consul to ship his produce directly to England. The arbitrary nature of the Consul's intervention was acknowledged by the British Foreign Office.[2] But meanwhile a local chief was forced by the Consul to accept a commercial practice which did much harm to the peace and stability of his state. Where the supercargoes were adversely involved, the Foreign Office hastened to assert that 'neither H.M. Government nor H.M. Consul...have any legal power to oblige the British supercargoes stationed in the rivers of the Bight of Biafra to adopt or to obey any particular code of trading regulations'.[3] The position was therefore a very sinister one. The supercargoes, who initiated the Courts of Equity, manipulated 'comey' payments and the 'trust' system, and in the process either procured the deportation of some local rulers or undermined the authority of the remaining ones, were themselves above the law.

The uncertainty and confusion caused by the lawlessness[4] of some of the British supercargoes led directly to the first attempt on the part of the British government to define formally the legal status of the Consul and the Courts of Equity, from the British

---

[1] Bindloss, *In the Niger Country* (London, 1898), p. 305.
[2] F.O. 84/1030, no. 23, Hutchinson to Clarendon, 29 April 1857.
[3] F.O. 84/1001, Minutes on no. 23, Hutchinson to F.O., 12 March 1856.
[4] F.O. 84/1356, 371, Livingstone's Memo to F.O., 3 December 1871.

standpoint. The Order in Council, dated 21 February 1872, is a wordy document and so the relevant portions only are summarised here. First, the Consul was empowered to carry into effect and to enforce the observance of the stipulations of any treaties and conventions between Britain and the Chiefs of Old Calabar, Bonny, Cameroons, New Calabar, Brass, Opobo and Benin rivers. Under this provision, the Consul could fine, imprison or banish British subjects who violated the provisions of the said treaties and conventions. Secondly, any local regulations made by the Consul were to be approved by the British Foreign Office. Thirdly, the Courts of Equity were given the role of providing assessors to assist the Consul in deciding the guilt or innocence of accused British subjects. Subject to the approval and guidance of the Consul, the local Courts of Equity were given limited powers to settle trade disputes between British subjects and the natives. But British subjects could forfeit the 'protection' of the Courts of Equity by refusing to be enrolled as members. Lastly, civil suits between British subjects and the natives could be determined by the Courts of Equity provided the natives were willing to submit to the authority of the courts.[1]

The Order in Council summarised above is invaluable for a study of the true nature of the British policy of informal sway during this period. In this respect, certain conclusions are inescapable. In theory, the British government apparently recognised that the city-states of the coast formed no part of Britain's dominion. The judicial and 'administrative' functions of the Consul were confined to British subjects. Then there was the typical vagueness of the document in respect of natives and British subjects who refused to accept the authority of the Courts of Equity. The previous actions of the Consuls in deporting kings, and the implications, were completely ignored by the Order in Council. The result naturally was that Consuls who chose to be energetic did what they liked with the local chiefs, and the Foreign Office asked no serious questions except where British subjects were directly or indirectly involved.

After the suppression of the slave trade, the basic purpose of the empire of informal sway was quite indisputably the growth of profitable commercial enterprise. This possibility was, from the

---

[1] For the Order in Council in full see Burns, *op. cit.* appendix E.

British standpoint, the most important feature of the British connection with the Nigerian coast. At the beginning of the nineteenth century only 150 tons of palm oil were exported from the coast. By the middle of the century, the export had reached 25,000 tons.[1] The Consuls carefully noted the spectacular progress of British business. According to Livingstone, there were sixty large trading establishments and a growing market for British manufactured goods.[2]

British enterprise was not confined to the Nigerian coast. The early calamities of the philanthropic projects up the river Niger did not for long obscure the economic potentialities of the Nigerian hinterland. The successful use of quinine in the Baikie expedition of 1854 opened the way to hinterland exploitation. Macgregor Laird, the pioneer of British enterprise in this area, obtained in 1857 a subsidy from the British government to enable him to maintain a steamer on the Niger. Laird soon had factories erected at Abo, Onitsha and Lokoja. This new enterprise naturally provoked the hostility of the coast British merchants, the coast native middlemen and their native allies along the Lower Niger.

British activities on the Nigerian coast and on the Lower Niger clearly belie the complacent assumption that the often quoted 1865 Resolution of the Parliamentary Committee represented before or after 1865 a consistent British policy towards the whole of West Africa. It is true that the triumph of the Manchester School of Free-traders in British politics inevitably led to the adoption of free trade and a measure of *laissez-faire* in imperial affairs. James Stephen of the Colonial Office could argue that 'in North America and in Australia we have vacant continents to occupy, and every shilling well expended there may be made to yield a large and secure return. But in Africa even if we could acquire the Dominion of the whole continent it would be but a worthless possession.'[3] To the British Parliament it was quite clear that territorial entanglements and profitable commercial enterprise were two

[1] *Parl. Papers* 1881, vol. XCIII. Value of exports, 1866 = £1,422,937; 1870 = £1,721,632; 1875 = £1,727,765.

[2] Diké, *op. cit.* p. 198.

[3] C.O. 267/159, Minute, 21 December 1840 on Governor of Sierra Leone to Russell, no. 34, 29 July 1840; also Bodelsen, *Studies in Mid-Victorian Imperialism* (Copenhagen, 1924), pp. 201–2.

different things. Here then lay the difference between the Niger districts and the formal British West African settlements.

The events which led to the appointment of the Ord Commission and the Adderley Parliamentary Committee do not require elaboration here. The famous Resolution of 1865[1] indicated no more than that Britain should cut her losses in the West African colonial footholds, presumably by withdrawing from them.

It is essential to note that the seven resolutions of the select committee have not up to now been carefully studied by historians of West Africa. The general tendency of the resolutions to look forward to the withdrawal of British authority from West Africa was explicitly qualified in the fourth resolution which stated that although the 'policy of non-extensions' would apply to all new settlements, there might be cases, in dealing with existing settlements, in which the 'policy of non-extensions' might not properly apply. The establishments involved were stations in Gambia, Sierra Leone, Gold Coast and Lagos. The figures representing the revenue and expenditure were in 1864–5 as follows:[2]

| Colony | Revenue from duties (£) | Expenditure (£) |
| --- | --- | --- |
| Gambia | 13,000 | 19,000 |
| Sierra Leone | 45,000 | 47,000 |
| Gold Coast | 4,000 | 9,400 |
| Lagos | 18,000 | 22,800 |

The discrepancy between revenue and expenditure constituted a liability inconsistent with the parsimony of the British Treasury. These colonies were 'mill-stones' but even then it is easy to exaggerate the willingness of the British government or Parliament to throw them off.

Did the British Foreign Office and the Admiralty shrink from the implications of the situation thus created? Was the situation not one that lent itself to the application of the Palmerstonian thesis of *pax Britannica*? During the decade after Laird's modest beginnings, the British Foreign Office deliberately encouraged trade expansion

[1] *Parl. Papers*, 1865, vol. I. Proceedings of the Parl. Committee on Col. Ord's Report, etc.

[2] *Ibid.* Also C.O. 147/2, F.O. to C.O., 28 November 1861. See Minute by Elliot, 30 November 1861.

on the Niger, even against the opposition of the local rulers. It enthusiastically accepted that '...if we can open out the Niger to the trade of this country, it will be another and a considerable step in the right direction'.[1] The possibilities of British trade in palm oil, cotton, groundnuts and ivory were therefore overriding considerations. In the circumstances, naval power was, as on the coast, an essential ingredient of the policy of informal sway. The local chiefs were given ample warning that the navy would be at hand to deal with those whose importunities hampered or jeopardised trade. At one time or another, Onitsha, Aboh and Idah were shelled and burnt to the ground. The aim of these operations was admirably summarised by the leader of the expedition against Onitsha. 'Our proceedings at Onitsha will have a most salutary effect up and down the Niger, and the Missionaries and Traders unanimously gave us their thanks....'[2]

Another positive step in furthering the policy of inland commercial penetration was the foundation of the consulate at Lokoja. Baikie had in an unorthodox manner installed himself as British Consul in the territory of King Masaba of Nupe.[3] His action was not repudiated by the British Foreign Office. In fact, steps were taken to regularise the new relationship with Masaba. The successors of Baikie were not energetic agents and so the consulate collapsed. Even then diplomatic missions were despatched to Masaba to persuade the Nupe ruler to protect British lives and trade.[4] Native protection or not, the navy was always available, and under the guarantee of naval protection, the British trade on the Niger apparently justified Palmerston's 'forward policy'.[5]

The Niger districts in no essential way shared the disabilities indicated above. On the contrary, the Niger and the Nigerian coast provided the spring-board for the type of expansion dear to the heart of the British Foreign Office. The growth of British trade here was a rewarding one. Where problems of sovereignty did arise, inexpensive consular 'influence' took care of them. It was here, therefore, that the British policy of informal sway found

[1] F.O. 97/343, see Memo by Wylde, 28 April 1864.
[2] F.O. 84/1541, no. 31, Easton to F.O., 3 November 1879.
[3] *Parl. Papers*, 1862, vol. LXI, p. 177. See Baikie's letter.
[4] F.O. 84/1351, Simpson to Granville, 21 November 1871.
[5] F.O. 84/1498, Admiralty to F.O., 13 December 1876.

fulfilment. There was no opposition to a 'forward policy'. In any case, the progressive deterioration of political stability in the city-states of the coast increased the opportunities for tightening the grip of the British Consul on the local rulers. It was not without some significance that the consular headquarters was transferred in 1872 from Fernando Po to the mainland at Old Calabar. There was no longer any question of the authority and goodwill of the local potentates, the occasional lip-service to native sovereignty notwithstanding. The state of affairs was not entirely the fault of the British Consul or the supercargoes, as two examples clearly demonstrate.

The return of King William Pepple to Bonny from his banishment did nothing to fill the political vacuum which the emergence of overmighty subjects in Bonny had originally created. The king had neither the resources nor the health to do more than retire to Juju Town and he died in 1866. His successor, King George Pepple, had no illusions about his impotence. If the records of Consul Livingstone are reliable, then the new king had begun his reign by begging the Consul 'to bring a Man-of-War and compel his chiefs to do whatever I thought fit'.[1]

The rivalry between the powerful Houses of Manilla Pepple and Annie Pepple and their allies had in no way abated. They were now under the headships of two dynamic ex-slaves, Oko Jumbo and Jaja. Oko Jumbo was already a powerful figure in Bonny politics when Jaja emerged in 1861 to lead the House of Opooboo 'the Great'. The British Consul at the time, Burton, while derogatorily noting that Jaja was 'the son of an unknown bushman, a common Negro', recognised the qualities in Jaja which were destined to produce remarkable achievements. Meanwhile, local European observers knew that although George Pepple was theoretically the king, everybody in Bonny looked upon Oko Jumbo and Jaja as the effective rulers of the city-state.[2]

If these two chiefs had co-operated, all might have been well for Bonny. The clash of personalities and of trade interests created a situation of which the logical outcome in 1869 was a civil war. The details of the civil war are of no consequence here. What is of

---

[1] F.O. 84/1277, no. 13, Livingstone to Stanley, 13 July 1867.
[2] Kingsley, *op. cit.* See appendix by De Cardi, p. 529.

significance is the way in which the civil war left Bonny at the mercy of the British supercargoes and the Consul. In the first place, the heavy guns and the war-canoes mustered by the rival Houses did not augur well for the trade business of the British merchants, who nonetheless took sides in the internal dispute. When Jaja temporarily yielded, it was to the Court of Equity, not to the king of Bonny, that he revealed his intentions.[1] The troubles of Bonny were by no means at an end.

Jaja secretly planned the evacuation of the chiefs attached to the Opooboo House. A site in the territory of the Andoni, north-east of Bonny, was chosen. Here Jaja founded a new kingdom which was to play a celebrated part in the history of the subsequent British attempt to incorporate the Nigerian coast into the British empire. The situation of Opobo—the new Jaja kingdom—placed Jaja in a strategic position which enabled him to control the traditional hinterland markets of Bonny. The supercargoes who had foresight enough to support Jaja transferred their business to Opobo. Between 1869 and 1870, a sort of commercial war raged between Bonny and Opobo. This was where the British Consul was bound to intervene. Bonny was so hardly pressed by Jaja's stranglehold that King George Pepple was dispatched to England to appeal to the British government. Meanwhile, the inveterate local opponent, Oko Jumbo, solicited the intervention of Consul Livingstone.[2]

The situation might have been comical had it not involved the political insolvency of the most remarkable of the city-states of the Nigerian coast. King Pepple in Britain protested that he was not seeking advice from the British Foreign Office on how to govern his state but was merely asking the British government to stop British supercargoes from having any business transactions with his 'rebel subject', Jaja. As was to be expected, the British Foreign Secretary, Granville, complacently agreed with Pepple and asserted that 'I am not in favour of our dictating terms of peace to these rival chiefs, for if so we make ourselves responsible for their being observed'.[3]

[1] F.O. 84/1308, Enclosure 2 in no. 24, Livingstone to Clarendon, 26 October 1869.
[2] F.O. 84/1326, Enclosure 1 in no. 7, Livingstone to F.O., 7 March 1870.
[3] F.O. 84/1343, no. 2, Granville to Livingstone, 25 January 1871.

The Consul was thus at first instructed not to interfere beyond safeguarding the lives and property of British merchants. The pretence that the Consul had no part to play in the politics of Bonny did not last long. In any case, to safeguard British lives and to interfere in the local political situation were in practice one and the same thing. The Consul was subsequently instructed to convey to the warring states of Bonny and Opobo that the side which prolonged the dispute would incur 'Her Majesty's serious displeasure'.

During King Pepple's absence in England, Consul Livingstone had apparently tried to undermine what authority the king still had in Bonny. Oko Jumbo and the leading chiefs, at the instigation of the Consul, practically disavowed the king's mission to England. It is easy to explain the Consul's antagonism to Pepple. In England, Pepple had blamed the political confusion in Bonny on the incompetence of the Consul. Livingstone's letters to the king were very abusive. He referred to Oko Jumbo, Waribo and Captain Hart as the king's superiors in office. With a note of ridicule, the Consul pointed to Pepple's change of his signature from George Pepple to 'Pepple Rex', and concluded that 'as "King" applied to you is entirely misleading to English minds, may I humbly suggest that the alliterative phrase "comey collector"...would be...appropriate'.[1] Pepple was not to be outdone by the Consul in vituperation. In his reply, the king argued that the term Consul as applied to Livingstone was misleading to both native and English minds. The term 'collector of fresh provisions' should accurately describe the Consul's public functions.[2]

In the long run, Livingstone was recalled, but he died at Bonny in November 1873. Before all this, the British government had dispatched Commodore Commerell with warships to settle the dispute between Bonny and Opobo. The intervention of the Commodore brought peace. The details of the Commodore's proceedings are not important, but it should be noted that the 'referees' were the British naval officer and the British Consul. The arbitrators were theoretically the king of New Calabar and British and native traders.

[1] *Bonny Local Records*, Livingstone's letter to Pepple from the British Consulate, Old Calabar, dated 9 July 1872.
[2] Pepple's reply, dated 18 July 1872.

44

The civil war in Bonny, Jaja's withdrawal from Bonny and his subsequent blockade of Bonny's route of access to the hinterland markets were indeed the proceedings of traders. The supercargoes had taken sides according to the prospects for good business which each side to the dispute held out. The way was thus open for consular and naval intervention. The treaty between Bonny and Opobo was to be enforced by the British Consul, on whom Article VIII of the treaty conferred the right to impose a fine not exceeding 1000 puncheons of oil on the local ruler who infringed the terms of peace.[1] The Commodore who settled the Bonny–Opobo dispute then undertook to recognise Jaja as king of Opobo. This recognition formed one of the stipulations of a Commercial Treaty with Jaja on 4 January 1873. Peace between the indigenous states of Bonny and Opobo became the responsibility of the British Consul.

While Jaja consolidated and extended his new kingdom, King Pepple of Bonny became more and more a shadow of a king. Pepple's message of greetings to the new Consul, Hartley, submissively accepted that 'now that you are placed at the head of affairs over this portion of the west coast of Africa appropriately called the Oil Rivers, I sincerely trust that firm and even justice will be impartially given to those to whom it is or may be done'.[2] The impotence of Pepple apart, the chiefs of Bonny who had helped to nullify the king's authority continued to intrigue against the king and against one another. Internal affairs came to a stage where even the Court of Equity, dominated by British merchants, threatened to deport the chiefs of Bonny. In 1881 Pepple took the unprecedented step of handing a letter of resignation to his chiefs. The main reasons were that ' ... you give me the name of king but refuse me the dignity. You enact and make laws as you please without my knowledge or sanction...you are all kings in your houses...'[3] Market disputes between Bonny and New Calabar were now, unlike before, referred to the Courts of Equity of Bonny and New Calabar, rather than to the indigenous rulers.

In internal affairs New Calabar provided a spectacle not unlike

---

[1] F.O. 84/1377, no. 2, Livingstone to Granville, 8 January 1873.
[2] *Bonny Local Records*, Pepple's letter to Hartley dated 20 October 1873.
[3] *Ibid.* Letter dated 7 December 1881.

that which had reduced the ruler and chiefs of Bonny to the status of being mere satellites of the British Consul. Up to 1879 the citizens of New Calabar had lived together under their king, Amachree. New Calabar had preserved a measure of respectability because the king had forbidden the 'trust' system which the supercargoes had exploited with disastrous political consequences in the neighbouring city-states. But then in New Calabar, as in the other states of the coast, the divisive competitiveness involved in the House system where trade was concerned was bound to reproduce in New Calabar the political instability already noted in Old Calabar and Bonny.

Will Braid, the head of the Barboy House in New Calabar, became very prosperous through the energetic trade activities of his sub-chiefs and boys. Naturally the king, Amachree, was not going to permit, without a struggle, the emergence of an over-mighty subject. He sought to destroy Will Braid by various devices, including arbitrary fines. Braid did not, like Jaja, precipitate a civil war. He quietly evacuated his House and occupied a new site on the main New Calabar route to the hinterland market.[1] The king's dispute with his wealthy subject led to the splitting up of the New Calabar kingdom. The king and his followers settled at Buguma. Another wealthy chief, Bob Manuel, founded his own settlement at Abonema, while Braid consolidated his position at Bakana. A kind of guerrilla warfare between the factions ensued on the creeks leading to the interior markets. Canoes and goods as well as men and women were seized in the undeclared war.

Whether a Consul was an imperialist or not, here was a situation he could not ignore. Consul Hopkins therefore had to intervene in order to restore the peace indispensable to the trade of the British merchants. He invited the warring chiefs on board a warship. Jaja of Opobo, the king of Okrika, and some Bonny chiefs were present as arbitrators. What emerged was a 'Perpetual Treaty of Peace between Chief Will Braid, the Head of Barboy House, and the King and Chiefs of New Calabar'. The Consul reserved to himself the right to impose a fine of 400 puncheons of oil on the side which broke any of the stipulations of the treaty.[2]

[1] Kingsley, *op. cit.* appendix 1, pp. 492–7.
[2] F.O.C.P. 4824, see no. 2, p. 3.

In a subsequent market dispute between Bonny and New Calabar, it was Consul Hewett who in 1881 decided which markets should belong to Bonny and which to New Calabar. King Amachree of New Calabar, in pleading for delay in the implementation of the Consul's partition, had to appeal through the local Court of Equity to the Bonny Court of Equity. In the absence of the Consul, the Courts of Equity controlled by British merchants had come to control the foreign relations of the local rulers.[1]

The internal political conditions and the trade practices which prevailed in the coast city-states have been discussed in considerable detail in order to show that before the European scramble for territory in the Bights of Benin and Biafra, the British had already, through the Consul, entrenched themselves on the Nigerian coast. The position of the Consul was, except in name, that of a governor. This situation helps to explain the ease with which Britain later secured the treaties which in 1885 provided the basis for the formal declaration of the Protectorate of the Oil Rivers. Before this, trade, influence and industrial pre-eminence had served Britain well in the Niger district. The growth of British trade and predominance had cost the British Treasury nothing. But the security of this inexpensive and informal sway depended on what has been called the indefinite self-denial of the oversea-minded European powers.[2]

Both France and Germany, not to mention the smaller powers, were to become actively aware of the economic potentialities of tropical Africa. As the Industrial Revolution gained momentum in western Europe, the nations involved attempted to buttress political nationalism with economic nationalism. The inevitable policy was a general adoption of high tariffs in order to exclude foreign goods. An important part of this policy was the determination to acquire exclusive control of tropical raw materials and markets. The French view of the new possibilities which Africa revealed was quite straightforward. 'Either we must found an African Empire, or in a hundred years we shall have sunk to the level of a second rate power.'[3]

The ramifications of French colonial ambitions in Algeria,

---

[1] National Archives (Enugu), Proceedings of the Courts of Equity, 1881.

[2] Robinson and Gallagher, *op. cit.* p. 394.

[3] Ireland, *Tropical Colonisation*, quotation from the French political economist, Leroy Beaulieu, p. 17.

Senegal and the Congo do not concern us here. Of greater importance to the subject was the challenge to the British position in the Niger districts. What originally roused the fears of British merchants was the exclusive tariff method, the damaging effects of which to British trade were experienced by the British merchants in the Gaboon, a territory secured to France by De Brazza. Thus, if British complacency and official inaction were allowed to hand over the Niger districts to France, the commercial business built up for nearly a century would be gone. The very idea was a nightmare to British merchants.[1]

The French did in fact appear on the Lower Niger and on the Nigerian coast. On the Niger, French plans were partly commercial and partly political. They began to unfold with a treaty between a French agent and the Nupe ruler who had succeeded Masaba. Land was acquired from Nupe in order to build French trading stations. By 1880 the French had built other stations at Loko (on the Benue), at Egga (on the Niger) and at Onitsha and Aboh. These apparently commercial activities had the full approval of the French government. The French objectives were expressed by the French Minister of Marine and Colonies as follows: 'On the Niger from the Delta up to its confluence with the Benue, our only aim must be to make sure of the freedom of our trade.... But on the Benue we can win a more privileged position by signing political or commercial conventions.... Such a policy, if it is skilfully pursued would give our traders a route to Lake Chad and to the rich markets of Adamawa and Bornu.'[2]

The year 1883, which saw the emergence of the imperialist-minded French Premier, Jules Ferry, and the virtual encirclement of British positions in the Gambia and Sierra Leone, also witnessed the appearance on the Niger of the redoubtable Commander Mattei who was loaned from the French War Ministry to direct the French enterprise on the Lower Niger. Thanks largely to the capital given by the French government, the French firms had been amalgamated into one company. As *agent consulaire*, Mattei progressively consolidated French trade which, in addition to the stations already noted, also possessed many floating stations.

[1] *Merchant Adventure*, John Holt and Co. (Liverpool) Ltd.
[2] Robinson and Gallagher, *op. cit.* quoted p. 166.

Fortunately for Britain, Taubman Goldie, who had an interest in one of the four British firms on the Lower Niger, proved equal to the French challenge.[1] To Goldie, the fear of the designs of the French was real, not hypothetical. In 1879 and 1882 he achieved the amalgamation of the British firms on the Niger, preparatory to a commercial war with the French company. All kinds of devices were employed. His ultimate aim was to buy out the French company and regain British predominance in the Lower Niger. This task Goldie achieved with unqualified success,[2] on the eve of the Berlin Conference.

The Anglo-French proceedings on the Lower Niger did not, except in one respect, seriously affect the more leisurely consular transactions on the Nigerian coast. The exception was the Brass city-state. Brass traders had done a great deal to develop the external trade of the Lower Niger. For many centuries Brass canoes had sailed up and down the river, touching places as far north as Lokoja. The palm-oil trade of Brass attained impressive dimensions after the middle of the nineteenth century. The attempts by British merchants, following the trail blazed by Macgregor Laird, to gain direct access to the Brass interior markets naturally roused the hostility of Brassmen. In this, they had the full support of the coast supercargoes. Full details of the bitter opposition to alien commercial penetration of the region behind the Niger delta are available in other sources.[3]

The Brass chiefs at first asked for no more than a reasonable partition of their source of livelihood. If Brass had 'the markets we have made between the river and Onitsha',[4] the English merchants were welcome to the remaining part of the river Niger. The solicitations of the Brass king were in vain. The Admiralty empowered its gun-boats to smash towns on the delta and above which attempted to obstruct British trading vessels sailing up the Niger. As already recounted, British and French trading stations were, after 1880, established along the Lower Niger, but not

[1] Flint, *Sir George Goldie and the Making of Nigeria* (Oxford, 1960), chs. II and III.
[2] F.O. 84/1814, Goldie to Anderson, private, 1 November 1884.
[3] Diké, *op. cit.*; Flint, *op. cit.*
[4] F.O. 84/1498, King Okyah's letter dated 7 July 1876, in Admiralty to F.O., 13 December 1876.

necessarily to the exclusion of Brass traders. The exclusion came later, but meanwhile the Brass chiefs invoked the assistance of the local Consul. In fact Hopkins promised to persuade the British government to secure for Brass the market from Abo to the sea. The Consul's promise remained a mere promise. It is hardly surprising that the Brass chiefs nursed a grievance against Britain and this was what the French tried to exploit. The French agent came within an ace of undermining the British position when the Brass chiefs temporarily accepted a treaty with France.[1] The grievance against Britain—and the attitude of Jaja—constituted the real obstacle to the ease with the British Consul in 1884 might have secured the desperately urgent treaties of protection. The Brass grievance was to express itself more aggressively in the next decade.

Apart from the birth of a Brass grievance, two other developments on the coast on the eve of the scramble should be noted. The first was the missionary penetration of the Cross river basin. The second was the consolidation of Jaja's dominion. It may be recalled that the Scottish missionaries' appeal to settle in Old Calabar had coincided with the slave treaty made between the rulers of the Calabar republics and the British naval commander, Raymond. The foundations of missionary enterprise seemed already laid when the chiefs of Calabar agreed that ' ... they are desirous of your coming amongst them, and are full of the scheme, hoping to have their children taught in English learning'.[2] The successful beginnings of missionary work in Old Calabar were the work of the remarkable missionary, Hope Waddell, who won the friendship of Eyo Honesty II of Creek Town and Eyamba V of Duke Town.

The reconciliation of the Egbo society and the slave organisations which threatened the very existence of the Calabar states in the 1850's was a tribute to the work of the Scottish missionaries. The powerful King Eyo of Creek Town, who died in 1858, left instructions that the traditional killings of slaves who would accompany his journey to the next world should not take place. For many decades, a missionary battle was waged against bar-

---

[1] Flint, *op. cit.* p. 52.
[2] McFarlan, *Calabar, the Church of Scotland Mission Founded 1846* (London, 1946), pp. 8–13.

barous customs. Naturally the chief stumbling block was the Egbo society, whose ideas about the status of women and the isolation of widows—to mention but a few examples—were contrary to those of the missionaries. The mission stations were to become the refuge of many a widow. The British Consuls lent the weight of their authority to the efforts of the missionaries.[1] The Rev. Hugh Goldie's scholarship proved complementary to the pioneering genius of the Rev. H. Waddell. Goldie produced an Efik translation of the Bible, an Efik Dictionary, and hundreds of hymns in the Efik language.

When more missionaries were available, the penetration of the Cross river basin began. Uwet, Okoyong and Umon were visited. These places were all strategically located to facilitate or frustrate Efik commercial enterprise in the hinterland. Although Efik attempts to dominate their hinterland neighbours usually ended in failure, the missionary penetration roused the suspicion of the Efik traders. On the other hand, the hinterland peoples believed that missionary enterprise was laying the foundation for the imposition of Efik authority. In spite of these difficulties, the missionaries entertained great visions of a vast network of missionary enterprise in Ibo, Ibibio and Ekoi country, access to which was provided by the Enyong and Calabar tributaries of the Cross river. Mary Slessor and Samuel Edgerley plunged into the Calabar hinterland. Through Edgerley's efforts, missionary teachers were established at Umon, Ikotana and Akunakuna. Slessor's main preoccupation was to be Okoyong,[2] a country of fierce fighters who had successfully defied the authority and commercial ambitions of the Efik.

It is hardly surprising that when Consul Hopkins in 1878 intervened in Old Calabar affairs to stop a multitude of traditional practices, including the murder of twins, the ostracism of the mothers of twins, human sacrifices, and the administration of poison oaths, he acknowledged that his action would have been impossible without the long residence and teaching of the Scottish missionaries.[3] The first steamer to patrol the Cross river was

[1] *Ibid.* pp. 62–3.
[2] See Livingstone, *The White Queen of Okoyong* (London, 1916).
[3] McFarlan, *op. cit.* p. 67.

4-2

provided by the missionaries. This was the *David Williamson*. British political penetration followed the lines already indicated by the missionaries. For many decades after 1884 the work of British political agents was based on the uncritical acceptance of the missionary view that the urgent task was 'to break down the inter-tribal barriers which closed the Cross river to trade and civilisation'.[1] In this region, therefore, the missionaries, more than the British traders, prepared the ground for the establishment of British political authority.

Whereas the missionary impact on Old Calabar facilitated British political designs, the rise and consolidation of the dominion of Jaja had exactly the opposite effect. The story of Jaja's commercial empire is briefly discussed here for three main reasons. In the first place, the empire of Jaja affords indisputable evidence of Jaja's organising genius. Secondly, Jaja's relations with Consul Hewett before the 'scramble' demonstrated that the mere presence of the British Consul should not necessarily have led to the collapse of indigenous authority on the Nigerian coast, provided of course that the British government did not resort to naval bombardment. Lastly, the consular charges against Jaja foreshadowed the reasons why the British government decided to proclaim a formal protectorate, as well as the difficulties which the British Protectorate regime was destined to aggravate owing largely to the equivocations of British policy.

The treaty which the British Commodore supervised and which brought the Bonny civil war to an end had been followed in 1873 by the recognition of Jaja as the king of the new state of Opobo. The 'Commercial Treaty' prohibited British merchants from direct trade transactions with Jaja's hinterland markets. Jaja's first task was to consolidate the port of Opobo. Assisted by the fourteen head chiefs who had accompanied him from Bonny, Jaja not only established the port of Opobo but also built up plantation settlements in the immediate neighbourhood of Opobo. Opobo's commercial expansion radiated in three directions. To the north was the famous oil market of Ohambele in Ndokiland. The oil producers from Bende and the Owerri districts brought their oil, through Ohambele middlemen, to the Ohambele market. Jaja

[1] *Ibid.* p. 98.

52

began by cementing a lasting friendship with the elders of Ohambele. He married a wife from there, and thus became a 'son-in-law' of the people of Ohambele. Then, through the instrumentality of the 'trust' system, the Ohambele middlemen traders became virtual trade agents of Jaja. In a similar manner, Jaja established a firm grip on the market of Azumini, fifteen miles from Aba. To these markets, Jaja appointed 'trade inspectors' from Opobo to regulate oil prices. In this way, he prevented the chaotic trade competition which had contributed substantially to the political ruin of Bonny. No one knew this better than Jaja himself.

To the north-east, Jaja established trading settlements on the creeks which discharge into the Opobo river. Here Jaja was brought into contact with the Ibibio groups in whose territories these trading stations were. Jaja's most important market was Essene. From here the ramifications of Jaja's trade enterprise embraced a large part of Ibibioland. It required a military expedition in 1884 to consolidate trade security among a very turbulent people. How turbulent the people were in this part of Jaja's commercial empire, the British were to find out after 1884.[1]

Jaja's eastern frontier at the Qua-Eboe river was both commercial and political. The security of the trading settlements and the trade routes which connected them with Opobo necessitated military expeditions organised by Jaja against the Annangs and the Ibeno aborigines. The first expedition in 1877, locally known as the Iköt Udö Öböng war, revealed the imaginative statemanship of Jaja. His rifles and cannon were too much for the dane guns of the Annangs. Nevertheless, after capturing the Annang war leader, Ogbo, Jaja treated him with incredible generosity, which secured on a friendly basis good relations with the Annangs to the north-east of Opobo. The 1879 and 1881 expeditions were directed against Qua-Eboe people who habitually plundered Opobo trade goods. After the latter chastisement, the leaders of the Qua-Eboe went to Opobo and signed a treaty in which they recognised Jaja's authority. This treaty, in which the late insurgents 'hereby declare that we are authorised to acknowledge Jaja as our king, and crave his protection, and to place ourselves under his authority for all time coming', was witnessed by the European trading agents on the

---

[1] F.O. 2/64, see Casement's Report, June 1894.

Opobo river, including De Cardi, Richard Hooper and three others.[1]

Jaja's exercise of authority on the Qua-Eboe precipitated a protracted but unnecessary controversy with Consul Hewett. The Consul's predecessor, Hopkins, had recognised Jaja's authority over the Qua-Eboe, and had therefore dissuaded the Efik rulers from their contemplated encroachment on the river in question. But in 1881 a British trading agent, George Watts, got himself involved by establishing a trade station on the Qua-Eboe without Jaja's authorisation. As was to be expected, Hewett and some British merchants rashly espoused the cause of Watts whose trade station was sacked by Jaja.[2]

Hewett began by disputing Jaja's claim to sovereignty over the Qua-Eboe. He resurrected an old Bonny treaty with the Ibenos in 1846 to support his contention that the area belonged to Bonny. Jaja's answer was simple but devastating. He pointed out that in 1846 Bonny had comprised the two royal Houses of Manilla Pepple and Annie Pepple, that the civil war had separated the two Houses, that during the war the Ibenos had sided with the Annie Pepple House of which Jaja was the head, and that in any case the Ibenos had reaffirmed their allegiance to Jaja in the treaty of 1881, after Jaja's expedition.

Consul Hewett changed his strategy. He now argued that Jaja's expedition against the Ibenos had been barbarous, and claimed, quite falsely, that the Ibenos were under the protection of the British government. No one in the Foreign Office seemed aware of the protection which the Consul alleged.[3] The British government ordered the Admiralty officers to investigate the situation on the Qua-Eboe. The naval inquiry vindicated the claims of Jaja. The British government, nevertheless, warned Jaja that they were not committed to recognising his sovereignty on the Qua-Eboe. The usual reference was made to the security of British lives and property. Jaja believed he had won his eastern frontier.

Hewett was not the man to accept defeat in good grace. Through-

[1] F.O. 84/1630, Jaja to Granville, 3 April 1882.
[2] *Ibid.* John Holt to Granville, 16 February 1882.
[3] *Parl. Papers*, Africa, no. 2 [C. 5365], encl. 2 in Hewett to F.O. See Hewett to Jaja, 24 May 1881. F.O.C.P. 4824, Granville's minute, 15 March 1882, on no. 20, Hewett to F.O., 17 February 1882.

out 1883 he persisted in his exaggeration of the alleged depreda-
tions of the Opobo warriors on the Qua-Eboe people. He went a
step further and tried to undermine Jaja's authority more directly
by entering into treaty relations with Eket, Ikoretu, Okat and
Okön. The Consul's endeavours were futile. Subsequently, two
British Admirals, usually more detached than the Consuls,
reported in 1884 on the local situation. Admiral Salmon asserted
that he thought British interests would be better served by keeping
on friendly terms with Jaja. Admiral Richards, who had also
served on the Oil Rivers but was now at the Admiralty, reiterated
his earlier opinion, conveyed to Consul Hewett, that Mr Watts
had been wrong in trying to establish a trade station on the Qua-
Eboe. Jaja had legitimate grievances because the Qua-Eboe
people were his subjects. If Jaja took severe measures against
their rebellion, civilised countries had done the same thing for
'less intelligible reasons'.[1]

The extraordinary thing was that Consul Hewett, who was
vilifying Jaja over the Qua-Eboe affair, was at the same time
implicitly acknowledging the beneficent pervasiveness of Jaja's
influence throughout the Oil Rivers. Early in 1884 Bonny and
New Calabar threatened to destroy Okrika. Hewett's attempts to
resolve the dispute failed. What was required was Jaja's intervention. The Consul, in spite of himself, agreed that 'if Jaja would
but assist, the matter would be settled; if he does not, I fear the
war may last a long time'.[2] Jaja did intervene in the interest of
peace. He summoned an arbitration conference in Opobo and
under his chairmanship the warring groups from Bonny, New
Calabar and Okrika accepted peace terms.

Another aspect of Jaja's position worth mentioning was his close
friendship with the Aro. He had some of them as Juju consultants
and others as diplomatic agents in the Ibo country. In some of his
military expeditions, the Aro willingly supplied Abam mercenaries.
The probability that Jaja's rule might ultimately have embraced
the whole of Eastern Nigeria, if the British had not intervened
in 1884, is a fascinating hypothesis. In fact, the very prospect

[1] F.O.C.P. 5004, Report dated 6 March 1884; 5063, no. 22, Salmon to
Villiers Lister, 5 December 1884.
[2] *Ibid.* 5004, no. 17, Hewett to F.O., 29 January 1884.

of this was a factor not less impelling than French and German competition in the British determination to proclaim a formal protectorate over the Oil Rivers in 1885.

While Goldie battled it out with the French on the Lower Niger and Consul Hewett nursed increasing apprehension that under the leadership of Jaja the recovery of the coast city-states might constitute an obstacle to British commercial penetration of the hinterland, the British Foreign Office was flooded with correspondence from the Chambers of Commerce of Liverpool, London, Bristol and Glasgow. The British government was warned of the danger of foreign encroachments on the region where British trade and influence had grown over a period of nearly fifty years. The merchants' importunities did not, however, indicate at this stage exactly what the British government was expected to do. One man on the coast had concrete proposals. Consul Hewett had in 1882 forwarded to the Foreign Office letters from the Cameroons in which the chiefs were alleged to be willing to surrender their country to the British Queen. Hewett argued that what had urgently to be done was to secure the control of the Bights of Benin and Biafra by establishing a 'protectorate', a Crown Colony, or a Chartered Company of British merchants.[1]

The leading members of the Gladstone ministry, although anxious to promote British trade, were rooted opponents of imperial expansion for its own sake. To Hewett's proposals regarding the region between the Benin River and the Cameroons, Kimberley, the Colonial Secretary, argued that the acquisition of such an extensive area would be a burdensome addition to the responsibilities of the British government. The coast was pestilential and the natives were barbarians. To subdue the savages, the British taxpayer would have to be called in to finance the military operations that might conceivably be involved.[2] Gladstone, the Prime Minister, was a notorious anti-imperialist. With utter unrealism, he seemed to argue that in the absence of the well understood and expressed wish of the people to be annexed, his government was opposed to annexations. According to the Lord Chancellor, with reference to another part of the world, annexation

---

[1] F.O.C.P. 4824, no. 9, Hewett to F.O., 14 January 1882.
[2] C.O. 806/203, appendix 1, Minute by Kimberley, 6 April 1882.

56

was 'morally unjustifiable, if it were done without demonstrable necessity'.[1] Two officials of the British Foreign Office certainly thought that the threat to British interests on the Niger and on the coast amounted to demonstrable necessity. These officials were T. Villiers Lister, Assistant Under-Secretary, and H. P. Anderson, Senior Clerk in the African Department. Their fight against official complacency finally won their chief, Granville, to the cause for which the merchants had long pleaded. A decision had to be made about the Oil Rivers.

The memoranda and counter-memoranda[2] which passed in 1883 through the Foreign Office, the Colonial Office and the Treasury reveal the true reasons behind official reluctance to commit the British government to the Niger districts. The stumbling block was the parsimony of the Treasury. Where no expense to the Treasury was involved, action to safeguard British interests was forthcoming. The consular status granted to an agent of Goldie's Company the better to liquidate French competition on the Niger provoked no controversy, because Goldie footed the bill. The situation on the Niger was in competent and inexpensive hands. But now the French and their gun-boats appeared at Bonny and Brass. Alarming news had arrived, and a decision could not much longer be shirked.[3]

Lister and Anderson urged the Foreign Secretary and the latter urged the Colonial Secretary that the region now threatened by France—the Oil Rivers—could pay its way as a colony. There was no question of yet another impecunious colony on the west coast of Africa. The Colonial Office had counter-proposals ready. The final decision taken by the Colonial committee of the Cabinet was to establish a protectorate in which the expensive paraphernalia of a Crown Colony establishment would have no place. A simple protectorate could exclude foreign competition and secure British trade. There would be time enough for dealing with the owners of the territories the fate of which was being decided in London. At first, presents had to be found for the local potentates whose

[1] Aydelotte, *Bismarck and British Colonial Policy* (Philadelphia, 1937), see quotations pp. 6 and 12.
[2] C.O. 806/214, Memo by Meade, 29 September 1883; F.O. 84/1655, Conf. Memo by Villiers Lister, 19 November 1883.
[3] F.O.C.P. 4825, Admiralty to F.O., 7 May 1883.

cooperation was needed for the necessary treaties of 'protection'. The little amount of money involved was indeed an investment because the region in question included 'those parts of the West Coast of Africa which lie between Capes St. Paul and St. John, in the Bights of Benin and Biafra, and which comprise the healthy regions round the Cameroons and the rich districts of the Niger and the Oil Rivers, with a trade which there is reason to believe would, if properly developed, render them a more valuable possession than the existing British Colonies on that Coast'.[1]

In May 1884 Consul Hewett was instructed to return without delay to his post on the Oil Rivers. He was to sign treaties with the local chiefs in the Oil Rivers, along the Niger and in the Cameroons. A few days before Hewett's departure, the German government had sent out an agent, Dr Nachtigal, to West Africa 'to gather information on behalf of the German Government'. In the event, Dr Nachtigal anticipated Hewett in the Cameroons and obtained a treaty of cession from the Cameroons chiefs on 14 July 1884. The Nigerian coast remained intact, a clear field for the implementation of Hewett's assignment of 'negotiating' treaties of protection with the chiefs of the coast city-states.

Hewett arrived at the coast with a model treaty and presents of gin, cloth and bright beads from the British government to their long-standing 'allies' and 'friends'. The treaties offered British protection, asked for British control of relations with foreign powers, stipulated full consular jurisdiction over British subjects and foreigners, and promised progress, civilisation and freedom of religion and trade.[2] In view of the authority already illegitimately exercised by successive British Consuls, Hewett did not anticipate much difficulty, and there were alluring presents to revive old friendships. He had, however, not reckoned with the deep-rooted trade grievance of Brass chiefs, or with the intelligence of Jaja of Opobo. The Benin River, New Calabar, Bonny and Old Calabar proved easy acquisitions.

The chiefs of Brass quite sensibly argued that before they 'put their hand to book', the British government must first protect

---

[1] *Parl. Papers*, no. 1, 1885 [C. 4279], F.O. draft to C.O. [part of text].
[2] Hertslet, *Map of Africa by Treaty*, I, 131–54. Also F.O. 93/10, 11, 16 for Treaties July–December 1884.

their traditional markets without which the people would be reduced to 'eating sand'. Hewett promised that this would be done. The chiefs, having learnt from past experience that consular promises did not usually produce any result, were prepared to sign only a provisional treaty. Hewett must have suspected that Jaja was going to be a difficult man to satisfy with glib promises. Jaja subjected Hewett to searching questions on the clauses of the treaty before him. He rejected them, but after a great deal of persuasion, agreed to sign a token treaty to show that he had no intention of accepting French or anybody else's authority. The treaty with Jaja nonetheless began with the obvious lie that 'in compliance with the request of the king, chiefs and People of Opobo', the Queen of England undertook to extend to the territory Her Gracious favour and protection. In the second treaty with Opobo in December 1884, Jaja refused to accept the article providing for free trade in his territory. However, between Goldie and Hewett, treaties were secured from the rulers of the Oil Rivers and the Niger districts. The Company's agents did in fact much better than the Consul, since the former obtained treaties in which the chiefs 'ceded' their territories to Goldie's company 'in perpetuity'.

A new danger to British interests was looming on the diplomatic horizon. British charges of duplicity against German action in the Cameroons and Anglo-French disputes about the Congo and the Niger were playing into the hands of Bismarck. France and Germany moved closer together in their determination to frustrate what Bismarck called Britain's 'dog-in-the manger' policy in Africa. The upshot was the Franco-German decision to summon a conference of the Colonial powers at Berlin in the winter of 1884 to discuss colonial questions. Through French insistence, the Niger question was included in the agenda of the Berlin West African Conference, 1884–5.[1]

At the Berlin Conference, the energy of Goldie on the Lower Niger proved invaluable to the British cause. This remarkable man had not only secured treaties with the riverain chiefs, but had successfully bought out the French company on the Niger a few

[1] *Die Grosse Politik*, III, no. 680, Bismarck to Hatzfeldt, 7 August 1884; *Documents diplomatiques français*, 1st series, 5, Courcel to Ferry, 25 August 1884; Crowe, *The Berlin West African Conference* (London, 1942).

days before the Conference began. Goldie was therefore able to claim that 'the Union Jack alone flew on the Lower Niger'. A memorandum prepared at the British Foreign Office by Anderson showed how tenaciously Britain was determined to press her claims to the Niger and the coast. It called attention to the British part in exploring the Niger from the time of Mungo Park. Britain had not spared money or lives in the task. The enterprise of British merchants was consolidating the work begun by the British government.[1]

In the end, the British delegation managed with considerable skill to nullify the original Franco-German project which sought to impose a joint system of international control of the Niger similar to that already approved by the Conference for the Congo. The responsibility of supervising the navigation of the Niger— theoretically free—was assigned to Britain, and not to an international commission. The German delegation was pleasantly surprised to find out that Britain was not in fact opposed to German colonial aspirations. British recognition of the German position in the Cameroons was easily followed by German acceptance of special British interests in the Oil Rivers. Internationally, British interests were secure on the Lower Niger and in the Oil Rivers. Britain had secured the region with great trade prospects and the best waterway into the interior. All that was left was to break the power of the coast middlemen and chiefs—but this could wait.[2]

[1] For details, see F.O. 84/1814 and F.O. 84/1816.
[2] Robinson and Gallagher, *op. cit.* p. 175.

# CHAPTER III

# A PAPER PROTECTORATE:
## 1885–90

The Berlin West African Conference of 1884–5 was in many ways a turning point in the history of British relations with the communities of the Niger districts. Hitherto, a vague and undefined form of British consular authority was exercised in the affairs of the indigenous inhabitants. The Berlin Conference secured for Britain international recognition of her paramountcy of interest in the districts. The Conference had, however, a wider significance. It proclaimed, quite unashamedly, the inauguration of European economic imperialism in tropical Africa. Up to 1884, Britain could argue that her advocacy of free trade was an essential ingredient in the policy of philanthropy which kept her in West Africa long after the cessation of the profitable slave trade. All nations were welcome to the self-appointed dual task of undoing the ravages of the slave trade and of laying the foundations of Christianity and civilisation. Leopold's 'great philanthropic enterprise' on the Congo was before 1884 assumed to be no more than the extension to Africa of the 'benefits' of European civilisation. In regard to eastern and central Africa, European intervention would be an answer to Livingstone's prayer for Heaven's rich blessing 'on everyone—American, English, Turk—who will help to heal this open sore of the world'.

From 1885 the European agents might still believe that they were working for the glory of God, but they were determined also to work for the glory of their native countries. The events which led up to the Berlin Conference and the underlying reality of the proceedings of the Conference broke the myth of piety which had hitherto surrounded European activities in Africa. In the words of Leonard Woolf, the nations of Europe fell upon Africa 'like a pack of snarling, tearing, quarrelling jackals'.[1]

---

[1] Woolf, *Empire and Commerce in Africa* (London, 1920), p. 44.

The situation which developed in Africa was of course not a new phenomenon in history. It was not without historical justification that a Russian sociologist, Novicow, noted in 1886, with respect to the prostration of Africa before Europe, that 'this subordination of the less fit individual and collective organisms to the more fit, this is justice in nature; an incorruptible but implacable justice which knows no pity....If one society is less perfect than another, the first must work for the second.'[1] Naturally no European power involved in the partition of Africa would have interpreted her action as crudely as Novicow. Animals may go directly for the victims they devour, but man attains the same objective with more subtlety and finesse.

During the Berlin Conference and subsequently, treaties of protection with indigenous African rulers figured very prominently in the transactions of Europe in Africa. It was assumed that the indigenous states involved thus voluntarily placed their sovereignty in the hands of the occupying European powers. Thus emerged what came to be called Colonial protectorates—the protection of uncivilised states. The legal and moral basis of these protectorates was the treaty or treaties purporting to effect the assumed transfer of sovereignty. Some European writers have argued that it is futile questioning the morality of these treaties because the alternative was conquest by force.[2] This kind of argument merely evades the question of the fraudulent basis of European rule.

It is obvious that certain conditions should have been satisfied before it could be assumed that treaties between European agents and African rulers had any moral validity. Lindley has suggested that the parties involved should have the capacity to enter into an agreement and that the nature of the agreement should be understood by the parties to it. It is not surprising that in Africa the whole process of treaty-making was hardly more than a farce.

According to Lugard, 'treaties were produced by the cartload in all the approved forms of legal verbiage impossible of translation by ill-educated interpreters'. Another European agent, Major

[1] Langer, *The Diplomacy of Imperialism*, vol. I, quoted p. 87.
[2] Flint, *op. cit.* p. 138. It is only fair to point out that Flint identified a few fraudulent treaties in the Benue region.

Thurston, has asserted that he had a 'bundle of printed treaties which I was to make as many people sign as possible. This signing is an amiable farce.'[1]

What requires explanation is not the farce of treaty-making, but the reasons why the European powers appear to have attached importance to it in the preliminary and subsequent negotiations for the partition of Africa. When these powers had dealt with Persia, Turkey and China, they had appreciated that a frontal encroachment on an ancient civilisation might prove difficult and dangerous. Their aggressive intentions had therefore to be cloaked in various devices. In tropical Africa, on the other hand, Europe believed she had come face to face with primitive savagery. She accepted as a moral postulate the assumption that the imposition of European rule on Africa was for the good of the Africans and of the world. Yet the outright acquisition of territory might have precipitated vexatious wars with the innumerable African rulers. Worse still, the European states might be at each other's throat. A way out was found in the diplomatic fiction of protectorates.

What then did Britain mean by a Colonial protectorate? The Indian states, which were earlier examples of British protectorates outside Africa, were 'semi-civilised' and well-organised states. They could organise formidable opposition to direct British intervention. Expediency therefore dictated that the treaties with the Indian princes were mostly 'treaties of alliance and friendship as between equals'.[2] Quite clearly Britain did not pretend to regard African rulers as equals. Even then, the Colonial protectorates established by Britain in Africa reveal no consistent pattern. British action was determined by local circumstances rather than by an ascertainable theory. The historian ought not, therefore, to generalise about Colonial protectorates.

It should be accepted that the term Colonial protectorate was one of which the meaning was indefinite. It had different meanings in different circumstances and in the mouths of different persons.

[1] Lindley, *The Acquisition and Government of Backward Territory in International Law* (London, 1926), pp. 11–18, 169–75; Lugard, *The Dual Mandate in British Tropical Africa* (1922), p. 15; Hobson, *Imperialism, A Study*, quoted (3rd ed., London, 1938), p. 260.

[2] Hall, *A Treatise on the Foreign Powers and Jurisdiction of the British Crown* (Oxford, 1894), p. 204.

For this reason, it is clearly not enough to say that the British political control of the communities of the Niger districts was based on the theory of a Colonial protectorate. Only the special circumstances surrounding the evolution of the protectorate established there by Britain explain the intentions and subsequent policy of the British government and its agents. The idea of a Niger districts protectorate was first mooted during the feverish months of 1882 and 1883 when British ministers were trying to make up their minds to keep out European competitors. To accept the responsibility of establishing a formal system of British Colonial administration would impose a burden on the British taxpayers. To this argument, Lord Kimberley added the further ones that the Niger coast was 'pestilential' and the natives 'unmanageable'.[1]

The Foreign Office and the Colonial Office were, however, agreed that some action should be taken to acquire political rights in the region which could exclude the French and the Germans. It was necessary to devise the cheapest way by which the exclusive British position and freedom of action could be safeguarded. The librarian of the Foreign Office was at this stage instructed to prepare a memorandum on protectorates. This was not the last of this type of exercise. Hertslet, the librarian, argued in his memorandum that in a protectorate the land was not British territory, the inhabitants were not British subjects, and the British Consul had no right to levy duties on exports and imports.[2] The negative attributes of the librarian's definition satisfied the immediate objectives of British policy in the Niger districts. Internal administration might be left in the hands of the local African rulers but foreign interference would at the same time be excluded and the British government relieved of administrative liabilities—at least for the time being.

The theoretical and moral implications of a protectorate relationship were not in the minds of the British ministers when they authorised their agents to collect treaties of protection from the chiefs of the Nigerian coast and the Lower Niger. The absurdities of the process of signing treaties mostly with illiterate

[1] C.O. 806/203, see appendix 1, 7, Minute by Kimberley, 6 April 1882, on Hewett's suggested Protectorate.
[2] F.O.C.P. 4824, Memo on Protectorates by Edward Hertslet, 24 April 1883.

groups roused no immediate misgivings on the part of the British ministers. During the Berlin Conference, in which Britain argued for 'freedom of action' in the Niger districts, an occasion arose for a clear definition of the political obligation to be imposed on powers claiming any part of the coast of Africa. The first proposition in this regard by France and Germany made no distinction between outright annexations and protectorates. The powers should establish and maintain 'an authority sufficient to ensure the maintenance of peace, the administration of justice, respect for rights acquired and, in case of necessity, freedom of commerce and transit....'[1]

The British delegation, as was to be expected, opposed the Franco-German proposition. The question was referred to the British Cabinet by the British delegation. Thus, for the second time, the British Cabinet found itself in a position to define what it proposed to do in the Niger districts from which it was determined to exclude European competitors. The British ministers involved set about producing memorandum after memorandum. Even the memorandum prepared by the law officers left the issue as obscure as ever. The Lord Chancellor, in his comments on the law officers' memorandum, produced a formula which seemed to satisfy the British Cabinet. He emphasised 'the recognition of the right of the aboriginal or other actual inhabitants to their own country, with no further assumption of territorial rights than is necessary to maintain the paramount authority and discharge the duties of an occupying power'.[2] The Lord Chancellor did not say what these duties were, nor did he indicate what was necessary for the maintenance of paramount authority.

In the end the Berlin Conference accepted the evasive British theory in regard to protectorates. A distinction was therefore made between annexations and protectorates. The British claims to the Niger districts were, from the standpoint of the European powers, vindicated. Furthermore, the freedom of action which the vindication guaranteed was based on the theory of a protectorate the precise meaning of which nobody, except perhaps the legal

---

[1] *Accounts and Papers*, vol. LV, 1884/5, Correspondence.
[2] F.O. 84/1819, Report of the Law Officers, 7 January 1885, and Lord Chancellor's Comment on the Law Officers' Report, n.d.

experts, understood. The situation with reference to the Niger districts left a vast scope for the interplay of many factors, sometimes altruistic and at other times selfish and calculating. The British government, the imperial agent on the spot, the British merchants and the local chiefs were to hold on to divergent interpretations of the implications of the British protectorate of the Niger districts.

It should be noted that Jaja, the king of Opobo and the most intelligent of the chiefs of the Nigerian coast, demanded from the British Consul a clarification of the term 'protection' which was contained in one of the clauses of the treaty between Opobo and Britain. Hewett's reply was explicit and unequivocal. 'I write as you request with reference to the word "protection" as used in the proposed treaty that the Queen does not want to take your country or your markets, but at the same time is anxious that no other nation should take them. She undertakes to extend her gracious favour and protection, which will leave your country still under your government.'[1]

There is no evidence that the other local rulers followed Jaja's example, but it is reasonable to assume that the Consul's reassuring letter to Jaja committed the Consul to this particular interpretation of 'protection' in its application to the local rulers of the Nigerian coast. It is true, of course, that the Consul had, before the treaties of protection, entrenched himself in a position of authority in Bonny, Old Calabar and New Calabar, where sectional strife and greed on the part of subordinate chiefs had undermined the stability of the traditional system of government.

To these sectional chiefs, the Consul's glittering presents, which were the reward for accepting British protection, must have constituted irresistible inducements to undertake a relationship with Britain they hardly understood. On the Lower Niger, the agents of the National African Company (later, the Royal Niger Company) did not pretend to obtain treaties of 'protection'. In most of the Company's treaties with the riverain states, the local rulers surrendered their country to the Company 'in perpetuity'. The British government asked no questions as long as the Company's

---

[1] F.O. 84/1862, see Hewett to Jaja, 1 July 1884, enclosed in Jaja to Salisbury, 5 May 1887.

66

activities successfully neutralised the French challenge in the area involved. Misgivings about the Company's proceedings came later.

On 5 June 1885 the following announcement appeared in the *London Gazette*. 'It is hereby notified for public information that, under and by virtue of certain Treaties concluded between the month of July last and the present date, and by other lawful means, the territories on the West Coast of Africa, herein after referred to as the Niger Districts, were placed under the Protection of Her Majesty the Queen from the date of the said Treaties respectively....' The protectorate was defined to include 'the territories on the line of coast between the British Protectorate of Lagos and the right or western bank of the Rio del Rey, and the territories on both banks of the Niger, from its confluence with the Benue at Lokoja to the sea, as well as the territories on both banks of the River Benue, from the confluence up to and including Ibi'. The notification in the *Gazette* concluded with the information that 'measures for the administration of justice and the maintenance of peace and good order in the Niger Districts' were being prepared.

In inserting this announcement in the *London Gazette*, the officials of the British Foreign Office were indeed not concerned with the implications of the political relationship which a protectorate theoretically postulated. The fact was that, according to the General Act of the Berlin Conference, the navigation of the Niger was to be free for the ships of all nations, and Britain undertook to protect foreign merchants.[1] The concern of the British government was therefore primarily to devise a cheap means of fulfilling the obligations imposed by the Berlin Conference. It is hardly surprising that when the *London Gazette* spoke of the measures in course of preparation for the administration of the Niger Districts protectorate, there was no reference to the wishes of the indigenous rulers.

The officials of the British Foreign Office believed that Goldie's company was capable of discharging on behalf of the British government whatever obligations were imposed by a protectorate. The man in charge of the African Department argued that 'the cheapest and most effective way of meeting the Berlin Conference

---

[1] *Parl. Papers*, 1886, vol. XLVII, see ch. v of the General Act of the Berlin Conference.

obligations would be by the employment of the National African Company, and in order to strengthen their position, it would be advisable without further delay to grant them the charter for which they had several times applied'.[1] The plan was not immediately implemented. Goldie was expected to come to terms with the independent Liverpool firms already entrenched on the Oil Rivers. This development did not materialise.[2] The charter which conferred political rights on Goldie's company was therefore for the time being to be confined to the Niger and Benue basins, excluding the Oil Rivers.

The negotiations for the charter became a protracted transaction, not because there was serious concern about the way a trading company might deal with the local inhabitants but because of disagreement about the precise form of the charter. It should, however, be pointed out here that one Minister, the Lord Chancellor, argued that the Company's treaties were fraudulent. He could not see how the local rulers could have understood treaties in which they handed over their territories 'in perpetuity'. He deplored a situation in which the British government appeared to give its blessing to a proceeding which was obviously trickery.[3]

The grant of a charter to a private company was thus one way in which Britain proposed to discharge the protectorate responsibility which she took upon herself. It is therefore necessary to investigate briefly the extent to which the British government satisfied itself that the chartered company would respect the rights of the local inhabitants and their rulers. It is true that at first the officials of the Foreign Office sought to retain some measure of imperial supervision over the administrative activities of the company. Goldie, on the other hand, insisted that the company's rights on the Lower Niger were derived independently from the treaties which the company's agents secured from the local rulers. The negotiations for the charter nearly broke down. The legal experts of the Foreign Office at this stage suggested that direct British sovereignty should be established and then Goldie's company might be used as an administrative agency.

---

[1] F.O. 84/1813, Memorandum by Anderson, 14 October 1884.
[2] F.O. 84/1880, Couper Johnstone and Co. to F.O., 10 August 1886.
[3] F.O. 84/1879, Memoranda by Permanent Under-Secretary of the F.O.; Granville and Lord Selborne, February and March 1885.

A change of government occurred with the fall of Gladstone in June 1885. Thereafter Goldie piled on pressure on the new ministry of Lord Salisbury by whipping up the clamour of the British Chambers of Commerce. According to these bodies, the Lower Niger was in a 'defenceless state', and the British government should set up an administration.[1] It was of course clear to Goldie and his friends that the British government was not in a position to ask Parliament for the money which direct British administrative control would involve. In the end Goldie won virtually all he originally demanded. The idea of the Queen's sovereignty was excluded from the projected charter. The company was empowered to exercise the Queen's jurisdiction over British subjects and foreigners—the latter including the indigenous inhabitants who were under Foreign Office consular rule but were now technically excluded from the company's districts.[2] As for the inhabitants within the company's jurisdiction, Goldie had no doubts in his mind that they had surrendered their territories by their treaties. The ill-defined control which Goldie conceded to the British Foreign Secretary could in no way be regarded as a safeguard for the integrity of the rights of the indigenous rulers. The British government's refusal to grant Goldie a specific right of trade monopoly was actuated more by the fear of German repercussions than by solicitude for the rights of the local people.

The preamble to the charter granted to the National African Company in July 1886 claimed that the company had acquired the Niger districts by acts of cession on the part of the local rulers. The condition of the natives would be improved by the 'beneficent' administration of the company. Lastly, the company, through its charter, would promote the commercial prosperity of 'Our subjects'.[3] The other references to the local inhabitants are contained in articles 7 and 8 of the charter. The company was required to avoid interference in religion, local laws and customs of any tribe, except on grounds of humanity. The charter said nothing about respect for the internal sovereignty of the local states. The

---

[1] F.O. 84/1742, see Resolutions to F.O. from Manchester and London, 17 September 1885.
[2] Flint, *op. cit.* pp. 80–5.
[3] *Parl. Papers*, 1899, vol. LXIII, C. 9372 (full text).

reference to the imperial right of intervention regarding the company's policy towards the inhabitants meant hardly anything in practice.[1]

In granting a charter to Goldie's company, the British government apparently extricated itself from any direct responsibility for determining the manner in which a large and strategic portion of the Niger Districts protectorate was to be governed. The supreme authority was the Board of Directors of what became the Royal Niger Company. Goldie was designated 'Deputy Governor' and in this capacity he was the political administrator of the company's Niger districts. Locally, the company's supremacy was represented in a triumvirate which included the Agent-General, the Chief Justice and the Commandant of Constabulary. In the districts, there were trading agents who at the same time combined executive, constabulary and judicial functions. A more oppressive and arbitrary economic and political grip on indigenous peoples could hardly have been devised.

It is on record that Goldie claimed that the local peoples would continue to be ruled 'by their legitimate tribal or feudal authorities'.[2] Some scholars have even suggested that Goldie initiated on the Niger the policy of indirect rule. These claims are clearly incompatible with a policy which in practice led to the burning down of villages and towns along the Niger, the imprisonment of their rulers, and the enforcement of iniquitous commercial regulations which drove neighbouring peoples to despair. The reaction of Brass chiefs and peoples to the rule of the Royal Niger Company will be discussed later. It is not without justification that British firms which opposed, maybe selfishly, the rule of the Royal Niger Company spoke of the 'Niger scandal' in reference to the activities of the company's agents.

Before turning attention from the Royal Niger Company's area of jurisdiction to the remaining portion of the Niger districts which came under the direct control of the British Foreign Office, it is necessary to point out that the British division of the whole region between the company and its own imperial agents was arbitrary and most harmful. Traditionally the Niger had been an

[1] Flint, *op. cit.* pp. 86–7.
[2] F.O. 84/1793, Goldie to Iddesleigh, 8 November 1886.

important unifying influence on the groups which made up Southern Nigeria. The coast city-states of Brass and New Calabar had always had close commercial links with Aboh, Onitsha, Asaba and Idah. Now the latter places and peoples were isolated from the coast peoples, thanks largely to the policy of the Royal Niger Company. People who are fond of referring to Nigeria as an artificial conglomeration of odd groups forget that British action in arbitrarily partitioning the Niger districts in 1885–6 effectively underminded traditional methods of trade and cultural contacts which linked widely separated groups in what became Southern Nigeria.[1]

It is time to consider the beginnings of British rule in the portion of the 1885 Niger Districts protectorate which was not comprehended in the Royal Niger Company's charter. This portion may be called the Oil Rivers protectorate, although the name was not officially adopted until 1891. The area originally comprised the Nigerian coast east of Lagos, and excluded the part of the Niger delta which the Royal Niger Company ruled. British paramountcy over the Oil Rivers was expressed in the instruction to Consul Hewett to establish a protectorate jurisdiction under the West African Order-in-Council issued in 1885.[2] What is interesting is that the administrative instructions to Hewett made a clear distinction between protectorates and annexations. 'The chiefs will, as hitherto, manage their own affairs, but will have always at hand Counsellors and Arbitrators in matters of difficulty or dispute....'[3] It is misleading to attach undue importance to the implied recognition of the rights of the coast chiefs to govern themselves. The fact was that the British government was as yet not ready to undertake the expense of establishing a Crown Colony machinery of government.

If the protection of local states had any significance for the British government, Brass, which was one of the states which sought the 'gracious favour and protection' of the Queen, afforded a wonderful opportunity for British protection. Brass markets and means of physical survival were arbitrarily handed over to the none

---

[1] Diké, *op. cit.* See ch. II for details.
[2] *London Gazette*, 5 June 1885.
[3] F.O. 84/1701, F.O. to Hewett, 30 December 1885.

71

too tender mercies of the Royal Niger Company. Yet the only reference to Brass in the instructions to Consul Hewett was that he should 'notice especially the state of affairs on the Brass River, where traders were being impeded by native chiefs and conditions had become so unruly that outbreaks of cannibalism had been reported'.[1] The emphasis was, as before 1885, on British trading interests and the excuse for intervention was alleged cannibalism —a convenient harmonisation of materialistic and humanitarian motives. Lip-service continued periodically to be paid to the theory that Britain did not intend to upset the internal authority of the indigenous rulers of the Oil Rivers. Practice was to be quite another matter.

If the analysis of British motives indicated above is borne in mind, the subsequent equivocations of the British government and the British agents on the spot become easily intelligible. A later Acting Consul, Johnston, was quite right when he summarised the nature of British rule in the Oil Rivers: '...our policy may for the present chiefly assume a negative character. So long as we keep other European nations out, we need not be in a hurry to go in.'[2] Indigenous rulers were safe as long as Britain was not ready to 'go in'. A lone Consul, without an army and without a civil service, had necessarily to play the role of 'arbitrator'. There is ample evidence that Jaja and a few other local rulers believed that the 'negative character' of British rule was one that could endure. They were therefore not prepared for the dramatic changes which were destined to cost them their independence.[3]

The 1885 Order-in-Council was unobjectionable. It merely conferred on Consul Hewett the power to set up consular courts which were to have jurisdiction over British subjects. The indigenous inhabitants were concerned with these courts only to the extent to which their rulers consented. The Consul was, however, also empowered by the Order-in-Council to make Regulations (to be called Queen's Regulations) for securing the observance of treaties with the local chiefs and for 'the peace and good govern-

[1] Oliver, *Sir Harry Johnston and the Scramble for Africa* (London, 1957), p. 93.

[2] F.O. 84/1750, Johnston to Anderson (Private), 13 November 1886.

[3] F.O. 84/1762, Johnston to Salisbury, 15 January 1886, for an elaboration of British future policy.

ment of British subjects or British-protected persons'. There was nothing new in all these powers. The 1872 Order-in-Council conferred on the Consul almost identical powers at a time when Britain had no legal standing in the Oil Rivers. Consul Hewett was himself baffled by the new document. He already had Courts of Equity and had before 1885 done more than merely regulate the affairs of British subjects. He therefore renamed the existing courts, put up notices to that effect, and hoped that what he had done 'will be considered sufficient for the purposes' of the new Order-in-Council.[1]

Thus began the formal British protectorate administration of the Oil Rivers. The illusion that in a colonial protectorate the internal sovereignty of the indigenous rulers was to be respected was apparently preserved by the nature of the task imposed on the British Consul. In the course of the months subsequent to the inauguration of the protectorate, Hewett was given an assistant in the person of Johnston, a man destined to play a decisive part in exploding the pretence which surrounded British political relations with the local rulers. Johnston as Vice-Consul on the Oil Rivers was also accredited to the German government of the Cameroons. He had his residence, not in the Oil Rivers territory, but on an island off Fernando Po. The stage was set for the events of the following five years. European writers have referred to this period as the 'paper protectorate'. This view is based on the assumption that it was the business of Britain to establish an elaborate Crown Colony administration in 1885. Britain had in fact no legal or moral right to do so.

In view of the vagueness, or perhaps dissimulation, which had from the start surrounded the theory behind a colonial protectorate, it is not without significance that Consul Hewett's first difficulties in his new role arose directly out of Chief Jaja's insistence on a scrupulous observance of the 'protection' treaty with Britain. Jaja had carved for himself a new dominion and within it he claimed and enforced his right to control the trade transactions of British merchants. He had always done this but the question was whether Consul Hewett, who had in 1882/3 vainly contested Jaja's sovereignty, would after 1885 resume his personal and political

[1] F.O. 84/1749, Hewett to F.O., 15 April 1886.

quarrel with Jaja. It should also be borne in mind that the fine distinction between protectorates and annexations had never impressed Hewett. If he had had the final word on how to rule the Oil Rivers, he would have established direct British authority and paid for it by imposing duties on exports, which he expected to yield a revenue of about £7500.[1] Hewett subsequently never stopped deploring the fact that he did not return in 1885 as the formal governor of the British colony of the Niger Districts.

In resuming his quarrel with King Jaja, Hewett's strategy was conveniently to forget that Jaja's treaty with Britain did not include the usual clause which stipulated 'free trade'. He also apparently forgot that in 1884 he had pronounced for Jaja's benefit a categorical statement that the Queen's 'protection' which Jaja was supposed to have solicited in the treaty did not involve any interference in his dominion and markets. A new interpretation of the protectorate treaty later emerged. The British government, in assuming the protectorate of the Oil Rivers, had in view 'the promotion of the welfare of the natives of all these territories taken as a whole by ensuring the peaceful development of trade and facilitating their intercourse with Europeans. It is not to be permitted that any chief, who may happen to occupy a territory on the coast should obstruct this policy in order to benefit himself.'[2] There is little doubt that the Consul's view was an accurate interpretation of the intentions of the British government. The latter, however, intended that the implementation was to come later. The Consul, on the other hand, wanted quick results.

The third party to the Hewett–Jaja controversy were the British merchants who had their own commercial interests primarily in mind. The merchants were anxious to circumvent Jaja's firm control of the hinterland markets of Ohombele and Essene. The manner in which the British merchants attempted to interpret the treaties of protection was contradictory but quite understandable. In Jaja's territory, in which they were excluded from direct contact with Jaja's hinterland markets, they identified the protectorate treaties with facilities for free trade. As regards the hinterland of

[1] F.O. 84/1634, Memo by Hewett, 12 December 1883.
[2] F.O. 84/1749, no. 4, see Memo by Hewett on Rosebery's letter, 15 April 1886.

Brass and New Calabar from which the Royal Niger Company excluded the Liverpool firms operating from the Oil Rivers, the British merchants on the coast were vigorous in their advocacy of the rights of the coast chiefs to their hinterland markets. In these areas, the true meaning of protection was 'that the rights of access to all markets the Natives have been accustomed to frequent should be continued to them and they so understand the treaties'.[1]

The attempts of the Liverpool firms to gain direct access to Jaja's Ibo and Ibibio markets were effectively checked by Jaja. The British merchants had either to pay 'comey' to Jaja and trade on his terms in his dominion or close down. Their failures in the hinterland markets were attributed to Jaja's terrorism.

The British Chamber of Commerce at Opobo took the initiative in inviting the commander of the British warships in the region to intervene on behalf of the British merchants. The memorandum submitted to the Naval Commander was entitled 'Protest of Traders against King Jaja's Rule in the Oil Rivers'. The Naval Commander came to the conclusion that the issue between Jaja and the British merchants was basically political. This was where Consul Hewett came in. He alleged that Jaja had broken his treaty with Britain because he refused free trade in his empire. His next extraordinary action was to impose a fine of 30 puncheons of oil on Jaja for 'breaking' the treaty. Hewett himself suspected that the Foreign Office would find it hard to condone the Consul's action. In reporting what he did, he endeavoured to gain the Foreign Office officials to his side by ingeniously suggesting that the 'free trade' clause in Jaja's treaty was omitted on 'sanitary grounds'. The first-fruit of British equivocation with respect to the Oil Rivers became manifest. The situation obviously provided one more occasion for the British Foreign Office experts to make up their mind about the precise relationship which a colonial protectorate postulated. The opportunity was not used.

In reply to Consul Hewett's Report, the Foreign Office pointed out that the Consul should not have imposed a fine on Jaja 'for breaking the Treaty'. If the Consul had to impose a fine, it should have been on the 'general ground' that Jaja's customs duties

---

[1] F.O. 84/1880, Petition to W. F. Lawrence, M.P., by Liverpool Merchants, 15 December 1886.

were arbitrary and vexatious. Hewett was advised to remit the fine on Jaja 'for the present'.[1] The Foreign Office obviously recognised that the charge that Jaja had broken his treaty was technically untrue. On the other hand, when the Foreign Office dispatch to Hewett suggested that excessive duties were a legitimate ground for fining a chief in his dominion, the Foreign Office experts were indeed far from giving their local agent any guidance for future action. It is probable that the Foreign Office regarded 'comey' charged by the local chiefs in the Oil Rivers as 'salary' for which the local chiefs were bound to keep trade routes open and secure for the British merchants. This view has in fact been expounded by one writer on the affairs of the region.[2]

It would be wrong to suggest that British equivocation was exclusively responsible for the difficulties which faced the British Consul in the Oil Rivers. The theory of a protectorate relationship presupposed the existence of local polities capable of maintaining internal peace and order. It has been shown in chapter II that, in many of the city-states of the Nigerian coast, various factors had co-operated to undermine the internal stability of the traditional systems of government. Thus in Bonny, Consul Hewett faced a situation in which the sectional chiefs—Warribo Manilla Pepple, Adda Allison, Oko Jumbo, and seventeen others—had completely undermined the authority of King George Pepple. The chiefs stripped the king of all his rights and at one stage actually imprisoned him. He was accused of 'fanning' a civil war similar to the one which in the last decade split Bonny and led to Jaja's secession. The British chairman of the local Court of Equity, R. D. Boler, in fact threatened to deport the king in September 1885. Having neutralised the authority of the king, the Bonny chiefs could not agree on how to share the 'comey' paid by the British merchants. They were in 1886 on the brink of a civil war.

During the long period 1849–85—a period described from the standpoint of British relations with the coast chiefs and communities as 'the invisible empire of informal sway'[3]—the British Consul had consistently intervened when internal conditions

---

[1] F.O. 84/1749, Lister to Hewett, 16 June 1886.

[2] Oliver, *op. cit.* p. 108; see also F.O. 84/1828, Rosebery to Jaja, 16 June 1886.

[3] For an elaboration of the concept of 'the invisible empire of informal sway', see Robinson and Gallagher, *op. cit.* ch. II; Diké, *op. cit.* ch. VII.

appeared to threaten peace and the security of British lives and property. It is therefore hardly surprising that after the assumption of official British responsibility, the British Consul should deem it his duty to intervene in Bonny in 1886. In the present situation of imminent civil war, the Consul selected five chiefs to form what Hewett called the new 'local authority'. Hewett's council of five chiefs had legislative, executive and judicial powers conferred on it by himself. Very wisely, he reserved the right to veto any law enacted by the 'local authority' which he found objectionable.[1]

As a practical measure, little can be said against the Consul's action in Bonny. He was quite right in excluding from the council the two chiefs—Oko Jumbo and Warribo Manilla Pepple—whose mutual hostility lay at the root of Bonny's political instability. There were, however, other issues involved in the Consul's action. His instructions in 1885 and the Order-in-Council of the same year gave Hewett no right to set up local governments in the protectorate. In the second place, the Consul had no right to impose a fine on Bonny for the self-appointed task of setting up a 'local authority'. For his services, Bonny was to pay Hewett 16 puncheons of oil. When the Consul reported his legally extraordinary proceedings to the British Foreign Office, the officials there naturally recognised that the Consul was exceeding his authority. The minutes made on Hewett's report do not show that the Foreign Office was prepared to clarify the legal implications of a protectorate, even at this stage. The head of the African Department observed that 'Hewett is trying to settle many large questions under his system of benevolent despotism—deposition of chiefs, markets, tenure of land, administration of justice, etc.'.[2] The Foreign Office made no attempt to guide the Consul in regard to the 'many large questions', but reminded him that the fine on Bonny should be credited to the Imperial Exchequer.

The affairs of Opobo and Bonny engrossed Consul Hewett's attention during the months which followed his reappointment as Consul in what was now an official British protectorate. But in the Brass city-state, the year 1885 witnessed the progressive

[1] F.O. 84/1749, Africa, no. 12, 12 July 1886.
[2] *Ibid.* Anderson's minute on Hewett's no. 12.

deterioration of relations between the indigenous rulers and the British merchants. It may be recalled that in Brass, as in the other city-states, the local Court of Equity, dominated by the British merchants, functioned as if indigenous authority did not exist. It sought to regulate trade and to impose its own judgement in disputes between the European traders and the local chiefs or their men. The record of the proceedings of the Brass Court of Equity available at the Enugu Archives throws light on the tense situation which persisted during 1885.[1] The king and chiefs naturally took no notice of the proceedings of an alien institution which was arrogating to itself the prerogatives of the king and chiefs in their own city-state and neighbourhood.

The first dispute between the local rulers and the British merchants arose from an alleged assault on a British merchant by a member of the Spiff House in Brass. The Court of Equity, in which no local chief was represented, decided to impose a fine of 100 puncheons of oil on the Spiff House. It should be borne in mind that hitherto, where the local chiefs were divided, it was usually easy for the Court to exact payment by enforcing a trade boycott against the offending chief or House. In the present dispute, the king and chiefs of Brass were unanimous in their opposition to the Court's ruling. The chairman of the Court of Equity, W. H. Young of Messrs Hatton and Cookson, could do no more than draft a protest to await the arrival of the Consul. The protest concluded with the question as to whether or not the Court of Equity had any 'authority or locus standi whatever'.

Another dispute was provoked in 1885 by the sudden death of a member of the House of Igbeta on board a ship. The Brass rulers believed that the victim had been struck dead by some intemperate European merchant whose surrender they demanded. A doctor's post-mortem examination, on the contrary, suggested that the young man died of a heart-disease. A 'national' meeting was summoned and it was decided that the European suspected of the murder of the Brassman should be handed over to them. Furthermore, the doctor was required to leave the state and the British merchants had to choose between the doctor and their continued

---

[1] The records bear the official stamp of the 'British Consulate for the Oil Rivers Districts'.

residence and trade in Brass. The issue was not quite settled when the third and most serious dispute developed between the rulers of Brass and the British merchants.

Apparently some of the local British firms had attempted to use their launches to trade beyond Fishtown Point. In other words, some of the British trading agents tried to deal directly with what was left of the hinterland markets of Brass. The king and chiefs of Brass thereupon demanded that the firms involved should sell their launches, pay in addition a fine of 100 puncheons of oil for their encroachment on Brass monopoly, and give securities against future infringements. In the absence of the British Consul, the British merchants in panic summoned the Senior Naval Officer of H.B.M. Squadron on the west coast. Commander Craigie arrived and summoned the Brass chiefs and the merchants to a meeting. He read out to the gathering what he called the 'Protectorate declaration'. According to this, the British Consul alone had the power to impose fines. Before withdrawing from Brass, Craigie seized a chief as a hostage because the chief had been 'guilty of turbulent and aggressive conduct on the beaches'.

In Brass there were, therefore, many complex questions which awaited Consul Hewett's arrival in 1886. The White Merchants' Court had imposed an uncollected fine on the important House of Spiff. The local rulers also had imposed their own fine on the leading British firms in Brass. Lastly a naval officer had removed a local chief as a political prisoner. When Hewett at last turned up, he held consultations, not with the rulers of Brass, but with the white members of the Court of Equity. It did not take the Consul long to come to the conclusion that the Court was right in imposing a fine on the Spiff House, but that the chiefs were wrong in demanding that the British merchants should pay for their encroachment on Brass hinterland markets. The Consul had not forgotten that the only thing specific in his original instructions from the Foreign Office when he assumed control in the protectorate was a reference to an allegation that the chiefs and conditions in Brass had become too unruly for the trade transactions of British merchants.

The Consul's partiality was therefore only to be expected. What seemed extraordinary was his argument that the Brass rulers' refusal to compel Chief Spiff to pay his fine amounted to a breach of their protectorate treaty obligations. On the basis of this obviously wrong assumption, Hewett advised the British government to deal severely with the rulers of Brass. Hewett justified his recommendation by suggesting that '...unless they receive some notification of your displeasure at their conduct and a warning to mend their ways in future, I feel sure that the authority of Her Majesty's Consular Officers in the District will be seriously undermined'.[1]

The western portion of Hewett's protectorate lay west of the Niger delta. The dominant indigenous ruler was Nana. Born of a Jekri father and an Urhobo mother, Nana possessed qualities of leadership and organisation not unlike those of Jaja of Opobo. He had built up a sort of feudal empire round his stronghold, Ebrohemie, off the Benin river. Nana's empire was basically commercial, but his relations with petty Jekri and Urhobo chiefs in the immediate hinterland had considerable political significance. The British merchants in the area recognised Nana's authority and conceded to him the right to regulate the 'comey' paid to his chiefs. No one questioned the position of Nana in this part of the Benin river basin. Yet, when Consul Hewett visited Nana's territory in 1885, he undertook the self-appointed task of solemnly proclaiming that he was making Nana the 'executive power through which decrees of Her Majesty's Government and of the Consular Court are to be exercised and enforced'.[2]

Consul Hewett's proceedings at Opobo, Bonny, Brass and the Benin river during the first two years of the existence of the official British protectorate reveal that the Consul behaved as if he were the governor of a British colony. He obviously did not appreciate the fact that the 1885 Order-in-Council which prescribed his legal powers in the protectorate also recognised the internal sovereignty of the indigenous states of the coast. The fault was not all his. The British government gave Hewett no guidance on the many occasions when he reported to the Foreign Office his high-handed proceedings on the Coast. The Consul was no doubt right in assuming that the true intentions of the British government

---

[1] F.O. 84/1828, Hewett to F.O., 1 August 1887.
[2] Burns, *op. cit.* p. 141.

indeed included facilitating the inland penetration of British trading interests. The insistence of the local chiefs on their traditional right to control European trade in their areas of influence was sooner or later bound to provoke direct British intervention. It should be recognised too that at least in one case—Bonny—the bickerings and petty jealousies of the local chiefs among themselves created a political vacuum which Consul Hewett inevitably had to fill, the 1885 Order-in-Council notwithstanding.

Whether or not the officials of the British Foreign Office who read and minuted on the reports by Hewett on the affairs of the Oil Rivers were already in 1886 beginning to have doubts about the applicability of the protectorate theory to the region is not revealed in their comments. There is also no evidence that the theory of government implied in the 1885 Order-in-Council was taken seriously by these officials or by Hewett. The latter, however, might quarrel with the coast chiefs, institute his own organs of local government, and prescribe punishments for the king of Opobo and the rulers of Brass, but he did not carry his pretensions to their logical conclusion. It is true he was often sick, but he had also lived sufficiently long with the conditions prevailing on the coast not to want to upset them seriously.

A political crisis had to await the arrival of a British agent of a different stamp. This man was Hewett's assistant, H. H. Johnston. This much-travelled Vice-Consul had clear ideas about the grand dimensions which the British empire in Africa ought to assume.[1] In the lowly position of Vice-Consul stationed on a tiny island off Fernando Po, Johnston had during 1885 and 1886 indulged in grand dreams of a hinterland colony of the Oil Rivers. In the latter year, he had sought and obtained Foreign Office approval for a tour of the hinterland bounded by the Benue to the north and the Cross river to the east. His aim was to assess the economic potentialities of an area that merely awaited the enterprise of British merchants. Johnston had a very low opinion of the coast peoples who, according to him, were 'by indigenous standards barbarians, who had acquired some crude wealth as traders and middlemen by exporting the produce of the interior, but had done

[1] Oliver, *op. cit.* see map on p. 102.

so by erecting a barrier between the producers and the outside world, a barrier which in the interests both of commerce and of civilisation must be speedily broken down'.[1] The Vice-Consul's interpretation of the Protectorate of the Oil Rivers was made clear in his assumption, clearly stated to the Foreign Office, that the protectorate arrangement was primarily intended to keep out the French and the Germans; and the British could 'move in when we want'.

At the end of 1886 Hewett left the coast on sick leave. Johnston became Acting Consul and was at last in a position to 'run the show' and deal with the 'barbarians' who impeded the inland penetration of British commercial enterprise. The posture of affairs in Opobo since 1886 obviously corroborated Johnston's views. The British merchants and the king of Opobo were engaged in the most serious of their periodic trade disputes. The merchants were questioning Jaja's right to determine his own commercial policy. They attempted to gain direct access to Jaja's hinterland markets at Ohambele and Essene, but Jaja had enough political hold on these markets to frustrate the pretensions of the British merchants. When the latter decided to reduce the 'comey' paid to the king of Opobo, the king retaliated by stopping their trade and made arrangements to ship Opobo oil direct to England. One of the British firms, Miller Brothers, dissociated itself from the attitude of hostility to Jaja's sovereignty. The firm traded on Jaja's terms and did excellent business at the expense of the firms of the African Association.

The Foreign Office was flooded with complaints from the British firms whose business was virtually paralysed by Jaja's firm policy. The firms argued that their launches had merely attempted to use the Opobo river for purposes of transit to markets outside of Jaja's domain. Had such freedom not been recognised by the terms of the Berlin West African Conference? Jaja ought not to be allowed to injure the trade of British subjects by imposing a monopoly outside his dominions.[2]

When Acting Consul Johnston arrived at Opobo, five ships

[1] F.O. 84/1762, Johnston to Salisbury, 15 January 1886, and Johnston to Rosebery, 17 June 1886.
[2] F.O. 84/1865, Couper, Johnstone and Co. to Salisbury, 23 June 1887.

belonging to the African Association were lying idle. To Johnston, this was intolerable. Within or without Opobo territory, the king of Opobo had no right to interfere with British trade. Apparently Jaja's slave origin disqualified him from any pretensions to the privileges of sovereignty. He was 'one of the most grasping, unscrupulous and overbearing of mushroom kings who ever attempted to throttle the growing commerce of white men with the richer interior'.[1] Whatever Johnston thought about Jaja as king, it became clear as the Jaja–Johnston dispute developed that two fundamental issues were at stake. What was the precise extent of Jaja's dominion? What was the exact nature of consular authority on the Nigerian coast? It has been explained in the previous chapter how Jaja, after consolidating the state of Opobo, had proceeded with vigour and imagination to extend his commercial and political influence northwards to the fringe of the Ibo country, north-eastwards to Ibibioland and eastward to the Qua-Eboe river. Jaja's relations with these outlying parts were based on friendship, marriage bonds and, in one or two cases, military predominance. With the Qua-Eboes, relations were cemented with a treaty in which the people recognised Jaja as their sovereign. Above all, Jaja's genius for commercial organisation gave the whole area under his influence a unity which a neutral observer could easily have recognised.

The problem of the precise demarcation of Jaja's dominion, especially in the context of the Jaja–Johnston dispute, was indeed not as simple as it seems in retrospect. It has never been easy to explain traditional African concepts of legitimacy and paramountcy by reference to European notions of sovereignty. There were systems of authority which in most cases did not become institutionalised in a sufficiently formal manner for easy comprehension by outsiders. In the case of Jaja's dominion, one would look in vain for a hierarchy or rulers and for legislative, executive and judicial organs with ramifications into all parts of the dominion. There was no bureaucracy. Any attempt at any precise territorial demarcation of what Jaja regarded as his domain would have been arbitrary and futile. Johnston and his supporters in the British Foreign Office who refused to accept that Jaja had a dominion

[1] F.O. 84/1828, no. 11, Johnston to F.O., 28 July 1887.

6-2

beyond the confines of the port of Opobo were confronted with a problem which social anthropologists have recognised as one of considerable complexity. In Opobo, the Acting Consul's precipitancy created a situation which left no room for a dispassionate inquiry into the nature and extent of Jaja's authority. Available documents in the British Foreign Office reveal that Lord Salisbury at least thought that such an inquiry was indispensable, but Johnston was too much under the influence of the British merchants to be anything but a prejudiced adjudicator.[1]

The second fundamental issue in the Jaja–Johnston dispute concerned an important aspect of Jaja's internal sovereignty—his right to 'comey'. Foreign merchants had to pay for the right to trade and for the protection which the local ruler provided. The origin of the 'comey' and the other less precise exactions from the merchants created considerable confusion as to the theory behind the payments. The rulers of the coastal city-states had no doubts in their minds that the exaction of 'comey' was a legitimate exercise of their sovereignty. They probably could not have expressed this right in legalistic terms. The European merchants in due course developed the argument that they paid 'comey' to the chiefs, not in recognition of the sovereignty of the local rulers, but because the latter promised to open up markets and to keep open the routes to these markets. It cannot be pretended that the issue was a clear-cut one. Furthermore, the manner in which some of the chiefs resorted to less creditable exactions, hardly far removed from disguised begging, tended to degrade their status as independent sovereigns, at any rate in the eyes of the foreign merchants.

Acting Consul Johnston naturally accepted the merchants' interpretations of 'comey'. In Opobo, the export trade had often attained the annual value of £160,000. 'Comey', assessed at four puncheons of oil in every twenty, produced for King Jaja a revenue of £30,000 a year. Johnston regarded this sum as salary paid to Jaja, and not as revenue which in European countries a ruler derived from custom duties. If Jaja failed to keep trade routes open, he should forfeit his right to 'comey'.[2] No merchants

[1] F.O. 84/1869, Minutes by Salisbury, 9 September 1887; also F.O. 84/1828, Minutes dated 24 and 25 September 1887.
[2] Oliver, *op. cit.* p. 108.

complained that Jaja's authority did not provide security or did not restrain Opobo men from sharp practices. His great offence was his 'rashness' in shipping Opobo palm oil direct to Liverpool and the success with which he frustrated the encroachment of British merchants on his hinterland markets. There were at least two parties who viewed Jaja's claims and actions differently. The firm of Alex. Miller Brothers recognised and avowed the justice of Jaja's cause. It accepted Jaja's right to regulate the trade carried on in his territory. Admiral Richards of the British Navy had always argued in favour of Jaja's policy. Writing to the head of the African Department of the British Foreign Office, Richards reminded him that 'the "middlemen" as you term the chiefs with whom for the most part we have treaties, have a clear and decided use.... The so-called "monopolies" I look upon as being dues fairly leviable for the security of the traders.'[1]

The divergencies of interpretation between Jaja and Acting Consul Johnston as to the nature of 'comey' and the boundaries of Jaja's domain must be borne in mind to make the events of 1887 intelligible. It is easy enough to suggest that Johnston was a fanatical imperialist who had no sense of equity or legality in the pursuit of his imperialistic ambitions. The British agent's behaviour and language were indisputably those of a lawless person, as Lord Salisbury later observed. Nevertheless, it is historically more objective to concede to Johnston the assumptions on which he based his policy, and these assumptions and policy had the consistent support of key officials in the British Foreign Office.[2] When Johnston arrived at Old Calabar to act for Hewett, there were instructions from the Foreign Office which required him without delay to remove alleged obstacles to British trade in Opobo. These instructions made no reference to possible complications arising from Jaja's sovereignty. Johnston had, therefore, a free hand.

Johnston saw his mission to Opobo clearly. The best way to safeguard peace and commerce in the British protectorate was to humiliate or banish Jaja. The British merchants who were 'about

[1] F.O. 84/1693, Richards to Lister, 5 December 1884.
[2] Particularly T. V. Lister, Assistant Under-Secretary, and H. P. Anderson, Head of the African Department and Lister's deputy.

to reap the long-waited-for and sadly needed profits of their praiseworthy enterprise'[1] were being frustrated by the machination of a slave-born upstart. As to the question of Jaja's claim to Ibo and Ibibio areas, Johnston was convinced that Jaja's hold on the people there was exercised through 'juju'. This was therefore no evidence of Jaja's suzerainty. The people in question were independent and were ruled by their own kings. The points mentioned here were all embodied in Johnston's assessment of the problems which confronted him in Opobo. At about the same time, the Acting Consul painted glowing pictures of the prospects of trade in the Opobo hinterland. 'The district of Ohambela is a very large trade centre for the Ibo country. I met people coming from Igara and other places on the Niger, and from Ikorofion on the Cross [Old Calabar] Rivers. The quantity of palm oil brought to the markets of Ohambela is amazing....'[2] Johnston's statement in respect of Igala was mere fantasy. The market of Ohambele was certainly an impressive one in the palm-oil trade—a trade developed by Jaja. There were Opobo stores there and Jaja's market inspectors, not 'juju'. The Ohambele people were themselves middlemen who needed and used Jaja's capital to bring in the palm oil from the Ibo country. The allegiance and indebtedness of Ohambele to Jaja were not expressed in European political terms. Johnston's visit to Ohambele was for him only a wonderful opportunity to explode the 'myth' of Jaja's rule. He assembled the elders of Ohambele and explained to them the advantages of direct trade with Europeans. Johnston believed that his explanations were eagerly accepted by his audience. He therefore promised to pay a second visit and sign treaties of protection with the Ohambele 'rulers'.

Johnston's next journey inland took him to Jaja's market, Essene, in Ibibioland. The Acting Consul produced another fantastically exaggerated report on the virtues of the Ibibio country. 'From the farthest point to which I penetrated inland, I could see the ground rising gently into undulating hills. Here is the country where white men may hope to settle and enjoy good health and it is from lands like these that run-away slaves and

---

[1] F.O. 84/1828, Johnston to F.O., 28 July 1887.
[2] *Ibid.* Johnston to F.O., 1 August 1887.

upstart kings like Jaja are trying to keep us from penetrating.'[1] It was one thing to paint alluring pictures of the opportunities for British trade and settlement, but quite another to make good the assumption that the areas involved lay outside Jaja's dominion. Johnston was certainly not the man to be content with half-measures. He collected treaty forms and proceeded once again to Ohambele in order to take the chiefs under direct British protection. But at Johnston's approach to the town, the chiefs and their people fled into the bush. This comic outcome of the Acting Consul's endeavours was to him very disconcerting and his reaction was immediate. Back in Opobo, Johnston issued an order stopping Jaja's trade and threatened a fine of £500 on any British subject who contravened the order.[2] The Liverpool firms fully endorsed the Acting Consul's action. This was to be expected. But the agent of Messrs Alex. Miller Brothers put in a claim for damages against Johnston at the rate of £1800 a month if the trade embargo was not withdrawn.

Jaja's protests and those of Miller Brothers reached the Foreign Office at about the same time as Johnston's report of his proceedings at Opobo. In addition, Jaja decided to send a delegation of his senior chiefs to state his case to the British government. The situation in the Oil Rivers had become alarming, even to the Foreign Office officials. Their reaction is very interesting. The Assistant Under-Secretary's view was that 'the cup of his [Jaja's] iniquity is now full'. He suspected, however, that his Chief, Lord Salisbury, might think otherwise. For this reason, he sought out Consul Hewett on sick leave and asked him to write in support of Johnston's high-handed behaviour. Hewett did not need much prompting. He proposed the one measure he delighted in—a fine of 200 puncheons of oil on Jaja. The fine was then to be followed by the deportation of the Opobo king. He concluded his recommendations with the hope that all the indigenous rulers in the Oil Rivers protectorate would then 'learn to respect the power and Majesty of the Queen'.[3] The Foreign Office officials were agreed that the British government had the right to deport King Jaja.

[1] *Ibid.*

[2] *Ibid.* Johnston to F.O., 20 August 1887. See also Alex. Miller Brothers to Salisbury, 19 August 1887.

[3] F.O. 84/1828, Hewett to Salisbury, 20 August 1887. See Minutes by Lister and Salisbury.

Lord Salisbury was the only man who kept a cool head. He pointed out that the whole case against Jaja was that he was alleged to have broken faith. The British were not entitled to parts of Jaja's country without Jaja's permission. 'If Ahombele really is under the dominion of JaJa [*sic*], he is only doing what a few years ago was done by France, China, and Japan and what is still done by Nepal, Thibet, Corea and Formosa.'[1] He advised that Jaja's claims to Ohambele and the other hinterland markets should be investigated. If Jaja's policy excluded British traders from countries under his control, the Consul should undertake to negotiate with Jaja in order to obtain the best terms possible. Salisbury refused to approve any action against Jaja until he had received the chief's embassy. He further affirmed that Johnston's language and proposals did not inspire him with confidence. He would prefer investigations by a naval officer who was likely to be less under the sinister influence of the British merchants. Lister protested in vain against Salisbury's views on the Opobo situation.

King Jaja's behaviour during the hectic months of August and September showed the restraint of a man convinced of the justice of his cause. No Opobo chief or servant threatened the person of the Acting Consul. No European's property was plundered. Against Johnston's hysterics, Jaja put forward reasoned arguments and legal proofs. There was the 1873 treaty with a British naval officer. There was the protectorate treaty of 1885. All recognised his right to regulate alien trade transactions in his territory. Jaja's arguments were embodied in a memorandum which Jaja forwarded through the delegation of Opobo chiefs who 'are men of considerable standing in my country, and leave it at great inconvenience to the country and themselves'. Jaja even included in his arguments an appeal to the British sense of fair play. 'We are sure of your Majesty's good intentions towards us, but if your Majesty have the least knowledge of the actions of these Europeans sent out by the merchants towards us poor niggers, as they generally call us, even in meetings held by some of your officials, your Majesty will actually see and feel with us.'[2] The suggestion in local Bonny records that

---

[1] F.O. 84/1869, see Salisbury's Minute dated 9 September 1887.

[2] *Parl. Papers*, vol. LXXIV, Africa, no. 2 [C. 5365], Petition dated 20 July 1887. Also Geary, *Nigeria Under British Rule* (London, 1927), appendix 1, pp. 275–93.

Jaja's emissaries stuttered and mumbled in confusion when confronted by the Parliamentary Under-Secretary cannot detract from the logic of Jaja's argument or the justice of his cause.

Meanwhile, it was becoming clear to Johnston that his embargo on trade could not be a final solution to the situation he had precipitated. Jaja must be deported and the Acting Consul must make a stronger case to justify the deportation. Three new charges were fabricated by Johnston. In the first place, the Opobo king was building up a large force. 'Jaja would, with his cannon, rifles and war canoes, his 4000 fighting men, and his own personal courage and tactical skill, become a mighty conqueror among the peoples at the back of Opobo.' The king, entrenched in the hinterland inaccessible to the British navy, would become a more formidable obstacle to the inland penetration of British interests. In the second place, Jaja was alleged to be disturbing the peace of the Oil Rivers. For instance, King Amachree of New Calabar had allowed Europeans to establish their factories in the hinterland at Isiokpo and Ndele. Jaja had then ordered him to rescind the permission and the king of New Calabar obeyed, to the detriment of British trade.[1] The most serious charge against Jaja was the 'discovery' by Johnston that the king of Opobo had dispatched an embassy to France. He might attempt to sell his country to that country and if the deal did not materialise, there was evidence (not revealed) that the Opobo king planned to plunder the European factories, kill the white men and retire to the inaccessible hinterland. To obviate the tragic consequences implied in the three charges, Johnston asked for permission to seize and deport Jaja.[2]

The Acting Consul's report seems to have impressed the Assistant Under-Secretary of the Foreign Office. In making his recommendation to the effect that the Acting Consul should be supported, he explained that if Jaja was not deported, all the chiefs of the Oil Rivers would become uncontrollable and civil wars would result in all the coast city-states. It is not easy to see how Lister arrived at these conclusions. At this point, Salisbury was in France on holidays, exactly at a time when the Jaja–Johnston dispute reached its climax. But he called for all the papers in the Foreign

[1] *Ibid.* pp. 35 and 80–1.
[2] F.O. 84/1828, Johnston to F.O., no. 17, 11 September 1887.

Office dealing with the Opobo crisis. The Prime Minister's reaction to the Acting Consul's charges and proposals was one of frank incredulity. His verdict on the situation was stated with great clarity. 'Nothing in the memorandum of the Department or in the papers sent with it throws much light upon the most important issue, namely whether JaJa [*sic*] is in any sense ruler of the territory of Ohambele, from which he has excluded our trade. If he is ruler, then, assuming we are dealing with him according to strict law, he is in his right.'[1]

Through some inexplicable confusion of papers in the Foreign Office,[2] an approval of Johnston's trade embargo was construed as approval by Salisbury of the Acting Consul's plan to deport Jaja. The Foreign Office dispatched an affirmative reply to Johnston's request before the memorandum in which Salisbury's utter condemnation of the Acting Consul was manifest reached the Foreign Office. The Jaja–Johnston dispute now moved into its final phase. The Acting Consul had at hand H.M.S. *Goshawk* with its sizable contingent of bluejackets. King Jaja was temporarily shaken and made promises calculated to mollify Johnston. The latter had all the advantage the show of force afforded. In spite of this, Johnston resorted to a very reprehensible strategem. He invited King Jaja on board the gun-boat for 'an exchange of views'. The king requested and received assurances from Johnston that he would not be detained against his wish, but Jaja had fallen into his enemy's trap. The upshot was the deportation of the king of Opobo to the Gold Coast, and subsequently to the West Indies. In the Gold Coast, Jaja was subjected to what was in fact an illegal trial, because he was not a British subject and was not amenable to the jurisdiction of a British court.[3]

A great deal of controversy has been provoked by the Jaja–Johnston dispute and the latter's act of perfidy in deporting Jaja in spite of assurances of safe conduct. Johnston's apologists find it difficult to exonerate him and the best they can do is to attempt to

---

[1] *Ibid.* Salisbury's Minutes, 24–28 September 1887.

[2] See Oliver, *op. cit.* pp. 113–15. No evidence is revealed of a deliberate manipulation of the despatches on the part of Foreign Office officials.

[3] The detention of a non-British subject was apparently legalised by the 'Opobo Political Prisoners Detention Ordinance, 1887', which was rushed through the Gold Coast Legislative Council, 6 October 1887.

explain that Johnston's whole policy was in agreement with the intentions of the British Foreign Office. It is, however, intended in this study to confine attention to the verdict of the British Prime Minister. As regards the basic issue of Jaja's right to the dominion he built up from almost nothing, Salisbury believed that Jaja's empire was *de facto* dominion, and any discussion of his title was irrelevant. '*De facto* dominion is the only thing of which we can take notice, for none of us are learned enough to determine the legitimacy according to the Native laws of a Guinea king.' As to the manner of Jaja's deportation, Salisbury observed that 'to invite a chief on board your ship, carefully concealing the fact that you have any designs against his person, and then, when he has put himself in your power, to carry him away, is hardly legitimate warfare, even if we had a right to go to war. It is called "deporting" in the papers, but I think this is a euphemism. In other places it would be called kidnapping.'

Why then did Salisbury not reverse the injustice perpetrated by the British Acting Consul? Why was a Naval Commander-in-Chief sent to try Jaja in the Gold Coast, and allowed to admonish Jaja to abandon all hopes of ever resuming the position he had hitherto held as king of Opobo 'as no future king or head chief will be elected'?[1] The Foreign Office archives provide the answer. Salisbury's lieutenants in the Foreign Office very ingeniously exploited the possible awkwardness that might arise from parliamentary inquisitiveness to mutilate the records of the Gold Coast trial and to manœuvre the British Prime Minister into the belief that 'we shall do more harm by dropping than supporting him (Johnston)...a singularly lawless personage'.[2]

The subsequent career of King Jaja in exile in the West Indies does not exactly belong to the history of the Oil Rivers protectorate. It is, however, difficult to avoid some reference to two circumstances in regard to the exile. The personality of ex-King Jaja could not be repressed even by the privations and agonies of exile. Everywhere he went, he carried himself with calm but impressive dignity. During the year 1888, Jaja's health began to deteriorate,

[1] F.O. 84/1828, Africa, no. 25, 2 December 1887.
[2] F.O. 84/1828, Minutes already cited, 24–28 September 1887; also Geary, *op. cit.* p. 281.

and in spite of medical certifications, British equivocation prevented him from ever reaching his native land alive. The episode is one of the most disgraceful in the records of British colonial history. The newspapers of the West Indies were not silent on the shabby treatment of a king whom Britain had no legal or moral right to deport, much less send to his grave in a desolate island in the Atlantic.[1]

The deportation of Jaja effectively exploded the myth that the protectorate treaties were seriously intended to safeguard the internal sovereignty of the city-states of the Nigerian coast. Even pretence dies hard, and so on many occasions subsequently there were still faint protests against measures adopted by the British agent in the Oil Rivers, on the ground that the 1885 legal basis of consular jurisdiction had not been changed. With or without authority Acting Consul Johnston was determined to put the finishing touches to his work of overthrowing indigenous independence. After the trial and elimination of King Jaja, the Acting Consul took Admiral Hunt-Grubbe on a tour of the Oil Rivers. The tour was nothing more than a show of force intended for the benefit of local rulers who might possibly not have appreciated the lesson which the deportation of the most dynamic and the most influential of their number was intended to convey. If Jaja had defied the Acting Consul and lost his patrimony, what coast chief would sanely contemplate the possibility of following Jaja's example?[2]

Johnston's first preoccupation was the organisation of organs of administration to take over the rule of the coast city-states. His justification for the unauthorised and illegal measure was, as he put it, that since 'the native Chiefs do not seem competent to administer the affairs of their country in a wise and just manner, it is necessary to create some scheme of local government'.[3] The scheme was an interim measure, Johnston conceded, but one which should pave the way for a regular British administration. The new organ of government was styled the 'Governing Council'. Johnston began with Opobo (where he had an excuse because Jaja was deported and his principal assistants were detained in the

---

[1] *The Barbados Herald*, Monday, 11 May 1891; The *Agricultural Reporter*, Tuesday, 12 May 1891.

[2] King George Pepple of Bonny studiously courted Johnston's friendship.

[3] F.O. 84/1828, no. 18, Johnston to F.O., 24 September 1887.

Gold Coast), but he later extended the system to Old Calabar, Bonny, New Calabar, Brass and the Benin River. The composition of the Opobo Governing Council provides a concrete illustration of the alien nature of the new system of government:[1]

| | | |
|---|---|---|
| *President* | H.M. Consul | |
| *Vice-President* | Samuel B. Hall (a British merchant) | |
| *Secretary* | William J. Kitchen (a British merchant) | |
| *Other members* | (*a*) *Opobo chiefs* | John Africa |
| | | Wago Dapa |
| | | Fine Bone |
| | (*b*) *British traders* | T. Y. Wright |
| | | F. D. Mitchell |
| | | R. Foster |
| | | Alex. H. Turnbull |
| | (*c*) *Ex-Officio* | The Senior Naval Officer |

There were therefore only three nominated local chiefs in a body of ten people. The executive offices were in the hands of aliens.

The Governing Council was to meet once a week. Its powers were limited to carrying out consular orders, the preservation of peace, the maintenance of highways and means of communication, the regulation of commerce, and the hearing in court of minor civil actions and criminal charges. Rates of fine, terms of imprisonment and the number of strokes of the cane permitted were all set out in Johnston's regulations. For public works, a tax not exceeding one shilling per person might be levied, not oftener than three times a year, on all persons residing in Opobo for a longer period than one month. Lastly, the Governing Council took over from the local rulers the right to collect 'comey', although half the value was to go to the indigenous rulers and half was to be used by the Council 'in the interest of the country'. Another far-reaching measure promulgated by Johnston was a regulation forbidding the importation and sale of machine-guns, cannon, guns, bullets and cartridges. He proposed a fine of £100 for the first offence, and deportation for the second. A reward of £100 was promised any informer whose co-operation led to the conviction of anyone, white or black.

[1] *Ibid.* Enclosure. See also F.O. 84/1839, no. 22, Johnston to F.O., 21 October 1887.

In Bonny, to which Johnston's system of Governing Council was extended, the internal political situation had since January 1887 assumed its former posture of normality. The explanation for the change from turbulence to stability lay in the 'friendship' which developed between King George Pepple and Johnston. The powerful chiefs of Bonny, Warribo Manilla Pepple, Adda Allison and Oko Jumbo, had from the time of the Bonny civil war almost reduced the king of Bonny to a nonentity. They had also through their petty jealousies produced internal political chaos in Bonny. At the beginning of 1887, thanks largely to King Pepple's friendship with and admiration of Johnston, the head chiefs were compelled to sign a declaration on 19 January. They renounced the claim to revenue and sovereignty, and recognised that the person of the king was 'sacred'. They pledged themselves not to go to war without the consent of the king. Lastly they exempted the king from the obligation to take part in any national ceremony which the king thought inconsistent with his Christian religion.[1] In all this, it is easy to see the influence of Johnston and there is little wonder that King George Pepple pledged his moral support to Johnston during the latter's celebrated quarrel with King Jaja. At the end of 1887 Pepple gladly accepted Johnston's new organ of government and was 'rewarded' with membership of the alien council. When George Pepple died in October 1888, no one bothered to recognise his heir, Prince William Pepple, because the office of king had ceased to have any significance in Johnston's new order.

As pointed out already, Johnston recognised that all his new measures were revolutionary and incompatible with the legal basis of his consular jurisdiction. In his report to the Foreign Office, he pleaded with the Foreign Office officials to condone any irregularity in his proceedings. The legal adviser to the Foreign Office, W. E. Davidson, observed that from the standpoint of the 1885 West African Order-in-Council and the treaties with the Oil Rivers chiefs, the Acting Consul's actions were *ultra vires*. The Permanent Under-Secretary, Sir Julian Pauncefote, after noting that the British government had no right to make laws for the natives, suggested that the time had come for the Foreign Office to decide the question 'as to our political status in these regions'. Lastly,

[1] *Bonny Local Records, op. cit.*

Lord Salisbury wished to know the grounds on which the Acting Consul had undertaken to establish 'a totally different regime politically and legally to that which is now in force'.[1]

It is misleading to accept the critical minutes on Johnston's report at their face value. There was of course impressive reference to the 1885 Order-in-Council and to treaties with the native chiefs, but the real concern of the British government was over the possibility of interminable court actions by trading agents who knew the legal limitations imposed on Johnston's consular jurisdiction by the Order-in-Council. If the Consul deported a British trading agent, the firm involved might sue the Consul for damages. Thus, although the Foreign Office dispatch to Johnston purported to disallow his measures and reminded him that 'H.M. Government have not assumed the administration of the Territories in question',[2] the misgivings of the Foreign Office had nothing to do with the fact that its agent was usurping the political prerogatives of indigenous rulers. In any case, the Foreign Office dispatch was a 'dead letter'. Johnston's Governing Councils continued to function, in spite of Foreign Office disapproval. As Johnston probably anticipated, no further awkward questions were asked by the Foreign Office so long as he did not deport a British trading agent.

Meanwhile, Johnston was preparing to implement plans which had been maturing in his mind. He now proposed in the new year to place the entire district lying east of the Niger, south of the Benue and west of the German Cameroons 'effectively' under British protection. This ambitious plan was in fact not fully carried out. The Acting Consul, however, did push his way up the Cross river, and concluded treaties with the independent states of Umon, Akunakuna and Ikomorut, 'besides making friends with and distributing British flags to the people right up the borders of Atam'.[3] Johnston encountered and noted the peculiarities of indigenous political activities along the Cross river (as the Scottish missionaries of Old Calabar had done before him). Each state claimed to control the bordering river section and demanded tolls

[1] F.O. 84/1839, see Minutes on no. 22 already cited.
[2] F.O. 84/1881, F.O. draft to Johnston, 10 February 1888.
[3] *Ibid.* no. 6, Johnston to F.O., 9 February 1888.

from its neighbours whose trade passed through the state. As a result, Calabar was at odds with Umon, Umon with Akunakuna, and Akunakuna with Ikomorut. The policy of exacting tolls was a traditional method of providing revenue in small hardly institutionalised states situated along the Cross river. Providing revenue was and is a legitimate exercise of sovereignty. Unfortunately, the smallness of the states in the Cross river basin and the informality of their political arrangements exposed them to the charge of indulging in 'anarchic freedom'. The Scottish missionaries of Calabar thought so. British agents in due course accepted the missionaries' views on the Cross river states and peoples.[1] But whilst the missionaries laboured patiently among the peoples, they expected the British government to adopt coercive measures. In 1888 Acting Consul Johnston could resort only to treaties of protection, but he did not fail to paint a bizarre picture in reporting on the situation on the Cross river. On one occasion, claimed Johnston, he was surrounded by a score of cannibals, and was then carried shoulder-high by the biggest of the savages who went off with him on a trot to the village. There Johnston was put on a crude bench in a hut to be stared at for an hour or so by hundreds of entranced savages. This grotesque scene vividly narrated by the Acting Consul drew but one significant remark from the head of the African Department of the Foreign Office. H. P. Anderson wondered whether 'these boisterous cannibals are fit for British Protection'.[2]

Before leaving the Oil Rivers about the middle of 1888, Johnston left on record a remarkable verdict on British relations with the peoples and states of the protectorate.

I do earnestly hope that our responsibility towards these peoples is going to be recognised.... Considering what very slight benefit has as yet accrued to them from our rule, it is surprising what loyalty the chiefs of the Oil Rivers have shown towards the British Government.... They have been cheated by British merchants, bombarded by British Captains and fined by British Consuls and yet they like us and stick by us and are proud of being 'all same Inglis man'....[3]

[1] Waddell, *op. cit.* p. 373; Goldie, *Calabar and its Mission*, pp. 100–1.
[2] F.O. 84/1881, no. 6, Johnston to F.O., 9 February 1888, and Minutes by Anderson.
[3] F.O. 84/1882, Memorandum on the British Protectorate of the Oil Rivers, 24 July 1888.

Comments on Johnston's verdict would make a fascinating academic exercise. What evidence had he of the loyalty of the chiefs whose independence he undermined? What responsibility did Britain seriously undertake towards the peoples? When Jaja attempted to control the activities of British merchants in his domain, did not Johnston side with the merchants, and was it not he who encompassed the ruin of Jaja?

Any judgement on Acting Consul Johnston's regime in the Oil Rivers protectorate must depend on one's point of view. He was an honest exponent of British policy. The legal experts of the Foreign Office made fine distinctions about treaties and Orders-in-Council, but Johnston knew that the protectorate theory was no more than a device to keep out other European powers. Therefore, when he did have the opportunity, he attempted to carry out what Britain would, except for the parsimony of the Treasury, have done in 1885 by direct British administration. To blame Johnston for refusing to pretend that the British government seriously intended to respect the independence of local rulers at the expense of British trading interests would be hypocritical. His critics in the British Foreign Office, including Salisbury, were perhaps not conscious hypocrites. From the standpoint of the Nigerian coast rulers, the regime of Acting Consul Johnston was disastrous. Thanks to his energy and perfidy, the greed of British merchants prevailed over treaty guarantees of the independence of indigenous rulers. It is with this standpoint that an adverse historical verdict should concern itself. There were no exonerating circumstances in the part Johnston played in the shameful episode of Jaja's deportation and death in exile.[1]

In June 1888 Hewett returned to the Oil Rivers, after the departure of his turbulent deputy. He was naturally not pleased with the fact that his deputy had in eighteen months achieved far more spectacular results for British rule than he himself could claim in more than three years. The officials of the Foreign Office had in many subtle ways contrasted Johnston's energy with his —usually to Hewett's disadvantage. Hewett's policy in the Oil

---

[1] For divergent judgements on Johnston, see Geary, *op. cit.* appendix I, and Oliver, *op. cit.* p. 121 (here the Assistant Under-Secretary speaks of Johnston's 'coolness and forbearance').

Rivers from June 1888 until his retirement in 1890 must be seen in the light of his ill-disguised envy of the flood of publicity which had marked Johnston's regime. After all Johnston was only Hewett's deputy. Hewett therefore began by picking out details of his deputy's legislative and executive measures for denigration. The regulation which forbade the giving of 'trust' by white agents to indigenous traders was, according to Hewett, vexatious interference in the question of debt by one to another. He questioned the legality of the decision of the Brass Governing Council to award to a trading agent, Townsend, a contract of £160 for the purpose of building a road between the beaches and the town. Hewett's report on his deputy's policy concluded with an obscure but pathetic question: 'What are the natives to believe as to law or power?'[1] The report caused considerable consternation in the Foreign Office. The head of the African Department came to the conclusion that Hewett's exposures were a convincing proof of the failure of the Foreign Office attempt at consular administration. He began from this time seriously to assess the alternatives to consular rule in the Oil Rivers protectorate. The operative word is 'seriously' because, as has already been pointed out, the consular administration was undertaken as a last resort. Throughout its existence the older proposals for company rule and a Crown Colony establishment were never entirely lost sight of.

Meanwhile, Consul Hewett was determined to do more than discredit Johnston's administrative regulations. He was aware that Johnston's unfulfilled hinterland tour project and Johnston's actual penetration of the Upper Cross river basin were highly commended by the Foreign Office officials. Now Hewett had his own opportunity to extend the 'boundaries' of the protectorate. He selected the hinterland of Bonny as his field of endeavour. Here was situated an important peripheral Ijaw/Ibo city-state, Okrika. Hewett's mission to Okrika was political and commercial. Okrika was to Bonny what Ohombele was to Opobo—a collecting centre for the palm produce from the hinterland. The friendship of the ruler of Okrika would safeguard the trade of Bonny. There was also the desirability of offering British 'protection' to Okrika. Hewett and the king of Okrika met and signed a treaty with the usual

[1] F.O. 84/1881, no. 25, Hewett to F.O., 20 June 1888.

clauses, in July 1888. Three months later, the new treaty state became involved in a war with an Ibo autonomous town further inland, and it was reported to the Consul, probably by Bonny traders, that Okrika people had captured many Ibos and 'eaten' 160 of them. Hewett went back to Okrika to investigate the alleged atrocity. The behaviour of Okrika, argued the Consul, violated the protection treaty with Britain which bound the king to refer all external disputes to the Consul. The king of Okrika advanced the counter-argument that he was under the impression that the relevant clause of the Okrika–British treaty applied to disputes between states under British protection, and not to states which had not accepted British protection and had no political relations with Britain.[1] Hewett knew that the Okrika king's contention was technically right. He, however, fined the king 100 puncheons of oil, which the king refused to pay.

Hewett, in the face of the new problem, attempted to initiate a dangerous policy. He summoned Bonny war leaders and proposed that they should accompany him to Okrika to subdue the king. Bonny chiefs knew better than to antagonise the ruler of Okrika.[2] Okrika was inaccessible to British gunboats, and so the fine imposed on Okrika was not paid until three years later when Major Claude Macdonald inaugurated a comparatively more effective administration. Hewett's impotence in the face of the defiant attitude of the king of Okrika, and what Johnston called his turbulent reception by the states of the Upper Cross river, foreshadowed the basic problems which British agents had to encounter when Britain decided to impose her rule on the hinterland peoples, peoples organised politically in sturdy autonomous villages, who believed in their own way of life, and were not subjected to the corroding influences of the trumperies of European civilisation.

Hewett's Okrika policy failed. He now turned his attention to Opobo where the political aftermath of Jaja's deportation was clearly visible—Johnston's Governing Council notwithstanding. The leading Opobo chiefs, exiled in the Gold Coast after Jaja's

[1] *Ibid.* no. 31, 6 October 1888.
[2] Hewett's strange precaution, 'viz. making some chiefs accompany the landing party who would be the first to pay the penalty of being shot in the event of the party being fired on', was elaborated in F.O. 84/1941, no. 29, 8 August 1889.

deportation, had been allowed to return. These chiefs seized the opportunity of the Consul's visit to present a petition soliciting his good offices on Jaja's behalf. The chiefs argued that Jaja's deteriorating health, his age and the effects of his absence on the affairs of Opobo deserved the British government's sympathy. Hewett's reaction was understandable. He was not to be expected to show weakness where Johnston's unequivocal firmness had virtually consolidated the pre-eminent authority of the Queen's representative. Hewett therefore chose to regard the petition of the Opobo chiefs as evidence that the exile of their king had not sufficiently cowed Opobo and her people. Early in 1889 Hewett invited the naval officer in charge of the West African Station to appear with gunboats and help to enforce new coercive measures which the Consul proposed against Opobo.[1] These measures included a fine of 300 puncheons of oil on Opobo; the deportation of Chiefs Sam Annie Pepple, Ogolo and Oko Jaja; the confiscation of all war canoes, guns, rifles and cartridges; the withdrawal of all Opobo traders from the hinterland markets; and the payment of £2000 as security for the good behaviour of the chiefs and people of Opobo for three years. If the terms were not accepted, the navy would blockade Opobo and starve the people into submission.

Lieut.-Commander Harrison of the local squadron and his superior, Admiral Wells, were unwilling to commit themselves to Hewett's proposals without the authorisation of the Admiralty. The Consul therefore sought approval directly from the Foreign Office. He repeated the old arguments that Opobo chiefs were obstructing free transit to the hinterland markets and that 'friendly natives' were losing confidence in the Queen's government. If steps were not taken to punish Opobo severely, all the consular districts would become engulfed in civil wars.[2] The Chairman of the African Association of Liverpool, Stanley Rogerson, sought an interview with the head of the African Department and reinforced Hewett's arguments that the work begun by Johnston in Opobo should be concluded.

The British government had already decided to send a Special Commissioner to investigate the problems raised by the Niger

---

[1] F.O.C.P. 4945, Incl. 4, dated 5 February 1889.
[2] *Ibid.* no. 46, Hewett to F.O., 9 February 1889.

Districts and the Oil Rivers. The Foreign Office was therefore inclined to a policy of conciliation rather than coercion. The controversy which Johnston's high-handed policy in Opobo had provoked had not quite died down. Jaja's progressive decline in health in his place of exile was not helping the conscience of the British government. In Opobo itself, some of the English firms were opposed to Hewett's new militancy. All the reports from the Oil Rivers were in fact being passed on to the Special Commissioner who eventually reached the Oil Rivers and visited Opobo on 4 March 1889.

Hewett's last task in the Oil Rivers took him on a protest visit to von Soden, the German governor of the Cameroons. The German governor had ordered a German warship to Calabar to arrest and remove King Eyo Honesty VII. The situation which led to this requires explanation. The arbitrary demarcation of British and German spheres of influence in 1886 cut off from the Efik their markets in the hinterland, north-east of Calabar. It was the capital supplied by the Calabar chiefs which helped to exploit the resources of this hinterland, whose inhabitants were often in debt to Calabar chiefs. All that King Eyo did was to have two men from the hinterland brought to Calabar as surety for the repayment of debts to Calabar. The Germans could not of course understand this traditional indigenous practice; hence their seizure of King Eyo. The missionary Goldie in Calabar construed the incident as evidence of the failure of the British government to afford the local rulers the protection and security which the protectorate treaties stipulated. The Calabar king was not released until two Calabar men were surrendered to the German governor. The British Consul delivered his protest note personally on 22 April. The German governor's reply took the form of a jibe at the British administration of the Oil Rivers. It was strange, said the governor, that when he arrived at the headquarters of the British protectorate, he found neither the Consul nor any one who claimed to speak for the British government.[1] The jibe was not lost on the British government.

Consul Edward Hyde Hewett left the Oil Rivers finally a sick man in the autumn of 1889. He had been the principal architect

[1] F.O. 84/1941, no. 17, Hewett to F.O., 30 April 1889.

of the British protectorate of the Oil Rivers. It was no small achievement that he successfully conducted, on behalf of Britain, very difficult negotiations in 1884, especially at Opobo and Brass. By means of these treaties Britain effectively excluded the French and the Germans from the most profitable field for economic exploitation in West Africa. It was not entirely Hewett's fault that he indulged in the illusion that he was a governor in a British colony. He was tireless in his efforts to expose the hollowness of the British pretence that the British role in the Oil Rivers protectorate was merely that of a paramount power with nothing to do in the internal affairs of the city-states. Hewett had lived long enough in the Oil Rivers to know the extent to which alien influences had corroded the fabric of the indigenous states. There were of course exceptions. The retiring Consul made mistakes in his relations with King Jaja of Opobo but these mistakes did not lead him to the extremes or the perfidy in which Johnston indulged. On the whole Hewett served his country well, primarily because without his tact and assiduity the Oil Rivers might conceivably have fallen into the hands of Germany during the panicky months of 1884.[1] The Oil Rivers indigenous rulers did not like him, but it would be unrealistic to expect the chiefs to have much affection for a man who laid the foundation of their final collapse as independent sovereigns. The British merchants in the Oil Rivers had no encomiums to shower on a man who, they thought, lacked the energy to deal drastically with 'recalcitrant' local rulers who prejudiced the profits of their trade. The attitude of the officials of the Foreign Office towards Hewett was contradictory. These officials expected results where the Order-in-Council they issued provided no room for results.[2]

When Hewett left the Oil Rivers, there was no assistant or deputy to take over British consular jurisdiction. There was no official British representative for at least three months. The city-states were not plunged into civil wars nor did the local inhabitants attempt to plunder British firms or threaten the lives of British subjects. The British Foreign Office had been fed for so long on the

---

[1] Ifor Evans, *The British in Tropical Africa* (Cambridge, 1929), p. 21; Keltie, *Partition of Africa* (London, 1922), p. 280.

[2] Robinson and Gallagher, *op. cit.* p. 394.

hypothesis that the absence of effective British rule meant chaos in the Oil Rivers. Therefore a consular officer on his way to assume duties in the Congo was intercepted with a peremptory telegram instructing him to take charge temporarily of the protectorate of the Oil Rivers. This man was George Annesley. He was in some ways more fortunate than his predecessors. The British Foreign Office for the first time authorised the appointment of 'consular agents' from among the British traders to assist the Consul. These consular agents were expected to receive no salary and to have no claims on the imperial government. In Old Calabar, Albert Gillies, a trading agent, accepted appointment in this capacity. At Bonny, another trader, James Munro, became the second consular agent in the protectorate. The records do not reveal how many were appointed altogether. Their powers were not defined and it is not easy to say what contribution they made to the administration. They probably presided over the governing councils in the absence of the Consul, and accompanied the Consul when he visited the district local rulers.[1]

Shortly after his assumption of authority in the Oil Rivers protectorate, Annesley's attention was directed to the affairs of the Cross river basin by Porteous of the United Presbyterian Mission of Calabar. The missionary reminded the Consul that the states of the Cross river had accepted British protection by their treaties with Johnston. In spite of this, their traditional feuds and the exacting of tolls had not abated. If Annesley's duty was primarily to encourage the development of trade by removing all obstructionist practices, and the missionary assumed that his construing of the Consul's duty was right, then there was much for him to do on the Cross river.[2] The logic of Porteous's arguments was unassailable, at any rate as far as the Acting Consul was concerned. The latter's decision to visit the places in question as far as Akunakuna was a natural one. It is misleading to refer to the states of the Cross river without the important reminder that the missionaries and the Consuls did not really regard them as such. Various derogatory terms were used, such as 'odd fragments of humanity' and 'boisterous savages'.

[1] F.O. 84/2020, no. 13, Annesley to F.O., 27 February 1890.
[2] *Ibid.* A. M. Porteous to Annesley, 27 February 1890.

The first local ruler on the Cross river north of Itu whom Consul Annesley visited was Andemeno of Enyong. The king explained that he had not in fact concluded a treaty with anybody. The situation of Enyong was a very strategic one. The Efiks on the coast and the Akunakuna on the Upper Cross river were great trading peoples. All that was required was an uninterrupted link between these two peoples in order to consolidate the advantages of the Cross river as a first-rate artery of trade. The position of Enyong and Andemeno's policy of exacting heavy tolls constituted a serious obstacle. The missionaries had already convinced the Consul that Andemeno's policy was outright blackmail. The Consul's intention in 1890 was therefore first and foremost to get the ruler of Enyong to conclude a treaty 'in order to prevent further outrages on his part'.[1] Andemeno, however, refused to see the Consul, let alone sign a treaty. He actually locked himself up in his house, and neither the Consul's persuasions nor his threats made any difference. The sequel is best described in the Consul's own words. 'As the Crowd around us became more aggressive I gave the king five minutes to come out, at the end of which I fined him one hundred boxes of rods and returned to our canoe followed by an armed mob.' Annesley did not stop to prescribe how the fine was to be secured, or to explain the grounds on which he imposed a fine on a ruler who had no treaty relations with Britain.

North of Enyong, the Consul made his way to the state of Ikotana. The king of this place had, according to Annesley, been 'a source of great annoyance to Johnston', because he had refused the offer of a treaty with Britain. On the present occasion, the king seemed more amenable to the Consul's solicitations. Obiakari undertook not to enter into any correspondence, agreement or treaty with any foreign nation without the knowledge of H.M. government. He also accepted the usual clauses in regard to free trade and good government. Encouraged by this success Annesley moved on to Akunakuna, and even successfully persuaded Obiakari of Ikotana to accompany him. Between Ikotana and Akunakuna there was an age-long territorial dispute which the Consul decided to settle once and for all. Annesley's solution was summary. The area in dispute was constituted an independent state and its people

[1] *Ibid*. Annesley to F.O., 27 February 1890.

were asked to elect a king. The stamp of 'permanence' was expressed in a treaty with Britain which offered the new state British protection.[1]

Annesley believed that his Cross river tour had been a great success. The one disappointment was King Andemeno of Enyong, who had locked himself up. As long as this king refused to be bound by any protectorate treaty, free transit on the Cross river could not be safeguarded. The Consul, back in Calabar, made up his mind to subdue the Enyong ruler. He first appealed to the Commander of H.M.S. *Peacock* but the latter firmly refused to commit his vessel to the uncertainties of the Cross river north of the Calabar republics. The Consul then summoned what he called a war council comprising Calabar chiefs, British traders and missionaries. If all co-operated, the Consul had no doubt that a military expedition against Andemeno of Enyong would be eminently successful. The Calabar chiefs, from past experience,[2] were a little sceptical. Rev. R. M. Beedie made an impassioned speech in which he declared that it was not the business of ordinary citizens of Calabar to fight in order to remove the obstacles to free transit on the Cross river. The British government which proclaimed the protectorate of the Oil Rivers should have provided the Consul with the means of discharging his responsibilities in the protectorate. The missionary was not of course concerned with the precise extent of the protectorate which Britain assumed in 1885. The council of war summoned by Annesley broke up in disorder after Beedie's impressive speech.

The views expressed by the missionary were echoed in the Consul's report to the Foreign Office.[3] Lord Salisbury commented that the Consul should be authorised to defray the cost of raising and equipping a native police force out of the fines collected by the Governing Councils. It may be recalled that these councils created by Johnston had been declared illegal but they nonetheless had continued to function. Rear-Admiral Wells meanwhile confirmed Annesley's views that 'the administration of the Oil Rivers

---

[1] As soon as Annesley left, the new kingdom of Uppem fell and the Akunakuna and Ikotana resumed their old feud.

[2] Goldie, *op. cit.* pp. 100–2, also p. 331; Waddell, *op. cit.* p. 373.

[3] F.O. 84/2020, no. 13 already cited. See Encl. Private letter from Annesley to Anderson.

Protectorate has got beyond the "Consul and gun-boat" stage'. With Foreign Office approval, Annesley proceeded to organise the police force which at first consisted of forty Krumen from Liberia who had for centuries served the European merchants and ships and could speak 'pidgin' English. This force soon earned itself the title of 'the forty thieves'.[1] The derogatory title illustrates the considerable hostility with which the local inhabitants regarded the new consular police force. The members of the force in fact constituted themselves into a new authority which openly showed utter contempt for the local rulers and indigenous standards of social behaviour. They were 'Consul men' and, therefore, were superior to the local chiefs and their men. It would be misleading to suggest that any local ruler was aware that the establishment of the force was yet another step towards the complete overthrow of the independence of the indigenous states. After all, it seemed less revolutionary than the setting up of alien governing councils in each of the coast city-states, and the consular force was no more than the land equivalent of the coercive force long exercised by the British navy.

The military prowess of the consular force was tested when Consul Annesley decided in June 1890 to chastise the state of Akwette, situated in the immediate hinterland of Bonny. It had been reported by Bonny traders that the people of Akwette were proving difficult to trade with. This state had no treaty relations with Britain, but it was offence enough that it constituted an obstacle to trade penetration. Thus, under the command of the Consul, the 'forty thieves' launched an attack on Akwette. The people of Akwette naturally rallied behind their ruler and repulsed the invaders with heavy losses to the consular force. In his report to the Foreign Office, the Consul said nothing about the reverse his force had suffered. He made two complaints. In the first place, '...there is no law properly speaking in this Protectorate...and I am continually asked "What is the law on this or that point? Consul so and so said this, Consul so and so said that—what do you say?"'[2] Secondly, Annesley blamed the missionaries who,

[1] F.O. 84/2111, Complaints to Macdonald enclosed in Macdonald to F.O., 1 September 1891.
[2] F.O. 84/2020, no. 29, Annesley to F.O., 19 June 1890.

according to the Consul, preferred the Bible to the sword—a probable reference to the speech of the Rev. R. M. Beedie of Old Calabar which had frustrated his war plans against King Andemeno of Enyong. The situation in the Oil Rivers had indeed come to a point where the Foreign Office no longer paid much attention to consular reports. The chaos, the contradictions and the confusions which resulted from the hypocritically negative nature of British intervention were too glaring to be ignored any longer. Salisbury now awaited with eagerness the report by the Special Commissioner, Major Claude Macdonald, who had been there for many months to investigate the affairs of the region.[1]

The consular regime which Britain inaugurated in the Oil Rivers under the 1885 West African Order-in-Council came to an end in 1890. This phase of British rule has usually been referred to by many writers on Nigerian history as the 'Paper Protectorate'.[2] The epithet 'paper' calls attention to the absence of the normal administrative paraphernalia of a Crown Colony regime. This argument is based on wrong assumptions. The Berlin West African Conference which 'legalised' European 'freedom of action' on the African coast made a clear distinction between annexations and protectorates. In the Oil Rivers Britain committed herself to the latter category. The duties of Britain as a paramount power, although not precisely defined, did not include intervention in the internal affairs of the indigenous states. The treaties which apparently gave Britain a moral right to be in the Oil Rivers contained specific assurances in regard to the integrity of the indigenous states and the preservation of their internal sovereignty. It was precisely for this reason that the Order-in-Council which prescribed the legal functions of the British Consul confined his jurisdiction to British subjects. If consular rule failed in the Oil Rivers, the reasons must be sought in the peculiar forces which operated. To dismiss a complex situation by merely blaming the parsimony of the British Treasury is to assume that Britain had in the Oil Rivers a *tabula rasa* where she could do as she liked. If the 'protection' treaties conferred a moral right, they also imposed a

---

[1] *Ibid.* F.O. Telegram, 6 December 1890. (The F.O. was already thinking in terms of sites for Customs and other governmental establishments.)

[2] Burns, *op. cit.* ch. XII; Oliver, *op. cit.* ch. IV.

moral obligation in respect of the scrupulous observance of their stipulations.

Hailey's verdict on British protectorate policy in Africa ingeniously evades the basic issues involved. 'Its primary concern was with the facilities which Native territories offered for the expansion of trade and it sought to limit its obligations to securing such order as was needed for this purpose. The policy was impossible in practice. The maintenance of order necessitated a control over the chiefs which prejudiced the traditional organisation of tribal authority.'[1] In the Oil Rivers, Britain's primary aim was indisputably trade. As to the question of maintenance of order, British agents were aware of the existence of well-organised city-states some of which had flourished for centuries. If there was progressive deterioration in the internal stability of some of these states on the Nigerian coast, British Consuls and merchants contributed substantially to this development. Jaja of Opobo and, later, Nana of the Benin river were not deported because they could not maintain order in their dominions. There were of course states like Bonny and New Calabar where internal petty bickerings played into the hands of the British Consuls and apparently afforded ample justification for the intervention of alien agents. It is nonetheless wrong to assume that the local rulers were unequal to the demands of independence and that British intervention was therefore inevitable.

The basic problem in the protectorate of the Oil Rivers was the conflict between theory and practice in British policy as interpreted by local British representatives. The Consuls from the start behaved as if they were governors, and it cannot be claimed that they received much guidance from the British Foreign Office officials. The latter had indeed regarded consular rule as a temporary expedient, and for this reason the moral and political implications of a protectorate relationship were at no time seriously analysed, much less understood. The Foreign Office, the British merchants and the local rulers held divergent views on the protectorate treaties. Above all, the requirements of British trade held primacy of place in British official thinking. Thus, any local ruler who stood in the way of the inland penetration of British trade had

[1] Hailey, *op. cit.* p. 467.

to be overthrown, whether or not the treaty with Britain safe-guarded his independence, and whether or not he ruled his state effectively. The confusions and contradictions which characterised the first five years of British consular rule were the direct result of the circumstances suggested above. These circumstances provide an explanation for the failure of the type of consular rule which operated between 1885 and 1890.

# CHAPTER IV

# SOUTHERN NIGERIA AT THE CROSS-ROADS

The time had come for the British government to cast aside all pretence about the motivations of its policy in the Oil Rivers. The actions of British consular representatives had almost completely undermined the independence of the protected states on the Nigerian coast, though Foreign Office comments would suggest that there was no legal basis for the actions of its agents. When at last the Permanent Under-Secretary observed that 'the first question to be decided is as to our political status in these regions',[1] it was clear that the British government was about to adjust the theory of the protectorate relationship to practice. Effective measures had to be devised for the control of an 'estate pegged out for posterity'.

The architect of the protectorate of the Oil Rivers had no doubts as to what he thought his government should have done long before the anomalies and contradictions which characterised the history of the protectorate came into the open. In 1887 Consul Hewett argued that 'so long as the country is only a protectorate we have the difficulty of contending against native laws and customs, and it will be impossible for our work to be thorough and our task to be quickly done as if the country was annexed'.[2] The Consul was, at least, aware of the dilemma which confronted the British government. On the one hand, it was clear that the basic motive for Britain's presence in the Oil Rivers was to consolidate the basis for the hinterland penetration of British trading interests. On the other hand, the treaties with the local rulers might have begun as a farce, but they undeniably involved legal and moral implications. The problem was therefore this. If, according to the British

[1] F.O. 84/1828, Minute by Pauncefote on no. 27, 13 December 1887.
[2] *Ibid.* Observations by Hewett on an alleged petition from the chiefs of Old Calabar, 19 July 1887.

agents, the protected states were incapable of governing themselves and chaos prevailed, to the detriment of British trade, was it not unrealistic to continue a policy based on the assumption that the treaties with the local rulers conferred on Britain only external sovereignty? In the exigencies of politics and trade in the Oil Rivers, was the distinction between internal and external sovereignty a tenable one? Could Britain, therefore, be charged with bad faith if she decided to abandon an unworkable political relationship?

The 1885 West African Order-in-Council was clearly out of date. Legal machinery had to be devised to provide a basis for the legitimate control of British subjects and the indigenous inhabitants of the protectorate of the Oil Rivers. The problem concerned the legal powers of the British Crown in regard to foreign semi-civilised and uncivilised territories. The Foreign Jurisdiction Act of 1843 was in the first instance enacted in consequence of the opening of some China ports to external commerce. The Act enabled British Consuls to cope with the necessity for controlling British subjects in these foreign ports. The Oil Rivers protectorate was technically foreign territory. Long before the promulgation of the protectorate, the foreign traders in the rivers had often behaved as if they were above the laws which the local rulers sought to enforce in their states. The Orders-in-Council, 1872 and 1885, did no more than attempt to regulate the jurisdiction of British Consuls over British subjects. The hands of the Consuls were tied, at any rate legally, in regard to the natives who were not British subjects. The misgivings about the legality of deporting King Jaja and the indecently rushed Ordinance in the Gold Coast before Jaja's trial clearly demonstrated the inadequacy for British purposes of the existing Orders-in-Council.

During the years 1887, 1888 and 1889, for reasons not directly connected with the Oil Rivers protectorate, the British Cabinet, the officials of the British Foreign Office and the law experts were occupied with the desirability of amending the Foreign Jurisdiction Act of 1843. As memorandum followed memorandum,[1] it became increasingly clear that the aim of the amendment was to equip the Crown with the legal power to act in protectorates even though

[1] F.O. 97/562. The volume contains memoranda and other information dealing with the legal problems of protectorates and paramountcy.

'they were not British soil'. The memoranda are themselves very illuminating, in view of the action which Britain was about to take in the protectorate of the Oil Rivers. The old question of the meaning of protectorates was reopened. Sir Alfred Lyall called attention, in his memorandum on Indian protectorates, to the hypocrisy which had unavowedly lain behind British policy in that part of the world. It had suited Britain, argued Sir Alfred, 'for obvious reasons' to pretend that native states from the largest to the smallest were foreign territory, although their rulers really held their separate status on the condition of obeying whatever commands the British government chose to impose on them.[1]

The view which apparently prevailed was that 'the Queen has jurisdiction within a Protectorate over all natives and over all foreigners residing therein or resorting thereto; and this is as a mere consequence of, or incidental to, the Protectorate, and without reference to the assent or dissent of the Native power in the one case or of the Sovereign of the foreigner in the other'.[2] It was in fact pointed out that Germany had not had any qualms in regularising her position in her own protectorates. By an imperial law of 17 April 1886, both natives and foreigners in a German colonial protectorate were made subject to the laws of the Reichstag. There was therefore no reason why the powers of the British Crown should not embrace exclusive control over foreign relations and responsibility for the internal peace of the British protectorates. The niceties of the legal distinction between annexations and protectorates were whittled down to a point where any distinction ceased to have any practical meaning. The upshot was that in 1890 the Act of 1843 was replaced by another Act which in effect 'was the machinery of a Protectorate and provided the authority for governing the countries'.[3]

While the legal powers of the British Crown in protectorates were being brought up to date, moral issues connected with colonial acquisitions were, by a remarkable coincidence, engaging the conscience of the imperialist powers at Brussels. The Brussels

[1] *Ibid.* Note by Sir Alfred Lyall, 29 January 1889.
[2] *Ibid.* see Confidential 5719, printed for the British Cabinet, November 1888. Also no. 7, Malet to Salisbury, 14 September 1887.
[3] Lucas, *The Partition and Colonisation of Africa* (1922), see appendix II, pp. 215-16.

Conference was the result of Lord Salisbury's initiative in writing to the Belgian king suggesting that the king should convene a meeting of the powers to consider the most effective means of combating the evils of slavery and liquor in tropical Africa. After all, the powers had originally justified their intervention in Africa by claiming that '...to open to civilisation the only part of our globe where it has not yet penetrated, to pierce the darkness which envelopes whole populations, is a crusade...worthy of this century of progress'. If Africa was a land of primitive savagery, the evils of liquor were not of Africa's own making. The carriers of European civilisation were themselves deriving huge profits by flooding tropical Africa with cheap, dangerous liquor. It was therefore time that Europe justified in the real sense of the word her presence in Africa. British intervention in the Oil Rivers had so far not vindicated, in the words of Britain's own agent, 'our responsibility towards these peoples'. The people had been cheated by British merchants, bombarded by British captains and very little benefit had accrued to them from British rule.[1]

In many ways the Brussels Anti-Slavery Conference 1889–90 was of a different character from the earlier International Conference on Africa in Berlin 1884–5. In Berlin the European powers were primarily concerned with 'pegging out estates for posterity'. They were making good their claims, as against one another, to African rivers and coastal stretches. Expressions like obligations to natives and the consent of natives to European occupation were brushed aside as matters hardly worthy of the serious attention of the assembled European statesmen. At Brussels, the prevailing mood was quite different. As a matter of fact, when the Portuguese delegation tried to raise questions of territorial claims, the powers objected to the inclusion of such materialistic matters in their discussions. The object of the conference was to concert efficacious measures for putting basic moral principles into practice.[2] These principles included the suppression of slavery and the obligation of European occupying powers to improve the material and moral conditions of the inhabitants under their control and protection.

The General Act of the Conference was signed by the powers on

---

[1] F.O. 84/1882, Johnston's memorandum, *op. cit.* 24 July 1888.
[2] F.O. 84/2010, Draft, Salisbury to Vivian, 12 November 1889.

2 July 1890. The first article of the Act has relevance to the present study. Specific measures were advocated with the view to fulfilling the obligations of Europe to the inhabitants of Africa. The measures recommended in the first article[1] were:

1. The progressive organisation of the administrative, judicial, religious and military services of the African territories under the sovereignty or protectorate of civilised nations.

2. The gradual establishment in the interior of strongly fortified stations in such a way as to make their protective or repressive action effectively felt in the territories devastated by slave-raiding.

3. The building of roads and railways 'so as to substitute economical and speedy means for porterage by man'.

4. The use of steam boats on inland waters, on lakes, in addition to fortified posts on the banks.

5. The establishment of telegraphic lines.

6. The dispatch of expeditions and flying columns into the interior.

7. The restriction of the importation of fire-arms and ammunition, which provided the instrument for both slaving and tribal war.

It is not proposed here to enter into an academic discussion of whether or not European political and judicial institutions represented in a true sense something better than the communal and traditional organisation of the 'primitive' African peoples. This must remain a matter for philosophical speculation. Two points must, however, be made in respect of the Brussels Conference. Its motivation was humanitarian whereas that of the Berlin one was mercenary. The recommendations of the Brussels Conference provided ample moral justification for the imposition of European political control on all acquisitions, including protectorates.[2]

It will be misleading to suggest that the amendment of the Foreign Jurisdiction Act and the recommendations of the Brussels Conference directly influenced British policy in the Oil Rivers protectorate. The British Foreign Office was already engaged in

[1] See F.O. 84/2010–2011 for Despatches from Vivian and Kirk on the Brussels Conference, and for the Commissions.

[2] Hall, *A Treatise on the Foreign Powers and Jurisdiction of the British Crown*, p. 207; Keltie, *op. cit.* p. 510.

discussing alternatives to the consular regime in the Oil Rivers. The important thing was that whatever the British government wished to do, the way was both 'morally' and 'legally' open. The problems connected with the choice of the administrative machinery for the control of the Oil Rivers protectorate assumed a superficial moral character, and the apparently serious discussions in the British Cabinet as to the nature of protectorates could provide corroborative data. But below the surface, the issues appeared to the Foreign Office officials and the British firms as practical ones of providing the foundations for effectively exploiting the resources of the territory. In the circumstances, the immediate British concern was to bring about some accommodation between the Royal Niger Company and the independent Liverpool firms of the African Association with the view to extending the scope of the charter of the Royal Niger Company. The Liverpool firms had, hitherto, been the bitterest critics of the almost diabolical manner in which the Royal Niger Company exploited its charter to engross the hinterland markets of the coast states of Brass and New Calabar. They recommended the territorial partition of the whole Lower Niger basin in such a way that the Royal Niger Company might be confined to the area north of Onitsha. The lower portion would then be restored to what it had always been—the natural hinterland of the coast. As the position was, the Royal Niger Company was grinding down the natives 'to most iniquitously low prices'.[1] The partition suggested by the Liverpool firms was ignored by the Foreign Office.

The possibility of amalgamating all the territories of the Niger districts under one chartered company administration was a more attractive proposition, from the standpoint of the British Foreign Office. The Royal Niger Company and the Liverpool firms opened negotiations with the view to uniting the Niger and Oil Rivers commercial enterprises of Britain.[2] The area comprehended in the proposed deal was legally one British protectorate because the boundary between the Royal Niger Company's sphere and the Oil rivers had deliberately never been defined. As the negotiations

[1] F.O. 84/1880, African Association to W. F. Lawrence, a Liverpool M.P., 3 March 1887. Also *The Liverpool Courier*, 1 January 1887.

[2] The reader may wish to compare the treatment given to this same series of events by Flint, *op. cit.* ch. 7, pp. 130–55.

proceeded the Liverpool firms abandoned their hitherto assumed posture of solicitude for native rights and markets, and accepted the argument that '...by fusion of interests', they could 'secure the administration and control of the country'. According to Goldie, all the merchants would then 'become our partners, our Co-Directors, and our co-rulers'.[1] The Foreign Office gave its wholehearted support to the negotiations. The difficulties and irregularities of the last years of one-man consular rule in the Oil Rivers did not cause the Foreign Office undue concern because, according to the head of the African Department, 'this paternal government can be only temporary. Sir George Goldie believes that Liverpool traders are now ready to join the Niger Co.'[2]

The British Consuls on the coast knew that the local chiefs would never voluntarily accept the extension of the Royal Niger Company's charter to their territories. Johnston argued that the interests of justice, commercial morality and 'our moral obligations towards uncivilised or backward peoples' were incompatible with chartered company administration. The Foreign Office documents show that little attention was paid by the officials of the African department to the protestations on behalf of native rights and markets.[3] As regards the protection treaties, Hewett spoke in vain to the effect that the chiefs 'look to us to protect their market and their rights', as stipulated in the said treaties. Indeed when the Permanent Under-Secretary did mention the need to obtain the consent of the chiefs of the Oil Rivers, it was rather a threat which was intended to accelerate the negotiations between Goldie and the Liverpool traders. That the accommodation between Goldie and his traditional rivals did not materialise and that the British government did not therefore extend to the Oil Rivers the scope of the charter of Goldie's company were not due to British anxiety about the possible repercussions chartered company rule might provoke in the Oil Rivers. The Oil Rivers chiefs had no spokesman in Parliament; their rights were a side issue.

Effective opposition to the amalgamation of the British trading interests, preparatory to the grant of a comprehensive charter,

[1] *John Holt Papers*, quoted by Flint, *op. cit.* pp. 104–5.
[2] F.O. 84/1828, Anderson's minute on no. 27, dated 15 January 1888.
[3] *Ibid.* Memo by Johnston on the British Protectorate..., 1888. Also F.O. 84/1881, no. 34, Hewett to F.O., 10 November 1888.

came from two outside sources. In defence of their own interests, the West African Steamship Lines, under Alfred Jones, rallied the support of the gigantic shipping interests of Britain. These interests constituted a formidable opposition which the British government could not afford to ignore. The interests were well represented in Parliament where many awkward questions might have to be answered. The principles from which the shipping interests argued against the proposed commercial merger had nothing to do with the basic rights of the local inhabitants. What mattered to the shipowners was the contingency that an amalgamated company might be powerful enough to establish its own shipping, to the detriment of the existing British shipping concerns.[1] The Foreign Office officials received a deputation led by Alfred Jones and the correspondence which followed amounted to an assurance that the interests of the shipping company would be fully protected, and there was only one way to protect these interests.

German intervention was equally decisive in frustrating the plans which Goldie and the Liverpool merchants almost brought to fruition. The German government had many reasons to entertain great hostility towards the Royal Niger Company and the possibility of extending the scope of its charter. The Germans had no illusions about the way the company's charter was being used to obviate the operation of the 'free-transit' clause of the General Act of the Berlin Conference. There was in addition the specific case of the bitter quarrel between the Royal Niger Company and the German trader-traveller, Herr Hönigsberg. The latter, having established close amity with Nupe, a powerful Moslem state on the Niger, proceeded to explode the myth that the rule of the Royal Niger Company was effective. The German, however, earned himself deportation from the Niger districts. The German government claimed damages from the Royal Niger Company on behalf of its citizen. To extend the charter of the same company would amount to ignoring the feelings of the German government and this the British government could hardly contemplate with

[1] F.O. 84/1863, African Steamship Co. and British and African Steam Navigation Co. to F.O., 24 May 1887. F.O. 84/1916, Memo by Julian Pauncefote, 23 February 1888; Draft by Anderson to the Shipping Companies, 15 March 1888.

equanimity. There was a further consideration. The 1886 boundary agreement between Britain and Germany stipulated that
differential duties should not be enforced in their respective
protectorates of the Cameroons and the Oil Rivers. The Royal
Niger Company was likely to extend its fiscal practices to the Oil
Rivers if its charter was extended.[1] The British government
conceded to Germany that 'a fresh start will be made'.[2]

When the proposed amalgamation of the Royal Niger Company
and the Liverpool traders fell through, it did not mean that the
British government had become convinced that company rule
was in principle unacceptable. After all, the influential paper *The
Times* was showering encomiums on company rule which was 'a
source of civilisation to the barbarous peoples and a benefit to the
overcrowded working classes of Great Britain'.[3] If the German
government opposed the extension of the charter of the Royal
Niger Company, it did not mean that it would necessarily be
against the Liverpool traders being given a separate charter in the
Oil Rivers. These traders had formed the African Association and
now asked for a charter of their own. Their Vice-Chairman had no
doubt that the Association was fully qualified to undertake the
government of the Oil Rivers. What more was required if 'we shall
go with commerce in our hands and good feelings in our hearts to
assist the natives on the sea board and in the interior and thereby
not only add to the welfare of the African native races but add to
the welfare of the world at large'?[4] The arguments put forward
by the African Association closely corresponded to those which
justified the grant of a charter to Sir William Mackinnon in East
Africa, 1888, and to Cecil Rhodes of the British South Africa
Company in 1889, although there was this difference that these
companies had secured treaties with the 'native' rulers in their
territories, whereas the treaties with the Oil Rivers chiefs were with
the British government. But what did this difference amount to,
in the face of the obvious desire of the British government to

[1] F.O. 84/1871, Memo by the German Foreign Office, 26 September 1887;
and R.N.C. to F.O., 20 October 1887.

[2] F.O. 84/2032, Malet to Salisbury, no. 77, 21 June 1890; and Enclosure no. 14,
Anderson to Malet, 21 June 1890.

[3] *The Times* (London), 4 January 1889.

[4] *Nigerian Pamphlets*, no. 3. Report of Meetings of the Chamber of Commerce,
3 March 1890.

employ inexpensive administrative agencies to discharge its obligations in the protectorates it claimed?

The Consul in charge of the Oil Rivers in 1890, George Annesley, commented sarcastically on the claim of the African Association that it had the experience and the facilities for dealing with native problems. What these facilities and experience were on the Oil Rivers 'no one knows', concluded the Consul. In addition to the Consul's disapproval of the plan to grant the African Association a charter, the Foreign Office was flooded with protests from the Chambers of Commerce of the leading cities in England and Scotland.[1] Once more, the steamship interests were up in arms and soon rallied the support of the Whig leader in the Lords. There is no evidence in the Foreign Office papers that the Department contemplated the endorsement of the political ambitions of the African Association.

The kind of administration which the African Association intended to set up must remain a matter of conjecture. The eloquent spokesman of these merchants deplored the unwillingness of the British government to confer administrative powers on the Oil Rivers traders. Morel argued that, in the first place, the people of the Niger delta and neighbourhood would not have accepted British protection and consular rule without the good offices of the agents of the Liverpool firms. Mary Kingsley claimed that the Liverpool merchants would have accomplished in the Oil Rivers the remarkable success of Goldie in the Niger districts where 'for nearly twenty years the natives...have had the firm, wise, sympathetic friendship of a great Englishman, who understood them, and knew them personally'. She poured scorn on the Crown Colony system under which the officials 'drift along with some nebulous sort of notion in their heads about elevating the African in the plane of culture'.[2]

The British merchants in the Oil Rivers had more practical reasons for opposing the third alternative open to the British government as regards the control of the Oil Rivers region. The Crown Colony system was bound to saddle the firms with taxes,

[1] F.O. 84/2020, Annesley to F.O., 29 October 1890. F.O. 84/1999, Hartington to Ferguson, 18 July 1890.
[2] See Morel, *Affairs of West Africa*, footnote on p. 28; Kingsley, *West African Studies*, pp. 360–1, also pp. 310–11.

British subjects from Lagos and elsewhere could not be kept out, and Goldie had most effectively laid down the regulations which saw to it that Lagos and Freetown merchants did not compete with the Royal Niger Company in the exploitation of the Niger basin. The merchants of the Oil Rivers were no more willing than Goldie to allow the competition of neighbouring British subjects. Lastly, the Oil Rivers merchants had for a long time been a law unto themselves in the Oil Rivers, and were therefore hardly expected to welcome a formalised system under which they were to be ordered about by ubiquitous Crown Colony officials. The threat of a Crown Colony system in the Oil Rivers was Goldie's trump card in his ultimately futile negotiations for the amalgamation of the British Niger and Oil Rivers interests. If the officials of the Foreign Office had had their way, the Oil Rivers might have been converted into a colony in 1887, at a time when Goldie and his new allies were seeking the extension of his charter. The head of the African Department argued that he had been assured on all hands that the Oil Rivers territory could pay its way. The most obvious advantage of a Crown Colony system, he pointed out, was that difficulties like that over Jaja would be eliminated once and for all.[1] These views fully harmonised with those which the British Consuls in the Oil Rivers had reiterated almost *ad nauseam*.

The revenue potentialities of the Oil Rivers were assessed by the Consuls. According to them, a duty of 3*d*. a gallon on spirits alone could produce a revenue of £14,000. There were other statistics available if further proof was needed of the 'qualification' of the Oil Rivers for a Crown Colony administration. The British West African Colonies individually produced less trade than the Oil Rivers. The trade of the Gold Coast was worth £813,000, Lagos £950,000, Sierra Leone £941,000 and Gambia £217,000. The Oil Rivers trade was estimated at nearly £2,000,000. The whole point was that the Foreign Office or the Colonial Office should ignore the notorious parsimony of the Treasury as the latter was unlikely to be asked for more than the initial capital for launching the Crown Colony administration in the Oil Rivers territory.[2]

[1] F.O. 84/1838, Memo by H. P. Anderson and T. V. Lister on Hewett to F.O., 15 October 1887; also F.O. 84/1916, C.O. to F.O., 18 February 1888.
[2] *Nigerian Pamphlets*, no. 3. Report of Meeting, *op. cit.*

In the midst of what are best described as arguments about the best way to consolidate British rule in the Oil Rivers, Lord Salisbury decided, as mentioned on p. 100, to send a special commissioner to the Niger districts. To suggest that the problem of governing the Oil Rivers protectorate was uppermost in the mind of Salisbury in deciding on an inquiry would be extremely misleading. In view of the awkward diplomatic position to which the policy of the Royal Niger Company exposed the British government, 'the position of the Royal Niger Company' was specially emphasised in the instructions issued to the special commissioner. There was, however, some reference to the Oil Rivers. As regards these '...If you should report against the Charter, you should at the same time inform me whether, in your judgment, the Oil Rivers should be annexed to the Colony of Lagos, or should be endowed with a separate Colonial administration, or should continue to remain under the present Consular jurisdiction'.[1] There was not the slightest suggestion in the instructions that the special commissioner should consult the chiefs of the Oil Rivers protectorate as to the type of government they were willing to accept in the place of the independence which the protection treaties 'guaranteed'. That consultation with the chiefs in fact took place was due solely to the initiative of the commissioner. The Commissioner himself revealed this in a later correspondence.[2]

The new personality introduced into the affairs of the Oil Rivers Protectorate was Major (later Sir) Claude Maxwell Macdonald. Born in 1852, he was educated at Uppingham and Sandhurst. He entered the 74th Highlanders and subsequently came into prominence in the Egyptian campaign in 1882. After a long spell as military attaché to Sir Evelyn Baring in Cairo, Macdonald served as Consul-General at Zanzibar from 1887 to 1888. Then at the beginning of 1889 he was appointed Commissioner to the Niger Districts and his connection with the Oil Rivers, which lasted till the end of 1895, began.[3]

On 1 March Macdonald arrived in the Oil Rivers and proceeded to obtain the views of the chiefs and the agencies involved in

[1] F.O. 84/1940, Instructions to Macdonald, 17 January 1889; also F.O. 84/1881, F.O. to Macdonald, 15 December 1888.
[2] F.O. 2/63, Macdonald to Kimberley, 21 August 1894.
[3] See the *Dictionary of National Biography*.

commercial and missionary enterprise in the Oil Rivers. He visited Bonny, Opobo, New Calabar, Old Calabar, and Brass, in the order in which these states are enumerated. Macdonald deserves great credit for the way he set about his business, but it is too much to claim, as Flint does, that Macdonald's proceedings amount to 'a rudimentary kind of plebiscite'.[1] The chiefs were asked to choose between Chartered Company Administration and a Crown Colony system. A choice between two inevitable evils does not amount to a voluntary surrender by the chiefs of the independent status of the states of the Oil Rivers. The upshot of Macdonald's inquiries and his recommendations could not conceivably be described as 'government by consent'. The replies of the local chiefs which the Commissioner fortunately recorded throw significant light on the transactions which took place between these chiefs and the British Commissioner.

In Bonny, Macdonald met a delegation of chiefs headed by King George Pepple, who owed his elevation to primacy in Bonny affairs to the good offices of Acting Consul Johnston. The Bonny chiefs naturally expressed grave apprehensions about their land and their slaves. They were assured on these points. The choice of control preferred by Bonny was embodied in the letter which the Bonny chiefs handed over to Macdonald. 'After due consideration of the above clauses, we have to inform you that we strongly object to the extension of the Royal Niger Company's Charter to our river, or an independent Charter to any other Company of merchants. We have therefore decided to become a British colony.'[2] The Commissioner also consulted the agent of the firm of Harrison and Co., and Archdeacon Crowther, the African missionary head of the Native Pastorate Church. The former, Captain Boler, honestly confessed that the chiefs would never submit to be governed by a trading association. The missionary expatiated, as was to be expected, on the advantages to be derived from outright British annexation of the Oil Rivers territory. The Christian religion would be consolidated on the coast and extended into the interior places. Barbarous acts would be stopped and the lives of men, women and children,

[1] Flint, *op. cit.* p. 130.
[2] F.O. 84/1940, Confidential Report, Macdonald to Salisbury, 12 June 1889. See Enclosures.

particularly twins, would be saved. On the whole, concluded Crowther, 'the people...will be bettered in every way'.[1] The early tribulations and the slow progress of Christianity on the coast, the humiliations inflicted on King George Pepple by his powerful chiefs because the king had allowed himself to be converted to Christianity, and the alleged outbreak of cannibalism at Okrika, 30 miles north of Bonny, were powerful arguments.

Macdonald then proceeded to Opobo which since the deportation of its king two years back had not regained stability. The leading chiefs originally detained in the Gold Coast and then allowed to return had made it clear that what Opobo needed was the repatriation of King Jaja. This request had offended Consul Hewett. Thus when the special commissioner arrived, Opobo was being blockaded by H.M. gunboats in order to starve the Opobo people into complete surrender. Macdonald, however, managed to hold an interview with the Opobo chiefs headed by Chief Cookie Gam who acted as their spokesman. The coercive measures against Opobo and the expulsion of Opobo traders from the hinterland markets had produced the intended results. It was obviously dangerous for the chiefs to argue that their banished king was quite capable of controlling the political and commercial affairs of Opobo. The chiefs rather meekly expressed a preference for a 'Colonial administration', if the neighbouring states, and particularly Bonny, concurred.[2]

The Commissioner expected the agents of the Liverpool firms to echo the wishes of their employers. But this was in fact not the case. The agents of Stuart and Douglas and of Taylor, Loughland and Co. wished to convey their personal convictions, which they said were given in confidence because their employers were at that time importuning the Foreign Office for a charter. These agents stated unequivocally that the Opobo chiefs could never submit to the rule of the merchants, who in no small measure contributed to the deportation of King Jaja and the subsequent discomfiture of Opobo affairs. The agents of Miller Brothers tried to suggest that, although Opobo would never accept the extension of the charter of the Royal Niger Company, the chiefs were not necessarily averse to control by an independent corporation. If the agents meant control

---

[1] *Ibid.* Encl. 2, Crowther to Macdonald, March 1889.
[2] *Ibid.* Encl. 3, Chiefs of Opobo to Macdonald, 29 March 1889.

by their firm and its allies, there was something in what they said. They had been closely behind Jaja in the latter's fight to keep his independence. They had led in the protests against Jaja's deportation, and were, at the time of the Commissioner's visit, pleading for Jaja's return. What the agents really wanted was a charter with which they could consolidate their friendship with the able Opobo trader-chiefs and do very good business without the restrictions of Colonial rule. These arguments produced, however, no effects on Macdonald's thoughts.

At New Calabar, the feeling against the Royal Niger Company was most marked, and this hardly surprised the Commissioner. The hinterland markets of New Calabar, including the Oguta Lake, had been effectively cut off by that company.[1] At the interview with Macdonald, the chiefs expressed the desire to commence military operations against the Royal Niger Company. The Commissioner persuaded the chiefs to a more peaceful frame of mind by pointing out that the Royal Niger Company was better armed than New Calabar. The point made by Macdonald was appreciated, and King Amachree and his chiefs later sent a letter to the Commissioner in which they said that they would agree to a Colonial government because they believed that the Queen would not allow them to starve.[2]

Macdonald made his way to Old Calabar where he found a congeries of independent 'kingdoms' and 'dukedoms'. The rulers of these republics were of two categories. Those who were amenable to the influence of the Scottish missionaries readily accepted a Colonial administration which could exterminate what the chiefs called the evils of polygamy and the custom of Egbo. The more conservative chiefs sought guarantees in respect of the rights to their slaves, their land and their wives. All the chiefs agreed that they needed more effective protection against the German administrators of the neighbouring Cameroons. Unaware that Britain had already bartered away their hinterland markets in the 1886 Anglo-German boundary agreements, the Old Calabar chiefs imagined that a Crown Colony regime could recover their lost hinterland

[1] F.O. 84/1881, Hewett to F.O. no. 34, 10 November 1888.
[2] F.O. 84/1940, Macdonald's Report already cited. Encl. 4, Amachree and Chiefs to Macdonald, 4 April 1889.

markets in the Ekoi and 'Rumbi' country.[1] The fears of the Old Calabar chiefs were admirably summarised by the old missionary of the Presbyterian Church, the Rev. H. Goldie. He explained that 'we live with our strong-handed German neighbours, against whose inroads the British Protection does not afford much security'.[2]

The only jarring note came from the old King Duke IX of Old Calabar and his followers. This is best described in the Commissioner's own words.

A question was put to me by King Duke of Old Calabar, and a somewhat powerful following of chiefs, which I was rather surprised had not been put before in any of the other rivers. They wanted to know why there should be any change in the form of government. They were quite content to remain as they were, and had always done what the Consul had told them, and were quite capable of governing themselves subject to the protection of Great Britain.[3]

The Commissioner was most impressed by the European commercial agents he encountered in Old Calabar. They were, according to Macdonald, intelligent and honest. They had the realism to appreciate that problems like slavery and polygamy had to be handled with patience. In the circumstances a Crown Colony regime rashly inaugurated was not the real answer to the task of governing the protectorate.

From Old Calabar, the Special Commissioner proceeded to Brass to meet King Koko and his chiefs. Brass was the city-state most injured by the commercial ambitions of the Royal Niger Company. The Brass rulers had therefore looked forward with great eagerness to the coming of an emissary who bore the impressive title of a Special Commissioner. Perhaps, thought the Brass chiefs, there was at last the opportunity to obtain some redress for the inflictions of the Royal Niger Company. A long petition, denouncing the Royal Niger Company in unequivocal terms, was presented to Macdonald. The long history of Brass exploits on the Lower Niger and the close bonds between the state and the Niger communities were recounted. Lastly, it seemed that all Brass had so far got out of her

[1] See also F.O. 84/1828, Petition from Old Calabar, 19 July 1887, and F.O. 84/1941, no. 17, Hewett to F.O., 30 April 1889.
[2] F.O. 84/1940, *op. cit.* see Enclosures, 16–17 April 1889.
[3] *Ibid.* Duke IX to Macdonald, 17 April 1889.

acceptance of British protection was 'to feed on sand'. The white traders in Brass were naturally equally violent in their denunciation of the Royal Niger Company. In the circumstances, there could be no question of entertaining the possibility of extending the charter of the hated company. King Koko expressed his willingness to accept direct 'Queen's Government', although he had reservations about the domestic slaves who were the very foundation of Brass social and political structure.[1]

On the Benin River, the dominant personality was Nana. It may be recalled that in 1885 Consul Hewett conferred on Nana superfluous powers when the Consul appointed the paramount ruler 'the executive power through which decrees of Her Majesty's Government and of the Consular Court are to be exercised and enforced'. Nana had then accepted without question what amounted to a recognition of a position he effectively occupied. It was quite another thing when the special commissioner suddenly confronted him with a choice between chartered company administration and the Queen's government. Nana was nothing if not a trader and his trading 'boys' had heard none too pleasant stories about the activities of the Royal Niger Company on the Niger delta. On the other hand, Nana had encountered no difficulties with the sole Queen's representative who, if anything, had gone out of his way to honour him. The Benin River chief, therefore, was not unduly worried about a possible threat to his independence. He expressed a desire for a Queen's government provided his or his chiefs' wives and slaves were not interfered with. Subject to these two stipulations Nana and the chiefs of the Jekri nation elected for a Colonial administration.[2] Macdonald left the Oil Rivers at the end of April 1889. He could not possibly have been left with any illusions about the opposition of the Oil Rivers chiefs to the idea of chartered company rule.

On his way back to England, the special commissioner called at the British Colony of Lagos. It is remarkable that at a time when nobody could have foreseen the future political identity of Lagos and the rest of Nigeria, the educated inhabitants of Lagos had already begun to identify their interests with those of the indi-

---

[1] *Ibid.* Encl. King Koko to Macdonald, April 1889.
[2] *Ibid.* Encl. Nana to Macdonald, April 1889.

genous inhabitants of the Oil Rivers and the Niger districts. It is of course true that many British subjects from Lagos had suffered at the hands of the Royal Niger Company in their attempts to participate in the exploitation of the resources of the Lower Niger. Nevertheless, the memorial drawn up on behalf of Lagos and presented to Macdonald revealed a comprehensiveness of vision and a solicitude for the welfare of the natives of the Oil Rivers and Niger districts which are impressive. The memorialists questioned the morality of the treaties which the agents of the Royal Niger Company collected from the territories. They condemned the iniquitous commercial regulations of the same company and concluded with the hope

that our interest and that of the peoples inhabiting the Niger and the Protectorate of the Oil Rivers, be taken into careful consideration in the matter, and that Her Majesty would be graciously pleased to withdraw the privileges conferred by the Charter granted to the Royal Niger Company in 1886, and adopt such measures as will bring both the territory of the Niger and the Oil Rivers under the direct rule and control of the Crown.[1]

Before examining the precise nature of Macdonald's 'consultations' on the Oil Rivers and his recommendations on the political fate of the communities, brief reference should be made to the Special Commissioner's scrutiny of the affairs of the Royal Niger Company in the region south of Idah which was later to become part of Southern Nigeria. Beyond Idah, Macdonald's inquiry does not concern the history of Southern Nigeria. The Commissioner began his Niger tour in July 1889. It is not clear what precise instructions he had from the Foreign Office in respect of the Niger Company's area of jurisdiction. Both the German and the Liverpool firms had made various charges against the company and these had been transmitted to the Special Commissioner. In view of the charges, it is probable that the Commissioner decided to investigate the title on the basis of which the Royal Niger exercised its jurisdiction. To what extent, too, had the company established a trade monopoly? Lastly, with what justice had the company's agent-general treated the German national, Hönigsberg, who attempted direct trade relations with Nupe? The first question only

---

[1] *Nigerian Pamphlets*, no. 2. Memorial of the Inhabitants of Lagos to Macdonald, March 1889.

is relevant to the present study because, as indicated already, the future components of Southern Nigeria were involved. What was the basis of the British protection exercised through the Royal Niger Company? What had this meant to the communities comprehended in the British protectorate of the Niger districts?

In regard to the first question, it should be easy to appreciate Macdonald's verdict that the Royal Niger Company had in the region of the Lower Niger an impressive number of treaties in most of which the indigenous rulers surrendered their sovereignty and territories 'in perpetuity'. In the Abo district alone, there were 32 treaties; in the Oguta district, 10; in the Anambara, 16; and in the Igara area, 46. The Commissioner was aware of the international complications that might arise if he exposed the hollowness of the company's treaties. Had they not been Britain's trump card at the Berlin Conference? Thus, against the ambitions of France and Germany, the Royal Niger Company had served Britain well. The inheritance of the local rulers was quite another matter. The Commissioner did not claim that he visited every local ruler in the Lower Niger in order to verify the extent to which the ruler understood the implications of his treaty with the Royal Niger Company. Macdonald encountered the rulers of the strategically placed town-state of Onitsha. The king and his councillors emphatically denied ever signing a treaty with the Royal Niger Company.[1] It is fascinating to speculate on the number of 'signatures' on the Niger Company's treaties which were genuinely put there by the legitimate indigenous rulers. The ruler of Idah explained that he signed the treaty with the company because he hoped to become prosperous. Instead, he 'had shrunk up and become dry'.[2] The Commissioner saw nothing fraudulent in the company's treaties, and this was indeed a remarkable verdict on the manner in which the company obtained many of its treaties.

The second question which Macdonald sought to answer concerned the manner in which the Royal Niger Company exercised the administrative privileges conferred by its charter. Here, also, the Commissioner did not make a comprehensive survey of the

[1] F.O. 84/2109, Report on the Administration of the Niger Territories by Macdonald.
[2] Flint, *op. cit.* quoted on p. 138.

company's administration in the Lower Niger. Nevertheless, he made some observations which throw light on the effects of the company's rule on the communities of the Lower Niger. In the Niger delta, the Ijaw who were supposed to have accepted the company's protection regarded that company as an enemy to be plundered whenever an opportunity offered itself. In return, many of their towns and villages were burnt down by the company. After all, the company had a well-equipped constabulary which was employed in punitive expeditions at least once a month. Onitsha, Obosi, Abo, to mention but a few, had at one time or another been burnt down by the Niger Company's constabulary. Apart from the wanton destruction of native towns whose rulers had the rashness to behave as if they were independent sovereigns, the irregularities of the company's judiciary were noted by the Commissioner. The officials of the company got away lightly with murders. Inexperienced British agents had sweeping powers over the lives of Africans. Where executive, judicial and commercial matters were one and the same thing, there could hardly be any distinction between civil and criminal offences, and the latter invariably meant long terms of imprisonment or the death penalty. It was clear to Macdonald that the judicial system of the Royal Niger Company's administration was basically faulty. In the previous year, the scandalous manner in which the company's agents had shot down many of its labour gangs had provoked the officials of the Foreign Office into pointing out that such 'an indifference for African life...is the worst possible recommendation for an extension of their [company agents'] powers over new and more populous regions'.[1]

The Royal Niger Company's administration was almost synonymous with the enforcement of its iniquitous commercial regulations. The Commissioner did not exactly charge the company with establishing a monopoly. He showed, however, that in respect of the company's policy, the inhabitants within and without the company's jurisdiction were subjected to the most rigid control in their commercial transactions. The indigenous traders from the Oil Rivers had the worst of two worlds. For purposes of trade, they

[1] For the notorious Zweifel case see F.O. 84/2000, Memo by Salisbury and F.O. to R.N.C., 26 July 1888; see also Flint, *op. cit.* pp. 147-9.

were classed as 'foreigners' and were therefore saddled with the preposterous licence fees if they wished to trade in areas which were for centuries their markets. At the same time, these traders could be imprisoned by the Niger Company as if they were subject to the company's jurisdiction. In Macdonald's opinion, the inhabitants of the Oil Rivers and those of the Niger Districts were legally in one British protectorate. One conclusion is inescapable from a close reading of the Commissioner's observations. By and large, the company's exercise of British protection amounted to rule by intimidation. The Commissioner's report on the administration of the Niger Districts was shelved by the Foreign Office. The recommendations for limited reforms were consigned to the limbo of the forgotten. The result was that the most strategically placed portion of Southern Nigeria remained under chartered company rule until 1900. The ill-will of the local communities—the heritage which company rule left behind—constituted an obstacle to the peaceful enforcement of direct British rule.[1] The Oil Rivers states and people escaped 'the paternal rule of that enlightened Englishman, Goldie'.

In his report on the Royal Niger Company, Macdonald might naturally have been anxious not to prejudice the British position on a vital portion of the Niger. In his report on the Oil rivers, the one thing which could not be suppressed or explained away was the hostility of the local rulers to any question of chartered company rule. The report which reached the Foreign Office in June 1889 stated in unmistakable terms that 'the opposition which the extension [of the Charter] would meet both in public and secretly from the chiefs and native traders—the number of quarrels and disturbances which would ensue would more than counterbalance any advantages to be derived'. Macdonald was convinced that the Oil Rivers territory could pay its way as a colony, but to organise a Crown Colony might be premature in view of what Macdonald called the unsettled condition of the region and the system of slavery which prevailed. The report concluded that

the best form of administering the district, at any rate for some years, would be by a strong Consular administration, with an Executive to maintain order and assist in opening up the country by means of, when necessary, armed police or constabulary. If such a form of government

[1] C.O. 520/2, Gallwey to C.O., no. 166, 12 June 1900.

were impossible for constitutional reasons, I am of opinion that the best form of government would be that of a Crown Colony.[1]

The possible constitutional objections to a consular administration with an executive to maintain law and order mattered very little with the British Foreign Office. The Foreign Jurisdiction Amendment Act and the recommendations of the Brussels Conference should have disposed of any qualms which might linger in respect of the rights of a paramount power in protectorates. It was thus wariness about expenditure and the existence of domestic slavery, not the implications of the protection treaties with the Oil Rivers chiefs, which were the obstacles to the immediate imposition of the Crown Colony system on the Oil Rivers protectorate. It may be argued that the chiefs themselves had opted for the Crown Colony system but the point is that no one in the Foreign Office thought much of the fact that the vast hinterland communities of the proposed colony had not solicited, much less accepted, British protection. This observation is perhaps mere sophistry. The realities of imperialism were quite another matter. Internationally, the Nigerian coast and the hinterland had fallen within the British sphere of influence. In this sphere, Britain enjoyed freedom of action, and freedom of action had nothing to do with the wishes of the inhabitants whose territories were partitioned without their knowledge.[2]

Macdonald's recommendation in favour of a strong consular administration in the Oil Rivers was endorsed by Salisbury who restrained the enthusiasm of his Foreign Office advisers for an immediate Crown Colony regime. Crown Colony regime or not, the decision by Salisbury to approve Macdonald's plan signalised the determination of the British government to establish and consolidate direct political control of the protected states of the coast and the communities of the hinterland. A strengthened consular executive regime was but the tentative beginning of the process. The author of the new proposals, Major Claude Macdonald, was selected by Salisbury to implement his own scheme. But first,

[1] Report by Macdonald, *op. cit.* pp. 93–5.
[2] Hobson, *Imperialism, A Study* (3rd ed., London, 1902), pp. 230–4; Lindley, *The Acquisition and Government of Backward Territory in International Law*, pp. 11–18.

he was instructed to prepare a schedule of a provisional establishment for the new consular regime in order to enable the Foreign Office to estimate the magnitude of the initial loan from the British Treasury. Macdonald's establishment, according to the summary which he submitted to the Foreign Office, included a high commissioner, his secretary, and six commissioners; one treasurer; one controller of customs and two assistants; two public works foremen; one chief medical officer, with subsidies available for medical officers already in the Oil Rivers; one superintendent of marine and one inspector of machines; one inspector-general of the constabulary assisted by two inspectors and three assistant inspectors, a paymaster and a quartermaster. In addition to the expenses involved in staff pay, Macdonald wanted money for steam launches, houses and £6000 for subsidies to local chiefs.[1] The British Treasury was therefore to be asked for a loan of £66,398 17s. 6d. To make the size of the loan less alarming, Macdonald pointed out that the prospective revenue of the Oil Rivers was £78,000, 'on a low computation'.[2]

The Foreign Office stripped Macdonald's proposed establishment of what it considered unessential items. In the event, it asked the Treasury for a loan large enough to cover the salaries of a commissioner at £3000, six deputy-commissioners at £600 a year each, and £10,000 for initial expenses. The Treasury was reminded that the new field of administration was potentially the richest in West Africa. Apparently the Treasury was unimpressed. The head of the African Department of the Foreign Office and his assistant decided to put pressure on Salisbury whose intervention would naturally be decisive. It was therefore through the influence of the Prime Minister that the Treasury agreed to grant the new administration in the Oil Rivers a loan of £14,000, on the condition that repayment with interest should start after three years.[3] Macdonald had cleared the first hurdle. There was a second. The Foreign Office gave Macdonald to understand that it was his job to find the men willing to go out to West Africa.

It is not easy today to appreciate the seriousness of the second

---

[1] F.O. 84/2019, see Reports and Minutes, May–December 1890.
[2] *Ibid.*
[3] F.O. 84/2110, F.O. Draft to Treasury, 9 February 1891.

task Macdonald was set. West Africa was 'the White Man's Grave'. European merchants, slavers and peaceful traders, had, of course, lived on the west coast for centuries, but they had also in large numbers succumbed to diseases and alcohol. Service on the west coast was anything but an attraction. The position has been described as follows: 'Not only has the European on leaving home a melancholy foreboding of a speedy termination of his existence, but his friends and relatives also reckon him from the day of his embarkation as among the dead.'[1] It is hardly surprising that the men who volunteered were men of the most peculiar qualifications. There were insolvent debtors who wished to keep out of the way. There were disgruntled army men from the Indian service. On one occasion, Macdonald informed the Foreign Office that 'I know some excellent men in the service who have no faults but impecuniosity and have tried to entice them but as they rightly say, in India, we would get £500 a year and command white troops, so it is not worth our while'.[2] Macdonald did, however, manage to get men some of whom rose in due course to high office. For instance, Ralph Moor, who became the first high commissioner of Southern Nigeria in 1900, was in 1891 for some inexplicable reason willing to proceed to the Oil Rivers at his own expense in order to organise a small force of Hausas as the nucleus of the constabulary of the Oil Rivers protectorate.

The consular executive regime which inaugurated direct British rule as finally approved by the Foreign Office was to comprise Major Macdonald, consul-general and commissioner on a salary of £2500 but also with an allowance of £700, and six vice-consuls each on a salary of £600. The haphazard selection of officials for service in the Oil Rivers continued for quite a time until an agency was established in London under Sir Alfred Jephson, who supervised the selection of men and supplies for the Oil Rivers administration. Sir Alfred was to approach his responsibilities with remarkable *bonhomie*. One recorded episode clearly illustrates the point. 'Here you are, my boy...here is a billet for you, if you like to take it. Sail next Saturday.'[3] Thus at the beginning of an

[1] Knowles, *Economic Development of the Overseas Empire* (London, 1928), quoted p. 251; also Mary Gaunt, *Alone in West Africa* (1913), p. 388.
[2] F.O. 84/2110, Macdonald to Anderson, 30 January 1891.
[3] Douglas, *Niger Memories* (Exeter, 1937), p. 1.

imperial administration in the Oil rivers, the political and military officers were indifferently chosen or seconded from their army units with the approval of the War Office. These were not men likely to possess the temperament or the diplomatic finesse necessary for imposing political control on a complex society with institutions hardly intelligible to an untutored European mind.[1] There were remarkable men among these first 'civil servants' of Southern Nigeria. The most remarkable was Major Macdonald himself.

[1] Blyden, *West Africa before Europe* (London, 1905), p. 36.

# CHAPTER V

# THE OVERTHROW OF
# INDIGENOUS AUTHORITY:
# FIRST PHASE, 1891–5

The choice of Major Claude Macdonald as consul-general and commissioner to inaugurate effective British rule in the Oil Rivers was in many ways a wise one. H. H. Johnston, the former Acting Consul whose career in the Oil Rivers had plunged the affairs of that region into turbulence, believed he had strong claims to the new appointment.[1] His energy and his profuse collection of data on the resources and peoples of the neighbourhood had impressed the Foreign Office men who were in charge of the African Department. Salisbury, however, had, at that time at any rate, an instinctive distrust of Johnston's methods. What the new task in the Oil Rivers required was not a rabid imperialist but a diplomat. As special commissioner in 1889, Macdonald's personal decision to consult the wishes of the local rulers in the vital matter of the political future of their states demonstrated the liberal attitude with which Macdonald approached the problem of establishing direct British authority. His first contact with the city-states had already endeared him to the chiefs of these states. The latter therefore accepted him as a man they could trust, just as they had sentimentally trusted the distant Queen of England. Macdonald, in his new role, persisted more or less in his belief in consultation as the most humanitarian way of bringing about changes which were naturally unpalatable to the indigenous rulers.

Before Macdonald left England for the Oil Rivers, he had to obtain Foreign Office approval of a systematised scheme for raising revenue in the territory he was about to rule. The Foreign Office understandably regarded the question as one of great urgency, and Macdonald was reminded that 'the system hitherto in force under

[1] Alex. Johnston, *Life and Letters of Sir H. H. Johnston* (London, 1929), p. 113.

135

which the coast chiefs have exacted "comey" must be finally abolished and revenue raised on a regular system and applied for purposes of government'. Under this system, the chiefs of the Oil Rivers were to become paid agents of the British local administration.[1] Macdonald scrutinised the tariffs operating in Lagos, the Niger Districts of the Royal Niger Company, and the German Cameroons. The agreements between Germany and Britain in respect of their spheres of influence stipulated that differential duties proposals should be notified to each other in advance, but Macdonald did his best to conform to the German Cameroons scale of duties. The following table gives the relevant statistics,[2] which are also interesting because they reveal the principal imports into the West African territories at the time.

| Items | Lagos | Niger | Cameroons | Oil Rivers |
|---|---|---|---|---|
| 1. Wine, ale, beer (cost of 1 dozen) | 9d. | — | 6d. | 6d. |
| 2. Brandy (a), gin, rum (b) (per gallon) | (a) 1s. (b) 6d. | 2s. | Below proof 6d. Above proof 1s. | 1s.+1d. a degree above proof |
| 3. Unmanufactured tobacco (per lb.) | 2d. | 6d. | 1d. | 2d. |
| 4. Gunpowder per lb. | ¼d. | — | 1d. | 2d. |
| 5. Trade guns (each) | 2s. | — | 1s. | 1s. |
| 6. Lead | 4% ad valorem | — | — | 1d. |
| 7. Salt per ton | 5s. | 20s. | 4s. | 4s. |

The question of duties settled, Macdonald took a second decision before he sailed to the Oil Rivers. This decision was born of his instinctive understanding of the minds of the chiefs of the coast states. It might be an affront to the dignity of the local chiefs, thought Macdonald, if he arrived unannounced at the Oil Rivers and proclaimed himself the new ruler of the territory. He therefore sent out two of his six prospective vice-consuls, Captains D. C. Macdonald (no relation of the Consul-General) and F. Synge, to visit the Oil Rivers and hold meetings with the principal chiefs at Old Calabar, Opobo, Bonny, New Calabar, Brass and the Benin River. At these meetings, the vice-consuls were instructed to recall Macdonald's consultations with them two years back. The special commissioner was coming back, now as 'the big Queen's

[1] F.O. 84/2110, F.O. Draft to Macdonald, 18 April 1891.
[2] F.O. 84/2111, see Enclosure in Despatch, 4 May 1891.

man'. Major Macdonald obviously realised that the question of abrogating the long-established 'comey' system, the one remaining evidence of indigenous sovereignty, was one of great delicacy. He had therefore proposed to undertake the explanations in regard to the new customs regulations when he himself arrived.

On 28 July 1891 Major Claude Macdonald, with his staff of six vice-consuls, arrived at the Oil Rivers. There followed another round of meetings. Two days after his arrival at Bonny, he summoned the chiefs of Bonny and New Calabar to meet him. There are no records of what transpired between the Consul-General and the chiefs, apart from Macdonald's bare report that the chiefs gladly accepted the new customs duties. The new ruler then set out for Old Calabar, arriving there on Sunday, 1 August. Macdonald believed that most of the Old Calabar chiefs were 'pillars of the Presbyterian Church' and for this reason he thought it would be unwise to hold a meeting on a Sunday. On Monday, the kings, duke and chiefs of the Calabar 'republics' all 'signed a paper' to signify their assent to the duties. The Consul-General went through this performance at Opobo, Brass and the Benin River and reported back to the Foreign Office that his first task was successfully accomplished.[1]

The significance of the new system of customs payments was apparently lost on the chiefs. There are two possible explanations. In the first place, the new duties were levied on imports and not on exports with which the chiefs and their 'boys' were preoccupied. In the second place, the promised subsidies in lieu of 'comey' softened the blow which the abolition of 'comey' might have dealt to the purse of the merchant princes. For the rest, if the new 'Queen's man' defrayed the expenses of administration and 'opening up and development of the country generally', that was his own business. The exaction of 'comey' from European merchants had always been a tricky transaction. The chiefs were therefore being relieved of a burden, and without forfeiting their right to remuneration under a new name. And why not, when the fine issues of sovereignty had long ceased to have any meaning in

[1] F.O. 84/2111, Macdonald to F.O., 1 September 1891. (From Anderson's minute, it is clear that what the F.O. feared was not the opposition of the chiefs but the intrigues of 'discontented Liverpool traders'.)

the affairs of the coast? Subsequently, the threat to withhold the payment of subsidy became a powerful weapon in the hands of the British administrators with which to retain the loyalty and co-operation of influential chiefs or to bend them to the will of the new rulers.

During Macdonald's procession through the important river mouths, he formally introduced his vice-consuls to the chiefs in whose states the vice-consulates were established. At Old Calabar, the capital, the Commissioner had under him T. A. Wall as vice-consul, and Roberts as treasurer. Major-General Hammil was installed as vice-consul for Bonny and New Calabar, Armstrong for Opobo, Captain Macdonald for Brass, Captain Synge for Warri, and Captain Gallwey for Benin River.[1] In addition to the six vice-consuls, Macdonald was able, thanks to the efforts of Ralph Moor, to raise a constabulary force of 165 men. These men were recruited from the Gold Coast but also included a considerable number of Hausas. Ralph Moor did not think that the inhabitants of the Oil Rivers were 'fit elements for training'.

The only place where the new administration had any buildings was at the capital, Old Calabar. Macdonald did not mince words in describing what was to be his seat of government. 'The Consulate, Old Calabar, fortunately located on a hill some 200 ft. above the river, was a barn-like structure infested with white ants, mice, etc.'[2] Macdonald's vice-consuls did not have any government building in their stations. They operated from hulks. One of the early vice-consuls has explained that a consular hulk 'was not a convict settlement as in the old days of the Australian hulk, but was merely an ancient sailing vessel which had seen its day; it was moored in the river and was used by the traders in lieu of a house, as it could be moved about to suit their requirement'.[3]

Thus were Macdonald and his vice-consuls poised on the coast, ready to carry out the instructions from the British Foreign Office. It is quite remarkable the way the Foreign Office officials continued to indulge in equivocation. In their comprehensive instructions to Macdonald, the Consul-General was required to ascertain the old

---

[1] Gallwey later became successively Governor of St Helena, Gambia and South Australia.

[2] F.O. 2/63, Enclosure in Despatch to F.O., 19 August 1894.

[3] Douglas, *Niger Memories*, p. 33.

treaties made with 'Native chiefs' and to ensure that the chiefs understood them. He could amend and extend these treaties, consolidate the protectorate and bring all the territories under a uniform system of administration. As regards internal affairs, Macdonald's object should be, 'by developing legitimate trade, by promoting civilisation, by inducing the natives to relinquish inhuman and barbarous customs, and by gradually abolishing slavery, to pave the way for placing the territories over which H.M.'s protection is or may be extended directly under British rule'. This portion of the instructions notwithstanding, Macdonald was reminded that it was not advisable to interfere unduly with 'tribal government' and that the chiefs should continue to rule their subjects and administer justice to them. What Macdonald could do in these respects was to keep a constant watch to prevent injustice and check abuses. The chiefs should be made to understand that they would forfeit their powers by misgovernment. In any case, the Consul-General was authorised to take over the judicial and administrative powers of the chiefs if such a step was essential 'for the benefit of the natives'.[1] He was also empowered by the Order-in-Council of 1889 to legislate by means of proclamations.

Major Macdonald with his skeleton staff proceeded to carry out the Foreign Office programme. The difficulties were obvious enough. In the first place, the new administration was confronted with a territory cut in two by the Niger basin which was under the jurisdiction of the Royal Niger Company. The boundary between the two administrations was at last defined by the Foreign Office officials in the sanctity of their rooms in the Foreign Office.

(1) On the west of the Nun the line starts in the middle of the mouth of Forcados River and follows the river to the mouth of Warri Creek, and thence follows that creek midway to a point $2\frac{1}{2}$ miles below the mouth of the creek leading to Oagbi and Ahiabo. From that place the line runs north-east for ten miles and then due north for 50 miles.... (2) On the east of the Niger the boundary is formed by a straight line from a point midway between Brass and Nun and terminating at Idu....Idu itself is to be under joint administration.[2]

---

[1] F.O. 84/2110, F.O. Draft Instructions to Macdonald, 18 April 1891. See also Lucas, *op. cit.* Foreign Jurisdiction Act, 1890, pp. 215–16.
[2] F.O. 84/2110, F.O. to Macdonald, 29 July 1891.

An arrangement more calculated to lead to difficulties can hardly be imagined. The Macdonald administration was excluded from the most important access to the hinterland. The exclusion of Brass communities from their traditional markets was made final. It is no wonder that Brass chiefs remained aggrieved and 'only too glad to pay off old scores against the Royal Niger Company'.

Two issues threatened to mar the goodwill which generally existed between Macdonald and the chiefs. In Brass, for instance, the complaints against the Royal Niger Company produced considerable tension during Macdonald's visit in his new capacity. The Brass chiefs signed the document which abolished their 'comey' on the understanding that Macdonald, 'the big Queen's man', would do something about Brass's exclusion from its traditional markets. The tension in Opobo arose from the circumstances surrounding Jaja's last days and death in exile. It may be recalled that in the spring of 1889, Jaja's health had begun to cause anxiety in St Vincent Island in the West Indies. When the Foreign Office suggested that Jaja might be removed to the Gold Coast, the governor of the latter protested and argued that as the lawyer who defended Jaja during his trial was still in the Gold Coast, Jaja's presence in the colony might give rise to renewed intrigues which the colony could hardly afford. On the 16 June 1890 a Foreign Office telegram to Consul Annesley announced that 'Medical report from St Vincent states that Jaja's life may be endangered if his detention there is much prolonged. Her Majesty's Government therefore wish to allow him to return. What precautions would you think necessary?' Annesley wrote back to explain that his eleven years' experience as Consul among negroes had convinced him 'that kindness, combined with justice and firmness, goes a long way'. Every chief in Opobo expected that King Jaja would shortly return to Opobo, but, thanks largely to the influence of the African Association of Liverpool, the British government took shelter in vacillation. Jaja was already suffering from chronic bronchitis and in February 1891 he was transferred from St Vincent to Barbados.[1]

This was where Macdonald came in. Jaja's last plea to the British government that 'I feel I cannot last long and that is the

[1] The *Barbados Herald*, 11 May 1891.

140

reason which leads me to ask you to send me back to Opobo' was too much for Macdonald's liberal mind. Before the Commissioner and Consul-General left Britain for the Oil Rivers, he advised that King Jaja should be allowed to return. But on 7 July 1891 Jaja died at Santa Cruz, in the Spanish island of Teneriffe. The news of Jaja's death was received in Opobo with bitterness and sorrow. When Macdonald presented himself as the Queen's man, the chief's first request was that the Commissioner should arrange the return to Opobo of Jaja's body.[1] Macdonald gave the Opobo chiefs and people complete satisfaction in the matter. On 12 August he announced the return of Jaja's corpse for interment at Opobo, and shortly after the body arrived in the S.S. *Benin*. The Opobo town bell, erected by Jaja in 1879, tolled and mingled with the wailings of Jaja's subjects.

Apart from the specific grievances which Macdonald encountered at Brass and Opobo, his programme which involved the developing of legitimate trade was bound to provoke the old question of the role of the coast chiefs as middlemen. The chiefs were naturally not anxious to see their source of wealth and livelihood undermined by the opening up of the immediate hinterland to free commercial intercourse. In any case, the innumerable creeks which afforded access to the hinterland could be navigated only in canoes which the coast chiefs and their trading boys used. The stepping up of exports in palm oil, palm kernel, cocoa, coffee, copra, rubber and ivory necessitated very drastic measures against time-honoured practices which included monopolistic privileges on the part of the coast chiefs, and the system of tolls on roads and creeks on the part of the inland inhabitants. There was lastly the problem posed by the harassing behaviour of the white traders. This point has been admirably summarised in the following words by one of the early administrators: 'Ousted by the administrator, and the "Do as I like—Go as I please" method supplanted by the "Do as I tell you" policy of the Government, the trader finds that his money bags are almost empty, and that he is no longer a law in the land. The direct result of this is to give him a grievance.'[2]

[1] F.O. 84/2111, Macdonald to F.O., 1 September 1891.
[2] *West African Pamphlets*, 43/2, 'The Government of Protected Races', p. 15; Douglas, *op. cit.* p. 25.

Macdonald recognised that his task was extremely complex and involved a situation which called for a display of tact, sympathy and wise discernment. He believed that a just and humane stewardship and visible solicitude for the contentment and prosperity of the people committed to his charge would in time produce rewarding, if not dramatic, results.[1] Meanwhile, Macdonald expected his vice-consuls to behave like the Tudor Justices of the Peace. They were in fact to be 'Jacks of all Trades'. Apart from their administrative duties which entailed travelling to open up friendly relations with the towns on the periphery of their stations, to assess their natural resources, to sign new treaties, and to collect intelligence reports, the vice-consuls supervised the collection of import duties and the postal services.[2]

The greatest challenge was the urgent need to extend British authority to the immediate hinterland of the coast. It may be recalled that the last lone Consul and his 'forty thieves' were repulsed in their attempt to overawe the ruler of Akwette, 30 miles up the Bonny river. Subsequently, the palm-oil trade at the centre had come to a complete standstill. Bonny chiefs needed the goodwill of the ruler of Akwette to be able to carry on any trade there. In October 1891 Macdonald decided to proceed to Akwette —his first venture inland. With his characteristic tact, he held a peace 'palaver' with the king and chiefs of Akwette. The latter were of course aware that a more militarily equipped British administration had been installed in the Oil Rivers. But, as in most other cases, Macdonald's manner of approach was the decisive factor. The Akwette rulers not only accepted a fine of 10 puncheons of oil for the Bonny trading establishments they had burnt down, but 'expressed a desire' to sign a protection treaty. The first important hinterland town was secured without bloodshed.

The vice-consuls were as active as their chief. In the Benin River, Gallwey in November 1891 undertook an extensive tour of the Itsekiri and Urhobo hinterland. He thought the Urhobo people were very ignorant and timid and therefore incapable of undertaking a treaty. Even if they undertook one, Gallwey doubted whether they had sufficient sense of honour to keep it. Besides, it

---

[1] See Morel, *Affairs of West Africa*, ch. x.
[2] Douglas, *op. cit.* p. 170.

was impossible to find out whether there was one head ruler of the Urhobo or many. One thing, however, was clear to Gallwey. The Urhobo were a great oil-producing people, although the Itsekiri acted as middlemen. In his report to Macdonald, Gallwey demonstrated his inability to understand the subtle way in which the Urhobo organised themselves into small autonomous political units under Ovies confirmed by the king of Benin. If there were no paramount chiefs, then the people had not attained the level of anything but anarchy. More serious was Gallwey's complete misunderstanding of the position of Chief Nana in the region. All he could advise was that Nana's monopoly of trade should be destroyed.[1] One important result materialised from Gallwey's tour of the Urhobo country—his advice that a constabulary post should be established at a small Urhobo village on the bank of the Ethiope river, about 55 miles from the vice-consulate. 'The anchorage here is deep and roomy, and the ground high, though one mass of forest. A most suitable spot to establish factories, especially as all the produce from the Sobo [Urhobo] markets passes here on the way to the towns near the mouth of the river.' When Macdonald visited the Benin river, he approved Gallwey's choice of a constabulary station, and the present township of Sapele came into existence. Chief Nana, the overlord of the region, did not oppose the action of the Macdonald administration, and so the second point in the hinterland was secured—also without bloodshed.

The vice-consul in Bonny, Kenneth Campbell, undertook a journey into the hinterland of Bonny in February 1892. The journey took him into the peripheral Ibo country. Calling first at Okrika, the vice-consul visited King Amachree who informed him that 'the Ibo people would die if they saw a white man and that much trouble would come to me...'. The naïve argument was, however, lost on Campbell who understood the true motives behind the Okrika king's solicitude. Amachree subsequently instigated the canoe men hired by the vice-consul to abscond. The king's success here later cost him his subsidy of £400 a year. The vice-consul managed to get into an Ibo town called Elebe

[1] F.O. 84/2111, Macdonald to F.O. no. 30, 12 December 1891. For details on the Urhobo people, see Salubi's paper in *Journal of the Historical Society of Nigeria*, I, no. 3 (1958).

(Elele-Nwa). His report on his journey was full of praise of the hinterland. 'The country through which I passed was very fine and appears to be most fertile. The farms are large and surround the towns... the oil palm tree is to be seen the whole way.'[1] Therefore, the sooner the administration moved in, the better.

From Gallwey, the vice-consul of the Benin River, came the most sensational news of the year 1892. In March the vice-consul successfully made his way to the city of Benin. Both Gallwey and the British traders on the coast had been fed by the Itsekiri traders with what were at the time enormously exaggerated accounts of the grandeur of the king of Benin and the extent of his empire. To get the king of Benin to accept the British protection was indeed to have acquired potential control of a large area of hinterland west of the Lower Niger. Gallwey reported he had achieved just this. According to his report, Overami (Ovonramwen), 'a most powerful king in the Protectorate', willingly signed a treaty in which 'Her Majesty the Queen of Great Britain and Ireland, Empress of India, in compliance with the request of the king of Benin, hereby undertakes to extend to him and to the territory under his authority and jurisdiction, Her gracious favour and protection'.[2] Gallwey did not give any details about his interview with the king of Benin. Whether or not the Benin ruler did require anybody's protection is a matter of conjecture. Meanwhile Gallwey was satisfied that his treaty would prove 'most beneficial towards the welfare of this particular country'.

Gallwey's report on his journey and successful mission to Benin City contained two assumptions which were destined to persist in British policy towards Benin and to lead to tragedy. The first assumption squared with the facts. In the Benin territory, there were vast possibilities for the development of trade in ivory, rubber, gum, copal, gum arabic, fibres, mahogany and hard woods, 'and probably coffee and cocoa'. Today Benin and its neighbourhood lead the rest of the country in the export of rubber and timber. Gallwey's assessment was, by and large, an accurate one. His second point about Benin was that he discovered 'manifold fetish restrictions' on trade. This was clearly a situation which required

[1] F.O. 84/2194, Macdonald to F.O. no. 14, 9 March 1892.
[2] F.O. 84/2194, Enclosure in no. 26, Macdonald to F.O., 16 May 1892.

careful investigation before it was made the basis of an aggressive policy towards Benin. In 1892, however, no military action was contemplated. It was to come in a matter of five years. The point is that Gallwey's belief that official Benin policy and its fetish practices constituted obstacles to trade was hardly compatible with his hope that the treaty with the ruler of Benin would open up vast trade possibilities. It is another question whether or not the clauses of the reported treaty meant anything to either Gallwey or the king of Benin. Gallwey's report in 1892 was good news.

The annual report for 1892 on the protectorate submitted by the Commissioner and Consul-General was extremely gratifying to the Foreign Office. The net revenue of the protectorate during the two years of its existence under Macdonald was £96,000 and £169,000 respectively. The Treasury loan of £14,000 with interest had been paid back. No serious conflicts with the natives had occurred and limited penetration of the hinterland had been accomplished behind Bonny and in the Benin River region. Lord Rosebery, who was then installed as Foreign Secretary, minuted on Macdonald's report 'O si sic omnes',[1] and why not? In recognition of his services to the protectorate, Major Macdonald received the K.C.M.G. in the New Year Honours awards. Macdonald had the opportunity to analyse the principles of his policy at a banquet in his honour arranged by the Africa Trade Section of the Liverpool Chamber of Commerce. Macdonald in his speech declared that '...to advance slowly, leaving no bad or unfinished work behind, to gain the respect and liking of the natives, by a firm and judicious conduct of affairs...are the means which, in my humble opinion, lead to success in Africa'.[2]

In the following year, 1893, a Foreign Office notice appeared in the *London Gazette* of 13 May, to the effect that the Oil Rivers Protectorate should be known from the date of notification as the Niger Coast Protectorate. The new name, Niger Coast, does not quite indicate the reasons for the change of name. What the Foreign Office wished to convey was that British control had been consolidated on the Oil River mouths and that the next stage was to extend

[1] F.O. 84/2194, The Oil Rivers Accounts Report, see minute by Rosebery.
[2] *Nigerian Pamphlets*, no. 5. 'Proceedings at a Banquet et seq.', 2 November 1892.

this control to the hinterland behind the coast. There was no doubt that British rule indeed functioned effectively in the Oil Rivers. The Commissioner was enforcing legislative measures in the formation of which the local coast chiefs had had no part. These measures included (i) the Post Office Ordinance, (ii) Medical and Sanitary Regulations, (iii) Customs Ordinance, (iv) the Constabulary Ordinance, and (v) the Niger Coast Fire-arms Ordinance. In each of the coast city-states, Macdonald created machinery for local administration. This was in a way a revival of H. H. Johnston's governing councils, but there was a vital difference. Johnston's councils had included European merchants as well as local chiefs. Macdonald's organs were called native councils, and the membership was confined to the leading chiefs in each city-state. In due course, minor councils were set up in the outlying districts to settle petty disputes. Whether alien or not, these councils were the beginnings of what came to be called 'indirect rule'.

Sir Claude recognised that the self-imposed responsibilities on the part of the British administration, in the Niger Coast protectorate, went beyond merely superseding the indigenous rulers and maintaining the traditional export trade in palm oil and kernels. There were opportunities for constructive activity in the form of introducing the culture of new export crops. For instance, the territory watered by the Qua-Eboe river was a plain which promised an excellent future in the way of cocoa and coffee plantations. The Commissioner had made a beginning by laying the foundations of a botanical garden at Old Calabar. Young coffee plants were distributed free of charge to Old Calabar chiefs who would clear the ground for their reception. To encourage the culture of the seedlings, Macdonald was willing to give subsidies for the number of years that must transpire before the plants reached the stage of fruition. The effects of this constructive policy showed themselves in the increase of coffee exported from the protectorate, that is, 2789 lb. in 1891/2 and 28,099 lb. in 1892/3. In the Qua-Eboe country, A. A. Whitehouse was installed formally as a consular agent, and within a short time there were extensive plantations of coffee and cocoa.[1]

[1] F.O. 2/63, Macdonald to F.O. no. 16, 25 April 1894. The Curator of the Old Calabar Botanical Gardens published a small pamphlet translated into Efik

The present and prospective demands of the British administration in the Niger protectorate clearly required an expanded establishment. As long as the revenue of the protectorate could cope with the emoluments of new officials, the Foreign Office was content to leave the matter in the hands of the local administration. The agency established in London by Macdonald was fully occupied with finding men and arranging supplies for the administration of the protectorate. In 1894 Macdonald already had under him 6 deputy commissioners and vice-consuls, 4 consular agents, 11 assistants to vice-consuls, 7 wing-officers for the protectorate constabulary, 3 treasury officials, 1 survey officer, 10 medical officers, and one officer each for the post office, the botanical gardens, customs, and public works. It is easy to imagine that the large increase in the number of assistants to vice-consuls should have led to spectacular consular penetration of the hinterland. The fact, however, was that the officers in charge of the river-mouth consular establishments were often away on sick leave, and all that could be achieved was a guarantee that there was always a British official available to carry on the 'all purposes' role of the vice-consul in each vice-consulate.[1] The Foreign Office and the protectorate officers were in the meantime satisfied with referring to the tasks of the administration of the protectorate as 'running the show'.

As already indicated, the ultimate aim of the protectorate government was, naturally, to extend political control beyond the sphere of activity of the coast middlemen to the rich agricultural and palm-producing regions of the hinterland. The administration was handicapped in this task: the Lower Niger and its basin lay within the jurisdiction of the Royal Niger Company; the creeks of the Niger Coast protectorate afforded but limited access to the hinterland; and for the rest, there were narrow forest tracks which led to nobody knew where. The early points of advance by Major Macdonald's administration were therefore in the direction of the creeks. In the Bonny district a government station was established at Akwette, 30 miles up the Bonny river. Degema, 30 miles inland

giving hints regarding the growing of coffee. The pamphlet was distributed to the chiefs free of charge.
[1] F.O. 2/63, Macdonald to F.O. no. 12, 19 February 1894.

on the Sombrero river, became the seat of the New Calabar vice-consulate. West of the Niger delta, in the western half of the protectorate, there were the new stations of Sapele on the Ethiope river and Warri on the Forcados river, both stations being approximately 50 miles inland. The advance was so far achieved without bloodshed. The change in the environment was invariably welcome to the administrators and the British traders. The records of a visitor to the coast contain a contrast between Warri and Bonny which probably reflected the views of the resident officials and traders.

Presently the swamps gave place to dry land, where tufted palms, great mahoganies, acacias, and cotton trees crowned the banks, and the beauty of the tropic forest unrolled itself....Warri stands about forty miles from the sea....This is certainly one of the finest Government and trading stations on the Niger...; but everything there is clean, new, orderly, and in this it differs widely from some of the others—Bonny, for instance, where squalor and filth abound.[1]

The advance stations were not necessarily consolidated seats of British authority. A great deal depended on the attitude of the neighbouring or surrounding inhabitants. Two examples will suffice to illustrate the position. At Itu, 60 miles up the Cross river, 'where the mangrove disappears altogether, being replaced by splendid forest trees and many clearings', a government station was established on the fringe of the Ibibio country. The Ibibio people might welcome individual white traders as guests in their country, but the arrival of people who claimed to be the new rulers of their country produced a different kind of reaction from the Ibibio. A British trading agent, John Harford, had recently opened a trading station on the Qua-Eboe. After a short period of local hostility, the leading Ibibio chief assured the trader of the future security of the trading station. According to the trader's account of what transpired, the burden of the chief's speech was that 'we have heard with sorrow of the way in which your people have been so ill used by our people, and it is a shame to us a stranger should be so treated who is trying to do his best to bring business among us'.[2] On the other hand, the attempt by a vice-

<hr />

[1] Bindloss, *In the Niger Country*, p. 143.
[2] Kingsley, *op. cit.* see appendix II, p. 595.

consul at Old Calabar to penetrate the Ibibio country from the Cross river to the Qua-Eboe in order to explain the new political order represented by the protectorate administration provoked the hostility of the Ibibio rulers. The vice-consul, Roger Casement, was left in no doubt about the attitude of the people to British political interference. Casement was therefore convinced that '...the inland people, whose present boast is that we dare not come near their country, will only see, in our clinging to the neighbourhood of the sea-shore, a fresh proof of their view that the white man has no power or wish to go beyond the guns of a man-of-war'.[1] The British station at Itu on the periphery of the Ibibio country was no more than a mere building where a touring vice-consul could stay for a short time and hold a 'palaver' if he succeeded in getting the chiefs of the immediate neighbourhood together; otherwise he issued warnings to the chiefs through any passers-by and returned to Old Calabar.

The situation in another advance British station, Warri, was remarkably different. The local political situation played into the hands of the vice-consul. Warri was the traditional capital of the Itsekiri, and, whether founded by a Benin prince or not, Warri was for centuries before the arrival of the British a virtually independent principality. In the second half of the nineteenth century the authority of the Olu was already becoming a thing of the past. The Itsekiri capital was overshadowed by new trading centres founded and controlled by dynamic Itsekiri upstarts like Nana of Ebrohemie. To the north and north-east of Warri lay the country of the Urhobo who were great oil producers and agriculturists. They were, however, never sufficiently integrated politically to resist the extortions of Benin rulers or the commercial stranglehold of the Itsekiri middlemen. The decline of Warri was the salvation of the neighbouring Urhobo groups, especially the groups which were not embraced in Nana's extensive trading empire. When, therefore, a British vice-consulate was established at Warri, the Urhobo of the neighbourhood welcomed the presence of a neutral arbitrator for their petty feuds with one another and with the Itsekiri. More important still, the oil producers could sell their oil, if they wished, directly to the European agents stationed at

[1] F.O. 2/64, Casement's Report on his hinterland journey, June 1894.

Warri. Major Copland-Crawford, the vice-consul, was in effect the ruler of that part of the hinterland.

Unlike at Itu on the Cross river, the consulate at Warri was the seat of effective British authority. The consulate was a 'handsome wooden building, white roofed, white walled...with cool verandahs, and the space underneath between its supporting piles turned into a spacious courtroom and offices'. Over the consulate floated the Union Jack. According to an eyewitness account, the vice-consul held court and dispensed justice. Although the prejudiced eyewitness painted the natives involved in the grimmest of colours, considerable light is thrown on the beginnings of the new political order in Urhoboland.

A big Yoruba sentry stood on guard...informed us, 'This is justice-palaver day, sah: Consul live inside.' Behind a big desk at one end of the room [otherwise 'occupied by a perspiring oily crowd...splendid specimens of animal physic'] a stalwart soldierly Englishman of middle age, whose face was wrinkled with lines of thought and anxiety, and probably suffering too, leaned wearily back in a chair, two big Yoruba soldiers with rifles in their hands standing like ebony statues beside him.[1]

The majesty of British rule was evident and the Queen's representative tried cases which included slave-stealing, wife-stealing, firing on trade canoes, and the adulteration of palm kernels with shells. And thus order was maintained and justice done.

The advance posts at the heads of the creeks were but points for further advance into the proper hinterland. Macdonald and his assistants recognised that the task was one that called for patience and tact. The problems varied, however, from place to place. In the western portion of the protectorate, the local officers tended to accept uncritically the traders' view that what was required was the elimination of the most powerful Itsekiri leader, who happened to have created a vast commercial empire, as a preliminary to the smashing of 'odious Benin'. In the Cross river basin, the journeys of the redoubtable vice-consul, Roger Casement, showed that the task involved no more than a willingness on the part of the protectorate officials to travel and win the friendship of peoples probably never before visited by a white man. When Casement journeyed overland from Okyong to Okurike instead of following the traditional route along the Cross river, the people of Okurike

---

[1] Bindloss, *op. cit.* pp. 145–7.

expressed surprise and conveyed their apprehensions in a manner that suggested humour rather than hostility. 'Hitherto, they said, they had only looked for the white man by the river, now they must expect him from the land as well, and if they should have trouble with the government again, where were they to run away?'[1]

Up to the summer of 1894, no bloodshed had stained the process of extending British rule. As far as Macdonald's speeches can be relied on, the Consul-General did not think in terms of warfare. By a strange coincidence the first serious military operation was undertaken by the protectorate administration while Macdonald was away on leave. The stormy period which developed in the second half of 1894 was the direct result of the determination of the British representatives to crush Nana of the Benin River. Whether or not Macdonald would have devised a method which circumvented a military clash with Nana is a matter of conjecture. Nana's difficulties with the British were long-standing, but that they degenerated to the point of open rupture was the measure of the rashness and lack of sympathy shown by Sir Claude's deputy, Ralph Moor.

Nana's pre-eminence was due partly to the thorough work done by his father, Alluma. The latter had not only overthrown his rival, the son of the queen of Warri, but by 1865 had founded and consolidated the new stronghold of Ebrohemie. Nana's mother was an Urhobo and this was a great advantage to Nana in his relations with the neighbouring Urhobo people. Nana seemed to have reconciled in his person the traditional frictions which bedevilled Itsekiri–Urhobo relations. Through remarkable commercial acumen, Nana gained considerable influence over other petty Itsekiri chiefs and over the surrounding Urhobo oil-producing districts west of the Forcados river. His wealth and prestige marked him out as the dominant personality in the commercial and political life of a large portion of the Itsekiri and Urhobo country. Urhobo traditions and local historians naturally tend to deny that Nana's position in the Urhobo country ever had any political significance.[2] These rather see Nana as no more than an

[1] F.O. 2/63, Report on the Niger Coast Protectorate, 21 August 1894, see pp. 33–43.
[2] See Salubi in *Journal of the Historical Society of Nigeria*, cited p. 190.

Itsekiri middleman trader who exploited the potentialities of finance to control the external trade of Urhoboland. Dominant Nana certainly was, yet he established no machinery of government which embraced Itsekiri-land and the portion of Urhoboland he controlled commercially. Numa the son of Nana's father's rival, remained Nana's Itsekiri rival and entrenched himself at Bateri. There was another Itsekiri rival in the person of Chief Dudu who founded Dudu town.[1] These disabilities notwithstanding, the first British agents believed that Nana was the governor of that part of the Oil Rivers, on behalf of the powerful ruler of Benin. The basis of this assumption is not clear, but British policy was at first based on that assumption.

Britain made the first contact with Nana when the latter signed in 1884 the treaty of protection on behalf of himself and the Itsekiri and Urhobo communities west of the Forcados river. After the formal proclamation of a British protectorate, the Consul, Hewett, ceremoniously, if superfluously, appointed Nana 'the executive power through which decrees of Her Majesty's Government and of the Consular Court are to be exercised and enforced'. Nana was subsequently given a 'staff of office', ostensibly as the Queen's special agent. Nana saw nothing sinister in what he regarded as flattering recognition of his predominance in the region. He acquired even greater prestige in the eyes of his local Itsekiri rivals and the commercially dependent Urhobo communities. His trade 'boys' naturally exploited their master's prestige to engross the trade of the oil-producing Urhobo country. British merchants who wished to do any business on the Benin river had to do so on Nana's terms. Thus, like Jaja of Opobo, Nana was bound to fall foul of the British merchants and then of the British political agents. In 1887 Hewett sent him a letter of warning which threatened deposition and the annexation of the Itsekiri country. Three years later, Consul Annesley confiscated Nana's 'staff of office', and Nana's protest to Lord Salisbury produced no result. The charge against Nana was that he interfered with the efforts of the European firms to establish business inland.

The vice-consuls who were appointed to the region in 1891 were

---

[1] Kingsley, *op. cit.* appendix 1, p. 458.

hardly settled in the new vice-consulates when they were flooded with complaints by the British merchants. These complaints were naturally embodied in the reports submitted to the Consul-General, Macdonald. The vice-consuls assumed that the smaller Itsekiri and Urhobo chiefs were anxious to repudiate Nana's authority and trade freely and directly with the European firms. They imagined that it was their primary duty to break Nana's trade monopoly, and referred with approval to the fate of Jaja of Opobo. Gallwey, the vice-consul, emphatically argued that as long as Nana was allowed to continue his 'reign of terror', no progress was to be expected.[1] If Gallwey and the merchants had had their way, a British gunboat might have been used against Nana, who, they said, was 'playing a very dangerous game'. In April 1894 Sir Claude Macdonald formally abrogated Nana's appointment as 'governor' of the Benin River. The letter forwarded to Nana explained that as the Queen's government had been established, he was no longer to be recognised as chief of the Itsekiri people.[2]

Nana was no fool. He began, rather belatedly, to regret his glibness in opting for a Queen's government during the 1889 tour of inquiry by Macdonald. Even his enemies, the British merchants, expressed surprise that Nana could not see in the downfall of Jaja of Opobo a contingency which was sooner or later to encompass his own ruin.[3] Too late, perhaps, Nana began quietly and secretly to accumulate all kinds of arms. Ebrohemie, his headquarters, was an ideal defensive position, amidst a network of muddy creeks and almost impassable morasses about a mile and a half from the north bank of the Benin river. The access to Ebrohemie was therefore through oozy swamp and tangled bush. An invading force had to wade through miry creeks, if it succeeded in cutting a way through the tangled vegetation which obscured the defences of Ebrohemie. At the mouth of the Ebrohemie creek, Nana had a grim stockade constructed.

Matters came to a head shortly after Sir Claude Macdonald left the protectorate on leave in the summer of 1894. The last straw was Nana's refusal to accept the price for palm produce stipulated

[1] F.O. 2/63, Report on the Niger Coast Protectorate, 24 August 1894.
[2] F.O. 2/64, see letter from Gallwey to Nana dated 21 June 1894.
[3] Kingsley, *op. cit.* appendix I, p. 466.

by the British trading agents themselves. Nana retaliated by stopping any trade relations with the merchants. Geary has pointed out that Nana's action was no more than a crude way of doing what a trades union might do to maintain the integrity of a strike. It is easy enough to see the analogies between the issue and Jaja's dispute with the British merchants in 1887. There was, however, a fundamental difference. Nana's behaviour was that of a businessman, whilst Jaja's was the exercise of his sovereign rights. The animosity which the British merchants felt against Nana can be gauged from a letter sent by a Mr Coxon to his employers in England. It recounted the various occasions on which the chief had openly 'insulted' the Queen's representative and concluded as follows: 'I think the egregious ass will find out shortly what Englishmen are made of....He is a d...d rascal!!!! I shan't be sorry when his power is completely broken. We will have a much better trade and more profitable too.'[1] Some of the white traders thought it expedient to accept Nana's terms—to the great annoyance of Macdonald's deputy who thought that, in yielding to Nana, the merchants prejudiced the prestige of the protectorate government.

The Foreign Office was baffled by what appeared to be a dramatic change in the peaceful career of the protectorate administration. Ralph Moor's dispatch as well as the trader's damning letter was forwarded to Sir Claude for his comments. The latter was aware of the inconvenience which Nana's predominance was beginning to cause the protectorate government determined to extend its political control to the hinterland. However, he held on to the view that tact was required in dealing with personalities like Nana whose only offence was their energy and their unwillingness to give up, without a struggle, their prescriptive rights. Macdonald dismissed the British trader's letter as 'somewhat highly coloured'. He concluded that the trader's view should not dictate British policy in the Niger Coast protectorate. Unfortunately for the peace of the area involved, Ralph Moor's views apparently coincided with those of the British traders. The Acting Consul-General proceeded to precipitate a showdown with Nana.

[1] F.O. 2/63, Moor to F.O., Enclosure in Despatch no. 23, 8 August 1894. Letter from Coxon to Pinnock, dated July 1894.

Here was the beginning of what Moor called a 'forward policy' which he pursued consistently when he became the head of the administration in 1896.

On 21 June Moor addressed a letter to Nana, summoning the chief to attend the vice-consulate at Sapele to answer charges against him. In the meantime, Nana's rival Itsekiri chiefs and as many Urhobo headmen as could be found assembled at Sapele where they were received in state by Ralph Moor and his escort. The local rulers protested their loyalty to the British and told a tale of wrongs suffered at the hands of Nana. Their wives had been stolen, their villages burnt and their canoemen murdered—all because the white man was indeed afraid of Nana. Nana's reply to the Acting Consul-General's summons was straightforward. 'Am I a servant of the Government? If the white officers would speak with me, let them come to Brohemie.'[1] Moor decided to send a second invitation to Nana and warned him that the order of the Queen's representative could not be ignored with impunity. To this the Itsekiri chief, probably beginning to appreciate the new posture of affairs, sought refuge in alleging that his brother was ill. He was prepared to send a representative. The Acting Consul-General lost his patience and ordered the blockade of the Ethiope river. Nana's trading canoes were to be confiscated and the appearance of war-canoes was prohibited.[2] Having adopted these stringent measures, Moor for the third time summoned Nana to a meeting at Sapele. Three days after the date scheduled for the meeting, Nana wrote to remind the British agent of the perfidy which had encompassed the deportation and ruin of Jaja of Opobo. There is no evidence that Moor contemplated following Johnston's nefarious example. Nana was, however, a keen student of local history and he obviously believed that history had the inconvenient habit of repeating itself. All he could commit himself to was a willingness to send his representative and a promise to carry out the wishes of the protectorate government in his future commercial and political activities.

The first thing to do, thought Moor, was to undermine Nana's political position. He therefore summoned all the petty chiefs of

[1] Bindloss, *op. cit.* p. 208.
[2] F.O. 2/63, no. 22, Moor to F.O., 6 August 1894.

Benin River and Warri districts and distributed to each and every-one of the local rulers treaty forms to sign. One treaty form was sent to Nana to sign for himself alone. In this way the original treaty which Nana had signed on behalf of the whole region would be nullified and the paramountcy the original treaty recognised would once and for all become undermined. Moor followed his political move with a military one. All the available troops of the protectorate constabulary were summoned to Sapele. On 3 August H.M.S. *Alecto* was sent up the Ethiope creek to blow up Nana's three-mile-deep stockade. This action and the blockade of Nana's stronghold might bring about Nana's surrender. Ralph Moor believed that as Nana and his followers 'grew nothing in or around the town itself but are dependent for supplies from up river I am in hopes that this course...may eventually bring about submission'.[1]

Nana did in fact have a sick brother, Berey. This brother died, and Moor suspected that slaves, in countless numbers, were being slaughtered in the ceremonies connected with the solemnisation of Berey's burial. From this point, Moor progressively built up a case in order to justify a military expedition against Nana which the Foreign Office was expected to approve. In the first place, Nana was reported to have set up himself as a fetish ruler, and rumours of sickening atrocities carried out at his instructions daily percolated to the vice-consulate. There were 'tangible proofs in the shape of decomposing corpses which floated down the creeks'. Then every act of insubordination on the part of any petty chief was ascribed to Nana's diabolical influence. For instance, a local Urhobo chief, in whose town there occurred a local fight, was summoned to Sapele. The chief refused to appear. The protectorate adminis-tration assumed readily that Nana must have been responsible for the Urhobo chief's refusal to attend the consular court at Sapele.[2]

The uncritical way in which Ralph Moor blamed every local defiance of the protectorate government on Nana is as baffling as his ignorance of the hinterland communities to which he was extending the benefits of British rule. In his reports, he described

[1] *Ibid.* Moor's terms in the event of Nana's surrender were (i) a fine of £500, (ii) surrender of Nana's arms and ammunition.
[2] *Ibid.* no. 23, Moor to F.O., 8 August 1894.

the Urhobo communities as Ijaw. Nor did he see any contra-diction in first claiming that the Urhobo chiefs were anxious to overthrow Nana's 'fetish rule' and then insisting that acts of insubordination by Urhobo chiefs amounted to demonstrations in favour of Nana. The immediate intention of the Acting Consul-General was, however, to justify punitive measures against recalci-trant Urhobo chiefs. Therefore, he dispatched a small contingent of the Niger Coast constabulary against the chief who had refused to appear at the Sapele vice-consulate. The troops were instructed to do precisely what the administration regarded as one of Nana's iniquities. The chief's village was razed to the ground, and Moor described the proceedings as 'exercising a form of "lex talionis"'. He hoped that the punishment inflicted on the Urhobo chief would have an excellent effect and would prove to the neighbourhood that 'neglect of the Government Orders entails serious consequences'. Moor concluded his report on the local situation by pointing out that 'it has too long been the custom of the people of Benin and Warri districts to say that they know no government but Chief Nana and it has now become necessary to convince them to the contrary'.[1]

The irony of the situation in the immediate neighbourhood of the vice-consulates of the Benin River and Warri was that, while the administration blockaded Nana and his trading lieutenants, the progressive deterioration of law and order in the Urhobo country was demonstrating that Nana's paramountcy did serve an extremely useful purpose in the hinterland involved. Nana's confinement left a vacuum which the protectorate government was not yet in a position to fill. Another misconception in regard to the situation in the immediate hinterland was the assumption on the part of the vice-consuls and the Acting Consul-General that as soon as Nana was neutralised, the palm-oil trade would flow abundantly and directly to the river terminals from the oil-producing areas. A few British traders who ought to have understood the mechanisms of indigenous commercial life were blinded by selfish considerations of immediate profit.[2] The indigenous system of trade, as indeed

[1] *Ibid.*
[2] The aftermath of Jaja's deportation from Opobo exemplified the point made here. The British merchants in Opobo were the first to admit their mistake in recommending the expulsion of Opobo traders from Opobo hinterland markets (1887–9).

all systems of trade, involved a series of markets and of middlemen. Nana's capital and trade 'boys' provided a vital chain which bound together the scattered hinterland markets to the port of export. Furthermore, they were an important factor in maintaining law and order in the miscellaneous markets. One result of the blockade of Nana was the breakdown of law and order in the hinterland markets. One example came to the notice of the Acting Consul-General himself.

In the market village of Efferonu in the Warri hinterland, the usual brisk business of oil buying and selling degenerated into a free-for-all scramble. The sellers from the surrounding districts apparently refused to have any dealings with any but Nana's boys who had long-established contacts with them and had in many cases advanced exchange trade goods to them. The local chief, Erigbe, who understood the basic cause of the dispute, intervened and drove away the upstart middlemen. For his action the chief earned himself the reprobation of being 'a staunch adherent and friend of Nana'. The Acting Consul regarded it as a demonstration in Nana's favour. His conclusion was that the sooner Nana was dealt with the better. The stage was therefore set for a final showdown with Nana.

It may be added that Nana had his own version of the crisis that arose between himself and the British administration.[1] According to him, the crisis was not one of the middlemen's opposition to European commercial penetration of the hinterland. He was an exponent of free trade and had introduced law and order by destroying with his 'Juju' the obstructionist tactics of the 'great [Ijaw] cannibals' in his country. The onus of responsibility for the crisis, Nana contended, rested with one Mr Locke, who at the material time was acting for Gallwey, then on furlough. Locke was a good friend of Chief Dawa, one of the rival chiefs who, with a Mr Gordon of the African Association, had been trying to embroil Nana with the protectorate administration. Nana also contended that the majority of European residents were against the war, an opinion endorsed by other independent observers.[2]

---

[1] Aborigines Protection Society Papers (Rhodes House, Oxford), Nana to Fox-Bourne, 5 November 1894.
[2] C.M.S. G.3/A.3/06, Dobinson to Baylis, 5 October 1894.

While warships and field guns from Lagos were awaited, the Acting Consul-General dispatched a reconnoitring party in the H.M.S. *Alecto* to probe the defences erected by Nana on the Ebrohemie creek. The attempt failed and on 25 August the party was forced back by the gun-fire of Nana's men, who in addition inflicted some casualties on the protectorate force.[1] Shortly after, H.M.S. *Philomel* and H.M.S. *Widgeon* arrived, and a force of 200 marines and 150 men of the protectorate constabulary were assembled under the supreme command of Rear-Admiral Bedford. News of these alarming preparations for a large-scale military operation reached the Itsekiri chief. Here was a contingency Nana had hardly bargained for. Defying a lone vice-consul and British traders, and using force where necessary to maintain his para-mountcy in Itsekiri and Urhobo villages, were clearly a different matter from facing an organised army of over 350 soldiers and marines. It is easy, therefore, to understand Nana's letter to the Acting Consul-General in which he made an abject apology. 'Please forgive me, I don't want to fight the Government. No Blackman fitted the Government.'[2] Ralph Moor was determined to teach Nana a lesson and in any case the reputation of the protectorate administration, tarnished by the failure of the reconnoitring party on 25 August, had to be restored.

Military operations against Nana began on 29 August. A graphic account of the first phase of the operations is as follows: '... a sudden detonation shook the forest, and amid a cloud of yellow smoke and a giant upheaval of mould and mud and foam, the impregnable stockade [Nana's Ebrohemie creek stockade] leapt into the air, and came down in a chaotic mass of splinters.'[3] There remained, however, the miry creek which had to be waded before the troops could gain access to Ebrohemie, otherwise protected by thick tropical vegetation. Nana's stronghold could not have been better chosen. Neither the British marines nor the Yoruba protectorate troops showed much enthusiasm in the idea of having to wade knee-deep through the oozy swamp of the Ebrohemie creek, while the surrounding thicket reverberated with the crash of Nana's

[1] One bluejacket killed; Captain Lalor of the protectorate constabulary fatally wounded; and two other officers and five men wounded.

[2] F.O. 2/64, Despatch 13 December 1894 (copies of Nana's letters enclosed).

[3] Bindloss, *op. cit.* p. 210.

flintlock guns. It was not till late in September that Rear-Admiral Bedford ordered assaults on the Ebrohemie creek. The sallies of 21, 22 and 23 September were frustrated by heavy gun-fire. It was therefore decided to cut through the mangrove on the eastern approach to Nana's stronghold. A massive advance against Nana was made on the 25th and Ebrohemie fell to the British.[1] Nana fled to Lagos, through a creek at the back of Ebrohemie, but the canoes containing his property and his letters were captured by the British troops.

The dislocation consequent on the protracted blockade and final defeat of Nana created a situation which Sir Claude Macdonald preferred to handle himself. Shortly after the arrival of Moor's telegram which announced the capture of Ebrohemie, the Consul-General cut short his leave and left Britain for the Niger coast on 13 October. His first assignment was naturally the trial of Nana in Lagos, but could Nana be tried in Lagos? The legal awkwardness was overcome when Nana voluntarily surrendered himself. The trial was a brief affair, and Nana was convicted on the grounds that he had violated his treaty with Britain and had also broken the protectorate laws. There were hardly any legal arguments about the precise way in which the protection treaty was violated by Nana or about the protectorate laws which Nana had sinned against. His punishment was deportation to the Gold Coast.

The trial and deportation of Chief Nana occasioned, in contrast to the case of King Jaja, no misgivings on the part of the British Foreign Office. The reference to the possibility of a Sierra Leone lawyer taking up Nana's cause was brushed aside by the head of the African department with the full approval of the Foreign Secretary, Lord Kimberley.[2] British writers, like Burns, give a one-sided account of the events which led up to actual hostilities against Nana.[3] It is of course futile to pretend that Ralph Moor was just a bloody tyrant who provoked an unnecessary war with the local Itsekiri overlord. The new political order which the protectorate administration symbolised had no room for indigenous rulers who

[1] F.O. 2/64, Moor to F.O. no. 28, 5 October 1894.
[2] The contrast with Lord Salisbury's reaction to Jaja's deportation, 1887, is almost absolute. See also F.O. 2/64, Macdonald to F.O. no. 49, 13 December 1894 and Minutes by Anderson and Kimberley.
[3] Burns, *op. cit.* pp. 160–3; Geary, *Niger Under British Rule*, pp. 109–10.

were prepared to defend their sovereignty. The nature of Nana's authority was inconvenient to both the protectorate rulers and the British merchants. Local Itsekiri and Urhobo historians do not indeed agree in their assessment of Nana's role in the area he dominated. The Urhobos understandably justify British action against Nana.[1]

The deportation of Nana meant the dissolution of his empire. According to reports of the protectorate administration, Nana had 2000 slaves as well as a number of villages under him. Nana's slaves were predominantly Urhobos but included, surprisingly, Yorubas. All these were now set free but were persuaded to settle in Nana's villages which the administration transformed into autonomous communities under headmen chosen by the British. The latter recognised, however, that the break-up of Nana's empire was not enough to guarantee peace and order in the vast Itsekiri and Urhobo hinterland. Itsekiri rivals of Nana were at hand and had the special recommendation of loyalty to the protectorate administration. One of them was Dore, son of Nana's inveterate foe, Numa. Chief Dore was probably the first person to fill a position, that of a political agent, which became increasingly important as the administration moved into a region of small, autonomous village communities. In the Urhobo country, two more political agents were later appointed and their activities will be discussed later. When Sir Claude Macdonald left Sapele on 8 November 1894, it was clear to him that the task of getting innumerable Itsekiri and Urhobo villages to accept the good intentions of the protectorate administration was hardly begun.

The Consul-General was pleased to note that during the difficult months of August and September, when the protectorate forces were preoccupied with the hostilities against Nana, the local rulers in the other city-states had remained loyal to the administration. He suspected, however, that the deportation of Nana and the confiscation of his slaves and property roused considerable sympathy for Nana on the part of Nana's middlemen colleagues in other rivers of the protectorate. The Consul-General fell back on his policy of consultation and explanation in order to restore undiluted confidence in himself and his administration. From

[1] For instance, Salubi in *J.H.S.N. op. cit.* p. 190.

8 to 22 November, Sir Claude visited all the city-states and held meetings with the chiefs at Sapele, Warri, Brass, Degema, Bonny, Opobo and Old Calabar. The Consul-General left no records of the proceedings and so it is impossible to say whether or not the local chiefs had had second thoughts, after the deportation of Nana, about their uncritical acceptance of the 'Queen's government'. The British representative was, however, able to report that the year 1894 came to a close with tranquillity restored everywhere in the portions of the protectorate where British rule functioned. His plans for 1895 concerned primarily the large Ibo groups of the hinterland.[1]

Sir Claude proposed to enter into negotiations with the Ibo groups with the view to establishing friendly relations with them. The Consul-General recognised that the Ibo were not organised into a large comprehensive state. For this reason, he asked the British Foreign Office for 500 treaty forms. Whether or not Macdonald assessed the number of autonomous Ibo communities at 500 it is impossible to say, but even then the modest number of treaty forms he asked for caused considerable surprise at the Foreign Office. The attitude of the officials of the Foreign Office apparently irritated the Consul-General and forced him into explaining his ideas about extending British rule to the Ibo hinterland. Macdonald asked whether Her Majesty's advisers were of the opinion that a mere declaration of a protectorate over the territories was sufficient to constitute them a British possession. If that were so, he could dispense with treaty-making. The Consul-General, however, believed that the extension and consolidation of British rule should be by right of treaty. The Ibo did not acknowledge any paramount chiefs, and he therefore insisted on getting the 500 treaty forms.

The attitude of the Foreign Office officials revealed their acceptance of the now discredited view that the absence of paramount chiefs was synonymous with the absence of any form of political organisation. They therefore argued that 'with such a changeling set of chiefs it seems hardly necessary to make so many individual treaties in our Protectorate, for each separate treaty will probably be repudiated either by the signatory chief or his

[1] F.O. 2/83, no. 5, Macdonald to F.O., 14 January 1895.

neighbour'. The head of the African Department, while advising that Macdonald should have his treaty forms, warned that 'we would not allow repudiation'.[1] To the Consul-General, the picture of the Ibo country was not that of chaos. The limited advance made by his vice-consul in the Bonny and New Calabar hinterland into the periphery of the Ibo territory produced glowing reports. From areas in the Ibo country as far north as 100 miles up the Lower Niger neighbourhood came eyewitness accounts which held out both promise and danger. One example will suffice to illustrate the point being made.

...and here there is already a marked contrast with the races dwelling among the mangroves of the estuaries. The Ibo people, though they have little love for white intruders, seem to be a brave and particularly intelligent race....Their huts are scrupulously clean, and an Ibo village is remarkable for its orderliness and freedom from many things which sicken the white observer who enters a coastwise town.[1]

Sir Claude Macdonald was not destined to demonstrate how he might have implemented his avowed policy of peaceful penetration into and consolidation of British rule in Iboland. The early part of 1895 engulfed the protectorate in a storm precipitated by the attack on the Royal Niger Company's headquarters at Akassa by the chiefs and men of Brass. When the disturbances subsided, Macdonald was succeeded as commissioner and consul-general by Ralph Moor. The latter's 'forward policy' was diametrically opposed to Macdonald's empirical approach to the problem of imposing alien rule on groups fanatically devoted to their own way of life. Meanwhile the Akassa crisis was to absorb Macdonald's energies but was at the same time to reveal the humanity with which he attempted to mitigate the inhuman implications of imperialism.

There is no more conclusive proof of the hollowness of the theory of protection than the series of events which culminated in the Brass attack on Akassa. The callousness and hypocrisy of the British Foreign Office were exposed more completely than by the deportation and death in exile of Jaja of Opobo. The depressing story of the progressive reduction of the people of Brass to utter

[1] *Ibid.* See Minutes by Charles Hill and Sir P. Anderson.
[2] Bindloss, *op. cit.* pp. 293–4.

destitution and despair can be traced in the Kirk Report on the Brass disturbances.[2] As early as 1878 the Brass rulers had explained to Consul Hopkins that the activities of British companies in the Lower Niger were depriving them of their means of livelihood. The British representative made promises which never materialised. Then the occasion of the British eagerness to secure treaties of protection provided another opportunity for the Brass rulers to clarify the kind of protection they needed. The Consul, Hewett, secured the necessary treaty after giving the chiefs vague assurances. After 1884 Brass was included in the area over which the British government proclaimed a formal protectorate. In 1886 Hewett announced to the Brass chiefs 'that markets could not be divided nor given to anyone particularly, that white men and black men might trade equally in all markets'. It was precisely in the same year that the British government gave a charter to the Royal Niger Company, which proceeded to exploit the charter in a manner too well known to be elaborated here. The British government was fully informed of the hardships inflicted on Brass by the restrictive commercial regulations imposed by the Royal Niger Company with respect to the natural hinterland and the traditional markets of Brass.[2] The protests of the Consul were ignored, because what apparently mattered was the fact that the Royal Niger Company was performing imperial duties.

In 1889, for reasons not connected with the grievances of Brass, the British government had sent out Claude Macdonald as special commissioner to investigate imperial problems in the Niger Districts and the Oil Rivers. The Commissioner's report contains ample evidence of the iniquitous regulations with which the Royal Niger Company persecuted indigenous traders from Brass and New Calabar. The Commissioner argued that all the natives belonged legally to one protectorate and should have access to all the markets in the protectorate. The reforms which might have mitigated the hardships of Brass men were completely ignored by the British government.[3] Before Macdonald, appointed Commissioner and Consul-General, could find the staff to inaugurate a

---

[1] *Parl. Papers*, Africa, no. 3 (7977), 1895, See Annex C.

[2] F.O. 84/1881, no. 34, Hewett to F.O., 10 November 1888.

[3] Report by H.M. Commissioner, *op. cit.* Second Report dated 13 January 1890.

more effective British administration in the Oil Rivers, the agents of the Royal Niger Company saw to it that every approach to the Niger was barred. This policy was applied to all the channels which led to the Oguta Lake, and to the Forcados river to the west of the delta. The African Association of Liverpool felt the stranglehold as much as the people of Brass. This was the reason for the renewal of the Association's campaign of vilification against the Royal Niger Company. The Association warned the British government that the rulers of Brass were being driven into a situation in which they were bound to resort to desperate measures. As far as the British Foreign Office was concerned, the Royal Niger Company was fulfilling an imperial mission. It represented a new order and this new order meant progress. There was bound to be some discontent among the coast middlemen, but there was ample room for the Liverpool firm to exploit new fields.[1]

It fell to Macdonald, in his capacity as Commissioner and Consul-General, to negotiate with Goldie the boundaries between the western and eastern portions of the Oil Rivers protectorate and Goldie's territory. Goldie argued from a position of strength, because his agents were already in effective occupation of the river approaches which the boundary negotiations might modify. He knew also that the British Foreign Office officials were not unduly concerned about the hardships which an uncharitable boundary line could impose on the livelihood of Brass men. The result was that Goldie got all he wanted. To the east of the delta, the boundary was defined as a straight line from a point midway between Brass and the Nun and terminating at Idu. The boundary merely confirmed the position already held by the Royal Niger Company. In a dispatch to Macdonald, the Foreign Office included the meaningless suggestion that Idu should be under the joint administration of the protectorate and the Royal Niger Company.[2] It was convenient to forget that it was a Brass trader who ransomed the Landers at Abo and brought them to Brass. Now the British made the boundary not only shut out Brass traders from Abo and

[1] F.O. 84/2176, African Association to F.O., 3 October 1891; F.O. 84/2241, F.O. to President of the Liverpool Chamber of Commerce, 2 February 1892. See Memo by Anderson, Lister and Salisbury.

[2] F.O. 84/2110, F.O. to Macdonald, 29 July 1891. See also Kingsley, *op. cit.* appendix 1, pp. 470–1. For the original boundary, see p. 139.

the neighbourhood but confined them to the uninhabited patch of hinterland south of Idu.

During the first few years of the Macdonald administration, every vice-consul appointed to Brass conveyed to the Consul-General ample evidence of the destitution to which the rulers and people of Brass were being reduced by the destruction of their means of livelihood. The Brass complaints were invariably an appeal that those who had undertaken to protect the city-state should recover for it its traditional markets. The British Foreign Office was regularly informed about the deterioration of Brass's prospects. Macdonald's report for 1894 explained to the Foreign Office that 'the markets which the Natives of Brass formerly visited to procure produce, lying now within the territories of the Royal Niger Company...they [the natives] are deprived of a means of subsistence, and are therefore, perhaps not unnaturally discontented and somewhat troublesome.'[1] After the tragedy of the Brass attack on the Royal Niger Company's station and the subsequent destruction of Brass villages by British forces, the British Foreign Secretary, Lord Kimberley, could afford to express his astonishment in the following terms '...But the most serious part of the matter is the [apparently] total absence of any attempt to remove an undoubted grievance well known to, and acknowledged by Sir C. Macdonald. Has no report been made to the F.O. on this subject and if so, were any steps taken?'[2]

Lord Kimberley soon discovered that the Foreign Office had done nothing to relieve the sufferings of Brass chiefs and traders. If anything, the officials of that department went out of their way to defend the Royal Niger Company—their main argument being that 'the Company had not violated its charter'. The people of Brass received considerable help, moral and material, from the Liverpool agents in their attempt to survive through smuggling. In any case, it was owing to the Liverpool opposition to the Royal Niger Company that any questions were asked by members of Parliament at Westminster. By 1894, however, Goldie had successfully neutralised the Liverpool African Association's

[1] F.O. 2/63, Report on the Niger Coast Protectorate, 21 August 1894. See also F.O. 84/2194, no. 12, Macdonald to F.O., 8 March 1892 and F.O. 84/2259, Memo by Anderson, 26 April 1893.

[2] F.O. 2/83, see Minutes on no. 9, 21 February 1895.

hostility.[1] The Steamship Company was bribed over to the side of Goldie, and later the assets of the African Association on the Niger were assimilated into the business of the Royal Niger Company. The people of Brass were left isolated—abandoned by their Liverpool allies and apparently also by the officials of the Niger Coast protectorate who exercised the Queen's protection. The sense of frustration deepened. On a visit to Brass in March 1894, Sir Claude met the Church Missionary Society resident pastor, Mr. Williams, who explained that his congregation of 250 had practically all returned to juju. The Brass converts argued that something must be wrong with Christianity if the rulers of the Royal Niger Company who professed it could callously allow Brass men, women and children to 'eat sand'.

Under the leadership of an old king, Ebifa of Bassambiri, or otherwise under the leadership of chiefs divided into Christians and pagans, Brass men could do no more than smuggle at great peril to their lives and property. But then the Royal Niger Company perfected its anti-smuggling measures. A ship was moored on the creek which gave Brass men access to the Oguta Lake or the Niger. From the ship, the company's agents fired on Brass canoes and often, too, confiscated canoes bringing yam and other provisions from the Niger territories. Under the leadership of a determined king, Frederick William Koko, Brass men decided to fight it out once and for all. The king summoned a mass meeting of all the able-bodied men and chiefs of Brass and arrangements were discussed and finalised for an attack on the Royal Niger Company's depot at Akassa.

The attack was organised with the utmost secrecy. King Koko actually refused to see Rev. Father Bubendorf who had arrived from Onitsha with the king's son. The latter was being educated by the Roman Catholic Mission. The Rev. Father was looked after by the king's secretary, but King Koko excused himself because 'he had to speak with other chiefs about palaver on the creeks'. Nevertheless, an anonymous letter reached the vice-consul in charge of the Brass district on Sunday, 27 January 1895. 'Brass people leaving tomorrow at noon to destroy Niger Company's factories and lives at Akassa on Tuesday morning, be sure you

[1] Flint, *op. cit.* pp. 197–8.

167

send at once to stop them. An Observer.' Vice-Consul Harrison, who had no troops in his station, dispatched the warning letter to the agent-general of the Royal Niger Company who by a strange coincidence was at Akassa on a tour of inspection. On Monday, the company's local chief, Joseph Flint, wrote back to the vice-consul to the effect that '. . . these rumours are generally in evidence at this time of the year, but this is the first notification I have received from the Consulate in Brass'.[1]

On Tuesday, Akassa was attacked by Brass warriors and almost completely looted. Flint and his two white companions stationed themselves at the head of the veranda stairway where a quick-firing gun was placed. The gun saved the lives of the white men. Meanwhile, the Kroo servants of the Royal Niger Company who did not flee into the bush were either butchered or captured by the men from Brass. The Brass warriors decided to withdraw when H.M.S. *Bathurst* appeared at the entrance of the Nun river. The firing which shattered the air at Akassa was heard at the Brass vice-consulate and Vice-Consul Harrison guessed that the worst had happened. On Wednesday morning, he saw the return of the warriors. 'Upwards of forty canoes laden with loot, with upwards of 1500 armed men on board passed the Consulate and factories—there was much tom-tomming and firing of guns. All proceeded to Nembe 25 miles from the Consulate.'[2]

Sacrifice to the supreme god of the Ijaw followed the conclusion of the Akassa expedition. Father Bubendorf was an eyewitness of the proceedings, and, according to the account he gave the Commissioner and Consul-General, the Kroo war prisoners were killed and eaten in the carnival. It is also claimed that some fourteen Kroo children were ultimately released by the Brass chiefs because 'their flesh is no [*sic*] sweet so young'. The Brass rulers knew they had some explaining to do, and so they hurriedly wrote to the Vice-Consul to say that they had no quarrel with the Queen or her servants. Sir Claude shortly arrived at Brass and called on the chiefs to surrender to the government or be declared outlaws. He blamed them for taking the law into their own hands. King Koko replied thus: 'At first we were encouraged by you to be patient.

[1] See F.O. 2/83, no. 9, Macdonald to F.O., 21 February 1895 and Enclosures.
[2] *Ibid*. See also Kirk's Report, *Parl. Papers*, Africa, no. 3 [C. 7977].

But in your last visit here you said in the meeting that you have nothing to do on the Niger Company's matter again. Better to die on their guns and sords [*sic*] than starvation.' Koko's case was that the attack on Akassa was no more than a reprisal for the injuries Brass men had suffered at the hands of the company whose agents killed and plundered even innocent provision sellers. 'If the Queen of England was acting in like manner as the Niger Company, the whole of Africa would have died through starvation.'[1]

Whatever King Koko and his chiefs said in exoneration of their conduct, it was clear to Sir Claude that Brass men had a case to answer. In Britain Goldie, after temporary stupefaction at the news of the Niger, went into the attack. The work of the Brass men was the work of cannibals. The company's workshop and machinery had been destroyed and its stores looted. That was not all; the company's servants had been butchered in cold blood and eaten. In the circumstances, there could be 'no doubt open outrage must be punished'.[2] But while British forces were being assembled at Brass, Sir Claude tried to persuade the Brass chiefs to submit. Kimberley was prepared to accept the conditions that the Brass chiefs should pay a fine, surrender their canoes and guns, and restore the company's property in their possession. But the Brass chiefs continued to send vacillatory replies to the Consul-General who reluctantly came to the conclusion that a punitive expedition was inevitable. Goldie did everything to exploit the fact that the protectorate administration had shown little humanity in the deportation of Jaja of Opobo. His accusation that Macdonald was being hypocritical in his efforts to find a peaceful settlement of the Akassa crisis is, however, unfair. The men Goldie should have charged with hypocrisy were the officials of the British Foreign Office who approved the deportation of Jaja as a monopolist and then turned a blind eye to the iniquities of Goldie's company.[3]

The punitive expedition against Brass was led by Rear-Admiral Bedford. A few days were spent surveying the approaches to Fish Town and Nembe. Even while the reconnoitring was going on, Sir Claude persisted in his efforts to persuade the rulers of Brass

[1] F.O. 2/83, Enclosure 4 in no. 9, Macdonald to F.O., 4 February 1895.
[2] F.O. 83/1374, see Minute by Kimberley on Goldie to Kimberley, 8 February 1895.
[3] See F.O. 2/83, Macdonald to Hill, 26 March 1895.

to accept Kimberley's terms for a peaceful settlement. King Koko temporised, but there was evidence that defensive stockades were being erected at Nembe by Brass warriors. There was therefore nothing left but to order a mass attack on the Brass villages. The news that government forces were approaching plunged the villages into considerable excitement. According to local records, war songs were chanted and people encouraged one another by recalling that the Brass god of war was always there in an emergency. Was this god not already incarnated in King Koko under whose leadership Brass had only recently struck effectively at the persecutors of women, children and peaceful traders? A fleet of armed canoes sallied forth from Nembe to take the offensive. As the Ijaw did not seem to believe in the value of taking the enemy by surprise, the advance of their fleet was accompanied with tom-toms and conspicuously displayed flags. There is no mention of a naval battle in the official accounts of the Nembe expedition, but local traditions insist that a brisk naval encounter with the protectorate vessels took place.[1]

The main attack on Nembe was made on 25 February. Fish Town was occupied but was found deserted. It was burnt down. On the following day the town of Twon, where the houses of the chiefs were, was razed to the ground. On Macdonald's instructions, the houses and plantations of the ordinary people were left intact. On the whole, Brass warriors and their leaders did not accept defeat lying down. Every chief's house had been turned into a stronghold and in some cases the chiefs stood fighting until they were shot down. After the capture of Nembe, the Brass men did not capitulate but withdrew to continue resistance in the surrounding bush. Rear-Admiral Bedford and Macdonald thought that sufficient punishment had been inflicted on the 'rebels' and ordered a general withdrawal of the protectorate forces.[2] The next phase of the struggle was one of diplomacy. Macdonald attempted to isolate King Koko. He wrote to the chiefs of Nembe to the effect that the government was prepared to accept reparation, without inflicting further punishment on the people of Nembe, but he

[1] Alagoa, J., unpublished MS, 'The Small Brave City-State' (a history of Nembe).
[2] F.O. 2/83, no. 11, Macdonald to F.O., 28 February 1895.

excluded King Koko '...for whose capture alive I offer a reward of £200. This chief I have ascertained has been the leading spirit in this movement.' Macdonald concluded his condemnation of King Koko with the obviously false statement that the king had not used the subsidy he received for opening new markets.[1] The movement which the king led was the direct result of the inability of Brass men to find new markets in place of the old ones.

The Consul-General's policy of demanding reparation without further bloodshed was condemned by Goldie as a capitulation to cannibals. The Foreign Secretary, Kimberley, declared that he was not particularly pleased with the way Macdonald was treating the whole affair. Thus, in spite of the fact that Brass women and children were starving in the bush and that an outbreak of small-pox was decimating the local population, the Foreign Office insisted that Brass men must surrender their guns. Macdonald's humanity shines out in a private letter to one of the officials of the Foreign Office:

Just got the Foreign Office telegram saying I must make the Brass men disgorge their rifles—more joy! I start tomorrow with that intention. Jaja was deported...because he was a big monopolist...now we have wiped the floor with the Brass men because they have endeavoured to go for the biggest monopolist of the crowd—the Royal Niger Company. As I dare say you are aware, in the vast territories of the Niger Company there is not one single outside trader, black, white, green or yellow. The markets are all theirs. They can open and shut any given market at will, which means subsistence or starvation to the native inhabitants of the place. They can offer any price they like to the Producers, and the latter must either take it or starve. And why, in heaven's name, why? Because they must pay 6 or 7 percent to shareholders.[2]

In his next dispatch which took the form of a telegram, Macdonald gave a full picture of the condition of desolation to which Brass and her people were reduced. '...towns are destroyed, trade almost ruined, women and children starving in the bush; hundreds have been killed; small-pox has been raging; the rainy season is beginning. I have seen all this and visited the town destroyed. I most strongly deprecate further punishment in the

[1] *Ibid.* no. 1, 28 February 1895.
[2] F.O. 2/83, Macdonald to Hill (private), 26 March 1895.

name of humanity....'[1] There were people too who began to ask awkward questions in Parliament. Macdonald's humanity and the pressure from British members of Parliament triumphed when the British government decided to appoint a Commissioner to investigate the grievances of Brass men.[2]

In Brass, the work of pacification proceeded quietly. The chiefs of Brass were willing to co-operate with the Consul-General, especially after it was announced that the British government was at last prepared to investigate their grievances against the Royal Niger Company. The fine imposed on Brass was assessed at about £500 and the Consul-General explained that this amount was compensation to be paid to the dependants of the Akassa victims of the Brass attack on the company's station. The people surrendered their war canoes and what was left of the plunder carried away from Akassa. Macdonald was suspected in the Foreign Office of attempting to soft-pedal the grievous sin of cannibalism in which the Brass men had indulged after their exploit. It was no justification that this practice of eating human beings was in existence 'from time immemorial'.[3]

The man chosen by the British government to investigate the circumstances leading to the Akassa raid by Brass men was Sir John Kirk, a former Consul-General at Zanzibar. In that capacity, he had achieved considerable reputation both for his fight against the Slave Trade and for his advocacy of British interests against the encroachments of Germany. Sir John was therefore in a way a humanitarian and an imperialist, and his main recommendation was the belief of the British government that he would be impartial in his new role as Commissioner. Sir John Kirk's assignment was by no means an easy one. There were charges and counter-charges which had to be unravelled. The most constructive part of the instructions issued by the British government concerned the desirability of producing a scheme for the joint collection of custom duties by the Royal Niger Company and the Niger Coast protectorate administration. As the draft instructions went from one department to another, it became increasingly clear that the British

---

[1] F.O. 2/86, Macdonald to F.O. (telegram), 9 April 1895.
[2] *Ibid.* Kimberley to F.O. (telegram), 10 April 1895.
[3] F.O. 2/100, Macdonald to F.O., 1 May 1895.

government attached considerable importance to the outcome of Kirk's inquiry.[1]

Sir John Kirk arrived in the Oil Rivers on 8 June, and before the end of the month his investigations were completed. The details of his findings and recommendations do not serve any purpose in this study because they had no immediate influence on the course of events in the Niger Coast protectorate. The Liberal ministry which sent out the Commissioner lost office before the Commissioner's recommendations could be implemented. The new Colonial Secretary, Joseph Chamberlain, had his own ideas about how British 'undeveloped estates' should be run. Anyway, Sir John Kirk thought that Brass men had a legitimate grievance against the Royal Niger Company, but since the company's regulations were theoretically approved by the British government, the Royal Niger Company might be exonerated. If there was anyone to blame for the whole affair, it was the British government. In the interest of peaceful co-existence, Kirk recommended 'a common tariff and a common arms law throughout the whole maritime zone that will do away with all inland customs frontiers'. The effect of this recommendation would have been the abolition of the Royal Niger Company's iniquitous licensing system, and the coast traders of Brass might have secured their traditional inland markets.[2] As pointed out above, nothing of significance materialised from Kirk's efforts. The Brass question, in fact, remained unsettled except that the Niger Coast protectorate administration paid the Niger Company compensation amounting to a sum just over £20,000.[3] The local agents of the company were chastened enough to be willing to undertake limited local negotiations for the benefit of Brass.

Sir Claude Macdonald's handling of the Akassa crisis did him great credit. It was not easy to defend plunder and cannibalism on the part of the Brass king and chiefs, but the Consul-General knew only too well that the offenders had reached the limits of human patience and endurance. Macdonald's humanity recognised too that there was a limit to the punishment which could

[1] F.O. 83/1378, Minutes and Draft Instructions to Kirk, 6 May 1895.
[2] F.O. 83/1383, Kirk to F.O., 12 September 1895. See also Flint, *op. cit.* pp. 209–12.
[3] Paid in November 1897.

indiscriminately be inflicted on a whole community of men, women and children. He had, however, hardly completed the task imposed on him by the Akassa crisis when it came to his notice that the British commercial combines engaged in business in the Niger were once again entertaining political designs on the Niger Districts and the neighbourhood. Sir Alfred Jones of the African Steamship and the British and African Steamship Companies, John Holt of the African Association, and Sir George Goldie held several meetings with the view to forming a 'Trinity' capable of directing the administrative, commercial and shipping affairs of the whole of the Niger region. The administrative branch was to be under Goldie in London; commercial affairs would be directed by John Holt, and Alfred Jones was to be the undisputed head of all the shipping interests of the 'Trinity'.[1] A more colossal and all-embracing monopoly had hardly ever before been conceived. Goldie and his associates probably thought that the British government would enthusiastically accept a plan which not only saved it the problems of finance but also seemed to bring about the consolidation of British interests in the most profitable part of West Africa.

Sir Alfred Jones revealed the plan to Sir Claude Macdonald, probably because the latter was to be offered an enticing position as Governor of the territories embraced in the new scheme. Macdonald's reaction was immediate. He reported to the Foreign Office what he called 'these unholy designs', and concluded with a strong recommendation that these designs ought not to be countenanced. The Foreign Office entirely agreed with Macdonald's views. Sir H. Anderson, the head of the African Department, who had been particularly anxious in the years between 1886 and 1889 to secure company administration for the Niger territories, endorsed Macdonald's condemnation of the 'Trinity' and added that 'Sir George [Goldie] must know that he was talking nonsense'.[2] The frustration of the attempt by British business interests to control the future political destiny of the peoples of Southern Nigeria was indeed one of the most important services which did credit to Sir Claude's humanity and sense of fair-play. And it was,

[1] F.O. 83/1385, R.N.C. to F.O., 5 November 1895.
[2] F.O. 2/85, Confidential Memorandum by Macdonald, 8 November 1895. See also minute by Anderson.

too, no small achievement, from the British standpoint, that the first Commissioner and Consul-General virtually consolidated British rule on the Nigerian coast and made plans for the peaceful extension of this rule to the hinterland. The punitive expeditions against Nana and then against Brass were clearly not of Macdonald's making.

Before Sir Claude Macdonald left the Niger Coast protectorate at the end of 1895, he planned the administrative reorganisation of the protectorate.[1] His scheme envisaged the division of the region into three districts. Each district was to be under a consular officer, who in turn would be assisted by district commissioners and assistant district commissioners:

(*a*) Eastern Headquarters district embraced the Cross, the Calabar and the Qua-Eboe rivers.

(*b*) The Central district consisted of the Opobo, Bonny, New Calabar and Brass vice-consulates.

(*c*) The Western districts comprised the vice-consulates of Warri and Sapele, that is, the portion of the protectorate west of the Niger delta.

It should be obvious that the new pattern of administrative control involved the elimination of the separate identity of the traditional coast states, and was in fact the beginning of the artificial division of the territory into administrative units which cut across the traditional groupings of the various communities. It was the first step towards the amalgamation of the many groups in the region to produce a politico-territorial unit called Southern Nigeria. In 1895, however, much remained to be done to incorporate the hinterland.

While the British administration was imposing a new administrative pattern, the Consul-General attempted to preserve a measure of local identity in his institutions of local government. In each coast city-state a native council was constituted. The idea was presumably to reincarnate the traditional council of 'Heads of Houses' and give them both judicial and legislative powers to deal with what Macdonald called 'native affairs'. The native councils were expected to settle internal disputes in accordance with native law and custom, subject to the supervisory powers of the consular

[1] F.O. 2/85, Macdonald to F.O., 19 December 1895.

175

courts. The existence of the consular courts naturally meant that the native councils could never be an adequate substitute for the former independence of the city-states. The records of the proceedings of the councils show that the powers and the influence of the native councils were indeed derived from the representatives of British rule rather than from the consent of the people. There was the further disability that the British vice-consuls could not resist the temptation to recommend the chiefs for the membership of the native councils because the chiefs were friendly to the government and not because they held traditional authority. The later exclusion of King Koko from the Brass native council clearly illustrates the point. Lastly, the establishment at Old Calabar of a high court of the native councils under the presidency of the Consul-General was hardly in harmony with the antecedents of the coast city-states, but rather formed part of the new policy of administrative centralisation.[1]

Sir Claude Macdonald undoubtedly merited his elevation at the beginning of 1896 to the status of British Minister to China.[2] He had made a complete success of his task of imposing alien rule on the Nigerian coast with minimum friction. For this he possessed

[1] For regulations setting out the constitution of the native councils and minor courts, and statistics of criminal and civil cases, see F.O. 2/84, Macdonald to F.O. and enclosures, 12 July 1895.

[2] January 1896, British Minister at Peking. His term of office covered four critical years in the history of China. The China-Japanese war of 1894 had revealed to the world the military weakness of China, and European imperialism lost no time in exploiting the situation. Macdonald secured for England the leases of Wei Hai Wei and the Hong Kong extension. So successfully did Macdonald wage the 'battle of concessions' that the powers accepted the non-alienation of the Yangtse region, railway concessions to Britain, and the appointment of an Englishman as the Inspector-General of customs. For these successes, Macdonald earned the congratulations of Lord Salisbury, and the K.C.B. in 1898.

During the 'Boxer risings' of 1900, Macdonald was chosen by his European colleagues to assume command of the beleaguered legations which withstood Chinese assaults for many weeks. More decorations were showered on the British Minister, the G.C.M.G. in 1900, and the military K.C.B. in 1901.

In 1900 Macdonald was transferred to Tokyo, where in 1905 he was elevated to the rank of Ambassador. He took part in the negotiation of the Anglo-Japanese alliance of 1902, and his presence in Tokyo was invaluable to Britain during the Russo-Japanese war. Under Macdonald's auspices, the Anglo-Japanese treaty was renewed in 1905 and 1911. He was awarded the G.C.V.O., and in 1906 was sworn in as a privy councillor.

Macdonald retired from the diplomatic service in 1912, and died in London on 10 September 1915. (See the *Dictionary of National Biography*.)

the temperament, the tact and the patience. It was his conviction that British rule had but one justification—the improvement of the social and material conditions of the ruled. Profits for British interests were not synonymous with the interests of the communities whose independence British rule superseded. Macdonald was fully aware of the obstacles to the peaceful and complete imposition of a new order. Thus, although he entertained natural repugnance to the prevalence of what aliens called fetish practices and domestic slavery, yet he was convinced that 'all peaceful means should be tried before resorting to force'.[1] He was always prepared to champion the just claims of the inhabitants against the ambitions of his own countrymen. Herein lay his interpretation of British protection. A study of his career in the Niger Coast protectorate may well close with a reference to his great sympathy for the grievances of the people of Brass: 'It has been my unpleasant duty to listen to their grievances for the last three years and a half without being able to gain for them any redress.'[2]

[1] F.O. 2/85, Macdonald's comments on Moor's despatch, 12 September 1895, before the attack on Nana's town of Ebrohemie.

[2] F.O. 2/83, no. 9, Macdonald to F.O., 4 February 1895, before the British expedition against Brass.

# CHAPTER VI

# THE OVERTHROW OF INDIGENOUS AUTHORITY: SECOND PHASE, 1896–1906

The new head of the Niger Coast protectorate administration, Ralph Moor, was the officer who came out at his own expense to the protectorate in 1891 to organise the protectorate constabulary. He was undoubtedly very energetic and within a year he rose to be Sir Claude Macdonald's chief lieutenant and acted as Commissioner and Consul-General during the absence of his chief in 1892 and 1894. On these grounds, Moor seemed an obvious choice for the top post in the administration when it was known that Sir Claude was about to leave the Niger Coast for China. In fact, it was Macdonald himself who recommended to the Foreign Office that Ralph Moor should be his successor, and the Foreign Office which consistently regarded the Niger Coast protectorate administration as Macdonald's 'one-man show'[1] naturally accepted his nominee.

It is, however, surprising that Sir Claude should have recommended an officer whose temperament was diametrically opposed to his own for the delicate and complex task of extending British rule to the hinterland. Moor's lack of patience and his eagerness for quick results were hardly in accord with Macdonald's conviction that '...to advance slowly...to gain the respect and liking of the natives...are the means which...lead to success in Africa'.[2] During the latter part of 1895 when Nana's relations with the protectorate administration deteriorated, Macdonald, who was on leave in Britain, urged pacific measures whilst his deputy, Moor, argued against any further delay in coercing the local chief. The result of Moor's policy towards Nana was the first large-scale

---

[1] F.O. 84/2194, Macdonald to F.O., 20 May 1892, see Minutes by Lister and Salisbury.

[2] *Nigerian Pamphlets*, no. 5, Macdonald's speech already cited.

military operation in the Niger Coast protectorate. At about the same time, Ralph Moor conducted an expedition up the Cross river, where Roger Casement's visit in the previous year had revealed that the problems confronting the administration in that region concerned petty local squabbles between town and town. Moor's solution of these problems took the form of shelling and destroying Ediba, the chief town of the Ikomoruts, shelling and destroying Obubura, and sending threatening messages to Afikpo, the chiefs of which had pleaded that they were frightened of the white man. In a private letter to Macdonald, Moor once again emphasised his dedication to the method of coercion. 'We want the men here as Afikpo will have to be smashed, I fear, directly I get down from the Rapids—they are not wheeling into line.'[1]

The Foreign Office reaction to the reports forwarded by Moor, as Macdonald's deputy, is interesting in view of the Foreign Office's uncritical acceptance of Macdonald's recommendation that Ralph Moor should succeed him. The shelling and destruction of towns along the Upper Cross river alarmed the head of the African Department who observed that 'it is unfortunate that most of the expeditions are marked by shelling and burning'.[2] Macdonald agreed with the Foreign Office official, and proceeded to enumerate the qualities of patience and tact which the Niger Coast protectorate officials ought to possess in order to win the confidence of the local inhabitants and obviate the irony of establishing British protection by means of force. Lastly, in view of the later large-scale military attack on Benin, it is significant that Moor, as Macdonald's deputy, already harboured hostile designs against the ruler of Benin. In another private letter to Macdonald, Moor confessed that 'should we succeed in getting an invitation, [we] will take full advantage of it and act like soapy sponge— once we get in he'll find it hard to get rid of us again'.[3]

As already pointed out, Macdonald's choice of Moor as his successor was politically unfortunate. The programme for hinterland penetration was already outlined by Macdonald. The scattered

---

[1] F.O. 2/84, Moor to F.O., 11 September 1895, Encl. Private letter to Macdonald.

[2] F.O. 2/85, Moor to F.O., 26 October 1895, Minutes by Sir Charles Lloyd Hill. Also Macdonald's observations dated 29 October 1895.

[3] *Ibid.* Moor to Macdonald—private letter dated 9 October 1895.

vice-consulates originally established in the main coast city-states were in 1895 regrouped under three large districts—the eastern, the central and the western. Calabar, the headquarters, was to be the spring-board for the incorporation of the Upper Cross river and Qua-Eboe territories and peoples. In the central district, Okrika and Akwette in the immediate hinterland of Bonny and Opobo marked the approaches to the Ibo country. In the western district of Warri and Sapele, the kingdom of Benin was to be the major objective. As already mentioned, it is obviously a matter of speculation what Macdonald might have done if he had had to implement his own programme, but it is not without significance that he attached great importance to treaty-making, and for this purpose he was prepared to ignore the ridicule of Foreign Office officials and ask for as many as 500 treaty forms for Iboland alone. There is also no doubt that Macdonald regarded goodwill as a more effective weapon for expanding British authority than coercion. However, Ralph Moor became the Commissioner and Consul-General of the Niger coast protectorate in January 1896 and it became his responsibility to carry out the policy of extending British rule to the hinterland west and east of the Lower Niger.

The inauguration of Moor's regime saw the tightening of Foreign Office control over the Niger Coast protectorate especially in matters of finance. For the first time, the estimates for the year 1896 had to be submitted to the Foreign Office and the allocation of revenue was scrutinised before being approved. It was in the process of scrutinising the way the protectorate administration proposed to use its revenue that the Foreign Office African Department picked out the item of £1000 which appeared under Public Works recurrent and issued what amounted to a directive to the Consul-General. 'Attention should now be paid to further development of trade with the interior, which will best be effected by gaining the confidence of the natives. His Lordship would be glad to learn what steps are being taken in this direction.... The item of £1,000...is understood to be for making roads and other means of communication with the interior, and is therefore sanctioned.'[1]

Another evidence of increasing Foreign Office control was

[1] F.O. 2/99, F.O. Despatch no. 19, dated 5 March 1896.

connected with the appointment of J. R. Phillips as Deputy Commissioner, in which capacity he ranked next to the Consul-General. Ralph Moor's own choice for the position was H. L. Gallwey, who had done a great deal of pioneer work in the western district, including an alleged treaty with the king of Benin and the foundation of the township of Sapele. Ralph Moor was, however, overruled by the Foreign Office and his choice was cancelled.[1] Apparently the administration of the Niger Coast protectorate was ceasing to be 'a one-man show', but it would be wrong to assume that what did in fact happen in the protectorate was the result of directives issued from the Foreign Office. As in the days of Macdonald, the temper and convictions of the Consul-General continued to determine the character of British policy towards the groups with which British rule came into contact. Military expeditions dominated the history of the period 1896–1906 because Ralph Moor believed in the efficacy of punitive expeditions, and whatever the views of the Foreign Office officials, the local administration organised and carried through one expedition after another.

Ralph Moor's first year of office as Commissioner and Consul-General involved him in three main problems. In the first place, the crisis provoked by the Brass attack on Akassa and the recommendations of the Kirk Commission left things which had to be tidied up in the neighbourhood of the Brass hinterland. Then there was the perennial question of uninterrupted trade on the upper reaches of the Cross river. Lastly, the immediate hinterland of Bonny and Opobo had to be consolidated before any attempts could be made for the extension of British rule to Iboland. In dealing with these problems, Ralph Moor's methods and convictions revealed themselves. The Brass king, Koko, and his chiefs naturally expected that as a result of the Kirk inquiry, there would be considerable amelioration of their sufferings at the hands of the Royal Niger Company. In March, Moor held meetings with Sir George Goldie in an attempt to secure concessions for Brass traders. What the Consul-General was able to get out of the negotiations hardly satisfied the legitimate needs of Brass trade.

---

[1] *Ibid.* F.O. Draft, 6 June 1896. See also F.O. 2/100, no. 21, Moor to F.O., dated 25 March 1896.

The Ekole creek and the creeks connecting it with the Niger were to be open to Brass traders to within one mile of the Niger. The Brass king refused to accept that he had gone to war and been subjected to a long blockade by British troops just for this concession. Ralph Moor ought, too, to have recognised the inadequacy of the concession which he secured on behalf of Brass traders. Instead he chose to misinterpret the dissatisfaction of the local king. 'I do not consider the present attitude of the king and the majority of the chiefs with regard to the government such as to render it advisable that any assistance or concession be made to them.'[1] Moor went on to argue that King Koko deliberately declined all intercourse with the white man because he wished to retain his power as Juju-man and to pose as the absolute ruler of his country. In constituting a 'Native' Council for the Brass city-state, Moor ignored the king of Brass and selected chiefs who he believed were friendly to the government.

As regards the Upper Cross river, Moor was personally acquainted with the nature of the resistance against the new order which British rule symbolised. In 1895 he led a shelling and burning expedition against Ediba and other towns. In 1896 Moor was yet not convinced of the futility of shelling and burning towns. Therefore he approved another military expedition to the Upper Cross river. It would of course be wrong to suggest that the problems which confronted the administration in the region were easy to solve. Beyond Itu, both banks of the Cross river were occupied by towns belonging to different tribes, and these towns acknowledged no sovereignty outside their own bounds. Nevertheless, the Scottish missionaries stationed in Old Calabar were already doing excellent work in many of these towns, and what the government should obviously have done was to win the confidence of the rulers and persuade them that free trade along the Cross river was ultimately in their own interest. In the long run such a policy proved successful, but in 1896 Moor prescribed military methods. In February a force of 180 men of the Niger protectorate force under Captains Roupell and Cockburn made its way to Uwet and then to Ediba. The latter place was again shelled. Having had their principal town destroyed, the chiefs of

[1] F.O. 2/100, no. 18, Moor to F.O., 13 March 1896.

182

the Ikomorut were 'persuaded' to sign treaties of protection with the British. Treaties signed in the wake of shelling and confusion were of course not the best means of winning the confidence of the local rulers in the new administration.[1]

In the central district of the protectorate, Moor's immediate problems concerned two towns in the hinterland of Bonny and Opobo, Okrika and Akwette. As far back as 1892 Sir Claude Macdonald had persuaded the ruler of Akwette to accept a treaty with Britain and to pay a fine for alleged cannibalism. In due course a native political agent was stationed there with material for the erection of a small house. The native agent did not last long there because he was expelled by the Okrika chiefs, and in addition the material for a government house was thrown into the river. Early in 1896 reports reached Ralph Moor that human sacrifices had occurred in Okrika. As was to be expected, Moor proceeded to Okrika but, unlike Macdonald before him, he issued threats to the Okrika chiefs and left for Bonny to prepare for a punitive expedition against the town. The expedition launched on 2 June was accompanied by Moor, Gallwey and the local vice-consul, and comprised 105 officers and men of the protectorate constabulary. In the emergency which the arrival of troops created in Okrika, the king and the chiefs expressed their willingness to 'palaver' with the Consul-General. The latter's treatment of Okrika justified without question the alarming reports of the doings of the white man which did so much to retard what the British called the pacification of the hinterland. The king of Okrika and a priest described as 'the big juju man' were removed to Degema. According to Moor, this action was taken 'with the assent of the chiefs'. The juju houses in the town were burnt down, and a fine of £50 was imposed on Okrika for these 'services' by the troops. A 'Native' Council was set up which excluded the king of Okrika, but each chief selected was given a warrant of membership.[2]

While Moor was busy with the affairs of Okrika, a consular agent, Harcourt, 'toured' another peripheral area of the Ibo country. Accompanied by a force of fifty rank and file,

[1] In reporting these proceedings, Moor recognised the value of using native agents, in this case Chief Coco Bassey, who attempted to arrange 'palavers' as the best means of getting at the local view of the problems.
[2] F.O. 2/101, no. 51, 2 June 1896.

A. B. Harcourt held meetings at Akwette, Ohambele and Obegu. These proceedings were peaceful enough. The vice-consul received reports to the effect that the 'king' of the Ngwa was ready to assist the government in his part of Iboland. The only unsatisfactory incident was the refusal of the rulers of Obohia to have any dealings with the white man. Moor's immediate reaction was to authorise a punitive expedition against the town. Under Captain Roupell, 120 troops were dispatched. 'The place was occupied for four hours, the houses burnt, a certain number of coco-nut trees cut down, and a quantity of loot taken by the soldiers consisting chiefly of cloth, goat, fowls and manillas....'[1] The Consul-General indicated no disapproval of this hardly disguised brigandage.

The extraordinary thing was that while Ralph Moor was compiling the reports of the punitive expeditions launched by him or with his approval, he had before him a dispatch from the British Foreign Office in which Lord Salisbury asked for the specific steps which the Consul-General proposed to take in extending the Niger Coast protectorate. The Foreign Office document attached great importance to winning the goodwill and confidence of the local inhabitants to whose country British rule was being extended. In an attempt to answer Lord Salisbury's question, Ralph Moor committed himself to a number of measures which he claimed constituted his political programme:

(a) Small peaceful expeditions to explain the aims of the government and to open up friendly relations.

(b) The organisation of a native council of chiefs in all towns which accorded a friendly reception.

(c) Surveys with the view to determining the best directions for roads to the interior—with the resources of the area specially in mind.

(d) Treaties of peace and friendship but also the punishment of offending towns where accessible.

(e) Patrolling the waterways to suppress piracy.

The Consul-General concluded the enunciation of his policy with a lament that 'the "Consul" has been so grossly misrepresented in the past by European traders, native middlemen and

[1] *Ibid.* Despatch no. 38, received at the F.O. 13 June 1896.

others to serve their own ends that his coming is greatly feared by the natives of the interior....'[1]

Comments on Ralph Moor's programme will be interesting, but only a few observations are attempted here. In the first place, Moor's recent activities could not conceivably be described as peaceful expeditions. In the case of Okrika, to obtain the submission of the ruler after a show of force and then to deport him and the principal juju priest were clearly not the best way to obliterate the misrepresentations to which, according to Moor, the Consul had been subjected. The Consul-General was apparently unaware of the fact that the earlier deportations of the powerful coast chiefs including Jaja and Nana had invariably reached the ears of the hinterland communities, many of which had close links with the victims of British intervention. The secret of Sir Claude Macdonald's success was his determination to rule with the goodwill of the coast chiefs and peoples. To secure the same goodwill with respect to the hinterland groups was of course infinitely more difficult, but this should have been Ralph Moor's primary task. He professed to believe this but in practice he relied on shelling and burning villages.[2] There is some truth in his allegation that the middlemen were not anxious to see the hinterland opened to direct commercial intercourse with European firms, the establishment of which was bound to follow the acceptance of British rule. The Cross river region afforded an excellent example of the attitude of the indigenous middlemen. The Efik at the mouth of the Cross river and the Akunakuna at the upper portion of the same river were vigorous commercial communities which for centuries managed to dominate the trade of the Cross river basin. Situated midway between the Efik and the Akunakuna countries were the Umon. The first British attempts to establish political relations with the Umon were frustrated by a kind of whispering campaign conducted by Efik traders against the Consul. In the same manner the Akunakuna did their best to keep the Consul away from the multitude of towns and communities in and around the Aweyong tributary of the Cross river, in order to maintain the

---

[1] *Ibid.* Moor to F.O. no. 50, 14 June 1896.
[2] See F.O. 2/101, no. 80, 24 September 1896. King Ofen of the Npok people in the Qua-Eboe district was sentenced to 7 years' imprisonment because A.D.C. Bedwell alleged that he was greeted with jeers by the Npok people.

integrity of their commercial ascendancy. It is quite likely the Aro pursued a similar policy in respect of Ibo and Ibibioland, but as yet Ralph Moor and his assistants knew nothing about the Aro.

There are two other basic assumptions embodied in Ralph Moor's programme which led to tragic mistakes. The absence of paramount chiefs in the hinterland through whom the people might be persuaded to accept, or submit to, British rule apparently meant that anarchy prevailed, or at best that the people were ruled by wicked juju priests. The removal of the juju priests and the setting up of 'Native' Councils would be the beginning of any kind of government in the area. For this reason, no member of the protectorate administration bothered to attempt the study of the political organisation of the villages visited by the protectorate troops. Furthermore, the apparent isolation of the village communities one from another obscured the fact that vital ritual and defensive links bound the villages into a close fraternity. The shelling and burning of one village was therefore the best way to stiffen the resistance of neighbouring villages. The mistakes of the British pioneer administrators became increasingly obvious after 1900.[1] Meanwhile, the incompetence and the rashness of the vice-consuls and their assistants continued to bedevil the early relations of the officers with the hinterland communities. The following incident recorded by one of these officers is sufficiently revealing.

...found some brute had tried to injure my horse in the night; wound in his neck apparently with a matchet; was simply furious, and arrested the chief of the town and, later, two others, including the owner of the house where the horse stood. Set fire to the place, which at first rather alarmed the Calabar people in the market....Decided to send the two chiefs down to Obubura Hill to learn sense and manners...and throughout the district the horse received the greatest of respect.[2]

During 1896 Consul-General Moor must have recognised that little or no progress had been made towards extending the British protectorate. He therefore attempted to extend the policy of using native political agents initiated by Sir Claude Macdonald in 1893. In the Cross river area, Chief Coco Bassey was the first man who was appointed to this post, and he did excellent work for the

[1] Stopford Green, *Journal of the African Society*, no. 1 (October 1901).
[2] Douglas, *Niger Memories*, cited p. 173—quotes from an official diary. In April 1897 Ralph Moor cancelled Douglas's judicial warrant.

administration. An earlier attempt to appoint a native to Okrika produced no results because the Okrika rulers drove the man out of their city-state. Chief Coco Bassey, on the other hand, accompanied the British officials when they visited places such as towns in the Ikomorut and Ikum districts of the Upper Cross river. The British officers acknowledged that without Bassey's good offices it was unlikely that the chiefs of the towns would have agreed to receive the white men. Coco Bassey did not exactly become an officer of the protectorate government. The free service he offered the British created opportunities for him to do good business as a trader. He used his good sense to disarm native hostility to the government but at the same time he exploited the prestige which his 'familiarity' with the white man gave him in the eyes of the Upper Cross river inhabitants.[1]

In the central division of the protectorate, Cookey Gam, an Opobo chief, and Diko, a New Calabar chief, attempted to emulate Coco Bassey of the Cross river. There is no evidence that either chief made much headway in the Ibo country dominated by Aro influence. In the western division, Chief Dore, who was Nana's Itsekiri opponent and whose loyalty to the British stood out in contrast with Nana's recalcitrance, was the first political agent for the Itsekiri–Urhobo territory. His activities were later confined to the Warri district when another agent, Tom Fallodo, was appointed to supervise the affairs of the eastern Urhobo and Kwale countries. According to the official instructions issued to them, their functions consisted in explaining the intentions of the British government to the hinterland communities, encouraging the latter to promote trade, but also in playing the role of spying on the activities of the village communities. The Urhobo country offered both Dore and Fallodo excellent opportunities for rising to the pre-eminence hitherto enjoyed by Chief Nana, except that the new upstarts had the backing of the British vice-consuls and the prestige of the government. Their doings in the hinterland, especially in the case of Fallodo who was a Yoruba, often aroused the suspicions of the

[1] See F.O. 2/51, Macdonald to F.O., 12 October 1893. Coco Bassey died in 1898, and Ralph Moor regretted his passing away. Captain Roupell, in charge of the Cross river, conceded that 'the late Chief Coco Bassey during his lifetime kept these troublesome tribes in order with a wisdom and tact unusual in an African'.

British officials. There were accusations that Fallodo burnt and looted villages in Urhoboland.[1] Chief Dore on the other hand rose in importance and became the first President of the Itsekiri–Urhobo 'Native' Council. There is an interesting episode which throws considerable light on the relations between these native political agents and the Europeans whom they served.

Chief Dore was a neatly dressed man who carried himself with great dignity. He owned an impressive gig which flew the Union Jack. As his position was only semi-official, a number of vice-consuls were tempted to question the propriety of Dore's Union Jack. No action was taken about this because the vice-consuls conceded 'that this unlettered heathen had but to speak the word and a score of creeks would be closed to trade, or a horde of matchet-armed savages let loose to spread murder through the bush'. The same Chief Dore was in a party where British officials and British trading agents were regaling themselves with alcohol. When the party became riotous, Chief Dore quietly withdrew. The explanation vouchsafed by the Kroo steward is significant. 'Headman Dore savvy too much: the Lord give him sense. Suppose get drunk, then tell too much things about his bush to them so-so white man. Suppose trader man light matches on him [Dore's] jacket, then headman's boy dun chop that white man, and too much trouble live, sah.'[2] The whole episode does not indicate a great deal of mutual confidence between the protectorate officials and their semi-official political agent.

There was considerable uncertainty on the part of the vice-consuls as to the exact posture of affairs in the Itsekiri–Urhobo country. The lack of progress in the penetration of British rule was blamed on the machinations of the Royal Niger Company's agents who controlled the Forcados river or on the 'baneful influence' of Benin City. As regards the latter, the views of the vice-consuls were briefly that little could be expected from a region that lay on the fringe of a kingdom of darkness, 'where every kind of fiendish cruelty was rife'. Here was the beginning of the plan to destroy the kingdom of Benin.[3] In the meantime, the Assistant

[1] Political Papers, District Office, Benin, March 1898, pile 16/98.
[2] Bindloss, *op. cit.* pp. 195–6.
[3] F.O. 2/101, no. 50, Moor to F.O., 14 June 1896.

District Commissioners, who did not wish to leave all the touring to Dore and other native political agents, often encountered mixed receptions in the Urhobo villages. In some of these villages, the white man was very welcome and was entertained with dances and songs. He was also often loaded with presents from the chiefs, who took nothing in return because 'the sight of a white man was enough'.[1] In some villages where the rulers believed that the presence of a white man meant an invasion of the acknowledged 'world of the Oba of Benin', the vice-consul was given all kinds of excuses in explanation of the unwillingness of the rulers to accept a treaty. The native political agents blamed their own failure to open new markets in the hinterland on the alleged expectation of reprisals from Benin City. The conclusion was that the ruler of Benin not only forbade his people to trade but was determined to punish villages situated even at the head of the Ethiope river if they traded with the white man or received government officers.

There is indeed no way of verifying the allegation that the Oba of Benin forbade his subjects to trade. Considerable quantities of European goods certainly percolated into Benin, and there was no specific Benin religious taboo against external trade. What seems probable is that the deportation of Nana of the Benin River naturally intensified the suspicions of the Benin ruler and war lords towards the intentions of the white man in regard to Benin territory. In any case, no vice-consul attempted another visit to Benin after Gallwey's triumph in 1892. Sir Claude Macdonald believed that, after the removal of Chief Nana, it was necessary to reassure the chiefs of the coast. No such overtures were made to the ruler regarded as Nana's overlord. In fact, the protectorate officials began in 1895 to nurse plans for the overthrow of the kingdom of Benin. Ralph Moor, in a private letter to Macdonald already mentioned earlier in this chapter, confided that if he ever got into Benin he would 'act like soapy sponge'. Then as soon as Ralph Moor became the effective head of the protectorate administration, practically every report on the western district ended with one charge or another against the ruler of Benin.[2]

In October 1896 J. R. Phillips arrived to deputise for Ralph

[1] *Ibid.* no. 58, Moor to F.O., 18 July 1896.
[2] *Ibid.*

Moor who was home on leave. The new officer was hardly a month in the protectorate when he decided that the time had come to deal with Benin. In view of the one-sided British accounts of the events leading to the Benin disaster, it is necessary to trace all available evidence touching on British–Benin relations in 1896 and 1897. In November Phillips addressed the following letter to Lord Salisbury: 'I...ask His Lordship's permission to visit Benin City in February next, to depose and remove the king of Benin, and to establish a Native Council in his place and take such further steps for the opening up of the country as the occasion may require... but in order to obviate any danger I wish to take a sufficient armed force consisting of 250 troops, 2 7-pounder guns etc....'[1] To strengthen his plea for action against Benin, Acting Consul-General Phillips forwarded to the Foreign Office a letter from the local representative of Miller Brothers, James Brownridge. Part of this letter conveyed the information that 'so long as the King of Benin is allowed to carry on as he is doing at present, it means simply losses to the merchants, native Itsekiri trade as also the Protectorate'.[2] The Foreign Office passed on to Ralph Moor all the dispatches on Benin and called for his comments on them. Ralph Moor was not the man to miss any opportunity which lent itself to his advocacy of what he called a 'forward policy'. Therefore he vigorously argued for the immediate overthrow of the Benin ruler. '...further pacific measures are quite useless and only likely to damage the prestige of the Government with all the surrounding native tribes.'[3]

Ironically, Ralph Moor shortly afterwards forwarded another letter to the Foreign Office in which he conveyed the news from the coast that a protectorate official had successfully made his way to Bende in the Ibo hinterland without having to call on the troops. It is therefore baffling that the Foreign Office did not recommend a peaceful mission to Benin. What the department did was, in advising against the immediate undertaking of a military expedition against Benin, to point out to Phillips that the Niger Coast force could not be reinforced with troops from Lagos and the Gold

[1] F.O. 2/102, Phillips to Lord Salisbury, 24 November 1896.
[2] *Ibid.* Enclosure, Brownridge to Miller Brothers, Liverpool.
[3] F.O. 2/120, Moor's letter to F.O. dated 26 December 1896. See also another letter, dated 29 December 1896.

Coast because these forces were at the time preoccupied with the campaign against Ashanti. One conclusion is therefore inescapable. The British Foreign Office, Ralph Moor and his deputy in the protectorate were all committed in principle to war against the ruler of Benin.[1]

The events which occurred between January 1897 and the ambush of Phillips' party on its way to Benin expose Phillips to a serious charge of stupid obstinacy. When the Acting Consul-General could not obtain the troops for the deportation of the king of Benin, he changed his mind about the kind of approach he proposed to make to Benin. He was now prepared to take a small party including protectorate officials—Copland Crawford, Locke, Campbell, Captain Boisragon, Maling and Dr Elliot; European merchants—Powis (Miller Brothers) and Gordon (African Association); a Gold Coast chief clerk, a storekeeper, two interpreters, a dozen officers' servants and 220 Itsekiri and Kroo carriers.[2] Phillips also intended to take the band of the protectorate force but was prevailed upon to leave the band behind because any fanfare might give the journey the appearance of a military expedition. When the consular party reached Gwato on the Ikpoba creek, Chief Dore Numa, the native political agent, entreated Phillips to postpone his visit to Benin because the king of Benin was performing religious rites, or as Dore said 'making country custom', which did not permit the presence of foreigners. To admit foreigners was an abomination in the eyes of the indigenous ruler and priests. The Acting Consul-General ignored Dore's advice, but had the good sense to dispatch only messengers and presents to the king of Benin. The latter acknowledged the receipt of the presents and expressed good-humoured surprise at often getting presents purporting to come from the Queen of England. He also expressed disappointment at never having received any acknowledgements from the same Queen to whom he had sent presents. The Benin king concluded by promising to receive the consular party at a later date when he had completed the ceremonies in which he was engaged. Further, he was also thinking of sending a

[1] *Ibid.* F.O. Despatch, December 1896—see also Minutes by Chief Clerk Dallas on Moor's no. 13 of 8 February 1897 in F.O. 2/121. For typical British views see Burns, pp. 163–4; Geary, p. 114.

[2] F.O. 2/121, Gallwey to F.O. no. 1, 16 January 1897.

deputation to the Queen of England as a mark of the friendship between the 'two sole rulers of the world'.[1]

The Acting Consul-General's view was probably that the king of Benin was indulging in vacillation and merely putting off the day of reckoning. The free trade promised in the treaty of 1892 was never implemented, and in 1896 the trade between the Itsekiri and Benin was stopped by the Oba. In any case, the British officials and the British merchants had already convinced themselves that whatever it was the Oba of Benin was doing in the seclusion of Benin City was evil and also bad for the trade of that part of the protectorate. Nothing, therefore, could have persuaded Phillips and his party to abandon or postpone the ill-fated mission. The consular party left Gwato for Benin City on 4 January with guides supposed to have been sent by the king. At 4 p.m. the party was ambushed. Two of the protectorate officials, Captain Boisragon and Locke, escaped the tragedy by creeping into the bush. They wandered about for many days till they were rescued by an Ijaw man at a place 20 miles from Gwato. It was only after the most senior British official in the protectorate had interviewed the survivors that the details of the tragedy were learnt at first hand. Gallwey's dispatches dated 16 January and 21 January fully conveyed the gruesome details to the British Foreign Office.[2]

It is not easy to give a coherent account of the events in Benin City itself between the intimation of the proposed visit of the consular party and the ambush. The evidence of witnesses during the later trial of the king of Benin gives a very confused picture of the internal state of affairs. It is, however, enough to show that all was indeed not well. Oba Ovonramwen, who was crowned in 1888, did not succeed to an empire still possessed of its ancient glory and power. The Ishans were virtually in revolt. The Fulani incursions from Nupe were effectively dismembering the Kukuruku part of the empire. In 1896 the Oba was in fact engaged in military preparations for the reduction of Agbor, east of Benin City. Internally, the Benin ruler had apparently lost the firm control which the Oba traditionally had over his titled councillors. According to

---

[1] *Ibid.* Gallwey to F.O. no. 6, 21 January 1897.
[2] F.O. 2/120, Gallwey to F.O. no. 1, 16 January and no. 6, 21 January 1897. Also Boisragon, *The Benin Massacre* (London, 1897), and Bacon, *Benin, The City of Blood* (London, 1897).

one witness at the trial of the Oba in 1897, the Oba was willing to receive the British mission but his chiefs overruled him. It is of course possible that the aim of this witness was to protect his king from the vengeance of the British, by implicating the Iyase and the Ologbosheri. One witness claimed that the king's address to his councillors was something like this: 'If they [the white men] brought war to catch the king, or they came to play with him, the people must allow them to come...since he was born there had not been any white men killed in Benin, so no white man must be killed.'[1] Whether or not the Benin king issued the instruction embodied in the address, the role of the king in the crisis which engulfed his kingdom was not that of a master in his own house.

The report to the Foreign Office from the Niger Coast protectorate clearly indicated the sequel to the massacre of British officials on their way to Benin. The said report concluded that 'the destruction of Benin City, the removal and punishment of the king, the punishment of the fetish priests, the opening up of the country will prove a wonderful impetus to trade in this part of the protectorate, and at the same time do away with a reign of terror and all its accompanying horrors. If not already removed, the ivory at Benin should fully pay the cost of the expedition.'[2] The excuse for a large-scale military expedition into the hinterland was too good a one to be missed by the Commissioner and Consul-General, Ralph Moor. He cut short his leave in England and arrived at the coast on 3 February 1897. Military preparations were set in motion. Before long, an impressive force was concentrated on the Bight of Benin. A naval force included H.M.S. *St George*, *Phoebe*, *Philomel*, *Barrosa*, *Widgeon*, *Alecto* and *Magpie*. This naval force was further strengthened with H.M.S. *Theseus* and *Forte* from the Mediterranean Fleet. A hospital ship, H.M.S. *Malacca*, was expected with British marines. The protectorate force was placed under the command of Lieut.-Col. Hamilton, an officer sent from England. The Supreme Commander was Rear-Admiral Harry H. Rawson, who had arrived on 30 January.

The king of Benin and his chiefs undoubtedly knew what was

---

[1] For the evidence of witnesses at the trial, see Egharevba, *A Short History of Benin* (1960), pp. 56–8.

[2] F.O. 2/120, nos. 1 and 6 already cited.

coming, and so had every opportunity to place the city and its neighbourhood in a state of defence. But what happened? In the old days of Benin glory, the Oba would have had at his command what are best described as feudal levies from his chiefs and provincial representatives. In 1897, faced with the threat of a colossal military expedition against Benin City itself, the Oba showed a complete lack of leadership, blamed the chiefs alleged to have been responsible for the massacre of the consular party, and expected these chiefs to organise the defence of Benin. There is no evidence that the Oba attempted to utilise for defensive purposes the war camp which in 1896 he had built at Obadan for an attack on rebellious Agbor. The one 'positive' proceeding undertaken by the Oba, on the advice of his priests, was the slaughter of many human beings in order to ward off the impending punitive expedition.[1] There was but one exception to this picture of defencelessness on the part of the Oba and his principal chiefs. One Benin warrior rallied his followers and set up a defensive military post at Gwato, the western approach to Benin. It was here that the advancing British marines met with the only opposition encountered in the capture of Benin City.

Benin City is not accessible by any waterway. The Benin river divides into the Gwato and Jamieson rivers some twenty miles from Benin City. From the region of the two rivers, the villages to the north virtually belonged to Benin. Admiral Rawson, the Supreme Commander of the British expedition, divided his forces into three columns. One column was to hold the Gwato and the second took up position along the Jamieson. The protectorate troops and two marine divisions made up the third column which was to be the main attacking column and was concentrated on Warrigi, a point on the river nearest to Benin City and the base of operations. The Supreme Commander did not by any means underestimate the seriousness of his assignment and therefore issued orders of the day not unworthy of the famous battles in history.[2]

The first advance against Benin was made on 11 February 1897.

[1] Egharevba, *op. cit.* p. 52.
[2] F.O. 2/121, no. 13 of 8 February 1897. See Encl. Memo no. 1268 by Rawson.

The protectorate troops formed the spear-head of the advance. Ciri (or Siri) and then Sapoba were captured. On the second day, the village of Ologbo was taken. Subsequently one village after another was occupied; for instance, Ogage and Awoko. Benin City was not only eight miles away, but it was not until the 18 February that a general advance to Benin was ordered. All through the passage of the attacking column, the opposition encountered consisted of stray shots from the surrounding bush. The defence of Benin City itself comprised a stockade on the main road to the city and a rifle pit. These were themselves useless without Benin warriors to man them. In the words of the Commissioner, 'the final effort of the enemy was the discharge of two cannon from a large open space in front of the King's Juju Compounds'.[1] It is doubtful whether this last act of Benin defiance was undertaken on the instruction of the Oba. According to local tradition, the reliability of which cannot be confirmed or denied, the Oba dressed himself in his ceremonial outfit and sat in his palace to await the arrival of the British, but at the last moment he was prevailed upon to flee into the bush.

It is only natural that the British representatives who captured Benin could hardly resist the temptation to paint what they saw in the most macabre colours. According to the Commissioner, Ralph Moor,

the city presented the most appalling sight, particularly around the King's quarters, from which four large main roads lead to the compounds of the bigger chiefs, the city being very scattered. Sacrificial trees in the open spaces still held the corpses of the latest victims—seven in all were counted—and on every path a freshly sacrificed corpse was found lying, apparently placed there to prevent pursuit. One large open space, 200 to 300 yards in length, was strewn with human bones and bodies in all stages of decomposition.[2]

Captain Boisragon did better than the Commissioner. He asserted that the gruesome sights which Moor confined to the neighbourhood of the palace 'were met with all over the city'. It is of course useless denying that human sacrifice constituted the essential rite

[1] *Ibid.* no. 17, Moor to F.O., 24 February 1897. Enclosure—map of the layout of Benin City.
[2] *Ibid.* Also Boisragon, *op. cit.* p. 187.

in Benin religious ceremonies, and that before the British arrival, human beings were butchered in Benin as a defensive measure. Moor and the others had indeed no need to justify the British expedition. The massacre of the Phillips party provided all the excuse that the protectorate government required.

The tendency to exaggerate is also evident in the report of the Supreme Commander on the expedition which captured Benin City. In a reference to the part played by the protectorate troops, Rawson spoke of 'the exceedingly zealous and able manner in which the officers and men of the force have carried out their most arduous and trying duties. Hardly seeing the enemy...and bearing the brunt of the fighting, they have proved themselves a very valuable force....' The Commander did not say what forces were in fact opposing the advance of the British expedition into Benin. There is, however, no doubt that the local British chief was satisfied that the overthrow of the ancient kingdom of Benin opened up great possibilities for the destruction of what was widely believed to be 'a most appalling yoke of Ju-Juism'. The inhabitants ground down for centuries would at last show a desire for improvement. Moor indeed supposed that 'no worse state has ever existed in any country or at any time'.[1] There was no doubt in the Commissioner's mind that Benin citizens and the dependent peoples in the provinces would welcome the overthrow of the kingdom and would flock in to make their submission to the British deliverers. These hopes were destined to be dashed to pieces.

As already mentioned, when the British entered Benin the king and his chiefs had bolted, but the capital lay at the mercy of the British. The Admiral and the marines decided to retire, and Ralph Moor was left to devise a government for Benin City. It was of course intended to capture, without undue delay, the Oba, his chiefs and juju chiefs. In the meantime, the Commissioner left A. H. Turner as political Resident, Dr F. P. Hill as medical officer, and Capt. Roupell as O.C. of 120 troops. These symbolised the new order in Benin City. Before Moor left for Old Calabar, he took a very judicious decision in regard to future relations with the inhabitants of Benin and the neighbourhood. Benin was of course conquered territory, and the Foreign Office saw no objection to the suggestion

[1] Annual Report on the Niger Coast Protectorate, 1896–7, C. 8775, p. 14.

first made by Consul Gallwey that a fine should be levied on the people of Benin. Moor rightly argued that such a fine 'would be detrimental to the gaining of the confidence of the natives'.[1] In any case, it was expedient not to identify British rule with the imposition of hardships on the people and subordinate chiefs of Benin, who might easily be driven into the arms of their king and head chiefs still at large.

For the political Resident and the Commander of the troops stationed at Benin City there were two preoccupations. First, the diabolical influence which the British believed the Oba, even in flight, still had over his subjects must be undermined or exploded. Second, the Oba and the offending chiefs and juju priests must be captured and brought to trial. The second objective could subserve the first. The local British representatives therefore conducted both diplomatic and military warfare. To begin with, Resident Turner conveyed to the chiefs living in the vicinity of Benin the promise of a safe conduct to and from Benin. Eighteen chiefs responded favourably to the appeal and were conducted round the ruins of the Oba's palace. According to Turner, the ruins were 'an object of awe in their eyes'. From the ruins of their ancient ruler's palace, the eighteen chiefs were taken to the residency, which the British intended to be an impressive building. The contrast between the symbol of British power and the extinction of the Oba's authority was driven home. 'This pointed out the power of the white man and stressed a point which the black man had not properly grasped—that the white man had taken the country and meant to remain.'[2] Turner shortly afterwards proclaimed a rule to the effect that any village which did not make a submission during the following month would be considered as hostile to the white man.

Apparently the chiefs in charge of villages in the neighbourhood of Benin were not showing undue anxiety to secure the white man's goodwill by making their submission. The British Resident therefore attempted a direct appeal to the slaves owned by the village chiefs and heads. A new proclamation stipulated that any

[1] F.O. 2/121, Moor to F.O. no. 46, 30 April 1897.
[2] Calprof 8/2 (National Archives, Ibadan), Summary of Events in Benin City, March–April 1897, by Alfred Turner.

slave who arrived before his master to accept British rule would *ipso facto* become a free man. As Turner anticipated, slaves poured in to gain an undreamt-of freedom and the Resident was undoubtedly pleased with the results. He claimed that 'I have already made a large hole in the King's influence by freeing many of his slaves and receiving the submission of over thirty of the King's villages...the chiefs here have made an agreement with me not to lose their present position when the bigger and more important chiefs come in'.[1] The Resident's policy was a very realistic one. Slaves, petty chiefs and village heads were persuaded into having a sort of vested interest in the new political order. But nothing proved more conclusively the collapse of the rule of the Oba in Benin than the ease with which Resident Turner formed a 'Native' Council for Benin City. The Resident recognised with amusement the enthusiasm with which the principal chiefs of Benin, who had not fled or who had fled and returned, intrigued against one another in the 'Native' Council. The Iyasele was reported to have complained to the Resident that 'his master the king now was woman'. Whether or not the Iyasele of Benin was trying to win favour with the new masters, the Resident revealed what he thought of the Benin chief by referring to him as 'Poor Soapy'.[2]

The military aspect of the campaign against the king of Benin and his more resolute chiefs was to be a protracted affair. The capture of these last representatives of the ancient kingdom was more difficult than winning over the mercenary petty chiefs for whom it was enough to 'keep open house here to natives, smile at them all and they now begin to walk in without any sign of fear'— to use the Resident's own words. The military campaign against the fugitive chiefs took the form of dispatching flying columns under Lt.-Col. Hamilton to whatever village rumour alleged to be the hiding place of the Oba. Messages from the British Resident often got through to the king in hiding, and protracted negotiations ensued which, however, yielded no results.

Benin and the neighbourhood had to be governed whether or not the Oba was captured. A beginning had already been made in creating a 'Native' Council for Benin City. In June 1897 the

[1] Calprof 6/1, Turner to Moor, 4 April 1897.
[2] *Ibid.*

Commissioner and Consul-General, Ralph Moor, proposed two kinds of taxes to be levied on the Binis. It will be recalled that in April, he had opposed the policy of taxing Benin. But in June when a large number of chiefs and villages had made their submission to the new rulers, Moor believed it was safe to levy two kinds of taxes. As a matter of fact, he emphasised that his new taxes showed greater humanity than the former policy of the king of Benin. In any case, the country was a conquered one and he anticipated that his taxes would produce 'roughly in the current year about £1000'.[1] The taxes proposed by Moor were (a) a village tax which the chiefs were to collect for the government, and (b) a house tax which the chiefs had to pay in proportion to the number of their houses. With typical caution, the Foreign Office approved the taxes but warned that the officers deputed to enforce the new taxes should watch their effect on the natives very carefully. The caution was not necessary because, as Moor claimed, the country was indeed a conquered one.

Meanwhile, the Royal Niger Company's agents decided not to be outdone in the chase of the king of Benin. A patrol force of the company's constabulary under Lieutenants Carroll and Fitzgerald penetrated into the Benin districts. This 'neighbourly' gesture was duly publicised.[2] The company's agents had not gone into Benin territories solely to help the Niger protectorate administration. The fact was that the collapse of the Benin kingdom and the subsequent dissolution of its hold on the outlying Kukuruku and Ishan villages afforded the Royal Niger Company an opportunity for a scramble for territory. The company's agents distributed treaty forms in the Kukuruku country, the northern portion of the Benin empire—to the disgust of Ralph Moor who considered Benin and her empire as a prize legitimately won by the Niger protectorate administration.[3] The Commissioner's condemnation of the Royal Niger Company was ignored by the Foreign Office, where it was already well known that the powerful Colonial Secretary, Chamberlain, was maturing in his mind plans for the liquidation of the Royal Niger Company as a political factor on the Lower Niger.

[1] F.O. 2/122, Moor to F.O. no. 69, 21 June 1897. Also no. 73, 28 June 1897, and F.O. Draft 136, 29 July 1897.
[2] *The Times* (London), Friday, 9 July 1897.
[3] F.O. 2/122, Moor to F.O. no. 110, 15 September 1897.

The Oba of Benin, the apparent object of the general chase, got tired of incessant flight from one village to another and gave himself up. His arrival back in Benin City naturally caused considerable sensation. According to the Acting Resident's report, 'about five o'clock on the evening of the 6th [August 1897] a loud noise of drumming was heard and I was informed that the King was entering the city by the Sapoba road...'.[1] The king was accompanied by his followers, all unarmed, headed by a man holding aloft a white flag. As the Oba's palace had been burnt down, he and his followers spent the night with a member of the British-created 'Native' Council, Chief Obaseki. On the following day, the king and his entourage made their way to the residency to 'palaver' with the new rulers of Benin.

The Acting Resident could not conceivably have underrated the symbolic importance of the ceremony of submission about to take place. He therefore made sure that there was a large crowd of Binis to witness the humiliation of their Oba. The Oba, on the other hand, had turned up covered with his ceremonial strings of coral and hardly expected so large a crowd and was very agitated. There was no escape and so, supported by two chiefs, the king submitted to the British by rubbing his forehead on the ground three times. The formal trial of the Oba had to await the arrival of the Commissioner and Consul-General from Old Calabar. The officials of the British Foreign Office were not agreed on how the king of Benin and the chiefs were to be treated, but there was no difficulty in arriving at the conclusion that the chiefs directly implicated in the massacre of Consul Phillips' party should be executed.[2] Of these, two committed suicide, two were executed, and two, Ologbosheri and Abohun, continued the 'game' of hide-and-seek.

The trial of the king began on 7 September. The Commissioner and Consul-General had to his right and left the Acting Resident, the Officer Commanding the troops, and the Benin chiefs who were members of the 'Native' Council. There was as large a muster of people as possible. Before this assembly, Ralph Moor made an interesting declaration of policy in regard to Benin. 'Now this is

---

[1] Calprof 6/1, Roupell to Consul-General, 8 August 1897.
[2] F.O. 2/124, see Minutes by Hill and Bertie on Telegram no. 17, 27 March 1897.

the white man's country. There is only one king in the country and that is the white man. The only person therefore to whom service need be shown is the white man....Overami is no longer the king of this country....'[1]

After Ralph Moor's policy declaration, the Oba's formal trial proceedings began. The Commissioner's main concern was to determine the extent of the Oba's complicity in the ambush of Phillips' party. The Oba naturally insisted that he had nothing to do with the massacre. He claimed that he was the friend of the white man, that he had received a vice-consul a few years back with great hospitality, and that on many occasions he had exchanged presents with Queen Victoria. The Oba must have imagined that his last point ought to have created a good impression on his captors. How was he to know that the presents came from the local administration and were no more than a formal preliminary in the process of imperialist advance? Quite clearly, the most humiliating aspect of the Oba's trial was the cross-examination of the Oba's subjects and slaves on the evidence vouchsafed by the Oba. The latter's protestation of innocence was corroborated by other witnesses.[2]

The Commissioner presiding over the trial offered the Oba a choice between a chief's status in Benin City and banishment. If the Oba accepted the former, he would be assigned a number of villages and would accompany the Consul-General on a tour of Old Calabar and Yorubaland to enable the Oba to broaden his mind which, in the view of Ralph Moor, had for so long been shut out in savage isolation from the outside world. Presumably, the Oba suspected that the proposed tour was no more than a diplomatic manœuvre to deport him, like Nana of the Itsekiri river in 1894. On 9 September the Oba failed to appear for the resumed court sitting. It was then realised that the king had absconded and fled for the second time to the bush. The Oba's flight alarmed Ralph Moor, but not the members of the Benin 'Native' Council. The latter naïvely assured the Commissioner that 'Overami will not go to the bush; he has been there before and what is the use of his going back again'. This was precisely what the Oba did—the last

---

[1] F.O. 2/123, Moor to F.O. no. 120, 18 October 1897.
[2] See Egharevba, *op. cit.* pp. 56–8.

heroic gesture of the last independent representative of the long line of kings who had ruled Benin for many centuries. Ovonramwen must, however, have known that flight could not mean permanent escape, and it was not long before he was recaptured and marched back to the 'palaver' house. The Consul-General sentenced him to deportation to Old Calabar.[1]

The details of the ignominy which accompanied the Oba's banishment are fully recorded by Egharevba but the author gives no indication of his sources. Two episodes in the tale of humiliation may be noted. The ex-Oba had to be gagged and strapped to a hammock because he was unable to restrain his grief and resorted to agitated shouts and howls. Also, the Oba reportedly invoked the curse of 'the Spirits of the Binis' on the Benin people 'who ill-advised and cunningly sold me into the hands of the British troops in search of their own liberty and benefit'. The Oba's last words in Benin were: 'Oh! Benin, Merciless and Wicked! Farewell, Farewell.'[2] The overthrow and the deportation of the ruler of Benin were undoubtedly a remarkable step in the attempt to extend British rule from the coast to the hinterland. It was therefore no surprise that Ralph Moor succumbed to the temptation to exaggerate what the administration under his control did in fact achieve. According to him, the British local administration had, as a result of the Benin expedition, freed

a very large population of natives from a most appalling yoke of pagan Ju-Juism, which deadened every feeling of right and crushed out all desire for improvement....It is impossible in a report of this nature to detail the state of oppression in which these people lived and the absolute terror of the fetish and Ju-Ju of the King, but I suppose that no worse state has ever existed in any country or at any time.[3]

It is probable that the British local officials honestly anticipated that the removal of the Oba of Benin would be received with unbounded enthusiasm by the subordinate chiefs in the outlying provinces of the Benin empire. In these areas relations with Benin were anything but uniformly cordial. Nevertheless, the authority

[1] Ovonramwen died in Old Calabar in 1914. His son was recognised as Eweka II of Benin soon afterwards and installed as Oba.
[2] Egharevba, *op. cit.* p. 61.
[3] Africa, no. 3 (1898), C. 8775, Annual Report on the Niger Coast Protectorate for the year 1896–7.

of the Enogies in the Ishan and Kukuruku districts, and that of the Obis in the Ika districts, were derived from the Oba of Benin. The removal of the Oba therefore meant the collapse of the basis of indigenous political structure. The expectation that the Enogies would welcome British intervention did not materialise. The British had to do some pretty hard fighting at the leading Ishan centres of Irrua and Uromi. The administration did not immediately establish contact with the Ika groups, whose territory was largely dominated by the Royal Niger Company from Asaba. Even here, the removal of the Oba of Benin produced considerable disorganisation[1] and laid the foundation for the emergence of the Ekumeku society, the activities of which will be discussed later.

The energies of the protectorate administration of the Niger coast were concentrated in 1897 mainly, but not exclusively, on the western portion of the protectorate. The expedition against Benin City offered opportunities for a spectacular extension of administrative control. Elsewhere, the local officials continued to demonstrate their inability to win the friendship of the inhabitants of the hinterland. Even on the coast, where British authority had already been established for more than a decade, the protectorate officials tended to manipulate the Native Councils to serve their own ends. Any indigenous ruler who refused to become no more than a pliable tool was removed. The situation in the New Calabar district clearly illustrated this policy. King Amachree of New Calabar apparently dominated the Native Council of the district. The other chiefs accepted his leadership and often waited to see what action King Amachree proposed to take. Whatever the latter said, the other chiefs accepted. The kind of leadership exercised by Amachree was inconvenient to the British officials, who nonetheless professed to rule through the indigenous chiefs. The British policy was in fact to form 'Native' Councils of obedient chiefs. King Amachree was therefore removed, and the new members of the New Calabar 'Native' Council included chiefs Young Briggs, Bob Manuel, Reuben Standfast and Jack Braid, all of whom were reported to be willing to give 'every assistance to the Government'.[2]

[1] See Assessment Report by H. N. Newns, quoting from B.P. 16/14, Resident Watt's report, 5 October 1914.
[2] Calprof 8/2, Report on the New Calabar District, 31 March 1897.

The local administrators seemed incapable of realising that the deliberate and often inexcusable overthrow of the recognised rulers on the coast was hardly the best introduction of the new administration to the inhabitants of the hinterland. In the hinterland of New Calabar, British policy in New Calabar itself naturally roused the suspicions of the Isupo and Amaffa groups. The attempts to form a council of chiefs were unavailing. The people of Amaffa refused to have anything to do with the government and warned that they would shoot any Consul who showed his face. The District Commissioner explained in his report on the district that the present attitude of these hinterland peoples was due to the fact that they were 'uncivilised', were 'steeped in juju', and derived their knowledge of the white man from 'wild rumours'. The administration's answer to this kind of problem was a punitive expedition which was often described as 'a good tonic to the people'.[1] The expeditions settled nothing and in fact confirmed the suspicions entertained by the people that the arrival of the white man could mean only trouble.

In the region to the north-east of Opobo, the District Commissioner, Whitehouse, made a determined attempt to establish British rule. With an escort, Whitehouse made a journey from the upper waters of the Qua-Eboe river to Itu on the Cross river. He succeeded in summoning the neighbouring chiefs to a meeting and informed them that Her Majesty, the Queen of England, had graciously taken their country under her protection. The District Commissioner apparently thought it a waste of time to sign the usual treaties which preceded the declaration of a protectorate. The chiefs said nothing and returned to their homes. What they must have thought of the white man's proceedings was made clear when Whitehouse later reported that the natives of the area 'are a most truculent lot and evidently have no wish to recognise the Government'.[2] What was therefore obviously necessary was a military expedition to subdue the people. The expedition took place in due course; it became an annual affair.

The method used in the attempts to extend the protectorate by

[1] *Ibid.*
[2] F.O. 2/121, Moor to F.O. no. 56, 20 May 1897. See also F.O. 2/180, Gallwey to F.O. no. 185, 19 December 1898, and C.O. 444/1, Moor to C.O. no. 71, 14 May 1899.

intimidating the inhabitants militarily created considerable uneasiness to the Aborigines Protection Society. The Society was also concerned with the deportation of indigenous rulers. The Foreign Office forwarded to Ralph Moor the protest delivered by the Society. In reply, Moor declared emphatically, but falsely, that the policy in force in the protectorate in obtaining control over the natives was to open friendly relations with them by peaceful means. With this object the officers of the protectorate were continually travelling about, practically with their lives in their hands. They were doing all in their power to obtain 'the trust and confidence of the natives'.[1] The protestation of the Consul-General apparently satisfied the officials of the British Foreign Office where, during the same month, reports from the Niger Coast protectorate contained ample evidence that the local officials were resorting to or recommending military operations in order to establish British control in the hinterlands of New Calabar and Opobo.

From the standpoint of Britain the year 1897 had not been without solid achievements. As a result of the Benin expedition, an area of more than 3000 square miles, including rich forest resources like rubber, palm produce and timber, was open to British commercial exploitation and administrative control. The Consul-General obtained his due reward in the knighthood awarded him on the recommendation of the Foreign Office.[2]

The process of extending and consolidating British administrative control in the Niger Coast protectorate involved the territorial reorganisation of the areas already subdued and also the expansion of the political staff. In 1898 the protectorate was split into four divisions. The eastern division was under Gallwey, who was now designated Consul. Under him in the division were a Travelling Commissioner, a District Commissioner and four assistants. The central division, under Vice-Consul Leonard, included Opobo, Bonny, Degema and Brass, each under a District Commissioner and two Assistant Commissioners. Benin River and Warri made up the western division under the control of

[1] F.O. 2/121, Moor to F.O. no. 49, 6 May, 1897.
[2] F.O. 2/124, F.O. Draft, 3 September 1897. Ralph Moor received the K.C.M.G.

Vice-Consul Locke. There were District Commissioners and their assistants, in addition to the inevitable Travelling Commissioner. Lastly, the fourth division embraced Benin City and its neighbourhood under an officer styled the Political Resident. Fosbery occupied this position in 1898, assisted by an Assistant Political Resident and an Assistant District Commissioner. It was explained in the annual report that the increase of staff was necessary to keep in touch with the natives of the territories being constantly 'opened up every year'.[1]

Another administrative development was the creation of a Secretary's Department. The Foreign Office in approving the new office explained that Lord Salisbury was glad to know that it had been found possible to centralise the work of ruling the Niger Coast protectorate. There was, however, one feature of the new developments which apparently disturbed the minds of the officials of the Foreign Office. This was the increase in both the military and naval estimates. In regard to the military expansion, the Foreign Office expressed the pious sentiment that 'H.M.'s Government deprecate the extension of the Protectorate by force when the end can be attained by patience and the gradual introduction of civilised methods amongst the tribes of the interior'.[2] The Foreign Office did not indicate how the civilised methods were to be gradually introduced, and in any case the local British representatives had no intention of abandoning the only method they knew and believed in. The view of the local administration was summarised by Gallwey when he argued that 'in a country like this, experience has taught the Government that the only way to open up the country and to extend the influence of the Government is by means of [military] expeditions'.[3] The extension of British authority or what the local administrators called 'a forward move' was to depend exclusively on the expansion of the military establishment.

The year 1898 was therefore dominated by petty military expeditions in the different divisions of the protectorate. The appointment of Travelling Commissioners had given the impres-

---

[1] F.O. 2/180, Annual Report for 1897/8.
[2] F.O. 2/178, no. 26, 9 February 1898, and F.O. 2/177, no. 38, 5 March 1898.
[3] F.O. 2/180, no. 185, 19 December 1898.

sion that Sir Ralph and his subordinates were going to adopt a new policy of attempting to win the trust and confidence of the hinterland inhabitants, or at least attempt to explain to them the aims of the British government. That this was not to be the case was clearly revealed by the idiotic definition of the functions of the Travelling Commissioners. According to the annual report for 1897/8 already cited, the Travelling Commissioners' chief duty 'after civilising the natives would be to point out any new economic products and encourage the natives to develop them'.

The upper reaches of the Cross river received the first attention of the protectorate administration under Acting Consul-General Gallwey. This attention, as was to be expected, took the form of a formal military expedition of 120 troops under Major Milne, the Commandant of the protectorate force. Gallwey and Travelling Commissioner James accompanied the expedition. The local inhabitants against whom the undeclared war was waged included the Ekuris, Ibos, Asigas and Arums—all splinter groups who lived nearest the Cross river and, in accordance with long-established practice, imposed tolls on the Nkos, Ugeps and other inland groups which wished to trade on the Cross river. The riverside peoples rallied and offered very bitter resistance to the protectorate troops who sustained casualties of one officer and five men killed, two officers and twenty-three men wounded. The Commandant reported that 362 of the enemy were killed. In addition, whole towns were razed to the ground.[1] The expedition returned to Old Calabar, and the Upper Cross river region remained unsettled.

The reactions of the heads[2] of the African Department of the Foreign Office are worth noting. The Assistant Under-Secretary observed that '...trade is our object in West Africa and therefore the keeping open of trade routes'. His colleague grudgingly agreed but feared that '...the officials are very apt to stretch the keeping trade routes open, which is necessary, into opening new ones "vi et armis"'.[3] The need for removing obstacles to trade

[1] F.O. 2/178, Gallwey to F.O. no. 15, 25 January 1898.
[2] See F.O. List, 1898. Hon. F. Bertie, Assistant Under-Secretary, and Sir Charles Hill, Senior Clerk, Consular Department, Africa.
[3] F.O. 2/178, Letters dated 25 and 26 March attached to no. 26, 9 February 1898.

was recognised as supreme even if the removal involved the slaughter of the local inhabitants who were being civilised.

During the months of April and May, another expedition of 135 troops headed by three officers marched through the immediate hinterland of the central division. This division which, as pointed out earlier, incorporated the coast city-states of New Calabar, Bonny and Opobo lacked the advantage of a long navigable river which could afford easy access to the hinterland. The small rivers and their upper reaches, including the Sombrero, New Calabar, Bonny and Opobo rivers, had come under control. Okrika, Obunko, and Akwette, situated at the upper reaches, had all more or less been intimidated into submission to British authority. Beyond this rough line, advance entailed marching along forest paths. Nevertheless, the expedition of April and May achieved more constructive results than the tale of burning and killing which characterised the expeditions on the Upper Cross river in the eastern division. The happy change was owed largely to the emergence of a new type of political officer who recognised that contact with people in the hinterland who lived their own lives, and had caused no offence, demanded methods which had nothing to do with burning villages. These methods were applied by Acting Vice-Consul Fosbery[1] who, as political officer, accompanied the central division expedition.

Several towns were visited. The inhabitants of Egwanga, Essene, and Azumini accorded Fosbery a friendly reception. The officer explained that the troops had not come to make war. In each town a successful 'palaver' was held. In Mbolli and Ebubu, the headmen entered into treaty relations with the British representatives. The only disappointment occurred at Omokoroshi, where Chief Wagu refused to 'palaver' and fled. Fosbery's reaction was to advise patience where the normal officer would have fallen back on the more dramatic but hardly constructive tactics of warfare.[2] Shortly after the expedition, Fosbery was transferred to Benin, and the story of attempts to penetrate the hinterland were to become a tale of intimidation and punitive expeditions. In fact, a more pernicious strategy was devised. The Vice-Consul had

[1] Later Resident, Benin, 1901. Was highly commended by C.O. for avoiding punitive expeditions. See C.O. 520/7, no. 91, 5 April 1901.
[2] F.O. 2/179, no. 93, 2 June 1898.

208

received reports to the effect that chiefs of Ehea, on the fringe of the Ibo country, threatened to defy his authority, had closed trade routes to the coast and had put their town in a state of defence by digging trenches. The reaction of Travelling Commissioner James was immediate. It was one thing to attack a town with British troops and quite another to rally coast peoples to destroy a town in their hinterland. Travelling Commissioner James, District Commissioner Murray and his assistant, Roberts, collected levies from Opobo and other treaty towns for a punitive expedition against Ehea. The place was razed to the ground. After this a meeting was summoned in nearby Obegu, to which as many representatives of neighbouring villages as possible were invited by the British officials. It was reported that about 5000 representatives of the Ibo were present and were asked to witness the deadly consequence of defying British authority.[1] The Ibo representatives did not say what they thought about the proceedings, but obviously noted that coast peoples had assisted in encompassing the ruin of a neighbour village-state. It is reasonable to assume that many of the representatives, whom the British assembled, were Aro local traders. Travelling through the hinterland was not likely to be safer for Opobo traders after the kind of attack just described.

At this time, the British officials began to make references to the Aro of the hinterland. The first visit to Bende accomplished by Vice-Consul Leonard in 1896 had been received with jubilation by Ralph Moor, who then announced that he was making plans for establishing friendly relations with the Aro in 1897. Yet nothing was done up to 1898 to find out exactly who the Aro were and how they operated in the affairs of Iboland. It was vaguely known that they controlled the trade between the Ibo and the coast. Even then the minds of the British officials were obsessed with the efficacy of military expeditions. What deterred the Acting Consul-General from action was the fear that trade might be crippled if 'punitive action was taken in order to civilise them'.[2] If action against the Aro lay in the future, the situation around Benin division called for immediate attention in 1898.

Two Benin chiefs, Ologbosheri and Abohun, who were alleged

---

[1] F.O. 2/180, Gallwey to F.O. no. 163, 11 October 1897.
[2] Ibid. Annual Report by Gallwey for 1897/8.

to be the principal chiefs implicated in the Benin massacre, were still at large. As long as the chiefs were not captured and punished, the government's prestige in the Benin districts hung 'in the balance'.[1] The government's expectation that the deportation of the Oba would mean the submission of the Benin empire was not materialising. The fugitive chiefs found it easy to move from village to village without being betrayed to the British. A flying column of British troops was kept busy in the unpleasant task of trying to track down the Benin chiefs. Rumours flowed in that the chiefs were here, there and yonder. The villages involved in these rumours were visited and burnt down. The chiefs were reported to be indulging in human sacrifices. Lastly, the chiefs had allegedly collected all kinds of criminals, including prisoners released from the Royal Niger Company's territories and from Lagos. As if a sufficient case had not been made out against the recalcitrant Benin chiefs, the British officials added that Abohun's sister was involved in attempts to capture Bishop Tugwell, an Anglican bishop, who was travelling from Benin to Lagos. There were two sources of irritation over which the protectorate administration had no control. The war which the Royal Niger Company waged against the Emirs of Ilorin and Nupe accelerated the incursion of Nupes into the Kukuruku and northern Ishan areas of the Benin empire. Ewu, Irrua and Agbede were the principal centres invested by the Nupe aggressors. The local people were harried in turn by the Nupe and the flying column from Benin City. It was not clear what line demarcated the protectorate from the Royal Niger Company's territories and all that the protectorate officials could do was to indulge in vilification of the Royal Niger Company.[2] With the Lagos government there were similar but less acrimonious boundary problems. Akure, the Ekiti country, Owo and much of what is now Ondo division in the Yoruba country paid intermittent tribute to Benin. In 1898, was it the Niger Coast protectorate or the Lagos government which should control them? Meanwhile, the protectorate officials were convinced that the ruler of Akure was assisting Ologbosheri and Abohun in their defiance of British authority.

[1] *Ibid.* See Enclosure—Report by Assistant Resident Granville.
[2] See, for instance, F.O. 2/122, Moor to F.O. no. 110, 15 September 1897.

It was indeed not until the middle of 1899 that the administration succeeded in the immediate task of liquidating the rebellious chiefs whose freedom was incompatible with the political consolidation of British rule in the Benin districts. Ologbosheri was captured, convicted and executed on 28 June. A hastily summoned 'Native' Council in Benin justified the execution by passing a resolution to the effect that 'Ologbosheri was not sent to kill white men—and we therefore decide that according to native law his life is forfeited'.[1] Shortly after, Abohun was captured but for some obscure reason Sir Ralph Moor decided not to utilise the assistance of the Benin 'Native' Council. He intended to use Abohun, who was 'intelligent and of good character', in the government of Benin.

The year 1899 saw two important changes in the administrative set-up in the Niger Coast protectorate. These were the transfer of the control of the protectorate from the Foreign Office to the Colonial Office, over which Joseph Chamberlain presided, and the liquidation of the Royal Niger Company as a political agency of the British government. As regards the transfer, it had always been the wish of the Foreign Office to divest itself of the many problems created by the British acquisition of the vast territory, of which little was known apart from the city-states located on the coast. Great pressure was intermittently put on the Colonial Office, but the argument of the latter invariably was that an area in which slavery prevailed could not become a British colony.[2] The establishment of the West African Frontier Force by Chamberlain to deal with the French threat to the British claims in Borgu foreshadowed changes in British policy towards West Africa generally. Aggressive imperialism was to replace Foreign Office legal niceties and dilatory methods in regard to the effective control of areas taken under British protection.

It is not the task of this study to attempt to unravel the reasons why, in 1899, the British government decided to abrogate the charter of the Royal Niger Company.[3] The role of the company was, however, becoming increasingly inconvenient to the West African Frontier Force, which had been established in 1897, and to

---

[1] C.O. 444/1, Moor to C.O. no. 93, 2 July 1899; and no. 104, 20 July 1899.
[2] See F.O. 84/1828, *Africa*, no. 18, 1887, Minutes by Anderson dated 25 October 1887.
[3] See Flint, *Sir George Goldie and the Making of Nigeria*, ch. 13, pp. 295 f.

the Niger Coast protectorate administration. The warring activities of the Emir of Ilorin created difficulties for the British government in Lagos. The W.A.F.F. could take no action against Ilorin without the concurrence of the Agent-General of the Royal Niger Company. The area under the company was 'foreign country' and in this country the company had absolute authority in matters of native policy under the terms of its charter. All this was very galling to the officers of the W.A.F.F., who spoke scathingly of the company's employees as 'brutes'. These views were fully supported by Lugard.[1] The firms of Liverpool took a hand in the general vilification of the Royal Niger Company. Throughout 1898 the Foreign Office was flooded with letters from John Holt and others, which alleged that the Royal Niger Company was shipping into the hinterland large quantities of liquor and gunpowder in order to evade taxation if and when the area came under a new administration.[2] Questions were naturally asked in Parliament about these allegations. Goldie defended his company as best he could and found a champion in Mary Kingsley whose description of Crown Colony rule was 'a coma accompanied by fits'.

From Chamberlain's point of view, the existence of three separate administrations, with three different fiscal systems and vexatious boundary frictions, was not in the best interest of commercial development. The Foreign Office had always recognised this situation and had in co-operation with the Colonial Office set up what was designated the Niger Committee in 1898. This committee, under the chairmanship of Lord Selborne of the Colonial Office, included Goldie, Hill (F.O.), Antrobus (C.O.), Moor and McCallum of Lagos. The members prepared a report in which they agreed that, as regards the administration of the Niger territories, the object to be kept in mind was the eventual establishment of a Governor-General, but that owing to difficulties of climate and communications, the promulgation of a unified colony could not be recommended immediately.[3]

[1] C.O. 446/1, Lugard to Antrobus, 29 December 1898. F.O. 2/242, Goldie to F.O., 21 February 1899.
[2] F.O. 83/1606 and F.O. 83/1614, Letters to F.O. dated respectively 10 January 1898 and 19 October 1898. *Daily Chronicle*, 4 February 1899. Kingsley, *West African Studies*, p. 330.
[3] C.O. 446/3, Report dated 4 August 1898.

The negotiations for the transfer of the Niger Company's territories were taken in hand and concluded by June 1899. The company was generously compensated because it was assumed that the imperial government was acquiring from the company 'a ready-made and cheaply-won empire'. Lord Salisbury, in fact, expressed '...our deep gratitude and high esteem for the adventurers and patriots to whose efforts the preparation of this territory is due'.[1]

'...it is intended that certain of the territories formerly administered by the Company should be added to the said Niger Coast Protectorate, and that such territories, together with the said Niger Coast Protectorate, should henceforth be known as the Protectorate of Southern Nigeria....'[2]

It is very probable that the term Nigeria appeared for the first time in an official document in 1900. The territories administered hitherto by the Niger Company were portioned out between the new Protectorate of Northern Nigeria under Lugard and the protectorate under Sir Ralph Moor, which was designated the Protectorate of Southern Nigeria. The latter term did not include the hinterland of Lagos until 1906. The boundary between Northern Nigeria and Southern Nigeria was a line running west to east drawn roughly through Idah on the Niger. The emergence of Southern Nigeria was followed by the issue of a new Order-in-Council which set out the legal basis for the administration of the protectorate. The former Commissioner and Consul-General was renamed High Commissioner and empowered to provide, by means of proclamations, for the administration of justice, the raising of revenue, and generally for the peace, order and good government of the territory and 'of all the inhabitants therein'. The Order-in-Council took no account of the fact that the new protectorate contained vast tracts of territory, the inhabitants of which had neither solicited nor accepted British protection. For instance, the Niger Coast protectorate officials had not up to 1900 obtained any treaties from any major Ibo group. It is also of interest to note that an official of the Colonial Office entertained

[1] *Parl. Papers*, 1899, LXIII (C. 9372), on the Revocation of the Charter. F.O. 2/244, F.O. to the Treasury, 15 June 1899. See also Flint, *op. cit.* pp. 309–12.
[2] *Government Gazette*, no. 1, of the Protectorate of Southern Nigeria, 1900.

misgivings about the Ibos being handed over from the jurisdiction of the Niger Company to that of the protectorate of Southern Nigeria. This officer observed that 'I should not like to have to prove that the "treaties", the benefit of which we are taking over, would all bear scrutiny...'.[1] There was also conspicuously absent in the Order-in-Council the usual reference to the consent of the indigenous rulers in the matter of exercising British jurisdiction over their subjects. The High Commissioner was, however, advised to respect any native laws by which the civil relations of any native chiefs and tribes were regulated except where these laws were incompatible with the due exercise of British power and jurisdiction or injurious to 'the welfare of the said natives'.[2]

The acquisition of the Royal Niger Company's territories south of Idah imposed on Sir Ralph Moor the task of reorganisation. Southern Nigeria was split into four administrative divisions as follows:

(a) The eastern division which included Old Calabar, Opobo, Qua-Eboe, Bonny and Degema.

(b) The Cross river division.

(c) The central division, incorporating Akassa, Brass, Agberi, Oguta, Onitsha and Asaba.

(d) The western division, embracing Benin City districts, Sapele and Warri.

Each division was under the political control of a Divisional Commissioner, assisted by a Travelling Commissioner and a number of District and Assistant District Commissioners. The reorganisations which usually followed the extension of British rule involved fluctuations in the status of the coast city-states. Rival city-states such as Opobo, Bonny, and New Calabar were reduced to mere stations under petty British officials controlled from Old Calabar. In the central division, Akassa was for a time the headquarters to which Onitsha and Asaba were subordinated. In the same way, Benin city was controlled from Warri, the headquarters of the western division.[3] From the point of view of the

---

[1] C.O. 444/2, see Minutes on 120 Moor to C.O., 8 August 1899.

[2] *London Gazette*, 1900, 5 January. See also C.O. 444/1, Encl. in no. 52, 20 February 1900.

[3] For the distribution of the political officers, see C.O. 520/2, Encl. in no. 233, Moor to C.O., 22 August 1900.

British rulers, the increasing centralisation of authority was not inconsistent with the separate identity of the city-states in which 'Native' Councils were invariably established. These 'Native' Councils were, however, never anything more than instruments of local government which British officials manipulated for their own purposes. Under the Supreme Court Proclamation of 1900, a Chief Justice and District Commissioners' Courts were provided for and these exercised jurisdiction superior to the theoretical powers of 'Native' Councils. By and large, the executive paraphernalia usual in a Crown Colony were imposed on the protectorate of Southern Nigeria.

The liquidation of the Niger Company as an administrative agency on the Niger removed the most serious effects of the former arbitrary splitting-up of the Ibos west and east of the Niger. The traditional social and economic intercourse between the coast and the riverain groups could once more be resumed. The Ijaw and the Urhobo of the Forcados river area at last came under unified alien control. It is impossible to assess the full effects of the arbitrary, but effective, splitting of the groups which lasted from 1885 to 1900. In matters of commerce, the action taken by Brassmen in 1895 to deal with the Royal Niger Company clearly revealed the extent of the hardship imposed by the administrative arrangements which had hitherto operated.

The High Commissioner and his subordinates in charge of the central division had no illusions about the administrative problems which they were inheriting from the Royal Niger Company. The merits or demerits of the rule of the Niger Company over the riverain groups have provoked considerable controversy. Sir Ralph Moor was never tired of denouncing Goldie's methods. According to Sir Ralph, Goldie had claimed that the establishment of Residents and other political officers was contrary 'to the sound method of controlling barbarous Africa'.[1] The protecting power ought to confine itself to keeping the trade routes open. Sir Ralph suspected that Goldie's philosophy was motivated by a desire to keep down administrative expenses and thereby guarantee

[1] C.O. 444/4, Moor to C.O., 29 April 1899. See also Kingsley, *op. cit.* pp. 360–1, and Wellesley, *Sir George Goldie, Founder of Nigeria* (London, 1934), p. 34.

substantial dividends to the shareholders of the company. It was obvious to Sir Ralph in 1900 that the riverain peoples he inherited were not amenable to alien control. The High Commissioner's deputy, Gallwey, explained that the Royal Niger Company was in the habit of holding hostages from the troublesome towns in order to discourage these towns from raiding the company's trading establishments. The natives of Oguta were, on the evidence given to Gallwey by the company's agent who had lived there for more than ten years, particularly truculent and the company kept them sweet and quiet by giving them considerable sums of money every year as presents. The amounts paid out in 1898 and 1899 totalled £500.

Local traditions in Onitsha, Obosi, Oguta and Aguleri throw considerable light on the attitude of the local groups towards the Royal Niger Company. The company's activities were not much better than organised burglary, and therefore to plunder the company was an act of heroism. The natives suspected too that the company was hated by independent British traders and by educated Africans. The basic cause of indigenous opposition to the Niger Company, even after presents had been accepted in lieu of treaties of protection distributed by the company's agents, was the unwillingness of the local rulers and their subjects to accept alien control. In the circumstances, the revocation of the company's charter and the transfer of the territories to the protectorate administration made no difference to the attitude of the inhabitants towards alien rule. Sir Ralph and Gallwey knew this and were therefore unwilling to allow reinforcements for the British troops involved in Ashanti to be drawn from the central division. Sir Ralph's analysis of the political situation in the Division was that '...from an administrative point of view it is an unknown quantity, the "known" being that many elements that may create trouble and danger to life and plunder exist and that administrative control other than of a repressive nature has never existed'.[1]

Sir Ralph Moor's methods in the Niger Coast protectorate included punitive expeditions against towns and villages which were alleged to be unwilling to submit to British rule. His denunciation of the repressive rule of the Royal Niger Company

---

[1] C.O. 520/2, no. 166, Gallwey to C.O., 12 June 1900. See Minutes by Moor.

was absurd. While the protectorate was under Foreign Office control, the officials of the latter had invariably, in theory, deplored the policy of carrying fire and sword to defenceless hinterland groups who merely wished to live their traditional lives and to whom British intentions were never adequately explained.[1] In practice, the local officials were left free to carry on their work of military intimidation. It was not likely that the Colonial Office, more accustomed than the Foreign Office to quick results in the colonial field, would take a more humanitarian view of an aggressive colonial policy which the Aborigines Protection Society appropriately described as 'nigger hunting'. It should be recalled that Joseph Chamberlain, who presided over the Colonial Office, had in a famous speech at the annual dinner of the Royal Colonial Institute, 1897, upheld the necessity for punitive expeditions against indigenous African groups. 'You cannot have omelettes without breaking eggs; you cannot destroy the practices of barbarism, of slavery, of superstition which for centuries have desolated the interior of Africa, without the use of force....'

The British officials in charge of the protectorate of Southern Nigeria had nothing to fear from the Colonial Office when the African Association protested against the punitive expedition launched in the Qua-Eboe district in the year when the Foreign Office transferred to the Colonial Office the supervision of the affairs of the protectorate. According to the official report, the reason for the war of destruction was that the inhabitants of the district to the north-east of Opobo were known to be 'exceedingly unruly and turbulent'. Nine towns were destroyed, 175 others submitted and surrendered 1000 guns. A European trading agent stationed at Eket gave an entirely different picture of the proceedings. The Travelling Commissioner, Leonard, led the expedition overland from Opobo to Eket. From the latter place he issued a summons to the chiefs of the Qua-Eboe district to meet him before two o'clock the same day. When no chiefs turned up, Leonard hoisted a red flag and declared war on the people. The trader concluded his account with the lament that 'they have laid the country bare.... This will do the trade a lot of harm.'[2]

---

[1] See F.O. 2/178 already cited, Minutes on no. 26 of 9 February 1898.
[2] C.O. 444/4, Letter from Twist dated 15 February 1899.

Naturally, the people whose villages, plantations and yams were promiscuously destroyed could hardly engage in trade.

The protests of the African Association of Liverpool to the Colonial Office were forwarded to Sir Ralph Moor for his comments. The High Commissioner repudiated the point about the deterioration of trade by referring to trade statistics before and after the Qua-Eboe expedition, and concluded that 'there is no doubt that the action now taken will have far reaching effects in civilising the natives and doing away to some extent with their distrust of the government and each other....'[1] This piece of sententiousness apparently satisfied the Colonial Office. Thus, as long as trade was not jeopardised, and as long as the local administrators of the protectorate of Southern Nigeria were able to show that the natives were being 'civilised', the military activities of the administration were endorsed by the officials of the Colonial Office. The latter, however, on occasions urged pacific methods and commended local officials who reported successful 'palaver' with the inhabitants of new districts without resorting to warfare.

The outlook for the officials in charge of the protectorate in 1900 was far from rosy. In the headquarters division, very little of the hinterland of Opobo, Eket, Bonny and Degema had been subdued. In the Upper Cross river division, there was as yet no headquarters and no permanent British station, except Ediba, which was more or less a military camp. The High Commissioner believed that the political state of affairs in the division imperilled the greater part of the revenue derived from Old Calabar. The charges against the splinter groups and the independent villages clustering around the Upper Cross river were legion. Each village was a law unto itself. The Ekuri, Ungwana and Okurike were 'rude' to the Divisional Commissioner, Captain Roupell, who had in the previous year burnt down their villages. Beyond these groups, along the Aweyong tributary of the Cross river, there were the Ikwes, the Atam, the Indem and the Akaju who raided and harassed one another, and were in turn harassed by the Ibo of the Azar country. The territories between Benin City and the Niger river required, according to Sir Ralph, 'firm measures to bring [them] under

[1] C.O. 444/1, Moor to C.O. no. 71, 14 May 1899. See also Minutes on the Despatch.

218

government control'.[1] The British capture of Benin City and the fugitive Benin chiefs had not brought about the submission of Ishan, Kukuruku and Ibo groups formerly dominated by Benin City. Lastly, the numerous Ibo and Ibibio groups which occupied the region from the river Niger to the Cross river had not felt the weight of British authority. In regard to the area, the enemy were the Aro 'who are scattered all over this part, sometimes in twos and threes, sometimes in settlements from the Cross River to the Niger. Their influence is predominant over these pagan tribes, and as they have no good to say about the Government, their presence is a continual thorn in the side of the administration.'[2]

In the task of 'pacification' facing the protectorate administration, Sir Ralph Moor and his team were not without assets. The Niger Coast Protectorate Force had become the 3rd Battalion of the West African Frontier Force and had a strength of 1250 N.C.O.'s and men. The South African War temporarily made it difficult to find officers, but the Colonial Office officials were endeavouring to 'scour the highways and bye-ways' for them. The administrative and general staff of the protectorate were substantially expanded. The finances were good, even showing a surplus of revenue over expenditure to the amount of more than £22,000. In view of these facts, the High Commissioner argued that further development could not take place until government control was established. Tribal wars and disputes were liable at any moment to stop a great part of the existing trade. 'I cannot therefore urge too strenuously the necessity for prompt action in extending effective Government throughout Southern Nigeria, to which purpose, I submit, as much of the revenue as possible should be diverted.'[3] The issue of the effective political control of the protectorate was viewed by the Colonial Office in terms of profit and loss. Chamberlain and his principal assistants therefore agreed with Sir Ralph that surplus revenue in good years should be invested in extending British control, as was done in the other West African possessions. Investment in the context had only one meaning to Sir Ralph Moor—military expeditions.

[1] C.O. 520/3, Annual Report for the year 1899/1900.
[2] *Nigerian Pamphlets*, no. 16, 1909. Exploration in Southern Nigeria.
[3] C.O. 520/7, no. 56 of 5 March 1901.

Another advantage which the protectorate administration enjoyed arose from the fact that the indigenous groups whose independence was being threatened did not realise that the white man meant business. Local traditions in Iboland and in Ibibio-land show that the people had heard rumours about the activities of what they described as a new type of white men who claimed that they had come to rule. The indigenous groups had imagined that whatever the white man did on the coast, and even on the Niger, the intruders had no business in their own territories safely removed from the sea. The white men, they had heard, came in large ships. Well, these ships could not conceivably plough through the forest paths which afforded the only access to the homes of the hinterland Ibos and Ibibios. In any case, these indigenous groups, which had no political organisation that transcended the limits of a village, in a few cases the village group, gave no thought to defensive measures in the interest of their political independence. Even the Aro, who had reason to suspect that the encroachment of the white men might undermine their profitable role of middlemen, did not attempt to organise themselves or the Ibos and Ibibios for purposes of defence. This situation was hardly known to Sir Ralph Moor and his subordinates who were obsessed with the notion that 'the natives must be made to fully understand that the Government is their master and is determined to establish in and control their country'.[1]

Two diametrically opposed methods open to the British in their determination to extirpate the political independence of the indigenous peoples of Southern Nigeria were exemplified by the activities in 1901 of two types of officials who served under Sir Ralph Moor. The advocate of pacific measures in the imposition of a new pattern of politics on the hinterland was Fosbery, who had already done much constructive work in the hinterland of Degema and Bonny. In 1901 he proved once again that it was possible to establish contact with the indigenous peoples, explain to them that the government was interested in their welfare, and lay the foundations of local government without burning down and looting villages. In February he set out on an extensive tour of the Ishan districts incorporated, rather arbitrarily, in the central

[1] C.O. 520/10, Moor to C.O. no. 381, 24 November 1901.

division of the protectorate, and gave his exclusive attention to summoning the elders and chiefs of neighbouring towns. He usually explained beforehand that his aim was to examine the grievances of the villages concerned. In an area where each village had grievances against its neighbour, the presence of a neutral arbitrator was welcomed by the elders. It was for this reason that Fosbery was able to assemble a large meeting at Sobe. He found the elders 'most orderly in their demeanour and most anxious for the settlement of their old palavers'.[1] The news of the proceedings at Sobe spread very quickly, and Fosbery received invitations from the towns of Ojogbo, Ibewhe, Unwa, Uteku and Iyere. In these places, the elders undertook to build rest houses for Fosbery's visits in the future.

Sir Ralph Moor was undoubtedly gratified with the success of Fosbery because the latter was shortly promoted to the headship of the central division. In reporting Fosbery's activities, Sir Ralph claimed that the method of approach used by Fosbery was in conformity with the policy laid down in the protectorate. The Assistant Under-Secretary in the Colonial Office was obviously impressed by Fosbery's methods, and urged that officers like Fosbery should be encouraged to work through the chiefs and elders of the hinterland towns and not to have recourse to punitive expeditions.[2]

The method of fire and sword in imposing British rule was brought to Sir Ralph Moor's attention barely a month after the latter's commendation of Fosbery. The southern Ishan and Kwale districts of the central division were reported to be disaffected with the government. Further evidence of this disaffection was hardly thought necessary by the local District Commissioner when he had already accepted the story that a chief in the area who wished to be friendly with the white man had been murdered. Sir Ralph's reaction to the political problems in the districts was the suggestion that it might be necessary to seize and remove some of the more disaffected chiefs and 'generally to demonstrate the effective power of the government'.[3] It was in this aggressive mood that he issued instructions that a patrol under a military officer should scour the

---

[1] C.O. 520/7, Moor to C.O. no. 91, 5 April 1901.
[2] *Ibid.* See Minutes by Antrobus.
[3] C.O. 520/8, Moor to C.O. no. 131, 28 May 1901.

districts of Uromi, Kwale and the Aseh Creek. In contrast with the Fosbery 'expedition', the invasion of the territory indicated above was marked by sacking and looting. It is not without significance that the military commander of the expedition had a great deal to report, whereas the political officer who accompanied the troops hardly had anything to report in regard to the political settlement of the alleged disaffected areas. What took place is best described in the Commanding Officer's own words: '...23rd Went on with destroying...24th Took out party and maxim and drove enemy through and beyond Idumudeva and began the destruction of it...25th Took Company in morning and destroyed a large quarter of Awu...29th Completed destroying of Ekole. Raided farms for yams.'[1] The officer concluded that the first phase of the operations in the Ishan country was over. The people were beginning to come in and submit, although there might be a few more fights and a few more towns to be levelled. The country had had enough for the time being. The officer had no doubt whatever that his activities had produced the most salutary effects on the natives. For instance, when the Uromi people saw town after town levelled and even had no peace in their farm hiding-places, they said 'it was not the kind of war they had been used to'.

The Colonial Office made no comments on the report submitted by Sir Ralph Moor on the military intimidation of the Ishan groups, probably because it was faced with Sir Ralph's gigantic military plans for the subjugation of the Aro, east of the Niger. Joseph Chamberlain had spoken about not having 'omelettes without breaking eggs'. Sir Ralph Moor believed that if there was ever a case for carrying out Chamberlain's mandate, the Aro provided it. The protectorate administration rightly suspected that the vast Ibo and Ibibio groups, which occupied the territory between the Niger and the Cross river, did not recognise any paramount chiefs. To establish British rule among them involved occupying innumerable autonomous villages, a task at which Sir Ralph shuddered. It was, however, believed that these Ibo and Ibibio were not leaderless.[2] The Aro were the leaders, and therefore to subdue the Aro was the urgent business of the administration. No one knew

[1] *Ibid.* See Enclosure Report by Commanding Officer dated 9 May 1901.
[2] See chapter 1 above.

222

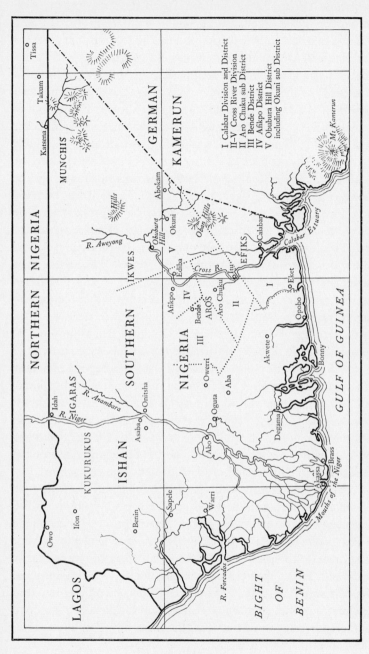

2. The Aro-Chukwu expedition and the Upper Cross River division

the precise nature of Aro hegemony, but that did not matter. What was believed afforded compelling reasons for dealing with the Aro.

In the first place, there was the Long Juju which was believed to represent all that was darkest and most terrible in native religious practice. The administration readily swallowed the stories brought to them by 'intelligent Efik'. For instance, when head-chief Okoroji of the Long Juju died, four hundred people were said to have been sacrificed to the Juju. All the towns under Aro influence were believed to have contributed victims—some ten, others five and so on. 'All were killed as offerings to the god, and then eaten by all the Aro people, the flesh being distributed throughout the late chief's country.'[1] In the second place, the Aro were believed to be incorrigible slave-dealers. Nobody was able to say how the Aro disposed of their slaves after the British had occupied the coast. The rumours of Aro raids against towns and villages constantly percolated to the government stations at the coast and its immediate hinterland. The need for supplying victims for human sacrifice and for currency apparently provided full scope for Aro slaving activities. In the third place, the Aro constituted an obstacle to the uninterrupted penetration of British trade. The coast middlemen had their trade centres at the upper reaches of the small rivers that run southwards to the sea. Beyond these, the Aro controlled the distribution of European goods to the hinterland. The Aro could do what Bonny men, Opobo men and so on could not contemplate—journey to every corner of Ibo and Ibibio country in complete safety. But neither the British merchants nor the coast natives were now content with Aro control of the economic resources of the hinterland.

From the standpoint of the British administration of the protectorate, the Aro were a thorn in the flesh. According to the evidence of native political agents, the Aro groups which traded in the neighbourhood of the Upper Cross river and the Atlantic coast were fully aware that the penetration of British authority would encompass the ruin of their profitable role of middlemen. When it was explained to them that British intentions included 'opening up the country and free trade generally', the Aro countered by suggesting that what the white man should do was to

[1] Partridge, *op. cit.* p. 59.

warn the Efik and other coast traders not to go beyond the centres at which they had traded for centuries.[1] The desirability of expanding British trade and humanitarianism thus joined hands to make the Aro issue one of paramount political importance for Sir Ralph Moor who continually urged that 'it is only by going to the heart of the matter at once and breaking up the power of the Aros that the country can be opened up and pacified'.[2]

The Colonial Office was, however, not persuaded that military action against the Aro was the answer to the problem. It argued that, although the officials on the spot ought to know best, they were sometimes too much in a hurry. Chamberlain agreed with this view and thought that 'this tribe' could be brought gradually under control without war.[3] There is no evidence that the administration did anything to negotiate with the Aro. There were Aro groups settled in Onitsha and other places along the Niger. After 1900 these river towns were under the control of the protectorate administration. Onitsha would have provided ample evidence of the fact that the Long Juju controlled by the Aro did not give the Aro political authority over the Ibo communities. The willingness, and ever-eagerness, on the part of Ibo and Ibibio communities to consult the Long Juju for the settlement of serious internal disputes and political subordination to the Aro who settled in small groups among them were two different things.

Sir Ralph Moor was determined to justify the need for a military expedition into the hinterland east of the Niger in order to achieve dramatic results comparable to those which had followed the Benin expedition west of the Niger. It is remarkable the way Sir Ralph and his subordinates built up a case against the Aro. In presenting to the Colonial Office the estimates for 1901, with the revenue showing a spectacular increase from about £160,000 to £350,000, Sir Ralph pleaded that as much of the revenue as possible should be diverted to extending the area under government control. This extension was the only guarantee against the falling off of trade.[4]

---

[1] Calprof. 6/1, vol. III, no. 24, from D.C. Old Calabar, dated 13 November 1896. See also statement by Magnus Duke. *Ibid.* 10/3, vol. II, no. 6, dated 23 June 1901, Report by C. R. Palmer.
[2] C.O. 444/2, Moor to C.O. no. 141, 9 September 1899.
[3] *Ibid.* See Minutes by Antrobus, the Earl of Selborne and Chamberlain.
[4] C.O. 520/7, Moor to C.O. no. 56, 5 March 1901.

It became the practice of the protectorate administration to ascribe every disturbance in the divisions of the protectorate to the baneful influence of the Aro. On a visit to the central division, Sir Ralph was 'reliably' informed that owing to pernicious Aro influence, the trade in oil at Oguta had fallen from 250 to 100 puncheons. At Atani, the Aro priests 'put juju' on the women, threatening them with sterility if they cracked the nuts of the palm for sale to the Europeans. In the eastern division, the Aro frustrated British efforts north of Opobo and in the Qua-Eboe country. The District Commissioner was reduced to having to distribute presents of gin and tobacco to the inhabitants in order to counteract the influence of the Aro. In a place called Ese Obong, the chief reported that he was being harassed by the Aro because he was friendly to the British government.[1]

In the opinion of the protectorate administration, the harm done by Aro iniquity was most serious in the Cross River division, a division in which military expeditions had virtually become an annual event. Here the Ibos who lived in the Ikwe country in the Upper Cross region were described as Aro and given the name of Inokuns which appears in official reports. The Inokuns lived at a good distance from the Cross river and could not be chastised by the constant military excursions organised by the government. The inability of the Divisional Commissioner to establish a government station in the neighbourhood was blamed on the Inokuns and the latter were alleged to draw their hostile inspiration from the Long Juju.[2] What was particularly galling to the administration was that the splinter groups on the Cross river, which often defied British authority, appeared to trust and like the Aro who lived among them. The only explanation which the local British officials could advance was that 'the wild tribes' were more frightened of the Long Juju than of British authority.

Sir Ralph Moor ordered that the protectorate troops in the Upper Cross river should be increased to 310 men. The inconvenient necessity was attributed to the fact that the Aro were instigating the Inokuns and the Ezza to the north to reduce the division to chaos in order to distract attention from the Aro

[1] See C.S.O. 1/13, Quarterly Reports from New Calabar and Opobo.
[2] Partridge, *op. cit.* p. 67.

country. All this 'emphasises the necessity for dealing with this Aro question at the first opportunity'. The last straw was the report transmitted to the Acting High Commissioner, Leslie Probyn, by a native political agent to the effect that the Aro had recently carried off many hundreds of Ibibios and sold them as slaves.[1] The event that was highly coloured by the Acting High Commissioner is still remembered in the neighbourhood of Mbiabon, about fifteen miles south-east of Itu. The Ibibio of the place had killed a leopard but had failed to comply with the tradition of surrendering the animal to the local Aro head. The district was therefore raided by the Aro. Probyn, who accepted the story as told by a native political agent, construed the Aro raid as a demonstration against the protectorate government and as an organised attempt to check the efforts of the natives of the Opobo and Qua-Eboe districts to carry their trade into the interior. The Aro had therefore committed unpardonable sins against humanity and commerce. Sir Ralph Moor, who was in England, saw the report and convinced the Colonial Office that the raid might 'be regarded as the technical justification for the expedition against the Aro...already decided to be necessary on more general grounds'.[2]

The impression given in the reports by British officials that the Aro were a 'tribe' whose conscious frustration of British good intentions was co-ordinated and directed by the Long Juju priests is notoriously wrong. This impression gave the widely scattered Aro settlements a coherence they never possessed. The prestige of the Long Juju afforded protection to individual itinerant Aro traders and to the distant Aro settlements, but the latter were not organised in a hierarchy reaching up to the Long Juju at the apex. The British reports included also a false assumption as regards the political status of Ibo and Ibibio communities. These communities, it was argued, would welcome British intervention in order to rid them of Aro tyranny. That many had not done so already was attributed to Aro intrigues which suggested that to submit to the white man was a calamity to be averted. The fact was that the Ibo and the Ibibio did not need Aro insinuations in their determination to preserve their independence and way of life.

[1] C.O. 520/8, Probyn to C.O. no. 200, 6 July 1901.
[2] *Ibid.* See Minutes by Butler.

The British discovered this after the Aro expedition.[1] From 1898 to 1901, during which the protectorate administration nursed its grievances against the Aro, every manifestation of opposition to British encroachment in any part of the protectorate east of the Niger, and sometimes on the Niger itself, was attributed to Aro influence.

The Aro head chiefs of Aro-Chukwu, the seat of the Long Juju and the home of the Aro, were unaware that the government of Southern Nigeria had decided on a colossal war against them. There are in Aro-Chukwu no traditions which can be construed to show that the local rulers of Aro-Chukwu consciously opposed British advance into the hinterland. The leaders were acquainted with the threats conveyed by native political agents who came in contact not with Aro-Chukwu but with Aro traders settled at strategic points on the trade routes to the coast. It is therefore among the Aro settlements on the periphery of the Ibo and Ibibio country that there exist old men who recollect the events which they believe led to the British military expedition. The account given below is the one narrated by Chief Claudius Abonta of Akwette, born in 1884 and educated at the Bonny Government School. The chief's story was corroborated by the old men still alive in the neighbouring towns.[2]

According to Chief Abonta, there was a very dynamic Aro trader named Okori Toti who controlled the trade between Bonny, Opobo, and the hinterland in the neighbourhood of Akwette. The people of the latter place preferred, however, to act as middlemen between the Aro and the coast traders. Okori Toti was determined to deal directly with Bonny and Opobo traders in the waterside market of Ajala Onwo. For this defiance of Akwette wishes, Okori Toti was fined 8000 manillas by the elders of Akwette. The Akwette Christians suspected that the Aro would bide their time and wreak fearful vengeance on the Akwette. They therefore hastened to inform the District Commissioner in charge of the Bonny district that Toti and his mercenaries were contemplating the destruction of Akwette, a town under British control. In another town called Obegu, the local traders owed money to the

[1] C.S.O. 1/13, see Encl. 2 in no. 36, Moor to C.O., 18 January 1903.
[2] The data used here are the result of field-work undertaken by Dr A. E. Afigbo, a post-graduate history scholar, 1962–3.

Aro who had provided the capital for the trade that passed through Obegu between the hinterland and the coast. In 1901 the Aro attempted to seize the debtors, in accordance with traditional trade relations. The people of Obegu, however, acted first, fully aware of the sympathy of the British local administration. The Aro in the local market were attacked and looted.

It became clear to the Aro of this neighbourhood that their whole position was being undermined by the inexplicable behaviour of their former trading partners. The Aro leader, Okori, did not associate the local incidents with the growing influence of British authority or with the growing defiance of the Aro among the local people which British influence encouraged. Okori summoned Abam mercenaries and raided Obegu, preparatory to the destruction of Akwette. The Travelling Commissioner hurried up to Obegu after the Aro raid, and rallied the frightened inhabitants. In an obvious reference to what the British had in store for the Aro, the Commissioner asserted that 'we white men are like a big tree. It takes time before we fall, but when we do fall the surrounding country side would know of it.' The incidents embodied in the narrative given here afford the only evidence there is that the Aro consciously and directly provoked the Aro expedition of 1901. Even then, the Aro involved were those that lived a long way from Aro-Chukwu.[1]

The British aimed at the control of the hinterland—not merely at the local Aro involved in the petty trade disputes of the towns on the periphery. Since the Aro were believed to be almost everywhere, the scope of the proposed British expedition was extensive. Three areas were specifically marked out. The first theatre of military operation was to embrace the Cross river and the hinterland of New Calabar, Bonny and Opobo. The second was the neighbourhood of Oguta. What remained of Iboland comprised the territory between Onitsha and the westernmost fringe of the Cross river. While the forces for the war were being assembled, Sir Ralph Moor set out the war aims as follows:[2]

    (i)  to stop slave raiding and the slave trade;

---

[1] After the Aro war, Okori Toti and his Abam ally, Uchendu, were publicly hanged at Obegu by the British. See C.O. 520/14, no. 135 of 4 April 1902.

[2] C.O. 520/10, Moor to Chamberlain, 24 November 1901—Memo of Instructions. See also C.O. 520/8, Moor to C.O. no. 181 of 25 June 1901.

(ii)  to abolish the Juju hierarchy of the Aro tribe;

(iii)  to open the country to civilisation;

(iv)  to stimulate legitimate trade;

(v)  to inculcate the use of currency in lieu of slaves, brass rods, and other forms of native currency; and

(vi)  to establish eventually a labour market as a substitute for the present system of slavery.

Joseph Chamberlain ordered the governments of Lagos and the protectorate of Northern Nigeria to dispatch contingents to supplement the 3rd battalion in Southern Nigeria. The officer who was to command the combined troops was Lt.-Col. H. F. Montanaro, now styled Officer Commanding Aro Field Forces. The Commander asked for 87 officers, 1550 soldiers and 2100 carriers. The forces were grouped in four columns based at Unwana (on the Cross river), Itu (also on the Cross river), Akwette and Oguta. Political officers were assigned to the army columns. Travelling Commissioner James was attached to the headquarters staff, Gallwey to the Akwette column, Woodhouse to the Oguta column, and Watt to the Unwana contingent. For the benefit of the political officers, the High Commissioner issued a subsidiary memorandum in which he defined hostile towns where the military officers would be free to do as they liked. A hostile town was one whose inhabitants resisted the passage of the troops, or which was evacuated by its people on the approach of the British troops. In any case, the government had made up its mind to overawe the hinterland communities and establish British control over one and all.[1]

Military operations were launched by the British early in December 1901. The Officer Commanding the Aro Field Force had probably been persuaded that he was faced with a war which required all the resources of his military training. He therefore issued directives to the sectional commanders and saw to it that regular bulletins were forwarded to the High Commissioner, who apparently awaited eagerly news of the fortunes of the Field Forces. To reinforce the grandeur of the expedition, opposition to the progress of the forces was exaggerated. In fact, Col. Montanaro expressed his surprise at the 'formidable' opposition shown by the enemy who proved 'to be a most persistent and

[1] *Ibid.*

dogged foe...'. He had had no idea that 'savages would make such a stand'.[1]

In actual fact, the military operation was little more than a farce. The Aro of Aro-Chukwu and many other Aro groups scattered in different settlements, as well as the autonomous Ibo and Ibibio villages, were completely unaware that a war was being contemplated or had been declared against them. In the circumstances, there was no organised defence on the part of the indigenous inhabitants. Opposition to the passage of the British troops was haphazard and was encountered mainly in towns and villages where the inhabitants were unwilling to surrender their guns, as demanded by the British. Honest eyewitnesses of the expedition have described the whole business as 'very tame' and, at best, 'a police and political excursion'.[2]

The operations were launched early in December 1901. Columns 1 and 3 started from Oguta and Akwette respectively, and on 2 December met at Owerri, and marched on to Bende on the 16th. Columns 2 and 4 began operations on the Cross river in the districts around Itu and Ungwana. Major Mackenzie, in command of the second column, received peace overtures from the chiefs of Ahofia, a place considered by the administration to be one of the staunchest allies of the Aro. The officer reported that here and at Ekole the inhabitants seemed 'inclined to accept our currency'. He impressed upon all who wished to remain friendly with the government that they must refuse to 'chop mbiam' with the Aro.[3]

Columns 2 and 4 proceeded to converge on Aro-Chukwu and entered the town without opposition on 24 December. All four columns assembled here on the 28th. The Supreme Commander, Lt.-Col. Montanaro, assembled all the Aro chiefs and people who could be found and explained to them 'the intentions of the Government'. As far as the officer could gather from the general attitude of the people, he was convinced that they were rather inclined to welcome the advent of the government. This notwithstanding, the officer set up a military commission which sentenced and hanged

---

[1] See C.O. 520/10 and 520/13, O.C. Reports dated 24, 28 and 31 December 1901.

[2] Douglas, *Niger Memories* (signed Memo), cited, p. 85.

[3] The equivalent of a mutual assistance alliance.

those Aro chiefs believed to be the 'ring-leaders' presumably of the Long Juju.[1] The Long Juju shrine was set on fire which Montanaro believed destroyed 'all traces' of the oracle. The description of the shrine left on record by British officers and missionaries is not a very pleasant one. A typical British picture is as follows: 'The approach to the Long Juju is through dense bush, which gradually becomes thicker and thicker until one arrives at the entrance of a deep oval-shaped pit.... One climbs down the precipitous sides of the rock into a narrow gorge and into running water....' The details of the macabre picture include two altars on which were piled human skulls and other relics of juju rites. The whole shrine was 'a gloomy cave of savage superstition'.[2]

When the task of destroying the Long Juju was completed, the troops were sent out in detachments to operate in several directions. During January 1902 the country west of the Cross river was traversed by the troops. Small engagements with the enemy were reported in the Obinkita and Qua districts. Early in February all the columns reassembled at Akwette from which a sweep was organised on a broad front into the hinterland of Opobo and New Calabar. Places such as Isiokpo, Iba, Elimini, Elele, Aba, Asa and Owerri were occupied without resistance. The troops again converged on Bende, and from here contingents were dispatched to continue the work of conquest to Obosi and Onitsha on the Niger.[3]

One incident revealed the stupidity and the cost of having given what should have been a political excursion an unnecessary military complexion. Two chiefs of Ikorana were tried by a military tribunal, charged with

knowingly doing acts calculated to imperil the success of a portion of His Majesty's forces—in that they (i) did fail to forward despatches to the officer commanding Uwet Column without delay and in that (ii) when asked by Mr. James, Political Officer, Aro Field Force, for information concerning a road from Ikorana to the Inokun Cuntry and to provide guides for the road, did conceal the existence of such road and did fail to provide guides for the same when called upon to do so.

The chiefs were found guilty and sentenced to five years and penal

---

[1] See C.O. 520/10 and C.O. 520/13 for Moor's reports and enclosures dated 10 December 1901 and 14 January 1902, respectively.

[2] Partridge, *op. cit.* pp. 55–6.

[3] C.O. 520/14, Moor to C.O. no. 183, 17 April 1902.

servitude for life respectively. The proceedings horrified even Sir Ralph Moor, and he condemned the military officers for punishing chiefs whose only offence was no more than refusing to take part in a war with which they were not concerned or being unwilling to betray people with whom they were probably connected by friendship and marriage. The legal experts of the Colonial Office could not see how the native chiefs could be amenable to the jurisdiction of a British military court. The trial was therefore declared illegal.[1] The chiefs were set free and returned as heroes to their Umon home.[2]

The area involved in the Aro expedition was estimated to cover 6000 square miles. The northernmost district of the protectorate between Onitsha and Ogoja was, however, not touched as originally intended. The nature of the resistance anticipated at Aro-Chukwu had been fantastically exaggerated and it was not thought expedient to disperse the protectorate forces too widely. In the territories covered by the expedition substantial results had been achieved. Twenty-five thousand war guns accumulated by the natives had been confiscated. On the whole, concluded the High Commissioner, 'the tribes...who have persistently resisted any interference on the part of the white man, have been taught a salutary lesson and have had clearly demonstrated to them the power of a Government that intends to rule them and control their country'.[3] The news of the defeat of the Aro and the destruction of the Long Juju naturally spread to every part of Iboland with which the Aro through their traders or Juju agents had been in contact for many generations. Local traditions suggest that the inhabitants of the area which escaped the expedition were warned that the government of the white man was invincible. This fact would explain why subsequently many of the towns and villages offered no resistance at the approach of military patrols. The best thing to do was to flee into the bush.

It was obvious to Sir Ralph Moor that the basis for the establishment and consolidation of the new political order which British intervention in the affairs of Southern Nigeria postulated required

[1] C.O. 520/13, see Charge Sheet in no. 66, 15 February 1902 and Minutes by Risley, Cox, Antrobus, Ommaney and Chamberlain.
[2] The men involved were Chiefs Abiakari and Ekpenyon-Ana.
[3] C.O. 520/14, Memorandum on the Aro Expedition dated 24 April 1902.

something more than the marginal and ephemeral success of the Aro expedition. The High Commissioner therefore set out on a political tour of the conquered area as soon as the dust of war had settled. On 26 and 27 March 1902 he held two meetings at Bende, to which he had invited the representatives of as many towns as possible. Eleven Ahoffia, eight Abam, five Aro and twenty-five Ibo towns were indeed represented at the meetings. Sir Ralph did his best to explain why the government had to enter their towns by force of arms. He then expounded the new methods of government which could guarantee peace and good order in their towns. Bende was forthwith made a district headquarters. Sir Ralph's report of the meetings does not contain any evidence that the natives, who listened to 'the big white man' in stupefaction, contributed anything to the proceedings.

At the end of March the High Commissioner made his way to Aro-Chukwu. There, of course, the Juju elders were already hanged or in flight. To Sir Ralph's astonishment, the women of Aro-Chukwu solicited his permission to re-establish the Long Juju which the women intended to control themselves.[1] The request, as was to be expected, was rejected by the High Commissioner. Aro-Chukwu was made a sub-district headquarters, and the political officers to be left here and at Bende were instructed to form 'Native' Courts 'for the settlement of individual and inter-tribal disputes'.[2] Two other towns in Iboland, in which the government proposed to establish visible signs of British rule, were Aba and Owerri. Two companies of the Southern Nigeria Regiment were stationed in these towns, and, preparatory to the elevation of the towns to the status of district headquarters, Sir Ralph's assistant, Gallwey, saw Chief Njemanze with the view to selecting a site for the proposed government station. What transpired at the encounter was recalled by Chief Njemanze when he was met by a postgraduate student.[3] The chief took Gallwey to a number of sites which the people of Owerri might consider leasing to the government. These were rejected by Gallwey. The latter at last pointed to

[1] The request was indeed an inexplicable one because, according to local tradition, women were always barred from any contact with the oracle.
[2] *Ibid.* no. 157 of 12 April 1902.
[3] See p. 228, note 2.

a fertile piece of land and, in spite of Chief Njemanze's objections, the Consul insisted that the site must be surrendered to the government. According to the chief, there was little he could do, confronted by troops who had for some time occupied themselves with looting yam barns. The site selected arrogantly by Gallwey is the location of the Owerri district office today.

The Aro expedition was the last major war launched by the British government of Southern Nigeria for the control of the hinterland. There were still vast areas into which British troops had not penetrated. First, to the east of Idah, lay the country of the Igala and the Munchi. Then there was the hinterland of the Onitsha bounded by lines roughly drawn from Onitsha to Oguta, Abakiliki and Ogrugu. Even then, the High Commissioner spoke in terms of 'a pause of one year...but any longer delay than this in establishing the absolute control of the local administration over the entire territories is not only unjust to those natives already recognising the Government and under Government control, but dangerous and damaging to the prestige of the local Administration'.[1] In the meantime, Sir Ralph urged the Colonial Office to approve a substantial increase in the civil establishment. He justified his request by calling attention to his assumption that the areas of the protectorate already taken over had had to be organised. He had had to do away with 'practically all the systems of the natives'. He had used the words 'native systems' for want of a better expression because it would have been more accurate to say 'that their want of system and methods has to be done away with and native government organised amongst them'.

The government's problems were by no means over even in the 'settled' districts. Detachments of the Southern Nigeria Battalion were stationed at the following places: Unwana, Obubura, Obokun, Okuni, Ediba and Aro-Chukwu (Cross river division); Aba Owerri and Bende (eastern division); Asaba, Oguta, Sabagreira, and Ida (central division); Warri and Benin City (western division). These troops were intended for 'mopping-up' operations and for petty military operations advised by the local political officers. Thus, what took place in a particular district depended on the temper of the political officer in charge of the district. A few examples will

[1] C.O. 520/15, Moor to C.O. no. 355, 8 August 1902.

illustrate the point. The District Commissioner in charge of Owerri district in 1902 was A.C. Douglas. In June he attempted a tour of the villages around the Owerri headquarters. At Omo Anum he and his carriers were surrounded at midnight in the compound they occupied for the night. According to his report he managed to escape between the hours of three and four in the morning. Thereafter a force of 60 men descended on the offending town. 'A chief was then caught and matters explained to him, and the live stock rounded up and taken as fine...on our return we came through the yam farms and destroyed them.'[1] This was quite typical of the method employed by political officers who saw in every inconvenient incident evidence of opposition to British rule.

In the Cross River division, the local British political officers anticipated that the Aro expedition would prove an adequate antidote to the hitherto insubordinate groups encountered in the area. It was indeed noticeable that the Aro expedition which included two columns based at Itu and Ungwana had immediately transformed the politics of the Upper Cross. It was hardly surprising that the indigenous groups were not anxious to see their towns burnt down and their elders hanged. They were fully informed of the fate of Aro-Chukwu. It was usual for the local British administrators to ascribe every manifestation of opposition to the interference of the white man to Aro instigation. It may be recalled that the itinerant Aro who appeared periodically on the Cross river to trade were given the name Inokuns in the official records, and were alleged to command more local respect than the British. Now that the Aro home town was in British hands, the British local officials liked to believe that the local people would recognise that the white man represented a force which had already proved itself superior to the Aro. The Assistant District Officer stationed at Ediba was able to report, a week after the Aro expedition, that he was being bombarded with protestations of friendship and goodwill from hitherto hostile towns. Ekuri, Ugep and Afikpo sent delegations to Ediba to convey their willingness to embrace the white man's ways.[2]

---

[1] *Ibid.* see Encl. in no. 365, 13 August 1902. See also C.S.O. 1/13, Encl. 1 in Moor to C.O. no. 36, 18 January 1903.
[2] Calprof 10/3, Report on Ediba, 31 December 1901.

Subsequently events showed that the local officials were too optimistic in their assessment of the local political situation. They gave too high a value to what was no more than the temporary stupefaction which gripped the groups, with whom the Aro had been in contact for generations, at the news of the complete defeat of the Aro. The riverain peoples recognised the vulnerability of their position, and among them British rule became in 1902 an established fact. To the north and north-west of the new government headquarters of Obubura Hills, there lay the territory of the Ikwe, the Ezza, the Akaju and the Indem. From the standpoint of the government, the work of political consolidation required that a government station should be established at Afikpo. Peace and uninterrupted trade in that part of the Cross river hinterland were beginning to be jeopardised by the Afikpo people who in 1902 refused to allow in their territory 'messengers from the white man'. The Ezza people in fact wished to convey to the white man that they, the Ezza, were stronger than the Aro, and so the white man should have no illusions about what to expect if he showed up in the Ezza country. It was clear to the British local military officers that the Upper Cross hinterland justified in 1902 a military expedition against the Ezza Ibo and the other unidentified groups which controlled the Aweyong tributary of the Cross river. But first, 'the Afikpos should be forced into fighting'.[1]

Sir Ralph Moor's reaction to the clamour for war in the Upper Cross River division illustrates the growing conviction on the part of many of the officials of the protectorate of Southern Nigeria that the policy which had culminated in the Aro expedition had proved to be unwise, expensive and reprehensible. Sir Ralph condemned the bellicose tendency of the military commanders of the Ediba post and advised the political officers to intensify their efforts to persuade the people of Afikpo 'to allow the Government to establish by peaceful means and provide a suitable site'.[2] If, however, it was found necessary to occupy the territory by force, the troops and carriers could live on the country until the submission of the people was obtained. After this, all provisions for the maintenance of the troops were to be paid for. It might

---

[1] C.O. 520/16, Encl. in Moor to C.O. no. 549, 1 December 1902.
[2] *Ibid.*

ultimately be expedient to deport some of the principal chiefs of the place to be held as hostages for the future good behaviour of their people. The threat of intimidation notwithstanding, it can be said that the High Commissioner was now disposed to accept the new method of approach first demonstrated by Fosbery, an officer promoted to the headship of the central division of the protectorate. In fact, the High Commissioner began to speak in terms of studying the native and appreciating his point of view. This, argued Sir Ralph in his instructions to new officers, would guarantee success in their work. The new method of imposing British rule was developed in the Cross River division by young Assistant District Commissioners, one of whom has left details of the manner in which the pacific approach was tried out. Diplomatic and political tours replaced the old policy of military confrontation. The District Commissioner, an interpreter and two native policemen represented all the show of force there was. A visit was preceded with a message to the effect that 'the Commissioner from Obubura is to come to visit you. He represents the big Government. I am your friend and protector, and stand between you and the big Government....'[1]

The indigenous people preferred this approach to the threat of military intimidation. They were perhaps not subtle enough to see that the results were in the end the same, except of course that their homes and farms, and possibly juju houses, were spared. The political officers more often than not found the elders of the place to be visited seated in the village open square, awaiting their arrival. The officers also discovered that where chiefs had in the past refused an invitation to appear at headquarters, it was because the chiefs were looked upon as the representatives of the ancestral god and were so valuable to their communities that they were not normally allowed to travel outside their villages. The sharing of kola-nuts or dried fish cemented the friendship between the villages and the white man, and the latter was sometimes asked to come again soon.

In the central division, W. Fosbery, the Commissioner in charge, enunciated the policy that 'my chief endeavour in dealing with the natives throughout was to allay the evident feelings of

---

[1] Partridge, *op. cit.* p. 303.

distrust shown towards the Government and to inspire that confidence which is so essential if law and order are to be maintained by pacific measures'.[1] Under Fosbery's influence the Ishan districts of the division escaped in 1902 a repetition of the military devastations of 1901. The Commissioner himself arranged meetings with representative chiefs drawn from the Ishan country. At the first meeting at Uromi, Fosbery conceived the idea of a regular council of chiefs from Uromi, Irrua, Ewu, Upogi, Opomo, Ubiaja and Uhoba. The Commissioner recognised, however, that the overthrow of the Oba of Benin had indeed removed the basis of the traditional authority of the Enogies of Ishan. Some chiefs still wielded substantial authority by the force of their personality. Others were, in the eyes of their people, mere nonentities. Fosbery hoped that the establishment of 'Native' Councils supported by the government could restore stability in due course. In the meantime, he concluded his meeting at Uromi 'with distributing three bags of American cotton seed among the towns...at the same time explaining its value'.[2] In the Kukuruku district of the division, Fosbery was satisfied that the king of Agbede was held in high esteem by his people. Here therefore was the man to use in opening up closer relations with the area. The king of Agbede was 'loyal to the backbone, and ready to place himself and his people at the service of the Government'.

Fosbery applied his pacific policy to the Ika peoples west of the Niger. In 1903 he visited Issele-Uku, Onitsha-Olona, Onitsha-Ugbo, Ogwashi, and Illah. It was the Commissioner's aim to establish at Asaba a centre for the regular meeting of Ika chiefs. In his progress through the Ika towns, there were, on occasion, unpleasant incidents. At Onitsha-Olona, Fosbery was told by the people that they did not want the white man and would provide neither food nor water. At Okpanam the chiefs summoned to meet the Commissioner appeared to be 'mostly young men garbed as in Asaba, with red Fez Caps, chalks smeared round their eyes and the usual paraphernalia of ivory horns and fans'. When the chiefs were asked to provide carriers for the Commissioner's party, they bolted. By and large, Fosbery was satisfied that the chiefs of most of the

[1] See Archives (Ibadan), File B.P. 1521, Report on Asaba, 16 September 1902.
[2] *Ibid.*

Ika towns were ready 'to turn over a new leaf and endeavour to live honest lives in the future'.[1] Fosbery was unaware that the young men of the Ika country were already reviving an underground movement for the expulsion of the white man from their country.

The Ekumeku society or Otuochichi,[2] the anti-government and anti-missionary activities of which assumed serious dimensions in 1904, began modestly as a local dispute in Issele in 1893. The king of this place, without the approval of his councillors or petty chiefs of Issele, yielded to the solicitations of the Roman Catholic Church missionaries and agreed to permit missionary work in the town. This incident brought to the surface the simmering hatred of the conservatives for the novel regulations introduced by the Royal Niger Company. These regulations included the prohibition of human sacrifices and the offer of protection to missions south of Lokoja. They could be enforced at Asaba where the Royal Niger Company stationed troops. In the hinterland of Asaba, things went on very much as before. The most formidable opposition to the spread of missionary work was centred on Ibusa, which was apparently the strongest of the Ika towns and was feared by the others. It may be recalled that the Ika communities had for centuries been under the political influence of Benin. Not unnaturally the towns had adopted the Benin hierarchical government structure, but the ruler called himself Obi, not Oba, as in Benin, or Enogie, as in Ishan. Many of the Ika rulers claimed Benin ancestry, and in the days of Benin glory the Ika kinglets were grouped in a fairly coherent feudal relationship with Benin. Thus, Issele-Uku claimed a status of feudal superiority to Ogwashi, Ubuluku, Ibusa and so forth. In the same way, the Obi of Onitsha-Olona liked to believe that he was recognised as overlord by the Obis of Onitsha-Ugbo, Onitsha-Uku, and Onukumi. With the decline of the central power in Benin city, the Ika rulers became virtually independent, and in each town the traditional hierarchy of Obi and councillors began to disintegrate.

Now when the king of Issele welcomed the Roman Catholic

[1] C.S.O. 1/13, Encl. 1 in no. 45, Moor to C.O., 28 January 1903.
[2] 'Ekumeku' suggests rapidity of movement—a sort of whirlwind. 'Otuochichi' suggests a society the proceedings of which are secret and nocturnal.

missionaries, the petty chiefs of the town challenged the authority of the king and invited the old rival of Issele, Ibusa, to espouse their cause. It can be seen therefore that the Ekumeku society was partly the result of internal politics and partly the product of the conflict between the old order as represented by traditional religious practices and the new order which missionary teaching symbolised. The rebellion of the chiefs of Issele against their king appeared to be also a demonstration against the work of the Roman Catholic Church.[1] The missionaries were naturally anxious to support the king, and it was through their representations that the Royal Niger Company dispatched troops in January 1898 to reduce Ibusa and the Issele rebels. The action of the company added a new enemy, from the standpoint of the 'conservatives'. The Ekumeku was in due course to direct its activities also against the alien government of the Ika country.

The Royal Niger Company believed it had nipped the movement in the bud when its force of 250 men burnt down half of Ibusa and dispersed the Issele rebels. In fact the defeat of Ibusa by the white man produced the same temporary stupefaction in the Ika country in 1898 which the Aro defeat produced east of the Niger in 1901. Several Ibusa chiefs were taken prisoner and brought to Asaba. Ibusa was constrained in the circumstances to accept the terms imposed by the Royal Niger Company. Missionaries were to be permitted to work in the town. The chiefs undertook to protect the missionaries. The petty chiefs of Ibusa were required to recognise one paramount ruler. The company's determination to station a garrison did not apparently materialise, but as soon as the terms of treaty were concluded, two Roman Catholic missionaries, Zappa and Scherer, proceeded to Ibusa to select a piece of land on which to initiate their missionary labour.[2] Shortly afterwards, missionary stations were flourishing at Issele, Illa, Ebu, Ezi, Ibusa and Okpanam.

It should be noted, then, that both at Issele and Ibusa, the fight against the old order was one based on the support of local rulers by alien agents against the determination of the younger chiefs to

---

[1] See Society of African Missions Archives (Rome), C. Zappa File—Zappa to Superior General, 26 January 1898.
[2] Ibid.

perpetuate traditional religious practices including human sacrifice. A few months after the chastisement of Ibusa, the Ekumeku society once again reared its head. It is difficult to describe the precise way in which the society was organised or where its headquarters was. All that can be said with a measure of certainty is that the members of the society were the younger chiefs and young men who did not want aliens to meddle in their affairs, political and religious. The outbreak in July 1898 began at Ezi and in a short time the mission stations at Ezi, Issele, Illah, Ibusa and Okpanam were razed to the ground. The missionaries escaped to Asaba. Once more, the Royal Niger Company dispatched troops which went from one town to another in the disaffected districts. The missionaries reckoned that as many as between 25 and 30 towns were involved in the Ekumeku uprising. The Royal Niger Company resorted to its usual policy of capturing a number of petty chiefs who were regarded as ring-leaders. These were imprisoned in the Asaba jail as hostages for the good behaviour of their people.[1] Between 1898 and 1900 the political state of affairs in the Ika country remained unsettled, and the Catholic missions continued to function only because the troops of the Royal Niger Company afforded them protection. In 1900, when the company's charter was abrogated, the hostages in the Asaba jail were released. They returned to resume their anti-foreign activities.

When the protectorate government took over the Lower Niger districts from the Royal Niger Company in 1900, it was clear to the officials that the Ika people had never accepted the white man's rule or his new order. The early comments on the reports prepared by the new officials often merely referred to the existence of 'many elements that may create trouble and danger to life and property'. It did not occur to anyone that the first duty of the new administration should be an attempt to investigate and understand the basic cause of disquiet in the Ika country. The issue of the devastating Ekumeku activities was specifically raised when the Roman Catholic mission demanded compensation for the destruction of its property at Illah when protection had been guaranteed to the mission. The Acting High Commissioner,

[1] C.O. 520/2, Gallwey to C.O. no. 166, 12 June 1900, and Minutes by Sir Ralph Moor.

Gallwey, used the occasion to issue a general warning to all the missionaries to the effect that if they persisted in operating in areas in which government troops were not stationed, they did so at their own risk 'as regards loss of life and property'.[1] The reaction of the Colonial Office expressed itself in the form of misgivings as to 'whether Foreign Missionaries should be allowed in British territories at all'.

The protectorate officials had no doubt in their minds that the political chaos in the Ika country and what the missionaries called the Ekumeku menace were part of the inability of the natives to govern themselves. Patrols by the military forces could deal with the situation as soon as the Aro expedition was concluded. In 1902 Fosbery, the newly appointed Divisional Commissioner and the most intelligent of the protectorate administrators, decided to undertake a political tour of the Ika country. This kind of tour, argued Fosbery, was preferable to indiscriminate military expeditions. The opportunity which the tour afforded the Divisional Commissioner to investigate the grievances or objectives of the Ekumeku society was lost, probably because Fosbery, like the other officials of the protectorate, complacently assumed that the natives, in their helplessness and political incapacity, were only too anxious to welcome the white man's rule. At Issele, he listened to the grievances of the king who argued that 'we have meetings in which we decide matters concerning the welfare of the country; these are already abolished by the Native Council members who base their authority on the white man. These men boast of having more respect from the European than the king.' The whole point of the king's argument was completely lost on the Commissioner. At Ibusa, the Roman Catholic missionary, Father Humberts, conveyed to Fosbery a blood-curdling description of the Ekumeku society. This society was a 'conspiracy which might equal the Indian Mutiny... brewing for the purpose of ridding the country of the white man'. At Ogwashi, Fosbery learnt that the local organiser was a man called Azu who was addicted to 'seizure, lawlessness and intimidation'. In the face of the type of evidence with which the Divisional Commissioner was confronted, it is

[1] *Ibid.* See no. 270, 11 October 1900, and Minutes by Strachey, Antrobus, Cox and Chamberlain.

hardly surprising that Fosbery echoed the notorious view of the head of the protectorate administration that 'a blow...will settle it [Ekumeku] once and for all'.[1]

In the meantime the government policy of arbitrarily but conveniently selecting the personnel for the government-sponsored 'Native' Councils in supersession of indigenous organs of government kept the old grievances fresh in the Ika country, and progressively united the traditional rulers and the young men in a common cause against all foreigners, government or missionary. Early in 1904 the whole Ika country literally erupted. Anglican and Roman Catholic mission stations were burnt down in Atuma, Akuku, Onitsha-Olona, Ezi, Onitsha-Uku, and Idumuje-Ugboko. The 'Native' Court buildings at Ogwashi, Onitsha-Ugbo, Illah, Ibusa and elsewhere were pulled down and destroyed. In these activities, the protectorate saw at last 'the flame of rebellion'.[2] The Ekumeku attacks were indeed directed against the foreign agencies in the Ika country, including African Christians suspected of foreign sympathies.

The protectorate government decided on strong measures against this 'Society of Africans, the motive principle of which is Africa for the Africans'.[3] The government's war aims included ridding the country of cannibalism, the slave trade, outrages, and crime. It was intolerable that a country 'peculiarly blessed by nature is practically closed to commerce and civilisation'.[4] It took approximately two months to suppress the Ekumeku society, at any rate to arrest all those alleged to be the ring-leaders. These 'leaders' selected from Ibusa, Onitsha-Olona, Ogwashi, Onitsha-Ugbo and Illah were imprisoned. The 'Native' Courts in these towns were suspended because the people did not 'deserve to have again extended to them the privileges conferred by these courts'.[5] The closure, rather than the reorganisation, of the foreign-inspired 'Native' Courts showed how little the government understood the

[1] Archives (Ibadan), see File B.P. 1521, Report on Asaba, 16 September 1902.
[2] C.S.O. 1/13, no. 48, Fosbery to C.O., 9 February 1904. C.M.S. Archives, C.A. 3/08, Dennis to Baylis, 19 January 1904 and *West African Mail*, 22 June 1906, on the 'Ekumeku' or 'Silent Society'.
[3] *Ibid.*
[4] C.M.S. Archives, *op. cit.* Copland-Crawford to Bishop Tugwell, 5 March 1904.
[5] C.S.O. 1/13, no. 57, see Encl. 4.

motives behind the Ekumeku society, one of whose aims was the liquidation of the 'Native' Courts. In the event the government had the advantage of superior force, and as in the other parts of the protectorate, the issue of indigenous independence versus foreign rule was decided by the naked application of brute force. The result was apparently satisfactory to the missionaries who were able to report that, as a consequence of the suppression of the Ekumeku society, attendance at divine worship and school soon passed 'anything we have ever seen before'.

The continued use of force by the British administration of Southern Nigeria in suppressing the Ekumeku movement in the Ika country or in dealing with the reported brigandage of a chief in the Anambra country cannot be blamed on Sir Ralph Moor. The High Commissioner in fact left Southern Nigeria in March 1903 on retirement. A dispatch from the Secretary of State expressed 'high appreciation of the arduous and valuable services which Sir Ralph Moor has, during the course of the last twelve years, rendered to the Empire in the Niger Coast Protectorate and Southern Nigeria'.[1] From the standpoint of British imperialism, the area annexed to Britain—the richest in economic resources in West Africa—was undoubtedly a tribute to Sir Ralph's energy and patriotism. His methods in achieving the grand results were quite another matter. Moral issues are involved and these lend themselves to interminable controversy, and no useful purpose will be served here in opening the controversy. On the other hand, it is only fair to say that, in his economic policy, Sir Ralph rendered an invaluable service to the people of Southern Nigeria. This will be examined in a subsequent chapter.

The first Acting High Commissioner, after Sir Ralph's departure, was Leslie Probyn, who was Secretary at Old Calabar. Probyn's reaction to reports that Assistant District Commissioner Boyle and his escort of 20 men had been attacked on their way from Idah to the Anambra creek was no different from that associated with Sir Ralph Moor's 'forward' policy. The territory involved was the northernmost portion of the central division. The local chief, a man

[1] *S. Nigeria Gazette*, 1903. See Chamberlain's dispatch dated 25 July 1903. (Sir Ralph Moor was found dead in bed at his residence, The Homestead, Barnes, on 14 September 1909. The inquest suggested suicide during temporary insanity: see *Dictionary of National Biography*, second supplement, vol. II.)

called Adukukaiku, had closed all the routes in his territory to trade and barred both Hausa and Yoruba adventurers who attempted from Idah to tap the resources of Adukukaiku's domain. The chief's behaviour was exaggerated into offences which included brigandage, slave-raiding, and harbouring various criminals escaping from the Idah prison. In Probyn's view, an area known to be rich in natural resources could not indefinitely be closed to commerce and civilisation. A small-scale military expedition was therefore organised. The Attah and chiefs of Idah, the heads of Yoruba and Hausa communities in Idah accompanied the expedition. The enemy's stronghold beyond Alede was strategically chosen in the middle of a swamp hidden by dense bush and palm. It was also trenched and stockaded on every side. The only access to the stronghold was a narrow track through which an invader had to wade knee-deep and, in addition, run the risk of injury from sharp stakes embedded in the track. British maxim fire was enough to destroy Akukukaiku's stronghold. His principal town, Okubo, was taken. Seventeen towns altogether were occupied and destroyed. A garrison was from this time stationed at Ogrugu, a town at the head of the Anambra creek. In the end, the chief was captured, tried by the Supreme Court at Asaba, and sentenced to detention in Old Calabar for a period of ten years.[1]

When W. Fosbery became Acting High Commissioner in the latter part of 1903 he apparently abandoned his earlier attitude towards punitive expeditions. It will be recalled that as Divisional Commissioner in charge of the central division in 1902, he had emphatically asserted that in the process of pacifying the territory which Britain pretended belonged to her 'the feelings of the natives must be taken into consideration'.[2] In 1903, when confronted with the Ekumeku movement in the Ika country, Fosbery approved military measures for the forcible suppression of the movement. It can only be assumed that, in Fosbery's view, the feelings of the natives should not amount to a rejection of British rule or to a repudiation of an alien way of life. The Ekumeku war notwithstanding, it can be said that after 1904 no large-scale expedition

[1] C.S.O. 1/13, Acting H.C. to C.O., 25 March 1903, see Enclosures 1 and 2. Also nos. 177 and 432 dated 10 April and 11 September respectively.
[2] C.O. 520/16, no. 574, dated 9 December 1902. See Report on the Central Division.

was organised for the subjugation of what was left of the protectorate of Southern Nigeria. The annual report for 1904 did in fact acknowledge that 'throughout the whole of the territory now under our control settled government has only been established by means of a show of military force'.[1] Military garrisons were established at Asaba, Idah, Owerri, Bende, Afikpo, Okuni, Obubura Hill, Ikot-Ekpene, Aba, Eket, Benin City and Warri.

From the military stations enumerated above, annual patrols went into regions not yet controlled or into districts where there appeared any manifestations of hostility to British rule. This policy of annual patrol was believed to be a new policy and it was later described by a Secretary of State as 'peaceful penetration'.[2] The new policy in actual fact meant no more than that indiscriminate military expeditions were to be avoided, and that as far as possible towns were to be occupied without hostilities. The emphasis was to be on the establishment of civil government and native courts. Under this policy, there were carried out various patrols known as the Anambra patrol, the Kwale patrol, the Mkpani patrol, the Ikwe patrol, the Onitsha hinterland patrol, the Ibibio-Kwa patrol and so forth. A special memorandum was prepared for the guidance of political officers accompanying the patrols. The officers were urged to explain the determination of the government to put down crime and to maintain law and order. The government would also assist in promoting trade and in developing natural resources. The officers were also to emphasise that '...it is the wish of the Government that they (the towns) should still continue to manage their own domestic affairs, and that Native Courts which will be established for this purpose, will be assisted with the advice of the District Commissioner'.[3] The memorandum concluded with the assertion that where opposition was offered in any town to the patrols, the troops would live 'on the country' until the natives submitted. Jujus were to be destroyed. In the Onitsha hinterland, the juju at Awka called the Agballa was singled out for destruction because of 'its baneful influence'.

The policy of military patrols, or what the Administration called

[1] Colonial Reports, Annual, S. Nigeria, no. 459, Egerton to Lyttelton, 1904.
[2] *Nigerian Pamphlets*, no. 16. See Steel, 'Exploration in S. Nigeria', 1909.
[3] C.S.O. 1/15, 5 A.D.M. 9/414, Confidential Despatches to Secretary of State, 1904.

'pacific penetration', was continued during 1905 and 1906—and indeed for many years after 1906 when Southern Nigeria was amalgamated with the colony and protectorate of Lagos. Official reports give specific reasons why particular towns were selected for visitation. For instance, in the western division, there was the Kwale patrol of 1904 because '...this particular portion of the country has always shown the greatest disinclination to come into touch with the officials and has always resolutely pursued its own course, retaining all its native habits and customs in spite of the many warnings received at frequent intervals...'.[1] Fines were imposed on the towns of the Kwale district visited and usually a number of chiefs were selected for detention until the fines were paid. The political officer accompanying the patrols concluded with impressing on the towns the duty of attending meetings arranged by the District Commissioner at central 'Native' Courts. In 1905 the murder of Dr Stewart near Ahiara necessitated the dispatch of a strong column to the Bende-Onitsha hinterland. The annual report for 1905 briefly conveys the information that the column, under Major Trenchard, secured the submission of the offending natives and confiscated 17,996 guns. Local tradition suggests that the townsfolk fled into the bush and when their hiding place was located by the government troops, revolving machine guns were deployed to mow down men, women and children.

Practically every town east of the Niger has its own traditions which recall the arrival of the military patrol, or, as the traditions call it, the arrival of the white man. The patrols were usually preceded by a summons to the town to send representatives to meet the white man at a government-controlled town. The summons was ignored and preparations were set on foot for the evacuation of men and property from the town. The strategy involved in this defensive evacuation was one already perfected during the long generations of sudden Abam raids instigated by the Aro. When, therefore, the military patrol arrived, it was confronted with a deserted town. Sometimes endless messages went to and fro between the visitors and the fugitives. If the commanding British officer ran out of patience, he ordered an attack which produced submission. Many towns are anxious to insist that

[1] C.O. 520/25, Encl. in no. 260, 3 June 1904.

their people did not submit without a fight. The chiefs who counselled negotiations with the white man are singled out for bitter denunciation in many a local tradition.[1] All in all, it is impossible to sift fact from fiction in these traditions, and no people have voluntarily painted their past history in colours of cowardice and ignominy. Superior military force was bound to prevail, and one and all submitted to British rule. What was left to be done was the consolidation of the new regime. This was merely a question of time.

[1] These traditions, now being collected by history post-graduate students, will be collated and edited in due course.

# CHAPTER VII

# THE 'NATIVE' COURT SYSTEM AND THE CONSOLIDATION OF BRITISH RULE: 1901–6

'If the tribal system is allowed to fall into decay it will be necessary to increase to an extent almost beyond the resources of the Protectorate the staff necessary for doing the work which is now done under the tribal system.'[1] The uninspired passage quoted here is interesting on two grounds. In the first place, it acknowledges quite frankly the primary reason behind the policy of building up 'Native' Councils in Southern Nigeria. In the second place, the British representatives indulged in the illusion that the 'Native' Councils were no less than the perfection of the indigenous systems of government. A great deal has indeed been written in praise of what came to be called indirect rule, in Nigeria and elsewhere. In Southern Nigeria, the administrators might easily have claimed some of the virtues of indirect rule for the system they were developing. Illusion and expediency therefore joined hands to lay the foundations of an alien system of local government which effectively undermined 'the tribal system' and produced chaos. In a way, the development of the ill-conceived local government institution illustrates the change which overtook the original conception of a protectorate.

It may be recalled that the first attempt to organise Consul-controlled local government machinery to supersede the indigenous organs of government on the coast had been made by Acting Consul H. H. Johnston in 1887. Having successfully completed the deportation of the most powerful chief in the Oil Rivers, Johnston saw an excellent opportunity of making British rule a reality in the protectorate. He therefore organised what he called

---

[1] C.O. 520/9, Confidential, no. 9, Probyn to C.O., 15 September 1901.

Governing Councils for Bonny, Opobo and so forth. The Councils comprised local chiefs and European traders selected by the Acting Consul, who also defined the legislative, executive and judicial powers of the Councils. Johnston's measures were, according to him, necessitated by his conviction that the native chiefs on the coast did not seem competent to administer the affairs of their country 'in a wise and just manner'. The British Foreign Office rejected Johnston's Councils and insisted that a 'Native' Council should be designed 'to make and enforce Native Laws and not to carry out Consular Orders'.[1] At the time, the Foreign Office preferred to hold on to the theory that in a protectorate the paramount power was confined to external as distinct from internal sovereignty. It was also true that the British government was in 1887 unwilling to encumber itself with the expense of running the administration of the Oil Rivers protectorate, especially when it was not certain whether the venture was going to be self-supporting. The repudiation of Johnston's local government councils was therefore not necessarily an indication of a carefully thought-out policy on the part of the British government.

There was no real inconsistency in what might appear as a drastic modification of the attitude of the Foreign Office to the indigenous system of government on the coast. In 1891 the British government took the first step in abandoning the policy of *laissez-faire* which hitherto dominated British relations with the Nigerian coast states. Detailed instructions to the Commissioner and Consul-General attempted to define the official view with regard to the integrity of the coast political organs.

It is not advisable that you should interfere unduly with tribal government, the chiefs should continue to rule their subjects and administer justice to them, but you should keep a constant watch to prevent injustice and check abuses, making the chiefs understand that their powers will be forfeited by misgovernment...in special cases...you will be authorised to insist on a delegation to you of a chief's judicial and administrative powers....[2]

Major Claude Macdonald could easily have found excuses for

[1] F.O. 84/1828, no. 18, Johnston to F.O., 24 September 1887. See also Minutes by Pauncefote dated 30 January 1888.
[2] F.O. 84/2110, F.O. Draft to Macdonald, 18 April 1891.

dispensing with the local institutions he found in operation. Promoting civilisation and local 'inhuman and barbarous customs' were hardly compatible with each other. In the event, Macdonald had neither the staff nor the temperament to dispense with co-operation of the chiefs who controlled the trade and politics of the city-states. The Commissioner's local government policy was therefore essentially a policy of compromise. The man himself often spoke of the importance of gaining 'the respect and liking of the natives, by a judicious conduct of affairs', and it was to be expected that he was aware of the sensibilities of the local chiefs whose powers were bound to be usurped by any drastic imposition of alien local government organs.

Indigenous government in the city-states was by no means uniform. Nor can it be pretended that stability was the order of the day. In Old Calabar the powers of the Egbo society often eclipsed those of the rulers. In Bonny the king could be a nonentity in the presence of dynamic and powerful heads of 'houses'. In the course of the nineteenth century, the traditional tribunals domi-nated by kings and juju priests were indeed cracking under the impact of growing materialism. In the face of the apparent political fluidity which prevailed, Macdonald attempted to use the services of those chiefs who wielded influence in the city-states. He there-fore revived Johnston's 'Native' Councils, although there was the basic difference that Macdonald's Councils excluded European traders. The 'Native' Councils were allowed to enjoy prescribed judicial and legislative powers in internal affairs. In the outlying districts, Macdonald constituted what he called Minor Courts.[1] How 'native' these Councils were Macdonald and his assistants never asked themselves. The administrators, however, firmly believed that they were doing nothing revolutionary. To rectify the deficiencies of indigenous institutions and gear them to the task of promoting civilisation could not be construed as revolutionary or unjust. It was the work of humanity. This much was clear to the British representatives.

By 1895 Macdonald's local government institutions were reportedly functioning at Calabar, Adiabo, Itu, Uwet, Bonny,

[1] F.O. 2/84, see Despatches 10–29, Regulations for the Constitution of a Minor Court; and statistics of criminal and civil cases.

Degema and in all the coast states in which British rule had become established. A remarkable appendage was the establishment at Old Calabar of a High Court of the 'Native' Councils as a kind of Court of Appeal. The first few years of British rule saw two parallel regimes—one 'Native' and the other alien. The 'Native' was at every level subordinated to the 'alien'. In each city-state and its environs, the 'Native' Council and 'Native' Court carried out the vice-consul's instructions, and at Old Calabar, the High Court of the 'Native' Councils was manipulated by the Commissioner and Consul-General. Theoretically, the 'native' organs constituted a vital link between imperial rule and the native peoples. In reality, the local institutions were from the first artificial bodies used by the British officials for their own purposes. The vice-consuls did not hesitate to remove from the 'Native' Councils those chiefs who appeared to be self-willed. It did not matter whether they were regarded by their people as their legitimate rulers. Two examples will suffice to illustrate the point. King Koko of Nembe, it may be reiterated, had led his people in the dramatic attack on the Royal Niger Company's station at Akassa. The venture was followed by a protracted punitive expedition which combined with hunger and smallpox to decimate Brassmen. It was a situation in which King Koko and his people saw the rule of the white man in its most vexatious form. It became quite clear to the protectorate government that the king was not prepared to forget his people's grievances in order to please the white officials. It was therefore with the view to eliminating the influence and authority of the king that the government reconstituted the 'Native' Council of Brass before the end of 1896. The official reason given was that King Koko had declined all intercourse with the white man in order to retain 'his power as "Juju Man" over the natives' and to pose 'as the absolute ruler of the country'. The formation of a 'Native' Council in Okrika followed the deportation of the Okrika king to Degema in 1896.[1]

The history of the 'Native' Council for New Calabar in 1897 affords an even more notorious example of the arbitrary way in which the British officials dealt with the personnel of the Councils.

[1] F.O. 2/100, Moor to F.O. no. 18, 13 March 1896. F.O. 2/101, Moor to F.O. no. 50, 14 June 1896.

King Amachree apparently continued to wield enormous influence over the chiefs of Abonema, Buguma, Bakana, Young Town and the neighbourhood. At the meetings of the Council, the chiefs waited to hear King Amachree's views on any measures proposed by the government and then they unanimously supported these views. The vice-consul then came to the conclusion that the king preferred the advice of juju men to that of the white man. King Amachree was forthwith sacked from the 'Native' Council which operated in his own domain. The vice-consul was indeed gratified when he discovered that the new members, including Manuel, Briggs and Braid, were keen to give every assistance to the government.[1]

The views of the protectorate government on the indigenous system of government on the coast were often contradictory. Sir Ralph Moor agreed that the coast peoples were 'formerly governed by so-called kings, all of whom are now dead'. Their successors were no more than middlemen traders whose hold on their 'boys' was increasingly tenuous. In the circumstances, the government believed it was rebuilding indigenous rule by selecting favourite chiefs to form 'Native' Councils. Having formed these Councils, the High Commissioner emphasised that the government should take all possible steps to maintain the position of the chiefs both as regards trade and members of their 'house', and that 'their native systems of Government should be strenuously upheld...'.[2] It is of course clear that the subtle dynamics of native political institutions of native rule were completely lost on the British representatives. The visible forms of native rule were expressed in the coast chiefs whose claim to pre-eminence was based almost exclusively on wealth derived from trade. As long as the government-selected 'Native' Council members afforded the dynamic leadership which the members of their 'houses' needed for the prosecution of trade, they could be expected to maintain native government. The part formerly played by juju priests was in any case inconsistent with the requirements of the new regime.

The policy of establishing arbitrary Councils on the coast and

[1] Calprof 8/2, Report on the New Calabar District, 31 March 1897.
[2] C.O. 520/12, Moor's report on his meetings with the chiefs at Old Calabar, Opobo, Okrika, Bonny, Degema, Brass, Warri, etc., dated 7 July 1901.

styling them 'Native' Councils could be defended on the grounds that politics and trade were intermingled on the coast and both were constantly in a state of flux. The organisation of local governments to replace the rule of the Oba of Benin had no such apology, except of course, and this ought to be borne in mind, that the protectorate government believed that everything about Benin rule was evil. In Benin City, a 'Native' Council was formed even before the capture of the fugitive Benin king. The members comprised those chiefs who made an early submission to the British, and these were not necessarily ones who enjoyed traditional authority. In fact the British representative in Benin, Turner, made an agreement with the loyal chiefs by which the latter would not lose their new position 'when bigger and more important chiefs come in'.[1] The Benin 'Native' Council members were mere British puppets whose chief spokesman did not want the Oba to have a place in the Council and was nicknamed 'Poor Soapy' by Resident Turner. There is nothing more fascinating than the manner in which the protectorate administration pretended that it was the Benin 'Native' Council, and not the British, which controlled the affairs of conquered Benin. The trials of the Oba of Benin, Ologbosheri and Abohun were conducted under the auspices of the Benin 'Native' Council and in accordance with native law and custom. Led by the High Commissioner, the Council proclaimed that according to 'native' law, a white man was equal to a chief and so the Benin chiefs responsible for the ambush of the white men had forfeited their lives. In June 1899 Ologbosheri was captured by the British troops and brought before the Benin 'Native' Council which declared that 'Ologbosheri was not sent to kill white men— and we therefore decide that according to Native Law his life is forfeited'. The remaining Benin chief, Abohun, was captured in July, but Sir Ralph Moor had already decided he could use him for the rule of Benin because Abohun was 'intelligent and of good character'. The Benin 'Native' Council could not in the circumstances apply native laws to Abohun's trial, which never took place. What the members of the Council thought of the justice they were supposed to dispense is a matter for speculation.

[1] Calprof 6/1, Turner to Moor, 4 April 1897. F.O. 2/123, no. 120, Moor to F.O., 18 October 1897.

By 1900 'Native' Councils and Minor Courts were functioning in all the portions of the protectorate subjected to British rule. Old Calabar had a High 'Native' Court and 15 Minor Courts, Opobo district a 'Native' Council and five Minor Courts, Bonny district two 'Native' Councils and one Minor Court, New Calabar district one 'Native' Council and three Minor Courts, Brass one 'Native' Council, Warri district one 'Native' Council and three Minor Courts, Sapele one 'Native' Council, and Benin City one 'Native' Council.[1] The subjugation of the Ishan, Kukuruku and Ika portions of the Benin empire was followed by the creation of the inevitable 'Native' Councils or Courts. At the time, the British officials knew absolutely nothing about the clan groupings of the Ishans or the Kukuruku. 'Native' Councils were arbitrarily established at centres where Enogies were thought to have influence over the surrounding districts. For instance, the Uromi 'Native' Court had the Enogie of Uromi as President and 15 representatives chosen by the administration from the surrounding villages. In 1905 the Ekpoma 'Native' Court was established for the village groups of Ekpoma, Opoji, Egoro and Urohi. In the Ika country, each town was found to be under an Obi, and the difficulty was to discover which Obi had paramount power over his neighbours. In the absence of thorough investigations, the choice of centres for the establishment of 'Native' Councils was bound to be arbitrary. For example, the 'Native' Court at Issele was boycotted by the surrounding towns because the latter had never been subordinate to Issele in the regulation of their political and judicial affairs. Even at Issele, the Obi was not a member of the 'Native' Council and he lamented that the 'Native' Council members 'boast of having more respect from the European than the king'.[2] The king explained that before the white men came, the Issele had meetings in which they decided matters concerning the welfare of the country. The 'Native' Councils set up by the government had put a stop to such meetings. The administration indeed took pains to point out to the chiefs of Ibusa, Asaba, Okpanam and so forth that the settlement of native affairs rested in the hands of

[1] C.O. 520/3, see Annual Report, 1899–1900.
[2] See File B.P. 1521 (Archives), Report on the Central Division, 16 September 1902.

the 'Native' Councils and that the latter could rely on the support of the government in upholding their authority.

The extension of the 'Native' Court or 'Native' Council system to Ibo and Ibibio country was destined to prove the greatest blunder of the British agents charged with consolidating British rule in this part of the protectorate. Two contradictory fallacies lay behind British policy. The first was the assumption that the Ibo and Ibibio had no form of government and that anarchy prevailed everywhere. The second concerned the efforts made in the early stages of penetration to 'find' the 'chiefs' through whom the British and their new order might be introduced to the people under the control of the 'chiefs'. Another fallacy which will be discussed in the next chapter was that the 'house' system which characterised coast social organisation extended to Iboland and Ibibioland.

Political officers who attempted to penetrate the periphery of the hinterland, before the Aro expedition, had invariably reported meeting 'chiefs' representative of towns in the interior. For instance A. B. Harcourt reported enthusiastically about his introduction to the 'king' of Obegu, and about his interviewing 'the kings and chiefs' of the various towns which the political officer's party traversed.[1] Another officer, Griffith, who visited a number of Ibibio towns assumed in his report that he had a most fruitful meeting with the most important chiefs in that part of the protectorate. Nobody seemed to recognise the inconsistency in the portion of his report where he detailed that the chiefs were seventy in number and represented thirty-three villages.[2]

It is easy to be over-critical of the implications in the reports. After all, these officers were aware that among the coast communities each state had a number of chiefs. The mistake was merely the complacent assumption that the 'chiefs' and 'kings' encountered in the hinterland were the rulers of their villages and towns. Then, when the Aro expedition was being planned, the High Commissioner, Sir Ralph Moor, convinced himself that the rulers of Iboland and Ibibioland were the Aro, and that once the latter's tyranny was overthrown, there would be no difficulty in

---

[1] Calprof 8/2, Report by A. B. Harcourt, 1896.
[2] *Ibid.* Report by A. G. Griffith, 5 July 1896.

getting the hinterland peoples to welcome the white man with open arms. As explained already, the progress of the expedition was accompanied by the establishment of 'Native' Councils.[1]

At the risk of repetition, it is intended to recapitulate briefly the Ibo and Ibibio traditional system of government. Generally speaking, the largest social unit comprised several localised kindreds, known as the *Umunna* in Ibo.[2] This unit was the village. In some cases a number of villages which believed themselves to be related constituted a village-group, the highest political unit based on a sense of common ancestry and the possession of a common territory, common customs and a common shrine, *Ala*, the god of the land. Within this framework, the heads of the lineage groups, known as elders, met informally and infrequently to interpret the 'laws' and sanctions handed down from the supernatural world through the ancestors. The communities did not recognise the elders as chiefs but merely as intermediaries between the dead ancestors and the living. Individually, each elder exercised within his own lineage an informal kind of domestic authority.[3] The work of government in the Ibo and Ibibio communities was not formalised or institutionalised and was full of subtleties which the impatient British conquerors had neither the training nor the disposition to attempt to unravel. The policy which aimed at upholding and using indigenous organs of government in the area under consideration should have sought out the *elders* in each village group, not 'find' the 'chiefs' through whom to rule. The latter represented the application of the protectorate policy of 'indirect rule'.

After the Aro expedition, a 'Native' Council of 'chiefs' was soon 'functioning' in each 'liberated' town, for instance, in Owerri, Aba, and Bende. When Aro-Chukwu was captured, the 'chiefs' who were exonerated of any complicity in the supposedly iniquitous manipulation of the Long Juju were constituted into a 'Native' Council. It is not without interest that a subsequent intelligence report on the Aro policy of the British revealed clearly that the representatives of the 1901 'Native' Council were arbitrarily

---

[1] C.O. 520/9, no. 320, 3 October 1901.
[2] Loosely translated, *Umunna* means the children of a common 'father'.
[3] Meek, *Law and Authority in a Nigerian Tribe*, pp. 88–9.

chosen and without any reference to their status under the old regime. The report concluded that '...Aro became yet another area wherein an artificial judicial body came into being, a body having behind it, in native eyes, no sanction but force represented by the District Officer and the police'.[1]

The Aro example is fairly representative of the history of the 'Native' Court system in Iboland and Ibibioland. In a number of places, local tradition points to more notorious instances of arbitrariness in the choice of the personnel of the 'Native' Council. In the towns around Awka and Aguleri, the story is that as the white man and his troops arrived, the elders, the women and the youngest age-groups fled to safety from the town or village. The more adventurous of the fighting age-groups stayed behind to find out what the white man was about. These young men therefore made the first contact with the political officers. The latter, understandably, assumed that the adventurers represented the vacated towns and it was from among them that the first members of the 'Native' Council were selected. In towns where there was actual resistance to the presence of the British, the elders, when captured, were considered *personae non gratae* and were therefore ignored for the purposes of the establishment of the 'Native' Council. Research students from the University of Ibadan have, during their field-work, encountered other methods of selecting the members of the 'Native' Council. In parts of Owerri, the community concerned deliberately nominated undesirables for appointment by the government, hardly realising that the undesirables would be invested with unprecedented powers over the community. In the Urhobo country where British penetration was more leisurely, the communities, in many cases, put forward their traditional rulers as personnel of the 'Native' Council. From these instances, it is clear that any generalisation is open to objection.[2]

The members of the 'Native' Council formed a link between the District Commissioner and the local community. They were gradually to acquire other powers, political and judicial. As a result a new aristocracy emerged with no local standing and to

[1] Shankland, Intelligence Report, no. 29017, 1933.
[2] Afigbo, *The Warrant Chief System in Eastern Nigeria, 1900–29* (Ph.D. thesis, Ibadan, 1964). Ikime, *Itsekiri-Urhobo Relations and the Establishment of British Rule, 1884–1936* (Ph.D. thesis, Ibadan, 1965).

17-2

which the natives accorded no recognition.[1] In the meantime, the protectorate government relied on the 'Native' Councils for the dispensation of justice among the natives, for the establishment of peace and good order, and for innumerable other purposes. In fact Sir Ralph believed that the 'Native' Councils were the means 'by which the natives are taught to properly govern themselves under the control of His Majesty's Administration'. His deputy went further and claimed that 'the most widespread powerful... influence tending to elevate the natives will...be found in the Native Councils, provided the latter are constantly supervised by European Officers'.[2] The importance attached to the 'Native' Council led naturally to the legislation enacted by the administration to define and regularise the new and artificial organs of local government.

Up to 1898 the protectorate records speak of four categories of court: the High Court of the 'Native' Council of Old Calabar and district; the 'Native' Council (the Court of the 'Native' Council); 'Native' Minor Courts; and the Consular Courts. The divorce between the 'Native' Courts and the unmistakably British court systems had not yet emerged. The Consular Courts were virtually at first local Courts of Appeal, and regulations were issued with the view to the 'observance of Native Customs in the Consular Courts'.[3] In the following year, a formal distinction was made between the 'Native' Council and the Minor Court, the former being 'allowed and encouraged to make necessary native laws affecting the tribes which they represent and over which they have control'.[4] These references and distinctions were only preliminaries to the formal legislation which in due course attempted specific definition of the relationship and powers of the categories of court enumerated above. The final act was the subordination of all the courts to the jurisdiction of the British Supreme Court of the protectorate.

It was Sir Ralph's deputy, Gallwey, who on his own initiative proposed four proclamations to define the position in respect of

[1] The term 'warrant chiefs' came to be applied to these new men of authority. Sir Ralph Moor used the term as early as 1896, but it acquired its notoriety in its application to the 'chiefs' of the hinterland Ibo and Ibibio.

[2] C.S.O. 1/13, no. 203, 17 May 1902. Also Annual Report for 1902.

[3] F.O. 2/180, Annual Report, 1897–8.

[4] Annual Report of the Niger Coast Protectorate, 1898–9.

the Supreme Court, Criminal Procedure, the Commissioners' and 'Native Courts'. Sir Ralph now thought that Gallwey's proposals involved complicated issues which he ought to handle himself.[1] Before Sir Ralph could come to grips with the business of formalising the Court system, the problems created by the mere establishment of 'Native' Councils on the coast, consisting of government-picked members, forced him to issue a proclamation which dealt primarily with the break-up of the 'house' system on which trade and political and social stability had traditionally depended. According to the preamble, Sir Ralph's aim was 'to maintain intact the Native System of House Government...the House Rule System has to be established which is in a way recognised by all the natives in the territories'.[2] In the 'houses' where the heads had lost authority under the new order, the High Commissioner entertained high hopes that he could, through the house rule proclamation, restore the former harmonious relations between the heads of 'houses' and their 'boys'.

The social implications of Sir Ralph's proclamation in 1899, which stemmed from the disintegrating effects of the 'Native' Council system, are not discussed here. The enactment of the second 'Native' house rule proclamation in 1901 was of special significance because it applied to the whole of the protectorate of Southern Nigeria. The stipulations, as far as Ibo- and Ibibioland, the Western Ibos and Urhoboland were concerned, were ridiculous. The basic assumption, as already pointed out, was that the 'house' system was characteristic of the social structure of the whole protectorate. Now, according to Sir Ralph's 1901 proclamation, any member of a 'house' who refused to submit 'to the...authority and rule of the head of his house in accordance with native law and custom' exposed himself to severe punishment by the government.[3]

Ignoring for the time being the social aspects of the 1901 proclamation, the political effects on the status of traditional administrative machinery are worth noting. The High Commissioner assumed formally the right to approve the appointment and dismissal of the members of the 'Native' Courts. Lastly,

[1] C.O. 520/2, Gallwey to C.O. and Enclosure in no. 247, 15 September 1900.
[2] C.S.O. 1/13, no. 34, 25 August 1899.
[3] C.O. 588/1 for Proclamations 1899–1901.

'where a "Native" Court is established in any district the civil and criminal jurisdiction of such court shall as respects natives be exclusive of all other native jurisdictions. . . .'[1]

Gallwey's earlier attempt to categorise the judicial organs at the disposal of the administration was fulfilled when a proclamation created (i) the Supreme Court, (ii) the District Commissioner's Courts, and (iii) the 'Native' Courts. Sir Ralph eulogised the 'Native' Court system unreservedly. 'The courts are not only the basis of the Judicial system but of the administrative and executive systems of the Protectorate.'[2] The extraordinarily contradictory situation which Sir Ralph did not recognise was the provision that the head 'chiefs' of towns who were not necessarily members of the 'Native' Courts had to ensure the attendance of people summoned to the Courts. Any neglect on the part of such 'chiefs' called for punishment by the government.[3] These enactments were coupled with increased powers for members of the 'Native' Councils ('warrant chiefs') to impose upon the traditional rulers of the hinterland. Examples of the grievances of the natural rulers in Ika country have been cited already. East of the Niger, the communities, when and where they could, continued to dispense justice in their traditional ways—these procedures were always of course at the risk of severe punishment by the government. The Ishan country provided a few illuminating instances of the indigenous opposition to the British-introduced 'Native' Court system. For instance, where before the arrival of the British the traditional rulers pronounced undisputed sentence on the culprit, the 'Native' Council under the District Commissioner indulged in elaborate procedures which were incomprehensible to the Ishan communities.[4]

The administration recognised that the Court system involved serious difficulties; some were understood, others were ignored. A few examples are sufficient to illustrate the general state of affairs. The administration believed that the 'Native' Court system was the only means of 'lifting up the primitive forms of

[1] Ibid.
[2] C.S.O. 1/13, no. 16, Moor to C.O., 7 January 1903.
[3] Calprof 9/2, Moor to D.C. Western Division, 22 May 1902.
[4] This information is owed to an aged Enogie who lived through the period of transition.

government' which Sir Ralph Moor thought did not deserve the designation of government. In this respect the choice of men and 'Native' Council members without reference to their traditional status within the hitherto autonomous villages or village-groups created two rival authorities. There were many occasions when the political officers discovered to their horror that in most places people took their cases to their traditional adjudicators rather than to the 'Native' Court. The 1903 proclamation included severe penalties for the boycott of the 'Native' Courts.[1] The ultimate result was naturally to destroy the old judicial system which the communities understood and venerated.

In the second place, the choice of the siting of the 'Native' Court took no account of the traditional links or absence of links which bound together the innumerable autonomous villages. Examples have already been given with respect to the Ika country, where traditional rival towns refused to attend Courts located in the one or the other. The solution which the administration attempted was to extend as rapidly as possible the number of 'Native' Courts 'to leave no excuse to the natives for not bringing their disputes for settlement'.[2] Even then, there was the problem of inadequate European staff to supervise the British-established 'Native' Courts. There was already ample evidence that the members of the 'Native' Councils, especially those whose power rested on the support of the white man, were turning the Courts into instruments of 'legalised' extortion, intimidation and injustice towards litigants or alleged offenders.

Sir Ralph had always insisted that political officers should preside over the proceedings of the 'Native' Courts, whenever possible. His political staff at the end of 1903 of 4 Divisional Commissioners, 4 Travelling Commissioners, 14 District Commissioners, and 38 Assistant District Commissioners could hardly be expected to cope with the requirements of effective supervision. Periodic visits and the inspection of 'Native' Court proceedings were the compromise achieved.

[1] Calprof 9/2, *op. cit.*; C.O. 588/1, The Native Court Proclamation, no. 25 of 1901, clause 12.
[2] *Government Gazette*, Supplement no. 30, 1904 (see Annual Report, Western Division, 1904). (It should be noted that the Commissioner in charge of a District was *ex-officio* President of the 'Native' Council of his district.)

In spite of the appointment of Court Clerks and Travelling Supervisors of 'Native' Courts, the integrity and effectiveness of the 'Native' Councils and Minor Courts remained in doubt. It is therefore not surprising that Sir Ralph instructed a Judge of the Supreme Court, M. R. Menendez, to undertake an extensive tour of investigation throughout the protectorate presumably under British control. The Judge was a man of considerable initiative and his tour is therefore of great interest.[1] The number of 'Native' Councils visited by the Judge amounted to sixty. It serves no purpose to list these Councils, but it is necessary to mention a few to show to what extent British rule had penetrated in 1903. The coast Councils naturally included Bonny, Opobo, New Calabar, Old Calabar, Nembe and Sapele. West of the Niger, in the hinterland, were Benin City, Ifon, Owo, Agbede, Uromi, Issele-Uku and Ubulu-Uku.

The Judge undertook to establish 'Native' Councils at Onitsha (with the Obi as Vice-President), Abo, Agberi, Omoku, Aguleri and Idah. He also preferred a measure of federation of small communities under 'Native' Councils to an innumerable number of Minor Courts to serve each autonomous community. He understandably failed to appreciate that detailed anthropological studies might alone provide criteria for any kind of federation of groups which attached great importance to their autonomy. The Judge's report concluded with the rather amusing story that while he was establishing the 'Native' Council at Aguleri, and while the first meeting of the Council was in progress, 'head hunters' were active five miles from Aguleri.[2]

It should have become apparent that the 'Native' Court system provided an important means of undermining traditional authorities, and thus served the purposes of the consolidation of British rule throughout the protectorate. Under heavy penalties, the traditional organs of government and of the judiciary crumbled and progressively ceased to function. The Members of the 'Native' Councils and Court Clerks, who 'knew the white man's ways', began to acquire a new prestige and wealth which the diehards

[1] C.S.O. 1/13, no. 16, Moor to C.O., 7 January 1903. See also Report by Menendez dated 4 January 1903.
[2] *Ibid.* (In 1903 the Government issued the Ordeal, Witchcraft, and Juju Proclamation.)

were not slow to appreciate. A 'warrant chief' became a man of importance through whom the wishes of the new rulers were conveyed, and through whom severe punishments and other penalties could be obviated. The Court Clerks also acquired these privileges and there are still many people living who made their fortunes by virtue of their role as Court Clerks and Court Messengers.

The main outlines of Sir Ralph Moor's policy were continued by his successor in 1904. Two years later the amalgamation of the Southern Nigeria protectorate with Lagos accelerated the decision to bring the 'Native' Court system, particularly in respect of its judicial functions, unequivocally under the Judicial Department and the Supreme Court in Lagos.[1] There was indeed no radical departure from Sir Ralph's 1901 proclamation and his increasing reliance on the Judges for the effective supervision of the judicial proceedings of the 'Native' Courts. Nevertheless, a few clauses of the 1906 Native Court proclamation deserve special mention, because they illustrate the complete control of the internal and external affairs of the communities which Britain had accomplished.

According to Clause 9 (a), the High Commissioner could appoint any member of the 'Native' Council to act as the President of the Court, in the absence of the District Commissioner; otherwise the District Commissioner remained the President of the 'Native' Courts. The membership of the 'Native' Council was defined to include the Divisional Commissioner, the Travelling Commissioner of the Division, the District Commissioner, the Assistant District Commissioner, and 'such other persons as the High Commissioner may from time to time by name or office appoint'.

By Clause 47 the power of 'Native' Councils was elaborated: Every 'Native' Council, subject to the approval of the High Commissioner, (a) could make rules embodying any native law in its district, with or without additions and modifications, as might be deemed expedient, (b) should regulate and promote trade in its district, and (c) should generally 'provide for the peace, good order, and welfare of the natives therein'. Lastly, the 'Native' Council could, subject to the approval of the High Commissioner, impose a fine not exceeding £100, or imprisonment for a term not exceeding two years with or without hard labour, or with or without

[1] C.O. 588/2, Proclamation no. 7 of 1906.

flogging, not exceeding fifteen strokes.[1] There were, in addition to the 'Native' Councils, Minor Courts with more limited powers. The personnel in regard to both courts tended to be the same, except that the Minor Courts comprised 'warrant chiefs' from the smaller territorial units. The traditional councils of elders were undermined or driven underground. The status of the elders as representatives of the ancestors progressively lost its former veneration.

Of course it is not being suggested that the administration set out deliberately to undermine the traditional system. But the point which is being emphasised is that the system was neither studied nor appreciated but written off as another instance of native primitiveness. Consequently what was regarded by the British as benevolent paternalism did not produce the results it was calculated to bring about. It is fair to add that the subordination of the 'Native' Courts to the Supreme Court Judges was a measure of the awareness of the administration that a great deal of injustice and terrorism might otherwise be inflicted on innocent but impecunious natives alleged to have committed an offence against the many but hardly comprehensible proclamations and regulations issued from the 'big white man in Calabar'. The Administration attempted another safeguard against the iniquities implied above. The Chief Justice or a Puisne Judge could at any stage of 'Native' Court proceedings order the transfer of the case to the Commissioner's Court or to the Supreme Court.

The supervision of 'Native' Courts by either the District Commissioner or the Judges was by no means effective, partly because of the increasing proliferation of the Courts and partly because of the enormous administrative work, including monthly reports and returns, with which the District Commissioner was saddled. Two examples will suffice. In Old Calabar, the headquarters of the protectorate, there were in 1905 (between January and September) 78 sittings of the 'Native' Council. The District Commissioner presided on only 24 occasions. In Creek Town, for the same period, there were 31 sittings and the District Commissioner could preside only once.[2]

---

[1] *Ibid.* See also C.S.O. 1/13, vol. XXXVIII.

[2] Conf. 152/5, Native Courts, Calabar; Owerri 122/16. Memo on Native Courts.

In fact it was the semi-educated Court Clerks who increasingly dominated the proceedings of the Courts. They understood much better than the illiterate 'warrant chiefs' the 'mysteries' of the regulations and procedures transmitted through themselves by the white man. Court Messengers, the agents of the Court Clerks who sent warrants of arrest through them, also became men whose presence caused a great deal of consternation in the community. The whole situation created by the 'Native' Court system provided limitless opportunities for intimidation and the acquisition of dishonest wealth which many a Court Clerk exploited to the full.[1]

Apart from the fact that the 'Native' Court system was an alien institution, nothing was more responsible than the behaviour of Court Clerks, the 'warrant chiefs' and the other agents, for the failure of the Courts to command the respect and the support of the hinterland communities.[2] The administration, on the other hand, and in spite of the disturbing reports by the Judges of the Supreme Court, continued to admire the system it created. For instance, the Commissioner of the Eastern Province had this to say about Native Courts: 'This system has worked well and the increasing demand for the establishment of new Courts shows the trust and confidence which the courts enjoy among the Native population.'[3]

In spite of the Commissioner's optimism, the administration had to cope with many problems arising from their alien system. In the first place, secret societies which exercised greater influence over the communities than the 'Native' Court continued to function in many places. Secondly, there were bold natives who designated themselves 'Consul men', kept courts in their homes and used their own boys as 'police'. With reference to this kind of impersonation, the annual report for 1906 noted that 'there appears to be little difficulty in securing some sort

[1] The number of convictions for bribery involving Court Clerks was an eloquent testimony that many abused the privileges which European rule introduced into traditionally well-organised communities.

[2] Afigbo, op. cit. ch. VII. In the preceding chapter, pp. 240 f., I discussed the 'Ekumeku' rising, west of the Niger.

[3] Southern Nigeria Annual Report, 1907, p. 36. See also Meek, Law and Authority in a Nigerian Tribe, p. 328; and Annual Report by J. E. Jull on Native Administration Affairs, Ogwashi-Uku District, 1935.

of "so-so" uniform—in one case a water bottle and revolver were secured. This together with a page from a hymn book or, as in another case, a pocket French Dictionary completed the equipment. Such men do a great deal of harm among the native population'.[1]

What is baffling is that the District Commissioners and the Assistant District Commissioners who were stationed in places that brought them closest to the communities did not seem to recognise, as their successors in the 1930's did, the false founda- tions on which the 'Native' Court system operated. The opportunities for the recognition of what was later called 'the necessity for intimate knowledge of tribal customs before attempting any but the most perfunctory relations with a primitive tribe' seemed completely absent in the most itinerant of the political officers of the protectorate. All that was said about a systematic inquiry into 'native' administrative systems, manners and customs was apparently wasted on the political officers whose districts had before 1906 embraced almost the whole of Southern Nigeria. A reasonably detailed survey of the functions of these officers will illustrate the point made here.

The administrative paraphernalia usual in a Crown Colony, rather than in a protectorate legally speaking, were almost complete in the protectorate of Southern Nigeria in the opening years of the twentieth century. The High Commissioner had under him a Colonial Secretary, Divisional Commissioners, District Commissioners and Assistant District Commissioners. The Judiciary comprised the Supreme Court, the District Commissioner's Court, and the 'Native' Courts under the presidency of the Divisional, District or Assistant District Commissioner. The military arm of the government was the third Battalion of the Royal West African Frontier Force. The Police, in 1902, comprised the Inspector, two Assistant Inspectors and 304 rank and file. The other executive categories of the Civil Service included the Customs, the Public Health, Public Works, the Marine, Prisons, the Post Office and others. The High Commissioner could, from Calabar, issue proclamations on all kinds of subjects, including the 'Native' Courts, but the officers who came into close touch with the com-

[1] C.O. 592/3, Annual Report on Eastern Province, 1906.

munities being ruled by Britain were the District Commissioners and their Assistants. The nature of the work of the latter therefore throws considerable light on the problems of consolidating the *pax Britannica*.

It has been pointed out that neither the territorial administrative units nor the locations of the 'Native' Courts and the headquarters of the district or sub-district bore any relation whatsoever to the traditional groupings of the indigenous communities. In addition, there were areas which the earlier period of intermittent military expeditions had not subdued or penetrated. A fortunate District Officer might find himself posted to a reasonably peaceful neighbourhood, and an unfortunate one might find himself in a 'disturbed area'[1] and would have to do as much fighting as administration. In spite of the absence of uniformity in the routine work of District Commissioners, all of them were burdened with multifarious duties. The records of one such officer throw abundant light on the general question raised in this paragraph.[2] It would be misleading to suggest that the military did not continue reasonably large-scale operations, despite a Secretary of State's description of this phase of British expansion as 'peaceful penetration',[3] but most of the District Officers accepted the Secretary of State's attitude towards a more salutary method of consolidation.

It can be gathered from Partridge's records that each new District Commissioner, or Assistant District Commissioner, was advised at headquarters to deal 'softly, softly with Nature's children of the bush, and [humour] them'. The initial instructions implied that small acts of courtesy 'were, in the very eyes of the natives, real proofs that their "big father" meant to protect and treat them well'. The realisation of these fine-sounding mandates depended partly on the mental disposition of the officer and partly on the degree of submission to British rule already achieved in any particular area. Invariably the fatal test which most officers seemed to have driven into their own minds was that it was the duty of the 'chiefs' to acknowledge the supremacy of the government by

[1] For instance, the Annangs (W. Ibibio) under Ekpe influence, 1904, and towns east of the Anambra river, 1904, and Abakaliki area, up to 1907/8.

[2] Partridge, *Cross River Natives* (1905).

[3] *Nigerian Pamphlets*, no. 16, Exploration by Capt. B. A. Steel, 1909. See Remarks by Col. Kemball.

coming out to greet the new District Commissioner or Assistant Commissioner.[1]

The duties imposed on these officers were indeed many. In the first place, the District Commissioner was responsible to the Divisional Commissioner for peace and tranquillity in his District and Sub-District. It was his job to transmit to the 'warrant chiefs' the many instructions and rules which arrived almost endlessly both from the divisional headquarters and from the High Commissioner. It was the District Officer who attempted to have the rules accepted by one and all without friction or rebellion. Another political aspect of the District Commissioner's work concerned the abolition of reprehensible native practices and customs, the removal of obstacles to freedom of trade, and lastly the 'civilisation of the natives'.[2] This assignment was sometimes phrased in official instructions as 'to open up new country'. The British officer concerned was here supposed to visit natives who had hitherto not had any contact with the white man or felt the effect of a military patrol. According to Partridge, who served in the Obubura district, patience, tact, common sense, good temper and a sense of humour were the qualities the District Commissioner or Assistant District Commissioner needed. In a peaceful area, the local communities looked forward with amusement to seeing a white man. The latter, accompanied by an interpreter and two policemen, would find the elders squatting in an open space shaded by trees— their traditional 'Parliament'. They made the District Commissioner a present of a goat, and the District Commissioner would in return distribute tobacco, cloth and other novel fineries. Friendship was thus consolidated.[3]

The idyllic picture of mutual understanding painted in the last paragraph could not conceivably be typical of the phrase 'to open new country'. For instance, in Ahiara in the Owerri district, Dr Stewart was murdered in 1905, and the murder by the Owa people of the Assistant District Commissioner Crewe-Read was reported in 1906. In these areas, 'opening up new country' took on a military complexion. In some towns, the people had ready

[1] *Ibid.* pp. 12–17.
[2] Southern Nigeria Annual Report, 1905. See General Observations.
[3] Partridge, *op. cit.* pp. 4–5.

defensive stratagems like trenches and stockades. In the circumstances, the District Commissioner was accompanied by troops to inflict severe punishment on the communities and hope that all would be well in the future.[1]

The judicial aspects of the District Commissioner's post, for which he received from the High Commissioner a judicial warrant, amounted to a sort of 'all-purposes' assignment. He was Justice of the Peace, the local sheriff and coroner. He was president of the 'Native' Courts, including both 'Native' Councils and Minor Courts. Lastly, he had his own District Court.[2] The other varied duties of the District Commissioner included financial returns, control of the local police detachment, the local post office and survey work.

The Divisional Commissioner was no doubt also saddled with a lot of paper work, including monthly reports on his division.[2] Periodically, however, he undertook a tour of the districts and sub-districts within his jurisdiction. The District Commissioner went to great lengths to guarantee that nothing untoward happened during the Divisional Commissioner's visit. The members of 'Native' Councils and Minor Courts as well as elders were summoned in advance and lectured in the following manner:

The Commissioner...is come to visit you. He represents the big Government. I am your friend and protector, and stand between you and the big Government. If you do as you are told, you will be protected from the soldiers...and plenty of trade will come to your country. The Commissioner goes about making peace between all tribes and towns and settling their disputes....The Government forbids certain bad customs which destroy peace.[3]

The High Commissioner's tour of the protectorate was very rare. He relied for his annual reports to the Colonial Office on the monthly and quarterly returns from the Divisional and District Commissioners. This explains in part the untrue but optimistic details about the spread of civilisation and the functioning of the 'Native' Courts.

The task of consolidating British rule was pursued with vigour

[1] See Annual Report, already cited, for details of the Onitsha hinterland, the South Ibibio and Itchi-Ogoni and Owa operations.
[2] C.O. 520/9. See circular issued from the Secretary's Office, 1901.
[3] Partridge, *op. cit.* p. 303.

not only in Southern Nigeria but also in the Lagos protectorate and in what was quite wrongly called the protectorate of Northern Nigeria. Before 1900, when the Royal Niger Company lost its charter and its territories, the existence of three administrative regions, one under the Colonial Office, the second under the Foreign Office, and the third under chartered company rule had proved a source of irritation to the administrators of the Niger Coast protectorate and of Lagos. The three administrations had different fiscal systems hardly consistent with the overall policy of the effective commercial exploitation of what became Nigeria.[1] There were idiotic boundary disputes between the Royal Niger Company on the one hand and the other two administrations on the other. Sir Ralph Moor was fond of recalling the Brass war and the alleged iniquities of company rule in his advocacy of amalgamation. Incidentally, there were boundary conflicts between the Lagos protectorate and the Niger Coast protectorate. The best example was, after the conquest of Benin in 1897, whether Yoruba tribes under Benin influence should come under the control of Lagos or the Niger Coast protectorate.[2]

The Colonial Office and the Foreign Office officials were often exasperated by the boundary and fiscal conflicts involving three territories supposed to be under the same Queen. It is therefore not surprising that in 1898 the British Cabinet set up what was called the Niger Committee. The committee, under the chairmanship of Lord Selborne, included Sir C. Hill (F.O.), R. L. Antrobus (C.O.), Ralph Moor, George Goldie and Sir H. McCallum (Lagos). The committee agreed that, as regards the future administration of the territories of Lagos and its protectorate, the Niger Coast protectorate and the company's territories, the object to be kept in view was the eventual establishment of a Governor-General. For the present, difficulties associated with the climate of the country and the absence of communication facilities ruled out the amalgamation of the three administrative and autonomous units.[3]

[1] F.O. 2/102, Moor to F.O., 24 November 1896; F.O. 2/122, same to same, 26 June 1897.
[2] The Owa of Ilesha equivocated when questioned on their traditional focus of allegiance.
[3] C.O. 446/3, Report of the Niger Committee, 4 August 1898. See also map no. 17887 in the Report.

Another idea in respect of some kind of amalgamation was suggested by Chamberlain. This was the division of the whole territory into 'Soudan' and 'Maritime' Provinces. Since Goldie assumed that the 'Soudan' Province corresponded with his existing sphere of jurisdiction, it was left to Ralph Moor and McCallum to find a basis for amalgamating the territories under their respective control. Each administrator, however, preferred to be master in his own domain. The whole issue was therefore shelved by Joseph Chamberlain in 1898. Sir Ralph had assumed he was the likely candidate for the governorship of the 'Maritime' Province, but Sir H. McCallum wasted no time in dispelling Moor's illusions.

After the abrogation of the Royal Niger Company's jurisdiction and the absorption of the Lower Niger into what became Southern Nigeria, Sir Ralph Moor once more in 1901 raised privately with Joseph Chamberlain the issue of amalgamating Southern Nigeria and Lagos. The Colonial Secretary authorised Sir Ralph to produce a concrete scheme. Sir Ralph proceeded with this task without consulting the new Governor of Lagos, MacGregor. The 'Maritime' Province of Sir Ralph's imagination would comprise seven administrative divisions, with Lagos as capital.[1] When MacGregor realised what Sir Ralph was about, he forwarded to the Colonial Secretary counter-proposals which envisaged the amalgamation of Lagos with Northern Nigeria. His strongest argument was that a railway was already begun from Lagos towards Northern Nigeria which served two vital purposes—co-ordinated economic exploitation and facilities for travelling. Once again the Colonial Secretary thought it expedient to shelve the rival schemes.

When both Sir Ralph Moor and MacGregor retired towards the end of 1903, the way was clear for Chamberlain to arrange for the union which had taken up so much time with futile discussions. Before examining the triumph of Chamberlain's hopes, it is necessary to show that in the Niger Coast protectorate from the inception of effective British administration, the policy of Sir Claude Macdonald and of Sir Ralph had progressively meant the amalgamation of the hitherto small city-states and the autonomous village communities into large administrative groupings. The inherent policy was not pronounced in the early years when a vice-consul was

[1] C.O. 520/7, Moor to C.O., 14 January 1901.

appointed to each important coast city-state and the energies of the administration were concentrated on using the city-states as points of advance into the hinterland. Local amalgamations went side by side with the expansion of the protectorate and the enlargement of the machinery of central administration. For instance, Macdonald in 1895 divided the protectorate already controlled into: (i) eastern headquarters district, embracing the Cross, the Calabar and the Qua-Eboe rivers, with Calabar as headquarters; (ii) central district, comprising Opobo, Bonny, Degema and Brass; (iii) western district, embracing the territories of the protectorate west of the Niger delta. The significance of these administrative unions was twofold. It was the first step in the gradual transformation of the administrative machinery of the protectorate into that of a Crown Colony. Far more important for the subject under discussion was that, for the first time, the city-states and neighbouring communities had to look to the district headquarters for instructions in regard to new proclamations and rules issued from Calabar—the establishment of 'Native' Councils notwithstanding.[1]

The elimination of the Royal Niger Company as a political agency and the extensive area under control after the Benin expedition provided another occasion for greater centralisation of administrative control. In 1900 the protectorate was split into four divisions—eastern, central, western and Cross River. Gallwey was in charge of the eastern division; Leonard, the central; Locke, the western; and Roupell, the Cross River division.[2] In the eastern division, for example, Old Calabar, Opobo, Eket, Bonny and Degema came under the overall control of Gallwey in Calabar. Naturally all the Divisional Commissioners had under them District Commissioners and Assistant District Commissioners, but all were supposedly local representatives of the 'big white man', the High Commissioner.

The policy of establishing organs of local government in the hinterland involved another aspect of amalgamation. It would have been impracticable for the administration to establish a 'Native' Council or Minor Court in each traditionally autonomous

---

[1] F.O. 2/85, Macdonald to F.O., 19 December 1895.
[2] C.O. 520/2, Enclosure in no. 233, Moor to C.O., 22 August 1900.

Ibo or Ibibio village, or even in each Ika community, west of the Niger, which had a recognised Obi. Thus the administration invariably selected rather arbitrarily or for adventitious reasons the location of a 'Native' Council to which surrounding, but hitherto autonomous, communities were expected to bring their disputes. The report by J. E. Jull, already quoted,[1] had emphasised that the attempt to blend diverse units into a centralised 'Native' administration produced an atmosphere of artificiality. The same verdict applies to the centralising policy of the protectorate government. The main aim in reiterating the points made above is to show that the amalgamation of Southern Nigeria and the Lagos protectorate effected in 1906 was by no means revolutionary.

As already mentioned, the retirement of Sir Ralph Moor of Southern Nigeria and the departure of MacGregor of the Lagos colony and protectorate at about the same time left the way open for the amalgamation of the two protectorates. The first step was the joint appointment of W. Egerton as High Commissioner of the Southern Niger protectorate and Governor of Lagos in 1904. In other words, Egerton was charged with the joint administration of two separate political entities. The new man indeed proposed to keep the two regions separate, and argued that the revenue and legislation of the two territories should be kept separate.[2] The Colonial Office repudiated Egerton's plans on two grounds. In the first place, the Colonial Office had always cherished the idea of removing the expense of duplicating administrative machinery. Secondly, the special arrangements made by Chamberlain in the Colonial Loans Act could not apply to a protectorate, and the latter would therefore be deprived of the facilities for raising loans on the London market for capital development on the security of a protectorate revenue.[3] One argument which the Colonial Office accepted was the removal of 'Old' from Calabar, on the ground that the foundation of New York in America had not led to the addition of 'Old' to York in the United Kingdom.

A royal commission of 1 March 1906 appointed Egerton, now Sir Walter, Governor and Commander-in-Chief of the

[1] Annual Report by J. E. Jull on Native Affairs, 1935.
[2] C.S.O. 1/13, no. 405, High Commissioner to C.O., 17 May 1904. C.O. 520/29, Egerton to Lyttelton, Confidential, 12 September 1904.
[3] *Ibid.* See Minute by Antrobus.

'Colony' of Southern Nigeria. The area was defined to include 'the island of Lagos and such portions of the neighbouring territories as have been annexed to Our Dominions'.[1] The new 'Colony' of Southern Nigeria was divided into three provinces: (a) the western province incorporating Lagos and the old Lagos protectorate; (b) the central province, with Warri as capital; and (c) the eastern province, with Calabar as capital. It should be noted that (b) and (c) were what was historically the protectorate of Southern Nigeria, now absorbed into the 'Colony' of Southern Nigeria.[2] The administrative paraphernalia of the Lagos colony naturally embraced the whole territory. There was the Governor and his Central Secretariat. Then there were Provincial Commissioners and Provincial Secretaries, Chief Assistant Secretaries, and Assistant Secretaries. The districts remained under District Commissioners and Assistant District Commissioners. A Chief Justice and three puisne Judges, Police Magistrates and Registrars were in evidence. The Attorney-General and Solicitor-General, the Financial Commissioner and Provincial Treasurers were clearly officers new to the old protectorate of Southern Nigeria. The 1st Battalion Southern Nigeria Regiment continued to be stationed at Calabar. The 2nd Battalion was in Lagos.

Two legal enactments were necessary to remove the irregularities, acknowledged by the Colonial Office, in amalgamating a British colony with a protectorate. By the Governor-in-Council Ordinance, 1906, the Acting Attorney-General provided an Ordinance 'to enable the Governor in Council to exercise certain powers vested, prior to the date of amalgamation of the Colony and Protectorate of Lagos with the Protectorate of Southern Nigeria, in the High Commissioner of the latter Protectorate'.[3] Another Ordinance proposed to enact that 'the Common Law, the doctrines of Equity and the Statute of general application which were in force in England up to the 1st of January 1900 should be in force within the jurisdiction of the Supreme Court of the Colony of Southern Nigeria till that date'.[4]

[1] *Southern Nigeria Gazette* (Extraordinary), 1 May 1906.
[2] Amalgamation Correspondence, Egerton to Lyttelton, 29 January 1905.
[3] C.S.O. 1/13, Enclosure 51/1906 in Governor to Elgin, 19 May 1906.
[4] *Ibid.* no. 185, 9 June 1906.

There is no evidence that the natives of the protectorate of Southern Nigeria protested in any way against the liquidation of their separate political existence. It was all high policy with which they had long ceased to have any concern. There was no substantial change in the status of the political officers—in fact, two Divisional Commissioners found themselves elevated to the status of Provincial Commissioners in the central and eastern provinces.[1] For the rest, the amalgamation meant incorporation into a regularised service typified by a Crown Colony.

Objections to the amalgamation came from the educated and more sophisticated inhabitants of Lagos. A public meeting was organised in Lagos on 6 June 1906. The speeches of the leading citizens of Lagos contained several issues, but as far as the amalgamation was concerned, there were two grounds of dispute. In the first place, a measure of Yoruba irredentism revealed itself in a preference for an amalgamation which would bring together the Yoruba of Ilorin and Kabba and the main Yoruba of the Lagos hinterland. In the second place, the Lagos citizens suspected that the 'Native' Court system, which operated in the protectorate of Southern Nigeria unequivocally under the presidency of British officials, might be extended to Yorubaland where the functioning Court system safeguarded the essential character of indigenous judicial organs for purposes of local government. The letter of protest was forwarded to the Colonial Secretary by the Governor.[2]

To complete the history of the British political relationship with a territory theoretically the protectorate of Southern Nigeria, it is necessary to discuss briefly the controversy forced on Sir Ralph Moor in 1902 by the demand of the British merchants for a legislative council in the protectorate. The High Commissioner's efforts to conserve the forests of the territory for the future benefit of the natives provoked the bitter opposition of the West African Trade Association. The merchants' demand was based on their claim to be in a position to veto or mutilate the enactments of the High Commissioner. Sir Ralph rejected the proposal on three grounds. In writing to the Colonial Office, he pointed out that the local agents would be the tools of their directors in England who

[1] *Government Gazette*, no. 2, 9 May 1906.
[2] C.O. 520/36, Enclosure 2 in Egerton to Elgin, 11 August 1906.

277

could think only of immediate gain. Sir Ralph concluded that 'the tendency in the past has certainly been to "suck the orange", employing the minimum of capital, putting nothing into the development of the Country...and taking everything possible out of it. It has been my endeavour and one of my difficulties in the past to combat this.'[1]

Sir Ralph's second objection was that it was impossible to find any one chief 'with any authoritative voice as representing native interests as a whole'. This objection was undoubtedly valid. The High Commissioner knew only too well that the former chiefs of the coast had become no more than a trading aristocracy. They might be members of the 'Native' Councils, but they had certainly ceased, in a political sense, to represent any but their own interests. As regards the hinterland, the arbitrarily selected agents for the personnel of the 'Native' Courts could not claim to represent anything but the authority of the District Commissioner. Besides, the traditional structure ruled out the type of political integration, by virtue of which there might be traditional functionaries who could speak for the whole protectorate. Sir Ralph's third objection was the difficulty of communication. The time it took a Divisional Commissioner to travel to the Districts and Sub-Districts was ample evidence in support of the High Commissioner's contention.

There was a further consideration to which Sir Ralph alluded indirectly. He made a distinction between absolute British rule for the native population and rule by the native population. He undoubtedly preferred the former, and in doing so, made vague references to the Lagos Legislative Council where he believed the enactment of 'necessary' legislation was held up by 'filibustering' native members.[2] Joseph Chamberlain apparently endorsed the arguments put forward by Sir Ralph against the establishment of a legislative council in the protectorate of Southern Nigeria. The Colonial Office, however, advised the High Commissioner to consult native chiefs and the European trading agents in lieu of a legislative council. The officials of the Colonial Office did not undertake to say how their advice was

[1] C.O. 520/16, Manchester Chamber of Commerce to Chamberlain, 1 May 1902. Morel, *Affairs of West Africa* (1902), p. 25. C.O. 520/15, Confidential, Moor to C.O., 21 September 1902.
[2] C.O. 520/10, Confidential, Moor to C.O., 14 December 1901.

to be implemented. After the amalgamation of 1906 the Lagos legislative council was empowered by the Southern Nigeria Protectorate Order-in-Council, 1906, 'by ordinance or ordinances, to legislate for the Protectorate'.[1] The legislative council then comprised mainly officials, but included three nominated educated Africans and three European unofficials. No native member represented what was, before 1906, the protectorate of Southern Nigeria.

There is no evidence to show that the natives of the protectorate protested against the new political order. The Governor of the new 'Colony of Southern Nigeria' was satisfied that the affairs of the old protectorate were progressing satisfactorily. The acting Governor's annual report for 1906 concluded complacently and optimistically that 'generally the progress of civilisation...has been most marked. The natives have shown appreciation of what the Government has done for law and order which have opened up their roads and rendered their lives and property safe.'[2] An uncritical acceptance of the implication of this report would be mere delusion. Considerable fighting to subdue portions of the protectorate continued until 1910.[3]

[1] C.O. 591/2, *Southern Nigeria Gazette* (Extraordinary), 1 May 1906.
[2] Southern Nigeria, Report for 1906, Acting Governor to the Secretary of State.
[3] Trenchard (later Lord Trenchard) led one of the severest of these expeditions.

# CHAPTER VIII

# THE FOUNDATIONS OF ECONOMIC AND SOCIAL CHANGE

...Cases have already come to my knowledge of Colonies...in which up to the present British Rule has done nothing, and if we left them today we should leave them in the same state as that in which we found them. How can we expect, therefore, either with advantage to them or ourselves, that trade with such places can be developed?[1]

The extract quoted above is part of Joseph Chamberlain's speech on 'our undeveloped estates', after his assumption of office as Colonial Secretary in 1895. For the speech, the British merchants on the Nigerian coast had nothing but appreciation. In his later endorsement of the urgency of the economic exploitation of the region, E. D. Morel, their chief spokesman after Mary Kingsley's death, argued, that internationally, Britain was secure in the territory. Commerce was the reason for their presence in West Africa. Its requirements demanded the 'constant vigilance, the most careful attention of the official world'.[2]

It is therefore hardly surprising that one of the instructions issued to Major Macdonald at the beginning of effective British administration in 1891 emphasised the part the encouragement of legitimate trade would play in civilising the inhabitants of the protectorate and in preparing the way for direct British rule. After all, the vindication of British claims to the Oil Rivers rested primarily on the preponderant commercial interests which British merchants had gradually built up since the outlawing and suppression of the slave trade. The very name Oil Rivers that was originally given to the territory suggests what remained for a long time the principal export which the merchants and the coast middlemen developed. The growth of this item of export trade is best illustrated by reference to a few statistics. In 1806 the amount

[1] *Hansard*, vol. 36, 1895, pp. 640 f.
[2] Morel, *Affairs of West Africa* (1902), p. 10.

of palm oil imported into Liverpool was estimated at 150 tons. In 1836 the amount had risen to 13,600 tons, as it was increasingly required for the making of soap, candles and different kinds of lubricants.[1] Export trade in due course developed in palm kernels, which came to be used for the manufacture of margarine in Britain. The export trade items and their value issued by the new administration for the first time reveal the position of the export trade in 1895:[2]

| Native products | Value in £ |
| --- | --- |
| Palm oil | 505,636 |
| Palm kernel | 295,312 |
| Rubber | 13,281 |
| Ebony | 5,458 |
| Ivory | 1,202 |
| Cocoa | 1,159 |

The government acknowledged that there were other sources for enhancing the export trade. These included coffee, kola-nuts, gum-copal and cotton, but exports of these products were then negligible.

In exchange for the native exports, the white merchants bartered spirits, tobacco, cotton cloth, guns and gunpowder, salt, brass rods, manillas and cheap metallic ornaments. Before the 1880's the merchants did all the transactions connected with their trade in hulks which were moored on the rivers. The name 'hulk' is still given by the inhabitants to the beaches where the hulks had been used.[3] The place of hulks was to be taken by 'factories' when the Europeans felt safe enough to do business with the coast people on land. A typical factory has been described as follows: 'A factory was on the edge of the river and usually consisted of a pier, a wharf, a large house and veranda containing quarters for the agent and clerks on the first floor, a shop or store on the ground floor, and stores, otherwise sheds, for produce and sleeping places for the Kroo-boys.'[4]

An important development which accelerated the volume of trade was shipping. The African Steamship Company and the British and African Steam Navigation Company, formed in 1852 and 1869 respectively, were amalgamated in 1890 and came under

---

[1] *Parl. Papers* (C. 7916), *Africa*, no. 9, 1895. Knowles, *op. cit.* pp. 84, 85.
[2] *Parl. Papers, op. cit.*
[3] For instance, the Onitsha 'hulk'.
[4] Geary, *op. cit.* p. 89.

the control of Elder Dempster and Company. The growth in the tonnage of British shipping in the trade with British West Africa is exemplified by the following statistics:[1]

| | Tonnage |
|---|---|
| 1884 | 1,157,000 |
| 1894 | 2,269,000 |
| 1904 | 4,674,000 |

The new administrators in 1891 were convinced that there still existed long-established practices which hampered a more phenomenal expansion of trade in a region blessed with rich natural resources in the hinterland. The first of these practices was 'comey'. The divergent interpretations of the levy by the local chiefs, the British merchants and the British political agent have already been discussed in the chapter on consular 'rule'. There were various other levies on the British merchants—work bar, custom bar, 'shake-hand', and topping—which the Macdonald administration refused to tolerate. Undoubtedly the innumerable levies, with obscure origins, had been a fruitful source of friction between the British merchants and the local rulers.

The conviction on the part of the administration that the local chiefs' levies were irregularities which hampered trade and the necessity to make provision for a government-controlled revenue were the grounds on which the administration justified the decision to abolish 'comey' and the other levies. Major Macdonald was instructed to do this and to compensate the chiefs with annual subsidies paid out of the government revenue. The government therefore proceeded to systematise the basis of import duties.[2]

When the administration was set up, the coast chiefs who controlled the river mouths were still monopolists in the sense that the trade from the hinterland passed through their hands. The European condemnation of this situation was not a new thing. The celebrated dispute between Johnston and Jaja centred on the question of European direct access to the hinterland to undermine Jaja's monopoly. To break up the coast monopoly was an im-

---

[1] McPhee, *The Economic Revolution in British West Africa* (London, 1926), see note 3 on p. 71.

[2] There is no documentary or oral evidence to throw any light on the chiefs' reaction to this significant change. See, however, F.O. 84/2111, A. P. Anderson's comment on Macdonald's Despatch, 1 September 1891.

portant item in the programme of the protectorate government. West of the Niger delta, the local vice-consuls encountered the 'biggest monopolist of all', Nana of the Jekri river, who was shortly disposed of. Direct trade between the Europeans and the protectorate was thus gradually getting nearer and nearer to the producing districts themselves. It would be misleading to give the impression that the limited advance inland achieved by the Macdonald government immediately disrupted the pattern of trade which had operated for centuries. The white merchants still found it easier to rely on the coast chiefs for the assembly and purchase of the principal exports, palm oil and kernel. In this respect, Nana's commercial empire might be broken up, but the petty chiefs remained monopolists. This was bound to be so until the protectorate government overran the hinterland and afforded the white merchants the security indispensable to the building of local trading stations.

First the Cross river and later the Niger offered opportunities for releasing the stranglehold of the coast chiefs on trade. By intermittent military expeditions and chastisement of offending towns, the government gradually succeeded in breaking up the tradition of each town on the Cross river demanding tolls before articles of trade to or from Old Calabar were allowed through. In due course, the advantages of direct trade with the Europeans were constantly preached by the District Commissioners in the up-country districts of the Cross river basin. 'You live far away from the white merchants of Calabar but the Government is bringing them up here to live and trade with you here. They cannot, however, come until there is peace everywhere....'[1]

In the areas of the hinterland without the facilities of river access, the administration recognised or were persuaded to recognise a different type of obstacle to trade expansion and the exploitation of the British 'estate'. The king of Benin was reported to have imposed an embargo on trade throughout the territories west of the Niger under his influence. Jekri traders who failed to honour the 'trust' (credit) from the white merchants at Warri or Sapelle invariably blamed their failure on the king of Benin's obstructionist policy. The merchants naturally urged on the

[1] Partridge, *op. cit.* p. 303.

government the need for action.[1] The fateful mission of Acting Consul-General Phillips was motivated by trade considerations.

To the east of the Niger, the government accumulated reports to the effect that the Aro were the 'thorn in the flesh' of the administration. They carried on the slave trade. They exploited the pervasive influence of the Long Juju to discourage the hinterland peoples from trading with the white man.[2] It did not occur to the vice-consuls who conveyed the information from the hinterland to the Consul-General that the coast traders were themselves anxious to deter the merchants from venturing into the hinterland. The Aro were themselves ubiquitous traders and their own interest was in harmony with that of the coast native traders in retaining their traditional monopoly of trade between the hinterland and the white traders. As in the case of the Benin tragedy, the Aro expedition was primarily motivated by the determination of the protectorate government to open unlimited access to European enterprise. Until these hinterland obstacles were eliminated, there could be little elasticity in the imports and exports. Nevertheless the trade of the protectorate increased substantially between 1892 and 1894.[3]

Macdonald recognised the danger inherent in the dependence of revenue on the trade items which were more or less traditional. His misgivings were justified in the slump in the prices of palm oil and kernel in 1895.[4] In his report to the Foreign Office, he accepted that '. . . it is the duty of the Administration to encourage in every way the development of other products which nature may have already bestowed upon the country, and also the cultivation of new ones suitable to its soil and climate'.[5] With this in view, Macdonald initiated projects which were ultimately to revolutionise the economic life of Old Calabar in particular, and the protectorate in general. A botanical garden was established in Old Calabar. The

[1] F.O. 2/102, no. 106, *op. cit.* See Letter to Brownridge.
[2] *Nigerian Pamphlets*, no. 16, *op. cit.*

[3]

|  | Imports (£) | Exports (£) |
|---|---|---|
| 1892–3 | 729,889 | 843,500 |
| 1893–4 | 929,332 | 1,014,087 |

[4] 1894–5, imports (£739,864); exports (£825,098). See *Parl. Papers*, 1895, *op. cit.*
[5] *Ibid.*

cultivation of coffee and cocoa was undertaken by the government as an object lesson for the chiefs, who were hitherto preoccupied with the palm-oil trade. Other inducements were offered in the form of subsidies and free issue of pamphlets explaining the best methods of cultivating the new crops. The attempt was a failure in the sense that, in spite of early promises of success, nothing important developed from the project.[1]

Sir Claude's successor later condemned the whole idea of a botanical garden, hardly anticipating he was destined to inherit one near Onitsha from the Royal Niger Company. Sir Ralph Moor preferred a Forestry Department, but events were to prove that the two departments were steps in the right direction. Sir Ralph particularly blamed the British merchants for 'gluing themselves to the coast', and being content with importing very cheap material. He therefore urged the merchants to introduce a more diversified class of goods of better quality. In his report on this aspect of the administration's problems, Moor admitted that it was the duty of the government to raise the standard of life among the natives, 'which can only be done by education and continuous intercourse and must, of course, result in greatly enlarged demands in the variety of the class of goods imported'.[2]

The basic problems in diversifying exports and in improving the quality of imports were many. Before 1902 the inhabitants of the hinterland continued their traditional way of living, with very limited demands for goods from outside sources. The absence of roads to facilitate the role of middlemen traders, coupled with the fact that the territory could not be surveyed before its conquest, constituted the main obstacles to spectacular trade developments. Nor at that time were the inhabitants interested in giving serious attention to exploiting their natural resources. The last point requires elaboration.

For the coast inhabitants, trade was the only means of wealth and even survival (at any rate in the circumstances of the period). It is almost true to say that at the same period a landless Ibo or Ibibio family was something quite inconceivable. There were few

---

[1] The Director of Kew Gardens was full of praise for Sir Claude's project. See C.O. 520/13, Moor to C.O. no. 105, 15 March 1902.

[2] C.O. 444/4, Letter by Agent at Eket dated 15 February 1899 and Moor's reply to C.O.

families which did not provide from their farms the main ingredients of subsistence.[1] The traders and itinerant blacksmiths among the Ibo were also farmers. By and large, the European goods that percolated through, for instance tobacco and liquor, were luxuries, not necessities. The later rise in population and land hunger, as well as the emergence of a non-agricultural group, are the end result of the changes the beginnings of which this chapter is attempting to analyse. The division of labour between the men-folk and the women-folk revealed the insignificance attached at that time to palm oil and palm kernel which happened to be the export prop of the protectorate.

Among the Ibo, agriculture was centred, and is still, on the cultivation of yams. This was a man's main business. There were other crops which included maize, beans, coco-yams, cassava and so forth. Around the household the women planted vegetables and other subsidiary crops. Now as regards oil palm, the most important crop from the standpoint of the protectorate government, the men, apart from cutting down the fruits, left the vital processes of extracting oil and cracking the kernel as a pastime for women. A change was bound to occur when the export of oil and kernel became the principal source of income and the sole means of purchasing the European goods which were increasingly regarded as essential to a comfortable way of life. The first administrators did not witness this helpful transformation in the early years of the twentieth century.

Another drawback in respect of the palm oil and kernel export was the very primitive method used for extracting oil and cracking the kernel. When the fruits were gathered, they were allowed to ferment and then mashed with the feet to squeeze out the oil. The amount of oil lost by the process has been estimated at up to 45 per cent.[2] According to Morel, 400 kernels when cracked amounted to 1 lb of exported kernel. It is easy to imagine the labour involved in cracking heaps and heaps of the palm kernel for the not inconsiderable export item it constituted, and Morel was right in adverting to the 'ignorance of those who say that the Native of West Africa will not work'.[3] The question of introducing

[1] Meek, *op. cit.* pp. 15–17.    [2] *Ibid.* p. 18.
[3] Morel, *Affairs of West Africa* (1902), p. 76. Dudgeon, *Agricultural and Forest Products of British West Africa* (London, 1911), pp. 62–4.

machinery for cracking palm kernels was discussed by the administration but nothing much came of it.[1]

Another attempt to diversify exports found expression in the foundation of the British Cotton Growing Association in 1902. The venture had everybody's blessing, and high hopes were entertained as to the potentialities of the Yoruba hinterland and Southern Nigeria for growing cotton, thus lessening British dependence on foreign-grown cotton. Cotton seeds were liberally provided and experiments began, as far as Southern Nigeria was concerned, in the Urhobo country and at the government 'plantations' at Nkissi, near Onitsha. The Urhobo experiment failed completely. On the whole, the Association had little chance of success, primarily because the low price of $1\frac{1}{2}d$. per lb of cotton hardly provided an inducement to the natives. The gathering of palm fruits, which paid much more substantial dividends, from the native standpoint, afforded greater encouragement than cotton planting.[2] In 1904 the Secretary of State, Lyttelton, urged the Association to change boldly from experiment to large-scale commercial production. The Southern Nigeria government was ready to assist with a subsidy of £5000 a year. The year that followed was one of optimism on the part of all concerned except the inhabitants who had to do the planting. [3]

It is easy to picture the hinterland communities as politically and economically self-sufficient units. This would be misleading. That there was no large-scale trade in the modern sense is hardly controvertible. Each village or village group was never entirely a self-contained economic unit. As Meek points out, 'the most striking feature of Ibo life is the keenness displayed by the women in petty trade'. Markets were indeed an important source of communication between villages and village groups, which were politically independent. Market days were so arranged that no clashes occurred on the dates of neighbouring markets. In due

[1] C.O. 520/2, Gallwey to C.O., Confidential no. 8, 27 July 1900. C.O. 520/8, Probyn to C.O. no. 233, 10 August 1901. (It was in this year that the government tried to use the 'Native' Councils as agents for educating the natives on the use of the machines. The move produced no results.)
[2] C.O. 520/16, Moor to C.O. no. 582, 14 December 1902.
[3] *West Africa*, 13 February 1904. Address to the Manchester Statistical Society by J. A. Hutton, the Vice-President of the British Cotton Growing Association.

course markets were to become centres of the district where people assembled as much for social as for commercial intercourse.[1] Charles Partridge, a District Commissioner, visited what might be regarded as a typical hinterland market. The articles displayed included yams, plantain, sugar-cane, pepper, salt, palm wine, kernel oil, beans, sleeping mats, groundnuts, native cloth and eggs. There was no evidence here of the permeation of European goods.[2] The Aro and the Ibo and Ibibio groups on the periphery of the coast were the first to devote attention to large-scale long-ranging trade, which was in our own time to become characteristic of the protectorate. In the period under consideration the government convinced itself that the great need was to encourage in the people the development of 'civilised' tastes, to implant 'new wants which form in every society the roots of civilisation'.[3]

In the face of almost stagnant trade returns, the administration was compelled on several occasions to raise the import duties to meet the exigencies of an expanding machinery of government. In 1895 the duty on spirits was increased from 1s. to 2s. a gallon, that on guns from 1s. to 2s. and on powder from 2d. to 6d. per lb. For the second time, in 1899, the duty on spirits was raised, to 3s. a gallon. The British merchants generally managed to have advance information of government's intentions and so anticipated the increases by stocking large quantities of the particular commodity in their factories. When the administration nullified the merchants' stratagem by imposing the new duties on accumulated stock, floods of protests from the African Association and the Miller Brothers inundated the Colonial Office. The protests contained an insinuation that the administration was favouring Freetown African merchants who were beginning to infiltrate into the commercial life of Southern Nigeria.[4]

The administration was faced with a dilemma. The burden imposed by increased duties on imports fell ultimately on the producers. The white merchants manipulated the rate of exchange

[1] The Nigeria Handbook (2nd ed. 1954), pp. 102–7.
[2] Partridge, op. cit. p. 249.
[3] Hobson, Imperialism, A Study (London, 1938), p. 227. Also see Geary, pp. 139–41, for table of imports.
[4] C.O. 520/5, African Association to C.O., 28 August 1899 and 27 January 1900.

in such a way that they evaded any losses on their part. The middle-men had little choice but to accept the merchants' decisions, especially at a time when the 'trust' system still operated. The middlemen in their turn would transfer the additional expense for European goods to the petty traders and producers. In this kind of situation there was little inducement to step up the production of the export items, or disposition on the part of the hinterland to cultivate 'civilised' demands for European imports.[1] In the last analysis, the government's declared policy of 'civilising' the natives by creating 'new wants' did not immediately materialise.

The real storm was to be let loose by the salt duty which the government introduced in 1900. Protests to the Colonial Office came not only from the firms but also from the Chamber of Commerce, Northwich, the Urban District Council of Winsford, the Middlewich Urban District Council in the County of Chester and the Weaver Watermen's Association. The main issue of contention was that a duty of 20s. per ton of salt damaged English trade and caused unemployment. There is no evidence that the protectorate administration's policy was motivated by any desire to protect local salt manufacture. The Chamber of Commerce, Northwich, however, referred to native salt which was 'of a very unwholesome character by solar evaporation'.[2] The Colonial Office supported the policy of the protectorate government, and replies to the protests from the various English bodies were brusque and unconciliatory.

On the whole, the table of revenue up to 1900 does not give a true picture of the extent to which productivity was being stepped up. The revenue showed increases by additional duties on imports, and the salaries of officials and the cost of military expeditions consumed the revenue. Little or nothing was done in the way of building roads in the place of forest foot tracks. As early as 1896 the Foreign Office, which then controlled the protectorate, had emphasised the importance of roads as arteries of trade. In respect of the estimates of the protectorate for that year, it again called attention to the desirability of opening up new markets by making roads and improving other means of communication with the

[1] Lugard, *op. cit.* p. 264.
[2] C.O. 520/5, Chamber of Commerce, Northwich, to C.O., 10 February 1900.

interior.[1] Up to 1900 the cutting of bush for the passage of troops in the attack on Benin, and the clearing of traditional tracks linking villages near the coast, through the agency of 'Native' Councils, constituted the progress made by the protectorate government towards fulfilling the request of the Foreign Office.

In the annual reports, the administration made references to currency as one of the factors retarding the development of trade. The officers assumed that the absence of British currency meant that all trade was by barter. The assumption was technically wrong. Jones is quite right in pointing out that over the centuries the local traders and their European counterparts had evolved a method of exchange through the mutual acceptance of units which served the purposes of currency. The earliest of these units was probably the iron bar, and according to James Barbot's reckoning:[2]

| One bunch of beads | = one bar |
| Sixty king's yams | = one bar |
| One goat | = one bar |
| One cow | = eight bars |

In time other units of exchange emerged. These included the manilla, the copper rod, the brass rod, puncheons of oil and cases of gin. The brass rod was generally about the size of a small stair-carpet rod, but bent over so that the two ends nearly met. This peculiar currency and a similar one called 'cheethams' were prevalent in the districts of Old Calabar. The manilla was a heavy horseshoe-shaped piece of metal.[3] The brass rods were popular in the hinterland and were in circulation, but for the sole purpose of making a native leg ornament known as 'nja'.

The origin of the manilla is associated with a fascinating local tradition. Brass fishermen had dragged up an old wrecked ship and collected a few strange pieces of the wreckage. They liked the look of these objects and therefore asked the Portuguese traders to get new copies of them. The Portuguese naturally lost no time in flooding the coast with manillas which the local traders accepted as currency and a unit of exchange. What passed for currency among the Edo, Ibo and Ibibio of the hinterland was the cowrie.

---

[1] F.O. 2/99, F.O. Despatch 19, 5 March 1896.
[2] Jones, *The Trading States of the Oil Rivers* (1963), pp. 91–2.
[3] See diagrams, p. 330. (It was used extensively in Bonny and New Calabar.)

There is considerable controversy as to the origin of the cowrie but Consul Campbell reported as far back as 1856 that the French and the Germans imported yearly 2500 tons of these shells. They made enormous profits, for according to the report the 'white Indian cowries' cost £60 at the source of supply and £80 on the Guinea coast.[1] What was described as Indian cowrie was smaller than the Zanzibar cowrie and was worth more in the Ibo market. The normal value of the cowrie is illustrated below:

$$
\begin{aligned}
&\text{40 cowries made a string} &&= \tfrac{3}{10}d. \\
&\text{5 strings made a bunch} &&= 1\tfrac{1}{2}d. \\
&\text{10 bunches made a head} &&= 1s.\ 3d. \\
&\text{10 heads made a load} &&= 12s.\ 6d.
\end{aligned}
$$

These statistics have been taken from a War Office 'Précis of Information' concerning the Lagos neighbourhood. There were naturally local variations but, from the table given above, 20,000 cowries were worth about 12s. 6d.

In a typical Ibo village, 6 cowries constituted the smallest unit, and bananas, for instance, cost 6 cowries each. As long as cowries remained the means of local exchange, there was little likelihood of the mobility of currency indispensable to the development of large-scale trade. A man might have buried thousands and thousands of cowries, but in terms of exchange value, he was hardly likely to have enough to buy European imports, such as Manchester cloth, salt, spirits, guns and powder.[2] As long as this was the situation it was not likely that the hinterland peoples would be interested in increasing the production and sale of palm oil and kernel. The trade between the villages at the one end and the European factors at the other passed through several categories of middlemen. As regards the coast, the older currencies had by the nineteenth century given pride of place to a case of gin as the unit of exchange. The unit was of high value and could conveniently be subdivided into 12 bottles each worth 1s.[3]

However cumbersome and primitive the unit of exchange on the coast, the European agents preferred the pernicious system to the introduction of more identifiable and definitive currency. For

[1] Talbot, *The Peoples of Southern Nigeria* (Oxford, 1926), vol. 1, pp. 57 and 62. Kirk-Green, 'The Major Currencies in Nigerian History', *J.H.S.N.*, vol. 2, no. 1, December 1960, pp. 136-7.

[2] Basden, *Niger Ibos*. See ch. xxx (Marketing).

[3] Jones, *op. cit.* p. 93. Diké, *Trade and Politics in the Niger Delta*, pp. 104-8.

instance, in accepting oil from the middlemen, the agents of the firms computed brass rods at the rate of four for a shilling, but required 5 rods as the equivalent of 1s. when handing out trade goods to the middlemen. The system enabled the merchants to dispose of what goods they liked and also to manipulate the mechanism of exchange in such a way as to make a double profit.[1] On the other hand, the huge quantities of cowries, rods, or gin which the middlemen had to carry up country made it inevitable that human beings (slaves) were also used as a kind of ambulatory currency. It has thus been observed that 'the very...commerce, which had been regarded as a liberator, was actually forging the chains more firmly on the slaves in the West African hinterland'.[2]

The High Commissioner of the protectorate of Southern Nigeria, Sir Ralph Moor, attacked the problem of currency by first trying to prohibit the importation of rods and manillas. He had on several occasions solicited the authorisation of the Foreign Office to fix a rate of exchange with the view to discrediting the undesirable and cumbersome currencies. The African Trade Section of the Liverpool Chamber of Commerce had at once protested when it was asked for its views by the Board of Trade to which the Foreign Office had referred the issue raised by Sir Ralph. The Birmingham Chamber of Commerce addressed a letter to Lord Salisbury, in which it emphasised that the city was interested in the manufacture and export of rods, and hoped 'that your Lordship will take steps to prevent' any prohibition.[3]

The Foreign Office did nothing and brass rods continued to flow into Southern Nigeria from Birmingham, through Liverpool. Sir Ralph Moor was not the type of man to surrender on an issue which so materially affected the economic development of a territory under his jurisdiction. Early in 1900 he complained to the Colonial Office in a strongly worded memorandum that he had no doubt in his mind that 'this barter trade assisted only by unwieldy and cumbersome currency' increased the difficulty of opening up and 'civilising' the territories 'enormously'. Commerce could not, while the existing systems prevailed, be regarded as a factor

[1] C.O. 520/8, Moor to C.O. no. 156, 12 June 1901. See Memo by Butler.
[2] McPhee, *op. cit.* p. 251.
[3] F.O. 2/182, Letter by the Liverpool Trade Section, 22 January 1898, and Birmingham Chamber of Commerce to Salisbury, 10 February 1898.

'assisting in civilisation'.[1] The High Commissioner was not naïve enough to assume that the mere prohibition of manillas and rods was all that was required. He therefore took up at the same time the question of establishing a bank in the protectorate which could provide the appropriate specie and call in redundant 'coins'. The Managing Director of the Bank of British West Africa, A. L. Jones, also head of the Elder Dempster Shipping Company, had approached Sir Ralph with the view to establishing a branch of his bank.

Other rival British combines were not to be cheated out of a potentially profitable venture. The Niger Company, the African Association and Miller Brothers anticipated Mr (later Sir Alfred) Jones by pooling capital to enable them to inaugurate the Anglo-African Bank Ltd.[2] Very sensibly, Sir Ralph pointed out to the Colonial Office that the competition of two gigantic monopolies was not in the best interests of Southern Nigeria. He also expressed his suspicion that the firms were fashioning a tool with which to establish a stranglehold on the commerce, shipping and banking of the protectorate. The Secretary of State therefore proposed a conference with the representatives of the three big concerns in order to 'warn [them] privately and in a friendly way'[3] that if they were working for a monopoly, he, Joseph Chamberlain, would do everything in his power to frustrate their designs. What Sir Ralph desired was that the big monopolies should not be in a position to prevent freedom of trade by making it impossible for the natives and the small European firms to have access to the facilities of a free cash circulation. The Colonial Office was not a little baffled that the same firms that battened on 'barter' were now anxious to provide the facilities of cash currency by forming a bank.

The three big firms did not abandon their evil designs on the protectorate very easily. They tried a new stratagem. They forwarded applications to the Colonial Office and solicited permission to import into Southern Nigeria, through the Crown Agents, an ever growing amount of specie. On the surface, they would be operating in accordance with the wishes of the High

[1] C.O. 520/1, Moor to C.O. no. 56, 24 February 1900.
[2] C.O. 444/4, The Anglo-African Bank to C.O., 17 November 1899.
[3] C.O. 520/6, Memo by Moor re the development of S. Nigeria, 7 June 1900. See also Minutes by Chamberlain, 1 July 1900.

Commissioner. The officials of the Colonial Office were not easily fooled. One of the most intelligent of the junior officials saw through the new proposal and noted in a memorandum that 'the Anglo-African Bank...might utilise unlimited facilities for the importation of silver to create a redundancy of the coin in S. Nigeria and so discredit the cash system which we wish to introduce in place of the barter system....'[1]

Meanwhile, Sir Ralph took a number of practical steps. First, he insisted that only silver could be accepted as import duties from the coast firms. In the second place, African employees of the government were to be paid in cash. Thirdly, Travelling Commissioners and District Commissioners were instructed to explain to the inhabitants the advantages of silver currency. The frequent military expeditions after 1901 helped in this propaganda campaign. One of the aims of the Aro expedition was to take new currency into the hinterland. The conservatism of the natives was not easy to overcome, especially when the military expeditions provoked deep-rooted, though futile, antipathy to everything associated with the new political regime. The report on the Asaba district by Fosbery illustrates the magnitude of the problem facing the protectorate government in the matter of new currency: 'Outside Asaba, the value of cash is unknown and in fact silver is regarded as a sort of juju and will not be accepted.'[2] The Divisional Commissioner had to be content with making 'various small dashes in silver to the women'.

A significant measure enacted by the High Commissioner to dispense with the use of slaves as currency was the Slave Dealing Proclamation of 1901. Before doing this, he consulted the 'chiefs' of Old Calabar, Opobo, Okrika, Bonny, Degema, Brass, Warri and Sapele. The 'chiefs' of these former city-states were the people whose traditional trading organisation and social structure would be affected in a revolutionary manner by the new legislation. When these chiefs were described as middlemen what it really meant was that their 'boys' (slaves) were used as traders and currency to bring down produce from the hinterland in exchange for the

[1] C.O. 520/5, Butler to Antrobus; Minute on Niger Company's letter, 2 June 1900. See also Niger Company's letter to the African Association, 21 May 1900.
[2] File B.P. 1521, op. cit. Report, 16 September 1902.

European imports. The Aro operated in precisely the same manner as intermediaries between the coast and the hinterland. The chiefs' fears that their 'houses' would break up did impress the High Commissioner, and he enacted other measures[1] calculated to arrest the prospective disintegration of coast society without reviving slavery. These measures will be discussed in their proper place— the beginnings of social change.

Early in 1902 Sir Ralph Moor persuaded the 'Native' Councils to pass a by-law abolishing brass rods and manillas as legal tender in native markets, with a fixed rate of exchange for silver. The Colonial Office was solidly behind Sir Ralph's policy, and Butler of the Colonial Office, with obvious jubilation, returned to his attack on those firms which had appeared obstructionist and selfish. 'The need of the country', concluded Butler, 'is a sufficient answer.'[2] Sir Ralph's avoidance of outright abolition of native currencies with 'compensation' was a very shrewd move. The natives who had hoarded a great pile of rods and manillas by way of savings suffered no injustice since they could exchange their savings for the silver prescribed by their new political masters. At the end of 1903 brass rods were worth $3d.$ each, manillas $1\frac{1}{4}d.$ and copper wires $\frac{1}{8}d.$ The native currencies died a gradual but certain death. For a while, the cowrie remained in favour for purposes of minor transactions in the native markets, as the three-penny piece was the smallest silver unit introduced by the government. The tenth of a penny was introduced later and was destined to discredit cowries.[3]

Apparently, Sir Frederick Lugard in Northern Nigeria was battling with the same problem as Sir Ralph. In his 1903 report, the former bitterly condemned the 'barter' system:

A factor which greatly militates against my efforts to promote the circulation of coinage—which should promote and facilitate trade...is the refusal of the sole European firm which has any large connection in the country to purchase any produce except with barter goods and

[1] For instance, the 'Native House Rule Proclamation, 1901' and the 'Master and Servant Proclamation, 1901'.

[2] C.O. 520/14, Moor to C.O., Telegram, 7 April 1902, see Minutes on Telegram. C.O. 520/16, Southern Nigeria Coinage Order, Treasury to C.O., 5 November 1902.

[3] A bag of cowries which constituted a man's load was worth less than a shilling in 1921. (See Basden, *op. cit.* p. 198 and Green, *Ibo Village Affairs*, note 2, p. 41.)

their unwillingness to accept cash when tendered by natives...for their goods. Presumably they thus hope to make a double profit.[1]

It is remarkable the extent to which Lugard's complaint corroborated Sir Ralph's earlier misgivings about the tactics of the European firms.

Although the Foreign Office had as early as 1896 reminded Sir Ralph of the urgency of road construction, it was merely reiterating a problem which the Commissioner appreciated but could do nothing about in the absence of substantial revenue and because of the inability of the protectorate government to float loans with the security of the British Treasury. After the substantial control of the hinterland had been accomplished, Moor took up seriously the questions of roads and railways in order to tap the resources of the protectorate effectively.[2] But it was the Colonial Office's decision to make loans available to the Lagos Colony that brought out quite emphatically the fighting qualities of the Southern Nigeria Commissioner on behalf of the protectorate.

The construction of a railway from the Lagos terminal had already begun in 1898. A short line only was completed to tap the local natural resources, forest and agricultural. The sand-bar which hindered entry by ships into Lagos harbour was notorious. Here was where Sir Ralph Moor began his fight. He argued that both Sapele and Old Calabar were superior to Lagos as depots for the external trade of Nigeria. He referred to the bar which blocked Lagos and contrasted this disability with the open estuary of Old Calabar into which steamers drawing 20 ft could enter. To strengthen his argument in favour of a Calabar railway terminal, Sir Ralph alleged that the Germans had completed plans for a railway from Rio del Rey to the neighbourhood of the hinterland of Old Calabar. The Commissioner's arguments were in vain. The Colonial Office counter-argued that the heavy expenditure already entailed in constructing the Lagos line was not to be sacrificed.[3]

The Lagos–Ibadan railway was ceremoniously opened on 4 March 1901. Both Lugard and Moor were invited to Lagos by the Governor, Sir William MacGregor, for a trip from Lagos to

[1] *Annual Report, Northern Nigeria*, 1903, p. 16. Partridge, *op. cit.* pp. 251–3.
[2] C.O. 520/7, Moor to C.O. no. 23, 17 January 1901.
[3] C.O. 520/1, Minutes by Antrobus on no. 92, 2 February 1900.

Ibadan. The trip left a tremendous impression on Sir Ralph Moor's mind. Railways were the only answer to the problem of exploiting the undoubted natural resources of his protectorate. As soon as he returned to his headquarters, he submitted a gigantic scheme of railway construction to the Colonial Office. The scheme envisaged two terminals at Warri or Sapele and at Old Calabar. The western line was to extend the Lagos line to Benin instead of to Northern Nigeria. The central line from Sapele or Warri was to link up with Onitsha, and the eastern line from Old Calabar would tap the resources of the Upper Cross river, and might even be extended up to the Benue river at Ibi. Subsequently, the last line might be extended northwards to Kano.[1] As to where the capital might come from, Moor had his answer—the Imperial Exchequer. Moor's reason for suggesting the source of the capital was clearly stated: 'The estate of Nigeria has been acquired by His Majesty's government at little or no cost beyond the monies paid to the Royal Niger Company amounting to about £865,000.'[2] Had the Colonial Secretary not outlined, in his speech on 'our estates', the duties of a good landlord? Moor's scheme and arguments remained on paper. Nonetheless the imaginativeness and boldness of the railway scheme do great credit to Sir Ralph. It is easy to imagine how, had his railway scheme been accepted, the economic life and habits of the inhabitants might have been revolutionised in the first decade of the twentieth century. Ormsby-Gore's later criticism of sluggish railway development in Nigeria in contrast with the dynamic railway policy of Guggisberg, Governor of what was then the Gold Coast, lends tremendous weight to Sir Ralph's foresight.[3]

The exploitation of the resources of the protectorate posed other questions of more fundamental importance from the standpoint of the inhabitants of the protectorate.[4] These involved issues of the method of forest resources exploitation and the ownership of the land. The two were closely bound up, but the collapse of Benin, the neighbourhood of which was known to contain an enormous amount of rubber trees, forced the administration to make a

[1] No railway was begun in Eastern Nigeria until 1912: from Port Harcourt to tap the coal deposits at Udi and Enugu.
[2] C.O. 520/7, Moor to C.O. no. 110, 25 April 1901.
[3] Ormsby-Gore, Report already cited, see ch. II.
[4] Meek, *Land Law and Customs in the Colonies* (Oxford, 1946), p. 145.

decision between large-scale foreign exploitation and native education to enable the owners of the land to exploit their own resources. The British capture of Benin was followed by an influx of speculators. The Commissioner foresaw the disastrous consequences of indiscriminate tapping of rubber, and so imposed regulations about rubber tapping as early as June 1897. Requests for large concessions were already being made by one Mr Bleasby, the African Association and Messrs Alexander Miller Brothers. Reporting to the Foreign Office, the Acting Commissioner warned:

What they would probably do would be to work their concessions with great energy so as to get as much out of it (*sic*) in the shortest possible time and having drained these resources, to seek concessions elsewhere...the Natives of the Protectorate...would be left with their country very much the poorer in certain products.[1]

Sir Ralph Moor, who was in England and was shown the dispatch, vigorously supported the spirit which inspired the Acting Commissioner's views. It was on this occasion that he stated the basic principle of his policy in regard to forest exploitation. 'The country can and should be developed by natives as regards its economic vegetable products especially...rubber.'[2] To understand the urgency with which the big firms asked for rubber concessions it should be mentioned that at the turn of the century there was a boom in the rubber trade, consequent on the demand for tyres for bicycles and the new types of automobiles.

The British had at first treated Benin land as having come over to them by right of conquest, but the native chiefs were closely associated with the first regulations which the government imposed to control rubber tapping. These regulations required that prospective dealers should obtain the permission of the Resident of Benin City and pay the sum of 10s. as licence renewable every six months. The chiefs were authorised to supervise all tapping in their areas and to receive half of the £50 penalty for any infringement of the regulations. The penalty was shortly afterwards increased to two years' imprisonment.[3]

The Forestry Department owed its establishment to the High Commissioner's solicitude for the protectorate's future. The effects

---

[1] F.O. 2/179, Gallwey to F.O. no. 121, 28 July 1898.
[2] *Ibid.* Minutes by Moor, 6 September 1898.
[3] C.O. 444/1, Moor to C.O. no. 48, 3 March 1899.

of indiscriminate forest destruction on the protectorate's potential source of wealth and on fertility were Sir Ralph's preoccupation. In 1899 Sir Ralph appointed Peter Hitchens Inspector of Forests. The Inspector naturally had his hands full with Benin rubber exploitation, but in 1901 a comprehensive forestry proclamation was enacted, based on the theory that 'the entire land in the territories is regarded as tribal property which cannot be alienated'.[1] No. 4 of the rules relating to the proclamation of 1901 set out the following conditions: (a) No concession was to be more than 9 square miles in extent, nor have a water frontage of more than one mile for every three miles. (b) No concession would last more than seven years. (c) The fees for concessions were £5 for the concession and £1 for each square mile. (d) Royalties amounting to 10s. on each tree felled were to be paid to the grantors, unless they failed to help in detecting offenders. From the forest management standpoint, the proclamation prohibited felling trees without regard to an imposed minimum girth of nine feet and height of ten feet. (e) A concessionaire should plant twenty seedlings for every tree felled. Sir Ralph's comprehensive programme was remarkable because he made provision for educating the natives in the methods of oil extraction, for the training of native staff for forestry and botanical work, and lastly, for reafforestation.

The proclamation was subjected to very severe scrutiny by the Colonial Office, which commented that nothing should be done to create the impression in the natives' mind 'that we are trying to take away from them their most cherished rights or to break the faith that has been pledged in treaties'.[2] The Colonial Office had no grounds for any misgivings because Sir Ralph had clearly explained that his policy was actuated solely by the desire to interpose the authority of the protectorate government between the cupidity of the combines and the 'ignorant folly' of the 'chiefs', as regards concessions and interests in land. The High Commissioner elaborated on the point that he had encountered no difficulty in obtaining the consent of the 'chiefs' where the reasons for legislation had been fully explained.

[1] C.O. 520/10, Moor to C.O. no. 418, 13 December 1901.
[2] *Ibid.* See 'summary' by Ezechiel. (This makes interesting reading in view of British policy in Kenya, and the protracted but futile legal efforts by the Masai to preserve the 'Reserves' assured them in treaties.)

Early in 1903 Sir Ralph secured the services of H. Thompson, a man who had had twelve years' experience in the Indian Forestry Service. He appointed him Conservator of Forests on a salary of £1000 a year. Because of preoccupation with the control of the flourishing trade in timber and rubber, Thompson and his officers could not find time for the more constructive policy of forest preservation.[1] The first report by the new Conservator of Forests drew attention to two abuses which Moor's 1901 proclamation had not provided for. First, there was the indigenous system of farming which is best described as shifting cultivation and meant the felling of trees for temporary farms. The second was the absence of a positive policy of conservation. The Conservator felt that the future was grim unless specific areas were set aside for the permanent practice of forestry principles. The existing proclamation only applied to forest lands at the disposal of the government, and this was confined to Benin territories. Whatever the shortcomings of Moor's policy, the views of one of the big firms illustrate the illusion from which Moor saved the protectorate: 'If the whole of the forest were cut down today, in 20 years there would be another forest equally large and valuable.'[2]

Sir Ralph's reaction to the request for mineral concessions was equally motivated by a desire to preserve to the local inhabitants the hidden resources of their territory. The first request had come from Messrs Lake and Currie, and the High Commissioner suspected that the capitalist A. L. Jones was behind the request for the concession to prospect for minerals. As a counter-measure, Sir Ralph proposed to establish a Government Engineer to head a Mining Department. The government as trustees of the inhabitants could then attempt prospecting, and pay subsidies to the land-owners to induce them to make roads. The Colonial Office's misgivings about Sir Ralph's proposals were concerned with the possibility of the protectorate government becoming compromised by being coupled with the vendors in the sale of concessions.[3]

---

[1] *Parl. Papers*, Cd. 3999, S. Nigeria, no. 51, for the phenomenal exports in timber, rubber and fibre. C.O. 520/7, see C.O. to India Office, October 1901.

[2] C.O. 520/6, John Holt to Antrobus, 21 September 1900. (There were similar views by the Liverpool and the Manchester Chambers of Commerce.)

[3] C.O. 520/9, Confidential, no. 39396, Moor to C.O., 23 October 1901, see also comments by Ommanney and Chamberlain. C.O. 520/16, Mining Regulation, section 7 of Proclamation no. 18, 1902, see Minutes by Risley, Cox and Antrobus.

Sir Ralph could well be satisfied that he had laid the foundations which safeguarded a substantial portion of the forest resources of the protectorate for posterity. There was indeed another source of satisfaction. The natives of Benin knew nothing before about the rubber industry, but had undertaken it under the guidance of officials, and had planted 50,000 rubber trees. In short, Sir Ralph's policy obviated the notorious Congo system in which the inhabitants became forced labourers in their own land and suffered mutilations and other indignities if they failed to bring in to the concessionaires the required quota of rubber or timber.

The Conservator's plans for future forest conservation involved the delicate issue of land ownership. The High Commissioner had observed earlier that the entire land of the protectorate was tribal property. This point requires elaboration. That the protectorate government did not proclaim the protectorate territory as Crown land was perhaps not entirely a matter of altruism. There was not, as in Kenya, the demand or the suitable site for European colonisation. In the circumstances, it was easy for the protectorate government to escape the 'Kenya system'.[1] Except in the coastal areas, the village members of autonomous political units owned land as coherent groups. The system of land tenure reflected this solidarity. Thus the land belonged to the group and its security was the responsibility of the elders. The individual could exploit the land he needed but did not thereby own the land. In the period under consideration, there were no visible signs that land ownership would become individualised and commercialised.[2]

In regard to the problems of land, the main concern of Sir Ralph was the regulation of concessions for the exploitation of forest products. Admittedly, the Royal Niger Company had acquired land rights by some of its 'treaties'. These were taken over by the protectorate government as Crown lands, except for specific areas occupied by the company's trading stations. The proclamations no. 1 of 1900 and no. 1 of 1903 stipulated that no aliens could acquire any interest in native land except under 'an instrument approved by the High Commissioner'. In due course the only land at the government's disposal was that which had

[1] Hailey, *op. cit.* p. 686. Meek, *Land Law and Customs in the Colonies*, p. 145.
[2] *The Nigeria Handbook*, *op. cit.* pp. 102–7. Hailey, *op. cit.* pp. 768 f.

expressly been acquired for 'public purposes'. Otherwise the only obligation on the local landowners was to seek (under the ordinances) the consent of the government when rights on land were being conveyed to aliens. Even then only leases not exceeding ninety-nine years were permissible. The administration did nothing that might disrupt the indigenous system of land tenure.[1]

Thompson, the Conservator of Forests, had not given up, in 1903, his idea of 'compulsory' land acquisition for the purpose of forest reserves. In 1905 he incorporated his ideas in a pamphlet entitled 'Rules of Procedure and Forest Organisation'. In the same year he became head of the amalgamated territories of Lagos and Southern Nigeria. His department included forestry, agriculture and the botanical departments.[2] His future career belongs to the history of the 'Lagos Colony of Southern Nigeria', but it may be mentioned that early success for Thompson's ideas was achieved in establishing early forest reserves in Ibadan and Onitsha. There was no element of compulsion, because both Moor and Egerton worked through native authorities. In terms of the future good of Nigeria as a whole, the importance of forest reserves has been admirably summarised in *The Nigeria Handbook*: '...the influence of forests and forest policy extend so far beyond their immediate location that it is merely a principle of common national safety.'[3] It is only fair to acknowledge the wisdom of Sir Ralph's policy in reconciling apparent irreconcilables. He strove to safeguard native land and resources and at the same time accomplish the setting aside of native land as forest reserves.

The permanence of the land policy of Sir Ralph was not to be threatened by European demand for land for purposes of settle-

[1] Modern agricultural developments have spotlighted the need for considerable modification in the indigenous system of land tenure, since small-scale uncoordinated peasant cultivation, especially of cash crops, is hardly equal to the need to earn more revenue, support a growing population, introduce new farming techniques, and carry the cost of the equipment necessary in the twentieth century to increase soil fertility and output and the other mechanics of large-scale land exploitation.

[2] *S. Nigeria Gazette*, May 1905.

[3] *The Nigeria Handbook*, *op. cit.* pp. 184 f. In the Gold Coast and Lagos the government encountered formidable opposition from the more educated and more sophisticated natives who refused to accept the government's definition of 'Crown Land'. Thus the point made in Thompson's pamphlet would have been found objectionable in those territories.

ment. The climate and the mosquito took care of this. As already pointed out, the chief problem in respect of native land was the regulation of concessions for the exploitation of mineral or forest resources. The Royal Niger Company managed to retain its mineral rights throughout Nigeria after the abrogation of its political jurisdiction.[1] After the First World War, Nigerian palm produce was jeopardised by the competition from the produce of the large-scale scientifically controlled palm plantations in the Dutch Indies. Should Nigeria therefore be allowed to continue the slow, primitive method of native gathering and oil production? Lord Leverhulme,[2] head of the 'soap-boilers of the world', had rational arguments on his side in demanding a freehold area in Southern Nigeria for scientific oil plantation and processing. He further demanded that the government should guarantee native labour in his prospective concessions. Here at last was a real crisis for Sir Ralph Moor's policy of safeguarding peasant proprietorship of their land. In view of the need to develop the resources of British oversea territories more effectively, Leverhulme could count on strong British parliamentary backing.[3]

The crisis which threatened Moor's policy and the natives of Southern Nigeria was averted by the firmness and liberalism of the new Governor, Sir Hugh Clifford, who arrived in Nigeria in 1922. In his address to the Legislative Council in 1925, Sir Hugh answered Leverhulme's attacks on existing land policy and concluded thus: 'I am strongly opposed to any encouragement being given by the Administration for which I am responsible to projects that have for their object the creation of European owned and managed plantations to replace or even to supplement agricultural industries which are already in existence, or which are capable of being developed by the peasantry of Nigeria.'[4]

The speech was like one inspired by the spirit of the late Sir

[1] According to the original agreement the Niger Company was to enjoy its mineral rights until the end of this century. By the late 1940's, when nationalist agitation was becoming very strong, the British administration, under Macpherson, successfully persuaded the company to forgo its privileges and receive £1 million as compensation.

[2] William Hesketh Lever, created Baron 1917, 1st Viscount 1922.

[3] Cook, *British Enterprise in Nigeria* (Philadelphia, 1943), pp. 262–6. See Leverhulme's speech on the occasion of a dinner in Liverpool in honour of Sir Hugh Clifford, 1924.

[4] *Legislative Council Debates*, Address by Governor, 1925, pp. 220–1.

Ralph Moor. The Kenya or Congo 'system' was averted and the consequences were to be far-reaching. In Nigeria the natives were confirmed in their possession of their land, and peasant proprietorship was safeguarded. This meant the economic autonomy of the inhabitants of Southern Nigeria, and this in turn led to the development of self-reliance, self-confidence and intelligence. In Kenya the creation of large English estates owned by English capital for the development of the country reduced the Kenyans to the status of wage-earners in their ancestral land. The economic subjection of the natives was complete, and economic subjection produced the inevitable evils of stagnation, economically and mentally, on the part of the native Kenyans. Ormsby-Gore endorsed Sir Hugh's stand in respect of Southern Nigeria in his report on West Africa.[1]

The social changes which the inauguration of alien rule either precipitated or accelerated were partly bound up with the legislation of government and partly with the results of other agencies which provided stimuli for social disintegration or reorientation. Examples of the latter include trade expansion, education and missionary activities. In considering government legislation, it is necessary to make a distinction between the coast and the hinterland. On the coast the political and social conditions of society had remained fluid for many decades before the imposition of British rule. In some city-states, kings had been superseded by new aristocracies. Royal 'houses' had collapsed while 'houses' headed by ex-slaves had attained both political and commercial ascendancy and provided the personnel of the 'Native' Councils established under the new regime. Old Calabar and Nembe might be exceptions to the point made here, but it has been noted already how the slaves had organised themselves to neutralise the authority of 'Ekpe' and the 'dukes'.

As the progressive consolidation of British authority undermined the traditional political influence of the 'house' system, the danger signs of anarchy, crime and social disintegration were visible enough to the new regime. The dilemma which confronted the administration was either to countenance a social structure based on thinly veiled slavery, or to undermine the working trade system by a policy of outright emancipation. The administration attempted

[1] Ormsby-Gore, report already cited, p. 107.

compromises through legislation, with indifferent results. In fact, some acts of legislation, on the surface, appear contradictory.

The earliest example of government social legislation was connected with Kalabari where the government feared that the loosening of 'house' solidarity was affecting trade adversely. According to the 1899 measure, which might be extended to the other city-states, the preamble stated that it aimed at '...the better maintenance and guidance of the trade systems of the New Calabar people...to maintain intact the native system of "house" government, and to establish cordial relations between the chiefs...and their boys, so as not to interfere with the rights of the chiefs or the responsibility of the boys'.[1] The system of 'topping' or trade-tax had long failed to 'satisfy all parties'. The fact was of course that the 'boys' were the people who went through the hazards of hinterland travel to bring down the exports, whereas the chiefs came in only at the last stage to deal with the European agents. A greedy chief gave little or nothing to the boys from topping. The boys naturally, in the light of the decreasing influence of their 'house' heads, were not averse to direct trade relations with the Europeans. The latter rather preferred the direct transactions to the rigmarole of entertainments and the request for various 'dashes' which the chiefs' visit to the factories involved.

The positive enactments of the 1899 measure are interesting in the sense that by them the government attempted to hasten a development which had hitherto operated automatically. The life of a trading boy (slave) was divided into three periods. The first period was described as 'probationary' and lasted from three to five years. During this period a newly acquired slave paid all the profits from his trade to the 'chief' of the 'house'. If he behaved well, by not cheating and by doing vigorous trade, he could be promoted to the second stage, that is, the 'taxed' period. In this category, which lasted from three to five years, the 'boy' traded for himself, but paid some tax to the chief at the rate of 10s. for each puncheon of oil, 4s. for each cask of kernel and 50 per cent on other exports sold to the Europeans. Lastly, there was the 'free' period in which the 'boy' became a 'free trader'. To accomplish the transition from one category to the next, the 'boys'

---

[1] C.S.O. 1/13, no. 34, 25 August 1899.

needed a certificate of good conduct from the District Commissioner and from the 'Native' Council.[1] The experiment in gradual manumission was apparently a failure because the 1899 measure was not extended to the other city-states and it became a 'dead letter'.

The decisive legislation was the Slave Dealing Proclamation of 1901. All the 'chiefs' and 'house' heads consulted at Bonny, Opobo, Degema and Brass unanimously and understandably opposed the legislation. This measure had long been expected by the Colonial Office, who had constantly argued that British rule was inconsistent with the existence of even 'veiled' slavery in the protectorate.[2] Sir Ralph Moor had, however, to face other realities which the Colonial Office could hardly appreciate. The sudden break-up of the 'house' system would produce anarchy and paralyse trade which for centuries had been built on the 'house' system. There was yet another consideration. The members of the 'Native' Councils were the new aristocracy who hardly did any trading themselves. To set their 'boys' free was to undermine the basis of the influence and usefulness of agents of local government. In the circumstances, Sir Ralph proposed other legislation to counteract the 'disaster' anticipated from his Slave Dealing Proclamation. To avert the anticipated chaos and to conciliate the chiefs, the High Commissioner rather hurriedly proposed and enacted the 'Native House Rule Proclamation of 1901'. It was intended to abolish the status of slavery and at the same time to retain the 'boys' in the 'houses' as house members and respectable traders.[3] The absurd aspect of the legislation was its extension to the whole protectorate, as if the Ibos, Ibibios and Edos had 'houses'.

The proclamation, without any reference to the realities of history, defined the 'house' as '...a group of persons subject by Native Law and Custom to the control, authority, and rule of a chief, known as a Head of House'. It proceeded to impose on any recalcitrant member of a 'house' a maximum fine of £50, or one year's imprisonment or both. Any vagrant member could be

---

[1] *Ibid.* It is worth mentioning that, through the influence of missionaries, the government had agreed to issue 'free papers' to domestic slaves treated with neglect for a long period by the head of the 'house'. See F.O. 2/85, Moor to F.O., 25 December 1895.

[2] C.O. 520/7, Moor to C.O. no. 72, 17 March 1901.

[3] C.O. 520/7, Proclamation no. 5 of 1901. C.O. 520/14, Moor to C.O., 24 April 1902.

arrested and imprisoned for one year. In the second place, employers were enjoined not to employ a member of a 'house' without the approval of the head of the 'house'. Any infringement of this section exposed the employer to a fine of £50 and/or imprisonment for one year. Thirdly, the members of a 'house' were protected by the provision that any 'house' head who neglected to perform his duties in regard to the economic and social welfare of his members was to be fined up to £50 or imprisonment for one year. The District Commissioners were entrusted with the task of supervising the operation of the proclamation in their districts.[1] No legislation could in fact defeat the inevitable movement towards a free egalitarian society on the coast. As a Bonny historian put it: 'Our king having ceased to function, our country has been steadily declining.'[2] The basic effort to sustain the 'house' system, by insisting that each trading member should pay 10 or 5 per cent of his trade turn-over to support the 'house', broke down completely. Sir Ralph's main concern was expressed as follows: 'If the tribal system is allowed to fall into decay it will be necessary to increase to an extent almost beyond the resources of the Protectorate, the staff necessary for doing work which is now done under the tribal system', for instance, supporting the poor and the aged and the maintenance of law and order. On his expatiation of the tribal system, Sir Ralph was quite out of date. His further attempt to make provision whereby the coast chiefs could, by paying a fee, obtain 'apprentices' from the hinterland 'tribes' failed hopelessly. The Colonial Office considered this expedient, whatever the local advantages, as 'veiled sale of these children into a servitude closely allied to slavery'.[3]

As the government became firmly established in the hinterland, the policy of conciliating the coast middlemen chiefs became less imperative. In due course, the members of a 'house' were officially allowed to buy themselves out of membership of a 'house'. It was the District Commissioner, not the head of 'house', who was empowered to fix the price of liberty. The price was in no case to exceed £50 or be less than £15. This took place

[1] *Ibid.* See also C.S.O. 1/15, 2. S.N. Confidential, 1901.
[2] Fombo—MS already cited.
[3] C.O. 520/12, see C.O. Draft to Moor, 20 August 1901.

20-2

after Sir Ralph's departure. It may be argued that Sir Ralph should have foreseen this contingency and saved himself the trouble of enacting proclamations which could not arrest the consequences of the imposition of alien rule.[1]

Although it has been suggested that the Native House Rule Proclamation, which theoretically applied to the whole protectorate, could have had no relevance to the social structure of the hinterland groups (excepting the riverain villages), the Slave Dealing Proclamation was destined to revolutionise social relations throughout the protectorate. The snag at first was that the proclamation was issued at a time when the new regime had not accomplished the political domination of the hinterland. The hinterland groups had an old system of domestic slavery, and when the 'Native' Court system extended the tentacles of British authority to every part of the protectorate, domestic slaves legally achieved their emancipation. Within their groups, they were still subjected to innumerable disabilities, but their former masters could not now use them for debt settlement or for sacrifices as they did hitherto. In this sense the change in the hinterland was similar to that which occurred on the coast.[2]

Another measure which materially affected the societies of the hinterland was the Roads and Creeks Proclamation of 1903. The avowed aim of the government was to continue the traditional practice of communal labour 'for the good of their country'. The government was quite right about this reference to communal labour. The absurdity of the government's legislation was evident in these clauses: every warrant chief had the right to call out any man or woman between the ages of fifteen and fifty to work on any road or waterway for any time not exceeding six days in each quarter; any 'chief' who failed to carry out the direction of the warrant chief exposed himself to a fine not exceeding £6 or to imprisonment for not more than six months; and anybody who disobeyed the chief was liable to a fine not exceeding £1 or to imprisonment for not more than one month. As far as the hinterland communities were concerned, the provisions of the legislation

---

[1] The Native House (Amendment) Ordinance was enacted in 1912.

[2] Talbot, *op. cit.* p. 236. Jordan (Rev.), *Bishop Shanahan of Southern Nigeria* (Dublin, 1949), p. 3.

amounted to reducing traditional behaviour and obligations to intolerable artificiality. The reverence which the elders enjoyed was desecrated by the executive powers given to picked men who had no place in traditional society. The appropriate age-group which needed nobody to remind it of its duty to clean up the village, market places and roads was the youth age-group.[1] Lastly, who were the 'chiefs' who had the job of summoning men between fifteen and fifty to do public works? There is no way of knowing how the law operated but it clearly constituted a revolutionary change from traditional willing acceptance of social responsibility to the group. The number of people who were penalised for infringement of the new law must be left to the imagination, as figures are not available.

The social effects of missionary enterprise on the lives of the natives of Southern Nigeria require only a very brief analysis, because a more detailed study of the subject will shortly become available.[2] By 1900 six major Christian missions were clearly well established in Southern Nigeria. In point of time, the United Presbyterian Mission of Scotland arrived first and concentrated its attention on the Efiks and along the Cross river basin. In 1846 mission stations were established in Creek Town, Duke Town and Old Town. Further up the river, the mission had stations at Ikonetu in 1856, and Ikorofiang in 1858. By 1900 the Okoyong, Umon and Akunakuna were already coming under the influence of the Presbyterian missionaries.[3]

As has been observed in an earlier chapter, the Church Missionary Society founded the first mission station at Onitsha in 1857. Apart from this, schools and churches were established in quick succession in Akassa, Osumari, Aboh and Asaba. In the years following the Benin expedition, the activities of the mission were extended to the Asaba hinterland in such places as Onicha-Olona and Illah. In the Niger delta, largely at the invitation of the local chiefs,[4] the C.M.S. began work in Bonny, 1864, in Brass, 1874, and

[1] Meek, *op. cit.* p. 200.
[2] Ayandele, *The Political and Social Implications of Missionary Enterprise in the Evolution of Modern Nigeria, 1875–1914.* (Ph.D. thesis in the University of London, June 1964.)
[3] McFarlan, *Calabar, the Church of Scotland Mission Founded in 1846,* pp. 62–3.          [4] *Ibid.* pp. 8–13.

in Okrika, 1880. In the hinterland, the Society of African Missions, with headquarters at Lyons, began Roman Catholic work in Lokoja and Asaba in 1884, and looked on the hinterland of Asaba as its main sphere of activity. In December 1885 the Society of the Holy Ghost Fathers, perhaps the mission destined to exert the greatest influence on the traditional life of the Ibo, began its work in the neighbourhood of Onitsha.[1] Partly at the instance of George Watts, the trader who had fought the protracted duel with Jaja for the commercial control of the Qua-Eboe river, the Qua-Eboe Mission, with its headquarters in Belfast, began work among the Ibenos and the Ibibio in 1887—the year Jaja was deported to the West Indies by the British. Lastly, in 1892, the Primitive Methodist Missionary Society, hitherto stationed in Fernando Po, moved to Oron and began the christianisation of the eastern Ibibio. One notable feature of the C.M.S. position in Southern Nigeria up to 1890 was that its pioneering work and the directorship of the mission's activities were in the hands of a 'native' Nigerian, Bishop Ajayi Crowther.[2]

For obvious reasons the missions began their work on the coast where British consular authority afforded security. The trader chiefs were more aware than their hinterland countrymen of the advantages of 'knowing book'. It may be recalled that the letter from the chiefs of Calabar to the Scottish Mission had expressed the hope 'to have their children taught in English learning'. King Eyo, who died in 1858, had left instructions that the traditional killings of slaves should cease. One of the main stumbling blocks to the missionary transformation of Old Calabar communities remained for a long time the Egbo society whose ideas about the status of slaves and women could not be reconciled with the preaching of the clergy.

At a time when European readers shuddered at accounts of African barbarism and practices, it is hardly surprising that the work of the missions in Nigeria was seen in the light of the words quoted by Coleman, '...when I carry my torch into the caves of Africa, I meet only filthy birds of darkness'.[3] Every

---

[1] Jordan, *op. cit.* The book deals exhaustively with the early work of the Roman Catholic Mission.      [2] Page, *The Black Bishop* (London, 1910).
[3] Coleman, *Nigerian Background to Nationalism* (California Press, 1958), p. 91.

aspect of indigenous social system and beliefs was supposedly bound up with witchcraft, human sacrifice, twin-killing, and of course slavery. In the circumstances the work of a missionary was conceived of as that of a revolutionary who must make an uncompromising and all-out attack on indigenous customs, including the very basis of social organisation. But as far as the Nigerian coast was concerned the first impact of missionary enterprise was on the slave section of the communities. In Old Calabar disobedience of their masters by slaves which began in the 1850's was a direct result of missionary emphasis on the equality of all men. Mission stations became the refuge of women and slaves who wished to escape the tyranny of the indigenous social system. In Bonny, New Calabar and Brass, the slaves, with the conscious encouragement of the missionaries, successfully claimed and asserted rights which contributed to the progressive undermining of the 'house' system. The early success of missionary enterprise in this respect may be easily exaggerated. The Consuls and other British political agents, as well as British merchants, did not always approve a movement which jeopardised trade and revenue.[1] The rights won by slave converts included freedom to worship the Christian's God on Sundays, to refuse to take part in the 'house' juju rituals, and to hold property not only *de facto* but *de jure*. To the coast communities, Christianity became a disruptive force, and contributed in no small measure to political strife in Bonny and Brass.

In the hinterland, the missions for some time clung to Onitsha and Obosi. Spectacular progress was quite impossible because of the bitter opposition of the natives. It is still a standing joke that the sites grudgingly given to the missions were areas which, according to the natives, were useless because they were affected by juju or some kind of evil spirit. The first children allowed to attend the mission schools were slaves or the children of slaves. West of Asaba, the Ekumeku society by its indiscriminate destruction of government and church property exemplified the local opposition to a new order. After 1900 the era of military expeditions, which from then on were the sole method of estab-

---

[1] The legal status of slavery was not abolished until 1901 and the Master and Servant Proclamation remained in operation until 1914.

lishing British rule, favoured the Christian missions. The missionaries followed in the wake of the military and administrative officers, many of whom believed that the missions could contribute to the destruction of the 'iniquitous' native system of political and ritual life.[1] In this respect the government and the Christian missions had common objectives. The joint achievement of the government and the missionaries has admirably been summarised by Basden: '. . . the heart of native law and custom has been pierced by the impact of British authority, and when the heart ceases to beat, the limbs no longer function.'[2]

The passage cited above is a considerable exaggeration of the progress of Christianity. The collapse of the indigenous system of government and subjection to new political masters were one thing, the acceptance of novel ideas about the Christian's God and the world was another. The government, which had coercive authority behind it, did not compel the natives to become Christians, but it certainly did insist on the prohibition of 'reprehensible' native practices. Here was where, indeed, government needed the missions, just as the latter needed government for the protection of lives and property. On the whole, the Ibo and the Ibibio and the fragmented groups of the Upper Cross river were the most vulnerable because village life collapsed more easily, partly through the instrumentality of the 'Native' Court system, than it did in the Ika and Bini territories and even in the coast city-states.

The institution of European-model schools was perhaps the most powerful weapon in the hands of the missions in revolutionising the lives of a not inconsiderable proportion of the inhabitants of Southern Nigeria. An Efik spokesman for missionary propaganda argued with his prospective converts that 'they [the white men] all get learning when young, but our children grow up like the goats. . . a school in our town to teach our children to saby book like white people will be very good thing'.[3] In 1873 a law was passed by Creek Town forbidding on 'God's day' markets, work, 'devil making', Ekpe processions, the firing of guns

[1] C.O. 520/15, Moor to C.O. no. 355, 8 August 1902.
[2] Basden, *op. cit.* Introduction, p. vii. See also Meek, *op. cit.* p. 326; Partridge, *op. cit.* p. 5.
[3] Hope Waddell, *Journals*, 16 April 1846.

and 'palavers'.[1] In Bonny, the Iguanas, the big lizard tribal 'animal totems', were ultimately destroyed. *Ikuba*, the tribal temple of skulls, had a new rival in the church building. In 1890 a house built by the government as a rest house became the centre of educational work in Bonny. The Rev. Hugh S. Macaulay, a grandson of Bishop Crowther, arrived from Onitsha to head the school.

A Jubilee sermon by an assistant bishop on St Stephen's day in 1947 based on a book, *The Romance of the Black River*, painted a macabre picture of Bonny before Christianity got to work:

...Bonny was surrounded by black mud and swamps, crocodiles and pythons. It was literally overrun with sacred Iguanas or monster lizards 6 ft. long. They were believed to be divine protectors of the town in which there dwelt the spirit of the dead....The moral and religious conditions of the place were dreadful. The dark bush around was the sacred abode of the 'juju' with its evil priest, degrading rites, and human sacrifice.[2]

A visitor to Bonny at the end of the century contrasted the heathen part of Bonny with the settlement about the church mission. As regards the latter,

the huts were clean and orderly, the inhabitants decently clad, and there was a general air of comfort and prosperity....The triumph was the greater that it had been brought about by mere force of example and humane influence, without the aid of either gunboats or Yoruba bayonets...there was hope of great results elsewhere.[3]

Even more symbolic of missionary educational enterprise was the Hope Waddell Institute of Calabar. But a Report by the High Commissioner indicated that most of the mission schools were in a state of collapse. The Commissioner gave no details as to the state of affairs, but singled out the Roman Catholic Mission and C.M.S. Schools in Onitsha, Hope Waddell and the school at Bonny.[4] In 1902 Messrs Miller Brothers agreed to contribute £100 a year to sustain the Bonny school. The government also planned to re-organise Hope Waddell to enable it with government assistance 'to provide higher education for at least 200'.[5]

[1] F.O. 84/1508, Enclosure in Hopkins to F.O., 28 August 1878.
[2] Walker, *The Romance of the Black River* (London, 1930).
[3] Bindloss, *op. cit.* pp. 285–6.
[4] C.O. 520/8, Moor to C.O. no. 157, 12 June 1901.
[5] C.O. 520/14, Moor to C.O. no. 145, 8 April 1902.

The pressure from the coast chiefs and the 'Native' Councils led to an independent government policy on the question of education. One suspects Sir Ralph forwarded with approval a letter from Eyo Honesty of Creek Town complaining about the incompetence of the Hope Waddell Institute. 'We beg therefore your Excellency to supply us with Government schools. Because we cannot rely on the Missionaries for the education of our children in Creek Town...it is disgraceful to us to see the foreigners [from Lagos and Freetown] coming in and occupied (*sic*) the offices and the benefits of our country....'[1] The issue raised about 'foreigners' was one that already preoccupied and later influenced Sir Ralph's policy in regard to education. As far back as 1900 he had expressed his concern over the situation in which the administration and the merchants had to employ foreign but educated clerks 'who spend as little as possible therein'. In addition the High Commissioner received almost every week requests for government schools from Asaba, Benin and other towns. He was convinced that local levies from the chiefs and from land concessions could provide adequate funds for running the schools. In any case, concluded Sir Ralph: 'I would submit that the provision of adequate educational opportunities for the natives is one of the primary duties devolving on local administrations consequent on the powers assumed by Her (*sic*) Majesty's Government in Nigeria....'[2]

Through the courtesy of Sir W. MacGregor, Henry Carr, the Inspector of Schools for Lagos, made an inspection tour of the existing schools in Bonny and Old Calabar. Carr's report emphasised that the missionaries looked upon schools primarily as the instruments for making converts. Other men viewed schools as instruments for making good and useful citizens. The criticism left a deep impression on Sir Ralph's mind, but he did not discontinue the policy of subsidising existing mission schools. The policy of founding government and native authority schools, while subsidising the missions' educational expansion, set the pattern of educational development which has remained unchanged. The annual report for 1906 revealed that there were thirty-one government schools in the 'Colony of Southern Nigeria', five in the

[1] *Ibid.* Enclosure in Moor to C.O. no. 173, 16 April 1902.
[2] C.O. 520/6, Moor to C.O., 10 October 1902.

western province, seventeen in the central province and nine in the eastern province.[1]

The children sent to school were potentially the fathers of a new generation of Nigerians. The new environment of school had little in common with the traditional way of life. It should, however, be emphasised that the full effects of European education and the creation of a new class little attached to the indigenous environment belonged to the future. The period of this study, however, saw the laying of the foundations for the new class.

Before concluding this chapter on the foundations of economic and social change, reference must be made to two issues directly connected with education: the press and native labour. There can be no doubt that the press has proved a powerful weapon for good or ill, according to the influence behind this particular medium of disseminating information.[2] In 1902 Sir Ralph Moor was already frightened by what he referred to as the 'reckless' press in West Africa—at a time when there were few people capable of reading in the protectorate of Nigeria. Lagos had then many weeklies, among which were the *Lagos Standard* and the *Lagos Weekly Record*. In Sir Ralph's favour it cannot be pretended that the Lagos papers were in any way restrained in their attacks on government policy. The High Commissioner did not want this development in his protectorate.[3]

In 1902, however, the Scottish mission at Old Calabar inaugurated a newspaper called *The Calabar Observer*. Moor thought that a mission publication should be encouraged because it would be in the hands of responsible and reliable people. The first edition of the paper Sir Ralph did not think inspiring. The leading article referred to the failure of an earlier attempt in 1885, *The Horn of Calabar*, in Efik, and then warned of 'the danger of the congregation of all and sundry from West Africa not averse to listen[ing] to garbled talk—talk which is apt to change matters quite trivial to matters of great importance'. The other pages of the first edition contained immodest claims for the Hope Waddell Institute as

[1] *Southern Nigeria Annual Report*, 1906. (It should be recalled that the Central and the Eastern Provinces together made up Southern Nigeria before 1906.)

[2] Coleman, *op. cit.* pp. 284 f.

[3] C.O. 520/7, Moor to C.O., 21 January 1901.

'beyond doubt one of the best equipped and most promising High Schools in Nigeria'. The most interesting part was a letter to the Editor, signed Pro Bono. 'My question is this: Why are the chain gangs used chiefly to keep the Golf Course clean, and seldom if ever to make any improvements in the Town?'[1] The Colonial Office reaction to Sir Ralph's misgivings was immediate. The enactment of 'The Southern Nigeria Newspaper Proclamation' was authorised and gave Sir Ralph 'the necessary powers for dealing with any particularly noxious specimen of the native press'.

The issue of wages for local labour was raised by Gallwey in the annual report, 1899–1900. The wages were unjustifiably higher than wages paid in East Africa. He considered the daily rate of 9*d.* to 1*s.* excessive. The natives, argued Gallwey, were not fond of work, and it was very difficult to get out of them anything like the worth of the money paid. On the whole, Kroo labour was preferable. In spite of Gallwey's low opinion of the calibre of local labour, the administration did an imperishable service to Nigeria in one respect. The Transvaal Chamber of Mines proposed to recruit labour from Nigeria as an 'experiment', in 1903. The Nigerians would serve for two years and would then be repatriated. It was largely owing to Sir Ralph Moor's uncompromising opposition that the idea was abandoned.[2] The press and labour questions were to assume great importance in the emerging Nigeria.

One minor point in the period under consideration, but one which loomed large in the period of the emergence of militant nationalism, concerns Sir Ralph Moor's policy in regard to European Reservations, not only in respect of habitation but also in regard to the provision of medical facilities. The policy of segregation was opposed by Governor MacGregor in Lagos but the Colonial Office dismissed the Governor's policy as mistaken and as being 'for sentimental reasons'. The Permanent Under-Secretary, Ommanney, described the Governor's policy as 'unfortunate'. 'He [MacGregor] does not always show the soundest judgment.' Sir Ralph naturally got his way and thus inaugurated

[1] C.O. 520/14, Enclosure in Moor to C.O. no. 265, 6 June 1900.
[2] C.O. 520/19, Probyn to C.O., Telegram, 8 May 1903. See also Minutes by Ommanney and Chamberlain.

the policy of European segregation from the natives in the protectorate of Southern Nigeria which persisted for many decades. The Assistant Under-Secretary at the Colonial Office endorsed the policy by emphatically stating that 'I think that the principle of these European Reservations is sound....'[1]

This chapter has attempted an objective analysis of the foundations of social and economic change. Much credit is due to the head of the protectorate government in avoiding unequivocally the Congo 'system'[2] in his land, forestry, and mining programmes. But it must not be assumed that some features of social legislation were not ill conceived. There is nothing but condemnation for the policy of racial segregation which had, and will always have, a strong and unmistakable undertone of 'the master race' hypothesis.

---

[1] C.O. 520/16, Proclamation no. 16 of 1902. See C.O. Minutes by Ommanney and Antrobus.

[2] Pim, *The Financial and Economic History of the African Tropical Territories* (Oxford, 1940), pp. 95-9.

# CHAPTER IX

# CONCLUSIONS

Nigeria, which is today one of the largest of the emergent African States, achieved its present territorial framework partly as a result of two amalgamations in 1906 and 1914, and partly as a result of Anglo-French and Anglo-German negotiations which were calculated to separate the spheres of exclusive influence of the European powers.[1] As if history has the paradoxical tendency of repeating itself, Nigeria is today split into four semi-autonomous regions. The area covered by this study comprises what are now the midwest region and the eastern region. There is considerable speculation as to the possibility of the union of these two regions on ideological and other grounds. If this contingency should come about, history would then have repeated itself and restored 'Southern Nigeria' to its original territorial integrity before 1906.

As regards Britain's association with the 'Nigerian' coast, 1884–5, the date of the Berlin West African Conference, was a 'dividing line'. Before 1885 Britain confined her attention to making amends for the iniquitous trade which she and the other European nations had indulged in, with incalculable harm to the Africans. Undoubtedly, the British operations connected with the suppression of the slave trade involved considerable expenditure in men and money.[2] In the Oil Rivers, after 1849, the sole representative of the British government was a lone Consul who had the job of persuading or forcing the local coast chiefs to abandon the basis of their great prosperity for many centuries. In the process, and with the backing of the British Navy, the phase of informal British authority was being unavowedly inaugurated. The motive behind the British policy was not, however, exclusively humanitarian. There was also the trade motive. Correspondence between

---

[1] Anene, *The International Boundaries of Nigeria, 1884–1906*, already cited.
[2] *Anti-Slavery Reporter*, London. Lloyd, *The Navy and the Slave Trade* (London, 1949). Burns, *op. cit.* pp. 277–8. Buxton, *The African Slave Trade and its Remedy.*

the local British agent, and successive British Foreign Secretaries, the petitions of British merchants, and the behaviour of some of the Consuls show abundantly that the gainful expectations from legitimate trade were never completely absent from British policy. The famous resolution of 1865 specifically recognised that the region of the Niger was one that promised ample economic rewards to British merchants and to Britain.

The phase of 'informal sway' could not survive the period which witnessed the industrialisation of the western European countries in the latter part of the nineteenth century. Tropical Africa abounded in a multitude of raw materials to feed the factories of Europe, and at the same time provided potential markets and consumers for all types of European manufacture including bad liquor, guns and cheap cloth. It was the British traders, not the statesmen, who first appreciated the value of exclusive colonial acquisitions. The merchants turned to their governments in order to 'peg out estates for posterity'. The undignified scramble for territories in Africa was the upshot. In spite of views to the contrary,[1] the intelligible explanation for British complacency before 1884–5 was what has been called 'the self-denial' of other potential competitors for the control of the Niger territories. Before the Berlin Conference, British uneasiness occasioned by German and French activities in the neighbourhood of the Guinea coast and the foresight of Taubman Goldie were the immediate causes of the decision of the British government to make treaties with the 'chiefs' of the Niger districts in order to vindicate exclusive British claims to the area. This was completely successful.

The primary British aim was to exclude foreign colonial competitors from an area of immense potential wealth in natural resources. The government had no intention of expending money in setting up a formal administration. The emphasis of policy was on trade exploitation with minimum expense to the British exchequer. The situation was admirably summarised by Morel: 'Commerce took us to West Africa; commerce keeps and will keep us in West Africa. It is the *fons et origo* of our presence in West Africa. The day it ceases to be so, West Africa ceases to be of use to

---

[1] Robinson, Gallagher and Denny, *op. cit.* See ch. I.

the Empire. It will become a costly plaything, and the British people are too essentially practical a people to care long for toys of that kind.'[1] It is not suggested that any British minister would necessarily have endorsed the views of a merchant, but the main point is the predominance of the trade motive in the period after the Berlin Conference. Here too lay the explanation for the method of establishing a more formal British control over the Nigerian coast.

The programme of signing treaties of protection with the local chiefs ostensibly laid the foundations of the protectorate of the Oil Rivers. There emerged a 'colonial protectorate'. Whatever the precise implications of a 'protectorate' in other parts of the British empire, and whatever the implications today, there is abundant evidence that in respect of the Nigerian coast, the British government was not unduly concerned with any clear exposition of what the protectorate of the Oil Rivers imposed on her. In the circumstances, the period between 1885 and 1890 has rightly been described as 'a paper protectorate'. The actions of British agents were full of anomalies, some of which the British government itself often repudiated. For instance Lord Salisbury described Johnston's treatment of King Jaja as 'illegal'.[2]

It is futile mincing words about British motives in preferring a protectorate to the outright annexation of the territory that grew to become Southern Nigeria. What is remarkable is the persistence of the pretence on the part of several Foreign Office officials and their legal advisers that a colonial protectorate was in a different category of British possessions from colonies. Every local British administrator at one stage or another raised the question of clarification.

The 'chiefs' of the coast city-states at no time questioned the implications of the policy of the first Consul-General in substituting subsidies for 'comey'. The acquiescence of the 'chiefs' was the first step in the eclipse of indigenous authority. The 'chiefs', most of whom had already undermined their traditional rulers, were not concerned with British intrusion as long as they received financial compensation which in any case did not involve the

---

[1] Morel, *Affairs of West Africa*, already cited p. 21. Knowles, *op. cit.* p. 104.
[2] Geary, *op. cit.* See appendix 1, pp. 275, 294.

hazards of 'comey' levy on British merchants. It is fascinating to speculate on how Jaja of Opobo, who had no misgivings on the issue of sovereignty, might have reacted to Macdonald's proceedings if he had survived his exile. Sir Claude Macdonald asked how the protectorate could be extended from the coast other than by treaty-making with the hinterland inhabitants. One of the Foreign Office officials wondered, in reply, how 'savages' could be expected to honour treaties. Sir Ralph Moor, after having overwhelmed the hinterland inhabitants by force of arms, complained to the Colonial Office: 'We are constantly passing laws and interfering with native authorities as if we had acquired full jurisdiction in all matters....'[1] He received a curt reply from the Legal Adviser of the Colonial Office to the effect that the 'Protectorate is not part of H.M.'s Dominions'. There were a great many learned memoranda in the Colonial Office on the subject of 'Protectorate' to which reference has already been made.[2] The fine distinctions between colonies and protectorates had little influence on what the local administrators chose to do. The local activities had ultimately the endorsement of the Permanent Under-Secretary of the Colonial Office when he wrote quite frankly at last that British policy should be to steadily pave the way 'for the annexation of the...Protectorates...but we shall have to proceed cautiously if disturbances are to be avoided'.[3] One conclusion is inescapable. Colonial protectorates in Africa were matters of administrative economy and expediency.

In one important sense the proclamation of the protectorate of the Oil Rivers did the inhabitants immense good. The alternative in the circumstances of the time was chartered company rule. The natives of Southern Nigeria who came under chartered company rule from 1886 to 1900 cherish nothing but abhorrence for the way the company brought 'civilisation' to them. A jurisdiction based on treaties in which 'we cede the whole of our territory to the National African Company (Limited) and their descendants, for ever...'[4] could be nothing better than fraud. Indeed the Lord Chancellor in Gladstone's government described the treaties as

---

[1] C.O. 520/16, Moor to C.O., 19 November 1902. See Minutes by Antrobus.
[2] Africa, no. 410. Confidential.
[3] C.O. 520/16, Moor to C.O., 19 November 1902. Minutes by Ommanney.
[4] Hertslet, *Map of Africa by Treaty*, vol. I, p. 137.

fraudulent. The Colonial Office in 1900 observed that it would not like to prove that the 'treaties', the benefit of which it was taking over from the company, 'would all bear scrutiny'. In reply to Moor's complaints about his inheritance from the Royal Niger Company, Antrobus of the Colonial Office had the last word: 'Sir R. Moor is not, like Sir F. Lugard, under any illusions as to the Company's administration.'[1]

The efforts of the African Association to obtain its own charter mercifully came to nothing. One cannot help shuddering at the thought of what might have been the fate of the various proclamations dealing with such far-reaching and fundamental questions as forest reserves, land and mining if commercial combines had had their way. Sir Ralph summarised the evil of commercial control in the succinct phrase 'to suck the orange'.[2] In successfully countering the selfishness which inspired the merchants' idea of exploitation, Sir Ralph rendered his greatest service to the protectorate of Southern Nigeria. The natives remained peasant owners of their land, but were increasingly made aware, through education, of the need for more intensive and more systematic exploitation of their own natural resources. The obvious advantages of forest reserves, against the cupidity of speculators, were guaranteed. In short, the 'Congo system' was never introduced into Nigeria. In this respect, the word 'protectorate' had profound significance in shaping the future of the inhabitants who were going through a period of transition. The administration did not hesitate to interpose its authority between the inhabitants and the British merchants when the latter persisted in practices or contemplated measures which might have done incalculable harm to Southern Nigeria. So, as Professor Seeley said of the British Indian empire, British rule began in trade, yet the rule was not planned by traders.

To eulogise the foundations of British economic policy should not, however, obscure two fundamental blemishes in the consolidation of British rule. In the first place, the complete reliance on conquest to establish the *pax Britannica* over peoples who merely

[1] C.O. 520/10, Minutes by Antrobus on Moor to C.O. no. 426, 16 December 1901.
[2] C.O. 520/13, Moor to C.O. no. 14, Confidential, 21 September 1902.

wished to continue their traditional way of life was inconsistent with the accepted conception of a 'protectorate'. The deportation of Jaja and the ruin of Nana were injustices inflicted on local rulers because British trade mattered more than the legitimate rights of the chiefs mentioned here. The military expeditions against the peoples of the hinterland occasioned unnecessary bloodshed and disruption which tact and patience might, possibly less dramatically, have obviated. The annual reports up to 1906 preserved the illusion that British occupation was welcome—innumerable instances of continued resistance by various indigenous groups notwithstanding.[1] The Foreign Office, and later the Colonial Office, officials regretted the need for military domination, but occasionally minutes by the officials suggested that there were indeed no alternatives to military subjugation in dealing with 'barbarians', especially when they impeded the expansion of British trade. To these strictures, two exceptions must be conceded.

For the Benin expedition Britain found ample justification in the ambush of the protectorate officials. The background to the expedition has been a matter of controversy. British writers judiciously emphasise the peaceful nature of Phillips' journey to Benin. On the basis of this thesis, Benin rulers could be charged with treachery. A full study of the documents shows, however, that Phillips and his predecessors had planned on many occasions the deportation of the Benin king. It cannot be denied that the expedition was bound to take place against a city the rulers of which seemed to have devoted most of their time to human sacrifice—the victims invariably coming from the neighbouring Ishan and Afemai communities. The liberation of these potential victims of very reprehensible practices on the part of Benin is in retrospect an act of humanity. The Oba of Benin is today the President of the House of Chiefs of the Mid-West Region, but Ishan children and the other neighbouring communities are no longer brought up with the idea that the Oba of Benin is the ruler of the world.[2]

[1] For instance, 1905–6, the Onitsha–Bende hinterland expedition, and 1908–9, the Niger–Cross river expedition.
[2] On the creation of the Mid-West Region, there were considerable misgivings about the possibility of making the Oba the Governor. The post apparently was too reminiscent of the terror of the old regime.

21-2

The expedition against the Aro presents problems of assessment similar to those of Benin. The British officials gradually built up a case for the expedition. On the other hand, Aro hold on innumerable Ibo and Ibibio communities had not always been in the best interests of the communities. The perpetuation of the internal slave trade, the exploitation of the reverence felt for the Long Juju fraud, and the use of Abam mercenaries to disturb the tranquillity of intergroup relations were aspects of Aro hegemony which no administration in a protectorate or colony could tolerate indefinitely. There were undoubtedly alternatives to a punitive expedition. Ormsby-Gore exaggerated the result of the expedition when he observed that the destruction of the Long Juju had left the people 'freer but leaderless'.[1] Nevertheless, Abam raids (or as, local tradition describes the raids, 'the flight from the Abams') are still recalled in many parts of Iboland with feelings of unmistakable terror. In this respect, the destruction of the pernicious influence of the Long Juju produced nothing but good in the lives of the communities.

A misfortune inflicted on the inhabitants by the British administration, particularly on the Ibo and Ibibio, had its roots in two fallacies. The 'house' system which the British administrators encountered on the coast was assumed to be the characteristic social structure of the hinterland. The system on the coast was passing through a period of political and social chaos, and had to be replaced by a British-sponsored system of local government. Worse still, the assumption that the hinterland peoples had no system of government, and that chaos prevailed, led naturally to the creation of the 'Native' Court system manned by natives who could not command the confidence of the local communities. The peace and solidarity of small but autonomous 'democracies' were disrupted. Further, the attempt to amalgamate the units into centralised but larger groups intensified the atmosphere of artificiality which the 'Native' Court system had from its origin. The pernicious consequences of the system were not entirely the fault of the British. The hatred generated by the way in which this new class of careerists—'warrant chiefs', court clerks and court messengers—exploited and terrorised their own

[1] Ormsby-Gore, Report already cited, p. 19.

324

people was not fully realised until the riots of 1929.[1] There were enough warnings for the British administrators to heed, and special reference has been made to the report of the Secretary for Native Affairs in 1922. The implied criticism naturally could not apply to the British officials who completed their task in 1906.

The social and economic changes which the impact of British rule precipitated are still going on, for good or ill. The penetration of the hinterland by both government and commercial enterprise meant the progressive decay of the coast towns which had seen centuries of great prosperity. The Ibo and Ibibio, who had traditionally lived in virtually isolated communities, have now taken to long-ranging trade, and the Ibo have gone further and now practically control the retail trade of most parts of Nigeria. What effects have these had on the homeland? It is a question which cannot be answered objectively. Meek has perhaps over-stated the case when he observes that '...if a backward people is suddenly confronted by a powerful modern state, and is not given the time and assistance necessary to enable it to face the new situation, it is liable to lose its stability, and indeed its soul'.[2] Southern Nigerian peoples have not become a disorganised rabble of self-seeking individualists. The traditional Ibo and Ibibio 'socio-centric' outlook could by slow evolution have given place to a wider one, but the process should have been based on solid indigenous foundations. The process involves a dilemma which still confronts the governments of today—how to reconcile the growth of individualism with the need to preserve the age-long sanctions of rural village life. This issue is coupled with the problems which the introduction of European education created.

No one can rightly claim that when the missionaries arrived they entertained motives other than the moral regeneration of a 'benighted people'. There were no material rewards which might offer inducements available to people in the government. A study of the early and often hazardous travels of the Scottish missionaries in the Upper Cross river reveals nothing but self-sacrifice, discomfort and often death. The life of Mary Slessor

[1] Afigbo, op. cit. See also C.S.O. 26/2, File 11857, vol. v. Annual Report, Warri Province, 1927, pp. 11, 21.
[2] Meek, Law and Authority in a Nigerian Tribe, p. 326.

among the Okoyong was an eloquent testimony to the manner in which the missionaries saw the task that lay before them. The reforms the missions achieved through persuasion are innumerable. The outstanding ones include the end of human sacrifice and twin-killing, and the gradual acceptance by the people of a world not 'filled with evil spirits'. Where the missionaries erred was in their lack of discrimination between the reprehensible aspects of indigenous life and innocent practices which formed part of the indigenous cultural heritage, provided sanctions, regulated behaviour, and safeguarded the solidarity of village life. The indigenous system was impregnated with evil, argued the untutored missionaries, and so the early Christians had to denounce their own people, their past, and their way of life. The converts to Christianity during the period of transition were indeed few, but the work initiated then bore fruit to an extent which it is for the statistician or the social anthropologist to measure.

The missions' greatest instrument, in what they regarded as the transformation of Southern Nigeria, was the school. The school not only provided the passport for employment but provided a fruitful field for indoctrination. The coast chiefs appreciated the value of the schools, and the hinterland peoples were not slow in doing the same. With the opening of unsuspected opportunities for earning ready wages, in contrast with the financially unproductive drudgery of farming or collecting palm produce, far-sighted families were determined that their children (not slaves as in the nineteenth century) should go to school, government or mission. The results are too obvious to require elaboration. The only question is the profundity of the change the missions and their schools have effected in the peoples' mentality and belief in the ways of their forefathers. The question is perhaps partially answered by this extract from the *Proceedings of the C.M.S.* of 1915:

Heathen people are ready to subscribe the money necessary to support a school teacher. The conscious need for Gospel, though it is shown occasionally, is most frequently obscured by the demand for education.... Our religious instruction is tolerated and accepted because it is compulsory and is a means of acquiring English, the language of trade, the law courts and government administration.[1]

[1] P. 14. See also C.M.S. G 3/A 3/011, Memo on education for Committee, by J. Brandreth.

The interval between 1906 and 1964 is indeed a long one. Today Nigeria is a sovereign state, whereas in the period discussed Britain had freedom of action. In retrospect, it is amusing to recall the views of the administrators on demands for a legislative council and African membership of the executive council. As far as the protectorate of Southern Nigeria was concerned, the demand for a legislative council came, not from the natives, but from the British merchants who had their own reasons to undermine the safe economic foundations which Sir Ralph Moor was trying to consolidate in the interests of the peoples of the protectorate. Benevolent paternal rule in this respect was amply justified in the results. The question of African representation in the executive council was raised after the amalgamation of Southern Nigeria with Lagos.[1] It is not surprising that the Colonial Office rejected the request. The succeeding Governors, including Lord Lugard and Sir Hugh Clifford, continued to persuade themselves that the destiny of the hinterland peoples could not be left in the hands of a few but vocal 'detribalised' educated Africans on the coast. What should be noted is that in a public speech, Sapara Williams urged, among other things, that the welfare of the people ought to be the goal of the government.[2]

There can be no doubt that the protectorate of Southern Nigeria began as an 'undeveloped estate' to be exploited by a wise 'landlord'. The early rulers were not unaware of their responsibility to the protected peoples. A speech made by Governor Egerton in 1905 is worth quoting in this respect: '...the more you develop British trade in a country the better it is for that country... the greater the trade the greater the revenue, and the greater the revenue, if it is well spent, the better the lot of the people we govern.'[3] The British 'landlord' did not do badly either. In 1906 imports from England amounted to £2,847,316. Local revenue exceeded expenditure by several thousands of pounds.[4] Southern Nigeria fully justified the original motive which inspired direct British imperial rule. The 'show' launched in 1891 with a Treasury

[1] C.O. 520/36, Egerton to Elgin, 11 August 1906.
[2] C.O. 520/3, S. Nigeria Government Gazette, 9 May 1906.
[3] Speech at a banquet given by the West African Trade Association in Liverpool, 5 October 1905.
[4] C.O. 592/2, Annual Financial Report. See also Appendix E in text.

loan of £14,000 was by 1906 paying handsome dividends in the form of enhanced British trade and the gainful employment of thousands of Englishmen. There are, however, two sides to the very much maligned word 'imperialism'. It is therefore not fair to insist on British gains without making some reference to the views of Joseph Chamberlain, the famous author of the phrase 'undeveloped estates', in his speech on the need to fight and destroy the scourge of the tropics—the mosquito: 'The man who shall successfully grapple with this foe of humanity, this malaria, these fevers desolating our colonies and dependencies in many tropical climates...will do more for the world, more for the British Empire, than the man who adds a new province to the wide dominions of the Queen.'[1] No sane Nigerian will deny the services rendered to Nigeria by British medical science in this fight against malaria.

Whatever the merits and demerits of imperialism as regards Southern Nigeria, 1885–1906, two things stand out prominently in this study of a period of transition imposed by the impact of British intervention. The first is the preponderance of the trade motive. The second is the almost exclusive use of military expeditions to intimidate the peoples of the protectorate into accepting British authority. These, in retrospect, appear reprehensible, but throughout the nineteenth and early twentieth centuries (and perhaps even today), trade was genuinely believed by British administrators, British merchants, missionaries and the British governments to be an indispensable instrument of civilisation. After all, trade was Dr Livingstone's prescription for 'healing the open sore of the world'. The expansion of trade has done and is doing Nigeria immense good. In launching military expeditions, the British administrators indulged in the illusion that they were doing nothing but good. The resultant disruption of local communities was something the British agents had neither the academic training nor the patience to analyse and understand. As they saw the situation, they were introducing 'order' into a society which was 'cannibalistic' and 'chaotic'.

Britain's 'freedom of action' in Southern Nigeria and the

[1] Quoted by Dr Ross in a letter dated 23 May 1899, addressed to the Secretary, Liverpool School of Medicine.

consequences should be judged, not by the motives, nor by the methods, but by the end object which is admirably summarised in the words of a journalist who combined in his mental disposition commercial and humanitarian instincts: '... to see Nigeria, at least, become in time the home of highly-trained African peoples, protected in their property and in their rights by the Paramount Power, proud of their institutions, proud of their race, proud of their own fertile and beautiful land.'[1] The extent to which Morel's optimism is justified by a Nigeria which is now independent and sovereign is an open question. The answer should, however, take into account not only the foundations laid in the period discussed in this book but also the constructiveness or vagaries of subsequent administrators and Nigerians themselves. Southern Nigeria had by subsequent amalgamations become two regions in the Federation of Nigeria. Foreign observers have claimed that Nigeria, by reason of her population and resources, is destined to lead the rest of Africa. Objective historians of Nigeria will undoubtedly accept that the basic problems, which are directly and indirectly connected with British intrusion, are that the political leaders of Nigeria have to 'weld Nigeria into one nation and... to develop her human and natural resources to a stage where she can support by herself a continual improvement in her standard of living'.[2] Britain, it may be for partly selfish reasons, laid the foundations, but she did not labour in vain. The future is entirely in the hands of Nigerians.

[1] Morel, *Nigeria: its Peoples and Problems*, cited, see chs. XIII and XIV.
[2] *The Sunday Times Weekly Review*, 10 May 1964, p. 30.

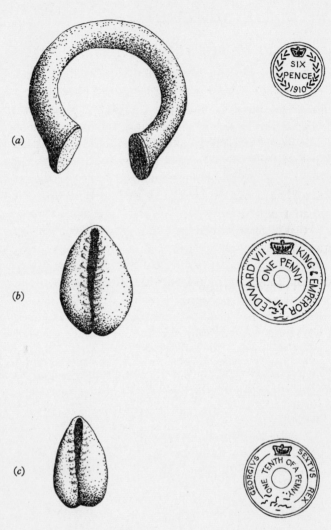

Native and British currencies (original size):
(*a*) manilla; (*b*) Zanzibar cowrie; (*c*) Indian cowrie.

# APPENDIX A

## OFFICIALS OF THE BRITISH FOREIGN OFFICE
## 1885–99

| *Foreign Secretaries* | *Date of appointment* |
|---|---|
| Earl Granville | 28 May 1880 |
| Marquess of Salisbury | 24 June 1885 |
| Earl of Rosebery | 6 February 1886 |
| Earl of Iddesleigh | 3 July 1886 |
| Marquess of Salisbury | 14 January 1887 |
| Earl of Rosebery | 18 July 1892 |
| Earl of Kimberley | 11 March 1894 |
| Marquess of Salisbury | 29 June 1895 |

*Permanent Under-Secretaries*

| Sir Julian Pauncefote | 23 September 1882 |
|---|---|
| Sir Philip W. Currie | 2 April 1889 |
| Sir Thomas H. Sanderson | 1 January 1894 |

*Assistant Under-Secretaries*
(supervising the African Department)

| Sir Thomas Villiers Lister | 10 October 1873 |
|---|---|
| Sir H. Percy Anderson | 1 January 1894 |
| Hon. Francis L. Bertie | 19 January 1896 |

*Senior Clerks*
(Consular and African, East and West)

| Sir Henry Percy Anderson | 10 October 1873 |
|---|---|
| Sir Charles Lloyd Hill | 1 January 1894 |

*Legal Adviser*

| William Edward Davidson | 27 July 1886 |
|---|---|

# APPENDIX B

| Secretaries of State | Date of appointment |
|---|---|
| Earl of Derby | 16 December 1882 |
| Earl Granville | 6 February 1886 |
| Viscount Knutsford | 14 January 1887 |
| Marquess of Ripon | 17 August 1892 |
| Rt Hon. Joseph Chamberlain | 28 June 1895 |
| Rt Hon. Alfred Lyttelton | 9 October 1903 |
| Earl of Elgin | 11 December 1905 |

| Permanent Under-Secretaries | |
|---|---|
| Sir R. H. Meade | 1 February 1892 |
| Sir Edward Wingfield | 1 March 1897 |
| Sir Montagu Ommanney | 7 June 1900 |

| Assistant Under-Secretaries | |
|---|---|
| Reginald L. Antrobus (West African Colonies and Protectorates) | 25 October 1897 |
| Hugh Bertram Cox (Legal) | 15 November 1898 |

| Legal Assistant | |
|---|---|
| J. S. Risley | 14 March 1901 |

# APPENDIX C

## TREATY WITH KING AND CHIEFS OF OPOBO, SIGNED AT OPOBO, 19 DECEMBER 1884*

Her Majesty the Queen of the United Kingdom of Great Britain and Ireland, Empress of India etc., and the Kings and Chiefs of Opobo, being desirous of maintaining and strengthening the relations of peace and friendship which have for so long existed between them:

Her Britannic Majesty has named and appointed E. H. Hewett, Esq., her Consul for the Bights of Benin and Biafra, to conclude a Treaty for this purpose.

The said E. H. Hewett, Esq., and the said Kings and Chiefs of Opobo have agreed upon and concluded the following Articles:

### Article I

Her Majesty the Queen of Great Britain and Ireland etc. in compliance with the request of the King, Chiefs, and people of Opobo, hereby undertakes to extend to them, and to the territory under their authority and jurisdiction, her gracious favour and protection.

### Article II

The King and Chiefs of Opobo agree and promise to refrain from entering into any correspondence, Agreement, or Treaty with any foreign nation or Power, except with the knowledge and sanction of Her Britannic Majesty's Government.

### Article III

It is agreed that full and exclusive jurisdiction, civil and criminal, over British subjects and their property in the territory of Opobo is reserved for Her Britannic Majesty, to be exercised by such Consular or other officers as Her Majesty shall appoint for that purpose.

The same jurisdiction is likewise reserved to Her Majesty in the said territory of Opobo over foreign subjects enjoying British protection, who shall be deemed to be included in the expression 'British subjects' throughout the Treaty.

* Taken from *Parl. Papers*, 1888, vol. 74, Papers Relative to the King Ja Ja of Opobo, etc. Africa, no. 2 [C. 5365].

## Article IV

All disputes between the King and Chiefs of Opobo, or between them and British or foreign traders, or between the aforesaid King and Chiefs and neighbouring tribes, which cannot be settled amicably between the two parties, shall be submitted to the British Consular or other officers appointed by Her Britannic Majesty to exercise jurisdiction in Opobo territories for arbitration and decision, or for arrangement.

## Article V

The King and Chiefs of Opobo hereby engage to assist the British Consular or other officers in the execution of such duties as may be assigned to them, and further to act upon their advice in matters relating to the administration of Justice, the development of the resources of the country, the interests of commerce, or in any matter in relation to peace, order, and Government and the general progress of civilisation.

## Article VI

[Free Trade article—not accepted by Ja Ja.]

## Article VII

All White Ministers of the Christian Religion shall be permitted to exercise their calling within the territories of the aforesaid King and Chiefs, who hereby guarantee to them full protection.

## Article VIII

If any vessel should be wrecked within the Opobo territories, the King and Chiefs will give them all the assistance in their power, will secure them from plunder, and also recover and deliver to the Owners or Agents all the Property which can be saved. If there are no such owners or agents on the spot, then the said property shall be delivered to the British Consular or other officer.

The King and Chiefs further engage to do all in their power to protect the persons and property of the officers, crew and others on board such wrecked vessels. All claims for salvage due in such cases shall, if disputed, be referred to the British Consular or other Officer for arbitration and decision.

## Article IX

This Treaty shall come into operation so far as practicable from the date of its signature.

Done in duplicate at Opobo, this nineteenth day of December in the year one thousand eight hundred and eighty-four.

(*Signed*)  EDWARD HYDE HEWETT
JA JA
COOKEY GAM
PRINCE SATURDAY JA JA
FINEBOURNE *his* × *mark*
JOHN AFRICA ×
HOW STRONGFACE ×
OGOLO ×
WILLIAM OBANNEY ×
BLACK FOUBRAH ×
SHOO PETERSIDE ×
SAM ANNIE PEPPLE ×
THOMAS JA JA ×
SAM OKO EPELLA ×
DUKE OF NORFOLK ×
WILLIAM TOBY ×
JUNGI ×
WARISOE ×
SAMUEL GEORGE TOBY ×

Witness to the above marks

(*Signed*)  HAROLD E. WHITE,
*H.M. Vice-Consul*

R. D. BOLER,
*Chairman of the Court of Equity*

# APPENDIX D

## BRITISH CHIEF LOCAL REPRESENTATIVES
### 1849–1906

| | | |
|---|---|---|
| J. Beecroft | Consul (Bights of Benin and Biafra) | 1849 |
| | Consul (Bight of Biafra) | 1853 |
| T. Hutchinson | Consul (Bight of Biafra) | 1855 |
| R. Burton | Consul (Bight of Biafra) | 1861 |
| C. Livingstone | Consul (Bight of Biafra) | 1864 |
| | Consul (Bights of Benin and Biafra) | 1867 |
| G. Hartley | Consul (Bights of Benin and Biafra) | 1873 |
| D. Hopkins | Consul (Bights of Benin and Biafra) | 1878 |
| E. Hewett | Consul (Old Calabar, Oil Rivers) | 1882 |
| C. M. Macdonald | Commissioner and Consul General | |
| | (Oil Rivers Protectorate) | 1891 |
| | (Niger Coast Protectorate) | 1893 |
| R. D. Moor | Commissioner and Consul General | |
| | (Niger Coast Protectorate) | 1893 |
| | High Commissioner (Southern Nigeria) | 1900 |
| W. Egerton | High Commissioner (Southern Nigeria) | 1904 |
| | Governor (The Colony and Protectorate of Southern Nigeria) | 1906 |

1  Prince Archibong II, Obong of Calabar, during Livingstone's Consulship

2  Chief Sunday Jaja, son of King Jaja; born in 1875 and educated in England

3(a)  European traders in 'native' attire

3(b)  The Bonny Consulate (partially dismantled in 1925)

4(a)  A city-state gig, 1901. When equipped with cannon it became a war canoe

4(b)  The steam yacht *Ivy*, 1898

5   Chief Nana with his family, in exile, after 1894

6 Ibani-Chuku, King of Okrika (deported in 1896)

7 Chief Young Briggs of Abonema, a coast 'warrant chief', with his son, 1905

8(a)   The Cable and Wireless Company building in Bonny, 1900

8(b)   Bonny School, 1909

# APPENDIX E

## SOUTHERN NIGERIA:
### EXPORT AND IMPORT FIGURES

#### (a) Exports

| Year | Exports to U.K. (£) | Total exports (£) |
|---|---|---|
| 1892–3 | 446,570 | 843,501 |
| 1893–4 | 494,246 | 1,014,088 |
| 1894–5 | 463,172 | 825,099 |
| 1895–6 | 538,637 | 844,333 |
| 1896–7 | 546,446 | 785,605 |
| 1897–8 | 497,589 | 750,223 |
| 1898–9 | 500,367 | 774,647 |
| 1899–1900 | 531,088 | 888,954 |
| 1900 | 672,900 | 1,133,604 |
| 1901 | 789,693 | 1,253,706 |
| 1902 | 820,057 | 1,254,696 |
| 1903 | 922,658 | 1,431,984 |
| 1904 | 1,079,544 | 1,718,717 |

#### (b) Imports

| Year | Imports from U.K. (£) | Total imports (£) |
|---|---|---|
| 1892–3 | 576,263 | 726,916 |
| 1893–4 | 697,484 | 929,333 |
| 1894–5 | 581,230 | 739,864 |
| 1895–6 | 575,448 | 750,975 |
| 1896–7 | 563,291 | 655,977 |
| 1897–8 | 504,802 | 639,698 |
| 1898–9 | 583,067 | 728,639 |
| 1899–1900 | 597,998 | 725,798 |
| 1900 | 927,905 | 1,115,583 |
| 1901 | 1,072,962 | 1,297,116 |
| 1902 | 1,004,958 | 1,246,480 |
| 1903 | 1,228,959 | 1,492,748 |
| 1904 | 1,416,554 | 1,792,468 |

# APPENDIX F

## ORDINANCES AND PROCLAMATIONS, 1894–1906

## (IMPORTANT EXAMPLES)

### *Ordinances*

|  | No. | Year |
|---|---|---|
| Medical and Sanitary | 1 | 1894 |
| Constabulary | 2 | 1894 |
| Customs | 3 | 1894 |
| Post Office | 4 | 1894 |
| Fire-arms | 5 | 1894 |
| Adulteration of Produce Regulations | 2 | 1897 |
| Observation of Local Law | 1 | 1898 |
| Constables' Wills and Distribution | 3 | 1899 |

(They are described as Ordinances and Queen's Regulations of the Niger Coast Protectorate and recorded in a Schedule to Proclamation no. 11 of 1900, i.e. Ordinance Extension Proclamation. See C.O. 588/1.)

### *Proclamations*

|  | No. | Year |
|---|---|---|
| Lands Acquisition | 1 | 1900 |
| Customs Tariff | 2 | 1900 |
| Supreme Court | 6 | 1900 |
| The Commissioners' | 8 | 1900 |
| Native Courts | 9 | 1900 |
| Spirituous Liquors Prohibition | 12 | 1900 |
| The Payment of Wages | 13 | 1900 |
| The Master and Servant | 3 | 1901 |
| Slave Dealing | 5 | 1901 |
| The Native House Rule | 26 | 1901 |
| The Police Proclamation | 4 | 1902 |
| The Native Currency | 14 | 1902 |
| The European Reservation | 16 | 1902 |
| The Mining Regulation | 18 | 1902 |
| Native Lands Acquisition | 1 | 1903 |
| The Public Lands Acquisition | 5 | 1903 |
| The Hospitals and Dispensaries | 7 | 1903 |
| The Public Health (Streets and Buildings) | 11 | 1903 |

## Proclamations (*continued*)

| | No. | Year |
|---|---|---|
| The Ordeal, Witchcraft and Juju | 13 | 1903 |
| The Roads and Creeks | 15 | 1903 |
| The Education Proclamation | 19 | 1903 |
| The Newspaper Proclamation | 26 | 1903 |
| Importation of Cowries Prohibition | 6 | 1904 |
| The Forestry Amendments Proclamation | 12 | 1905 |
| The Illiterates Protection Proclamation | 14 | 1905 |
| The Towns Regulation Proclamation | 15 | 1905 |
| The Unlawful Societies Proclamation | 16 | 1905 |
| The Native Court Proclamation, 1906 (C.S.O. 1/13), vol. 38 | | 1906 |
| Letters Patent and Order-in-Council— S. Nigeria Annual Report (Constituting the Colony of Southern Nigeria...) | | 1906 |

22-2

# BIBLIOGRAPHY

## A. PRIMARY SOURCES

### 1. *Nigerian* (including oral traditions and manuscripts)

The last few years have witnessed an increasing acceptance of oral traditions (with important qualifications) as valid source material for historical reconstruction. Thus, apart from the manuscripts of the local historians of Nembe, Bonny and Opobo, mainly based on collated traditions, many post-graduate students of the University of Ibadan's Department of History have, in their field-work in the hinterland in the eastern and western portions of the protectorate of Southern Nigeria, made an immense contribution to the material available to me.

### 2. *Nigerian government sources* (Ibadan, Enugu and Benin)

The most important of these sources are undoubtedly the series described in the National Archives as C.S.O. and Calprof. In many cases these sources suffer from the handicap of being out-letters to the F.O. or C.O., and do not therefore contain vital minutes which one finds in the comparable documents available in the P.R.O. (London). On the other hand, they contain internal administrative reports which throw abundant light on the local conditions within the protectorate.

Another invaluable government source consists of Intelligence Reports which began to be compiled in the 1930's. Although the work of amateurs, not of academic anthropologists, their analyses of indigenous traditional social and political organisation cannot be dispensed with. The Department of History and the National Archives have now agreed to bring together the otherwise dispersed reports on Eastern Nigeria to form one collection.

### 3. *Public Record Office* (London)

Most of the primary sources deposited in the P.R.O. are from official dispatches entitled 'Slave Trade' and 'Africa' in the Foreign Office records. After 1898 the Colonial Office records and miscellaneous correspondence are more relevant to the study. *Parliamentary Papers* have been used, but it cannot be pretended that they contain more than full or partial reproductions of the dispatches available in the F.O. and C.O. records. *Hansard* yields little, except for a number of important questions by Members of Parliament connected with Liverpool.

## 4. *Missionary sources*

The Waddell Journals by the pioneer in Calabar of the United Presbyterian Mission of Scotland are available in the National Library of Scotland in Edinburgh. Salisbury Square is the repository of C.M.S. records. The Roman Catholic Mission records have not been accessible to me, except for the files of individual missionaries of the Society of African Missions whose headquarters is in Rome. All the papers of this Society are now available, in microfilm, in the University of Ibadan Library

### Manuscript sources

1. *National Archives* (Ibadan)
   (*a*) C.S.O. series 1–28.
   (*b*) Calprof series 1–10.

2. *Public Record Office* (London)
   (*a*) *Foreign Office Records*
      F.O. 84 Series, Slave Trade Papers, Consular Correspondence, miscellaneous subjects, including presents to Chiefs.
      F.O. 93, Treaties, Benin to Ambas Bay, the Niger and the Benue.
      F.O. 97, Foreign Jurisdiction Consolidation and Amendment Bills.
      F.O. 2 Series, General Consular Correspondence (Africa, West Africa).
   (*b*) *Colonial Office Records*
      C.O. 444 Series, Despatches, etc. (Protectorate of Southern Nigeria).
      C.O. 520 Series, Despatches, etc. (Protectorate of Southern Nigeria).
      C.O. 806 Series: only 806/345, which deals with powers and jurisdiction of European powers in Africa, is relevant.
      C.O. 473/2–11, 1901–10, Blue Book of Statistics.
      C.O. 588/1, 1900–6, Proclamations.
      C.O. 591/1–7, 1900–10, Government Gazettes.
   (*c*) P.R.O. 30/29, Lord Granville Papers.
   (*d*) T 1, Treasury Records, 1887–9.

### Printed sources

(*a*) Foreign Office Research Library (London), F.O.C.P. Series.

(*b*) The British Museum Library, *Hansard*.

(*c*) Institute of Historical Research Library (London).
   *Parliamentary Papers*
      1865, XXXVII, 287, Col. Ord's Report on the West African Settlements.
      1865, vol. 1, Report of Committee on the above evidence, etc., 2 parts.

1885, vol. LV, Correspondence with Her Majesty's Ambassador at Berlin. Africa, no. 2 (C. 4284).

1885, vol. LV (West African Conference), Correspondence. Africa, no. 7 (C. 4284).

1885, vol. LV, Further Correspondence. Africa, no. 2 (C. 4360).

1885, vol. LV, Protocol and General Act. Africa, no. 4 (C. 4361).

1886, vol. XLVII, General Act. Africa, no. 3 (C. 4739).

1885, vol. LV, The Cameroons (C. 4279).

1888, vol. LXXIV, Papers Relative to King Ja Ja of Opobo, etc. Africa, no. 2 (C. 5365).

1890, vol. L, General Act of the Brussels Conference (C. 6048).

1895, vol. LXXI, Report on the Niger Coast. August 1891 to August 1894. Africa, no. 1 (C. 7596).

1895, vol. LXXI, Operations Against the Chief Nana, 1894, no. 3 (C. 7638).

1896, vol. LIX, Report by Sir John Kirk on Disturbances at Brass. Africa, no. 3 (C. 7977).

1897, vol. LX, Correspondence Relating to the War with Benin. Africa, no. 6 (C. 8677).

1899, vol. LXIII, Royal Niger Company (C. 9375).

1899, vol. LXIII, Correspondence, Benin Territory Expedition, 1899 (C. 9529).

(d) University of Ibadan Library—Annual Reports, Southern Nigeria, 1900–1910.

(e) Colonial Office Library, London: Official and Semi-Official Publications.

*Report on the Oil Rivers District, West Coast of Africa* (December 1888), by H. H. Johnston.

*Report of Visit to the Niger* (1890), by Major C. M. Macdonald.

*Memorandum as to Jurisdiction and Administrative Powers of a European State holding Protectorates in Africa.* Africa no. 410 (Confidential), 1891, by 'J. B.'.

*Report on Brass* (H.M.S.O.), Colonial Office, Nigeria (1896), by Sir John Kirk.

Hertslet, *Map of Africa by Treaty*, 3 vols. (London, 1909).

## B. SECONDARY SOURCES

There are many secondary sources which throw varying light on the problems discussed in the study. A comprehensive list is obviously impossible. Special attention has, therefore, been given to those books which have tried not to treat Southern Nigerian history as something on the periphery of British imperial history. There is a wealth of articles on the territory to be found in bound volumes at the Royal Commonwealth Society's Library in London. There is lastly the accumulation of the works of subsequent social anthropologists, which are available in the form of surveys and anthropological reports.

What follows is no more than a select bibliography. Works omitted but which have been quoted in the text have been acknowledged in footnotes:

ADAMS, J. *Remarks on the Country Extending from Cape Palmas to the River Congo* (London, 1823).

BACON, R. H. S. *Benin, The City of Blood* (London, 1897).

BASDEN, G. T. *Niger Ibos* (London, 1938).

BINDLOSS, H. *In the Niger Country* (London, 1898).

BLYDEN, E. W. *West Africa before Europe* (London, 1905).

BOISRAGON, A. *The Benin Massacre* (London, 1898).

BUCHANAN, K. M. and PUGH, J. C. *Land and People in Nigeria* (London, 1955).

BUXTON, T. F. *The African Slave Trade and its Remedy* (London, 1840).

COOK, A. N. *British Enterprise in Nigeria* (Philadelphia, 1943).

CROWE, S. E. *Berlin West African Conference* (London, 1942).

DIKÉ, K. O. *Trade and Politics in the Niger Delta* (Oxford, 1956).

DOUGLAS, A. C. *Niger Memories* (Exeter, 1927).

DUDGEON, G. C. *Agricultural and Forest Products of British West Africa* (London, 1911).

EGHAREVBA, J. *A Short History of Benin*, 3rd ed. (Ibadan, 1960).

FLINT, J. E. *Sir George Goldie and the Making of Nigeria* (Oxford, 1960).

FORDE, C. D. (ed.). *Ethnographic Survey of Africa*. Western Africa, parts IX and X (Oxford, 1955).

—— *Efik Traders of Old Calabar* (Oxford (for the International African Institute), 1956).

FORTES, M. and EVANS-PRITCHARD, E. E. *African Political Systems* (Oxford, 1962).

GEARY, Sir W. N. M. *Nigeria Under British Rule* (London, 1927).

GOLDIE, Rev. H. *Calabar and its Mission* (Edinburgh, 1890) and a new edition by Dean, J. T. (1901).

—— *Memoir of King Eyo VII of Old Calabar* (Old Calabar, 1894). (Both extremely useful eyewitness accounts.)

GREEN, M. M. *Ibo Village Affairs* (1947).

HALL, W. E. *A Treatise on the Foreign Powers and Jurisdiction of the British Crown* (Oxford, 1894).

HOBSON, J. A. *Imperialism, A Study*, 3rd ed. (London, 1938).

HODGKIN, T. L. *Nigerian Perspectives* (Oxford, 1960).

HOLT, C. R. (ed.). *Holt, J., 1841–1915: Diary of John Holt* (Liverpool, 1948).

JOHNSTON, A. *Life and Letters of Sir H. H. Johnston* (London, 1929).

JONES, G. I. *The Trading States of the Oil Rivers* (Oxford, 1963).

LANDER, R. L. *Journal of an Expedition to Explore the Course and Termination of the Niger* (London, 1838).

LEONARD, A. G. *The Lower Niger and its Tribes* (London, 1906).

LINDLEY, M. F. *The Acquisition and Government of Backward Territory in International Law* (London, 1926).

LIVINGSTONE, W. P. *White Queen of Okoyong* (London, 1916).

LLOYD, C. *The Navy and the Slave Trade* (London, 1949).

MATHIESON, W. L. *Great Britain and the Slave Trade, 1832–1865* (London, 1929).

MCFARLAN, D. M. *Calabar, the Church of Scotland Mission Founded 1846* (rev. ed. London, 1946).

MCPHEE, A. *The Economic Revolution in British West Africa* (London, 1926).

MEEK, C. K. *Law and Authority in a Nigerian Tribe* (Oxford, 1937).

—— *Land Law and Customs in the Colonies* (Oxford, 1946).

MOREL, E. D. *Affairs of West Africa* (London, 1902).

—— *Nigeria: its Peoples and Problems* (London, 1911).

PAGE, J. *The Black Bishop* (London, 1910).

PARTRIDGE, C. *Cross River Natives* (London, 1905).

ROBINSON, R. and GALLAGHER, J. with DENNEY, A. *Africa and the Victorians* (London, 1961).

TALBOT, P. A. *Life in Southern Nigeria* (London, 1923).

—— *The Peoples of Southern Nigeria*, 4 vols. (Oxford, 1926).

—— *Tribes of the Niger Delta* (London, 1932).

TEPOWA, A. 'A Short History of Brass and Its People' (in manuscript).

THOMAS, N. W. *An Anthropological Report on the Ibo-speaking Peoples of Nigeria* (London, 1913).

UMO, K. *History of the Aro Settlements* (Lagos, 1945).

WADDELL, H. M. *Twenty-Nine Years in the West Indies and Central Africa* (London, 1863).

WELLESLEY, D. *Sir George Goldie, Founder of Nigeria* (London, 1934).

WOOLF, L. S. *Empire and Commerce in Africa* (London, 1920).


## C. UNPUBLISHED THESES

AFIGBO, A. E. *The Warrant Chief System in Eastern Nigeria, 1900–29* (Ph.D., Ibadan, 1964).

ANENE, J. C. *The International Boundaries of Nigeria, 1884–1906* (Ph.D., London, 1960).

AYANDELE, E. A. *The Political and Social Implications of Missionary Enterprise in the Evolution of Modern Nigeria, 1875–1914* (Ph.D., London, 1964).

344

IKIME, O. *Itsekiri-Urhobo Relations and the Establishment of British Rule, 1884–1936* (Ph.D., Ibadan, 1965).

SCOTTER, W. H. *International Rivalry in the Bights of Benin and Biafra, 1815–1885* (Ph.D., London, 1933).

STILLIARD, N. H. *The Rise and Development of Legitimate Trade in Palm Oil with West Africa* (M.A., Birmingham, 1938).

TAMUNO, S. M. *The Development of British Administrative Control of Southern Nigeria, 1900–12* (Ph.D., London, 1963).


## D. PAMPHLETS AND ARTICLES IN JOURNALS

(*a*) *Nigerian Pamphlets* (Colonial Office Library)

African Association Ltd. *Application for Charter for the Oil Rivers* (1890), no. 3.

*A West African Monopoly By One Interested in Native Races* (1894), no. 7.

*Exploration in Southern Nigeria, by Capt. E. A. Steel, R.F.A.* (1909), no. 16. (A good account of the last phase of the military conquest of Southern Nigeria.)

*Niger Delta Natives*, by Cr. F. Darker (1905), no. 11.

*Royal Niger Company's Charter*, Memorial of the Liverpool Chamber of Commerce (1893), no. 6.

(*b*) *West African Pamphlets* (Commonwealth Society Library)

GALLWEY, H. L. *Nigeria in the Nineties* (1930), no. 43 C. (Views of a 'forward policy' pioneer.)

GOLDIE, G. T. *The Future of the Niger Territories.* An address to the London Chamber of Commerce, 6 July 1897, no. 8. British Priority on the Niger (1897), no. 150.

GREY, Major-General W. H. *Government Policy in West Africa, especially Nigeria.* An outspoken criticism, 1926, no. 161.

HARRIS, Rev. H. J. *Domestic Slavery in S. Nigeria.* A Report to the Committee of the Anti-Slavery and Aborigines Protection Society, 1911, no. 43/2.

JOHNSTON, H. H. *British West Africa and the Trade of the Interior*, 15 January 1889, no. 43/3.

LE MIS DE NADAILLAC. *Le Royaume de Benin: Massacre d'une mission anglaise* (Paris, 1898), no. 43/1.

LUGARD, F. D. *England and France on the Niger* (1895), no. 150. *Southern Nigeria and the English 'Humanitarians'* (Brussels, 1905), no. 43/1. (An out-and-out attack on the government and the organ of the Congo Reform Association.)

(c) *Journals* (magazine articles, most of which are compiled into vol. 150, Royal Commonwealth Society Library)

*Africa*, vol. x (October, 1937). Lord Lugard, 'British Policy in Nigeria'; *ibid*. S. Leith-Ross, 'Notes on the Osu System Among the Ibos of Owerri Province Nigeria'.

*Australian Royal Geographical Society, S. Australia*, vol. XVI (1914). Sir H. L. Galway, 'Pioneering in Nigeria'.

*Chambers's Journal* (March 1899), pp. 154–7. 'An Incident of the Niger Trade' (unsigned).

*Contemporary Review* (April 1898), J. Westlake, 'England and France in West Africa'. (Useful for the 'hinterland' problems.)

*Encyclopaedia Britannica*, 11th ed., vol. XII. 'Taubman Goldie' (unsigned).

*English Illustrated Magazine*, O. M. Dalton, 'Booty from Benin'.

*Geographical Journal*, vol. XC, no. 1 (1937). C. Daryll Forde, 'Land and Labour in a Cross River Village', S. Nigeria.

*Journal of the African Society*, vol. V (1902). Elijah Helm, 'The Cultivation of Cotton in West Africa'; no. XL, vol. X (July 1911), Rubert Boyce, 'Colonisation of Africa'; vol. XII (1912–13), Dr W. Asmis, 'Law and Policy in relation to the Native in the Gold Coast and Nigeria'.

*Macmillan's Magazine* (March 1900), pp. 379 ff. H. Bell, 'British Rule in British West Africa'.

*Manchester Geographical Society* (1905). W. E. B. Crawford, 'Nigeria'.

*Scottish Geographical Magazine*, vol. VI. A. S. White, 'The Partition of Africa'; vol. XXII (1906), J. Watt, 'S. Nigeria'.

*United Empire* (December 1914). R. E. Dennett, 'British and German Trade'.

*West Africa*. (November 1927) Alexander A. Cowen, 'The Story of Ja Ja'; (8 April 1944) W. Geary, 'Nigeria: Further Studies of its Past and Future'.

# INDEX

23-2

Aro (cont.)
  campaign against, 229–30; operations against, 230–2, 235
Aro Oracle, 15–16, 18; see also Long Juju
Aro-Chukwu (Chuku), 15, 16, 228, 231, 235, 258; sacred grove of, 17; Moor at, 234
Arums, the, 207
Asa, 232
Asaba, 235, 239, 242, 314; garrison at, 247; Niger Co. at, 203, 240; missionaries at, 309–10
Asaba district, 19, 71, 214, 256, 294
Ase, 5
Aseh Creek, 222
Ashanti, 26, 191, 216
Asigas, the, 207
Atam, 95; a chief of, 18–19
Atam, the, 218
Atani, 226
Attah (of Idah), 246
Atuma, 244
Aweyong river, 19, 185, 218, 237
Awka, 17, 247, 259
Awka district, 15
Awoko, 195
Awu, 222
Azar country, 218
Azu, 243
Azumini, 53, 208

Bacon, R. H. S., 22
Badagri, 21
Baikie, —, 32, 39
Bakana, 9, 46, 254
Bank, Anglo-African, 293–4
Bank of British West Africa, 293
Banyangi, the, 8
Barbados, 140
Barbot, James, 10, 23, 290
Barboy House, 46
Barrossa, H.M.S., 193
Basden, G. T., 312
Bassambiri, 9, 167
Bateri, 152
Bathurst, H.M.S., 168
Bedford, Rear-Admiral, 159–60, 170
Bedwell, A.D.C., 185 n.
Beecroft, John (Consul), 35, 336; appointed, 29–30; missions of, 30–1; as king-maker, 31–3, 34
Beedie, Rev. R. M., 105, 107
Bende, 16, 52, 190, 209, 231, 235, 258; Moor at, 234; garrison at, 247

Benin City, 144, 188, 206, 214, 314; kingdom of, 19–20, 180, 189; empire of, 20–3, 202, 256; war against, 190–5, 203, 323; government devised for, 196; garrison at, 235, 247; 'Native' Council at, 255–6, 264
Benin (district), 2, 8, 12, 145, 157, 209–11, 297–8; expedition from, 5; emigrations from, 6
  King of, 143, 179, 283; son killed in battle, 5; Phillips' designs against, 190–2, 323
Benin, Bight of, 4, 27, 47, 56
Benin river, 4, 38, 56, 58, 80, 93, 126, 136, 138, 153, 156, 194, 205; visited by Macdonald, 137; Gallwey's tour of, 142–3
Benin, S.S., 141
Benue river, 48, 67, 297
Benue valley, 8
Berey, 156
Berlin West Africa Conference, 49, 59–60, 62, 65, 67, 82, 107, 113, 117, 128, 318; leads to economic imperialism, 61; mercenary motives of, 114
Bertie, Hon. F. L., 207 n.
Biafra, Bight of, 4, 27, 37, 47, 56
Bida, 22
Bini, the, 19–20, 199, 200, 312
Birmingham, 292
Bismarck, Prince von, 59
Bleasby, —, 298
Boisragon, A., 191, 195; escapes ambush, 192
Boki, the, 8
Boler, R. D., 76, 122, 335
Bonny, 7, 9, 35, 38, 47, 54, 55, 57, 58, 66, 80–1, 93, 103, 108, 136, 148, 175, 205, 214, 274, 290 n., 306, 314; king of, 10, 32–3, 252; commerce of, 11, 98–9, 228; choice of site for, 16; slave-trading at, 23–4; treaty with, 27–8; civil strife in, 33, 42–5, 76–7; Governing Council at, 94; visited by Macdonald, 122–3, 137, 162; vice-consul in, 138, 143; hinterland of, 163, 181, 218; 'Native' Council at, 256, 264; missionaries at, 309, 311, 313
Bonny river, 147, 208
Borgu, 211
Bornu, 48

348

Bosman, Willem (1705), 36
Boyle, — (asst. D.C.), 245
Bradbury, —, 20
Braid, Jack, 203, 254
Braid, Will, 46
Brass, 5, 7, 9, 38, 57, 71, 80, 93, 136, 139, 175, 181–2, 205, 214, 256, 274, 294, 306; Lander's description of, 11; slave-trade at, 24, 28; growth of a grievance in, 49–50, 58, 140; hinterland of, 75, 115, 181; disputes at, 77–80, 163–73; visited by Macdonald, 122, 125–6, 137, 162; vice-consul at, 138; attacks Niger Co.'s H.Q., 163, 167–9; destitution of, 166–7; dealt with by Macdonald, 168–72; missionaries at, 309, 311
  Brass river, 72
Brazza, Count De, 48
Briggs, Young (Chief), 203, 254
Bristol, 56
Britain, 107, 112, 118; motives of in West Africa, 26, 65, 72, 108, 110, 280, 318; treaty policy of, 27–8, 63–4, 111; informal sway of, 29–60; 318–19; paramountcy recognised, 61; illegal treatment of Jaja, 92; sends Special Commissioner, 100–1; foundations laid by, 329
British and African Steam Navigation Co., 281
Brownridge, James, 190
Brussels, Conference at, 112–14, 131; humanitarian motives of, 114
Bubendorf, Rev. Father, 167, 168
Buguma, 9, 46, 254
Burns, —, 160
Burton, R., 31, 33, 42, 336
Butler, —, 295

Cabinet, British, 65, 111, 115
Calabar, 8, 24, 27, 180, 252, 274, 276; Consul's intervention in, 34–5; German warship visits, 101; chiefs of, 105
  Calabar river, 51, 175, 208, 274
Calabar, New, 7, 38, 55, 58, 66, 71, 93, 137, 175, 214, 290 n., 305, 311; slave trade in, 24, 28; king of, 44, 48; disputes of, 45–7, 108; hinterland of, 75, 115, 163, 204; visited by Macdonald, 122, 124; vice-consuls at, 136, 138; 'Native' Council at, 203, 253–4, 256, 264

Calabar Observer, The, 315–16
Calabar, Old, 38, 58, 66, 85, 93, 103, 196, 202, 214, 218, 252, 256, 274, 275, 283, 290, 294, 296–7, 304, 314; Consul transfers to, 42; missionary work in, 50–1, 311; visited by Macdonald, 122, 124–5, 137, 162; vice-consuls at, 136, 138; botanical garden at, 146, 284–5; High Court at, 176, 253, 256; 'Native' Council at, 264, 266
Cameroons, 38, 56, 58, 73, 101, 118, 136; Germans in, 58–60, 124–5
Campbell, Kenneth (vice-consul), 143–4, 191, 291
Cannibalism, 168–9, 172, 244; alleged, 72, 99, 123, 183, 224
Cape St John, 58
Cape St Paul, 58
Carr, Henry, tours schools, 314
Carroll, Lieutenant, 199
Casement, Roger, 149, 150–1, 179
Chad, Lake, 48
Chamberlain, Joseph, 173, 199, 211, 212, 219, 225, 230, 275, 278, 280, 332; on punitive expeditions, 217, 222; on amalgamation, 273; opposes trade monopoly, 293; on malaria, 328
Chiefs, 27, 36, 46, 81, 84, 170, 172, 238, 249, 251–2, 282–3, 294–5, 318, 320; of 'Houses', 9–10; 'warrant', 14, 260 n., 262, 265, 270, 308, 324; European names and dress of, 24; as hostages, 79, 242; dislike for Niger Co., 116; disregard of, 121; consulted by Macdonald, 121–2; object to company rule, 126; respect for Macdonald, 135; as paid agents, 136; as middlemen, 141; shown Benin City, 197; hanged (Aro), 231–2; as a trading aristocracy, 278
China, 63, 88, 111, 176
Christianity, 22, 27, 61, 122–3, 167, 312–13, 326; disruptive effect at coast, 311
Church Missionary Society, 309–10
  Proceedings of C.M.S., 326
Ciri (Siri), 195
Clifford, Sir Hugh, 303–4, 327
Coast (of Nigeria), 2, 17, 41, 131, 304; vegetation of, 4; communities of, 9, 25; city-states of, 26, 42, 76, 84,

354

355

357

Opobo (*cont.*)
visited by Macdonald, 122, 123–4, 137, 162; vice-consul at, 138; burial of Jaja at, 140–1; hinterland of, 181, 218; troops levied from, 209; 'Native' Council at, 256, 264; text of treaty with, 333–5
Opobo river, 38, 53–4, 82, 208
Opoji, 256
Opomo, 239
Opooboo, House of, 42
Ora, 21
Ord Commission, 40
Ormsby-Gore, W. G. A., 16, 297, 304, 324
Oron, 310
'Oru', the, 7
Osomari (Osumari), 18, 309
Osu (slaves), 17
Ottenberg, —, 12
Otuochichi, 240; *see* Ekumeku society
Overami (Ovonramwen), 144, 201–2; failing power of, 192–3; death of, 202 n., *see also* Oba
Ovies, 143
Ovonramwen, *see* Overami
Owa, the, 270, 272 n.
Owen, W., 27
Owerri, 8, 52, 231, 232, 234, 235–6, 258, 259; garrison at, 247
Owo, 264

Palm kernels, 281; method of cracking, 286–7
Palm oil, trade in, 39, 41, 49, 86, 141, 142, 146, 157, 281, 284–5, 291; extraction of, 286
Palmerston, Lord, 28, 29, 30
Park, Mungo, 27, 60
Partridge, Charles, 238 n., 269–70, 288; investigation of, 1
Patani, 5
Patrols, Annual, 270; policy of, 247–9
Pauncefote, Sir Julian, 94, 331
*Peacock*, H.M.S., 105
'Pepple' (Perekule), 10, 23–4
Pepple, Annie, 32, 42, 54
George, 33, 42, 43–4, 76, 94, 122–3; resigns, 45
Manilla, 32, 33, 42, 54
Sam Annie, 100, 335
Warribo (Waribo) Manilla, 44, 76, 94
William, 94
William Dappa (V), 32, 33, 42

Perekule, 10; *see also* 'Pepple'
Persia, 63
Phillips, J. R., appointed Deputy-Commissioner, 181; deputises for Moor, 189–90: mission to Benin, 191–2, 284, 323; ambushed and killed, 192, 196
*Philomel*, H.M.S., 159, 193
*Phoebe*, H.M.S., 193
Pires, A., tribute of to Benin, 22
Pitt, William, 26
Police, 268; absence of (Ibo), 13–14; Consular, 106; *see also* Constabulary
Port Harcourt, 297 n.
Porteous, A. M., 103
Portuguese, the, 113, 290
Powis, — (merchant), 191
Press, the, in West Africa, 315–16
Priests, among Ibo, 15
Probyn, Leslie, 227; as Acting High Commissioner, 245–6
Protection, British, nature of, 2, 63, 66, 163
Protectorates, colonial, 62–6, 73, 75, 76, 77, 320–1; distinguished from annexations, 65, 71, 74, 107, 112; theory of, 97, 112, 115, 163, 321; 'paper', 107, 320
of Niger Districts, 1, 67
of Oil Rivers, 73
of Southern Nigeria, 2

Qua-Eboe, 214
Qua-Eboe river, 7, 53–4, 83, 146, 148–9, 175, 180, 217, 274, 310
Qua-Eboe, the, 53, 55, 83

Railways, Moor's plans for, 296–7; Lagos line, 273, 296–7
Rawson, Admiral H. H., 193–4; reports on Benin expedition, 196
Raymond, — (naval officer), 50
Resolution of 1865, 39–40
Rhodes, Cecil, 118
Richards, Admiral, 55, 85
Rio del Rey, 67, 296
Rivers, *see* Aweyong, Benin, Benue, Brass, Calabar, Cross, Enyong, Ethiope, Forcados, Gwato, Jamieson, Niger, Nun, Opobo, Qua-Eboe, S. Barbara, Sombrero
Roads, importance of, 289–90, 296
Roads and Creeks Proclamation, 308
Roberts, — (official), 138, 209

358

Rogerson, Stanley, 100
Rosebery, Lord, 145, 331
Roupell, Captain, 182, 184, 187 n., 196, 218, 274
Royal Anthropological Institute, 2
Royal Niger Company, 4, 66, 71, 120–30 passim, 136, 139, 147, 171, 188, 199, 203, 215, 216, 301, 303; charter and constitution of, 70; negotiation with Liverpool firms, 115–18; German hostility to, 117–18; grievances of Brass against, 125–6, 140, 164, 172–3, 181; headquarters attacked, 163, 167–9, 253; obstructionism of, 165; anti-smuggling measures of, 167; charter revoked, 211, 213, 216, 272; compensated, 213; in Ika country, 240–2; botanical garden of, 285; see also National African Co.
Rubber, 141, 144, 205, 281, 297–8
'Rumbi' country, 125

Sabagreira, 235
Sacrifice, Human, 210, 242, 308, 311; in Benin ceremonies, 22–3, 194, 195; abolition of, 31, 35, 326; at Okrika, 183; to Long Juju, 224
St George, H.M.S., 193
St Vincent Islands, 140
Salisbury, Marquess of, 69, 85, 95, 97, 105, 107, 113, 121, 131, 132, 152, 206, 331; handling of Jaja case, 84, 87, 88–91, 320; critical of Johnston, 95, 97, 135; promotes Brussels conference, 113; asks Moor for programme, 184; thanks Niger Co., 213
Salmon, Admiral, 55
Salt, duty on, 289
Santa Barbara river, 5
Santa Cruz (Teneriffe), 141
Sapele (Sapelle), 9, 148, 175, 180, 214, 283, 294; foundation of, 143, 181; Moor's meetings at, 155, 156; Macdonald's meeting at, 162; 'Native' Council at, 256, 264; as potential depot, 296–7
Sapoba, 195
Scherer, — (missionary), 241
Schools, Government, 314–15
Mission, 312, 313–14, 326
Secret service, absence of (Ibo), 13–14

Secret societies, 267; among the Ibibio, 15; in Calabar, 34
Segregation, policy of, 316–17
Selborne, Lord, 212, 272
Senegal, 48
Sierra Leone, 40, 48; trade value of, 120; a lawyer from, 160
Silver, as currency, 294, 295
Slave Dealing Proclamation, 306; social effect of, 308
Slave trade, 9, 22, 61, 244, 284, 318, 324; effects of, 23–5; abolition of, 26–8, 31
Slaves, 9–10, 161; Aro traffic in, 17, 224; settled at Freetown, 26; as heads of Houses, 32; plantation (Calabar), 34–5; traditional killing forgone, 50; in Brass, 126; suspected slaughter of, 156; Turner's appeal to, 197–8; as currency, 292, 294; trading boys, 305–6; escape to missions, 311
Slessor, Mary, 51, 325–6
Sobe, 221
Sombrero river, 148, 208
South African War, 219
Southern Nigeria Regiment, 276
Spiff, Chief, 80
Spiff House, 78, 79
Spirit world, authority of, 12–13
Standfast, Reuben (chief), 203
Stephen, James, 39
Stewart, Dr, 248, 270
Stuart and Douglas, 123
Subsidies, 132; payment of, 30, 146, 282; withholding of, 138, 143
Supercargoes, 34, 36–7, 49; at Opobo, 43, 45
Synge, F. (vice-consul), 136, 138

Talbot, P. A., 5, 11, 18
Taxes, imposed on Binis, 199
Taylor Loughland and Co., 123
Theseus, H.M.S., 193
Thomas, N., work of, 2
Thompson, H., as Conservator of Forests, 300–1, 302
Thurston, Major, 63
Times, The, 118
Tolls, 141, 283; disapproved by British, 19; in Cross river states, 95–6, 104, 207
Townsend, — (trading agent), 98
Transvaal Chamber of Mines, 316

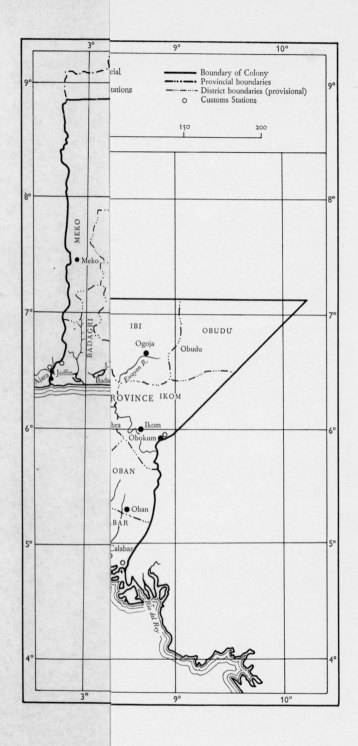